LANGUAGE PROCESSIN
SECOND LANGUAGE DEVELOPMENT
PROCESSABILITY THEORY

STUDIES IN BILINGUALISM (SiBil)

EDITORS

Kees de Bot
University of Nijmegen

Thom Huebner
San José State University

EDITORIAL BOARD

Michael Clyne (Monash University)
Kathryn Davis (University of Hawaii at Manoa)
Charles Ferguson (Stanford University)
Joshua Fishman (Yeshiva University)
François Grosjean (Université de Neuchâtel)
Wolfgang Klein (Max Planck Institut für Psycholinguistik)
Georges Lüdi (University of Basel)
Christina Bratt Paulston (University of Pittsburgh)
Suzanne Romaine (Merton College, Oxford)
Merrill Swain (Ontario Institute for Studies in Education)
Richard Tucker (Carnegie Mellon University)

Volume 15

Manfred Pienemann

Language Processing and Second Language Development

Processability Theory

LANGUAGE PROCESSING AND SECOND LANGUAGE DEVELOPMENT

PROCESSABILITY THEORY

MANFRED PIENEMANN
Australian National University

JOHN BENJAMINS PUBLISHING COMPANY
AMSTERDAM/PHILADELPHIA

The paper used in this publication meets the minimum requirements of American National Standard for Information Sciences — Permanence of Paper for Printed Library Materials, ANSI Z39.48-1984.

Library of Congress Cataloging-in-Publication Data

Pienemann. Manfred, 1951-
    Language processing and second language development : processability theory / Manfred Pienemann.
        p.   cm. -- (Studies in Bilingualism, ISSN 0928-1533 ; v. 15)
    Based on a paper presented at a workshop held in Washington, Sept. 1992.
    Includes bibliographical references and index.
    1. Second language acquisition. 2. Psycholinguistics. 3. Grammar, Comparative and general. 4. Interlanguage (Language learning) I. Title. II. Series.
    P118.2.P54   1998
    401'.93--dc21   98-23896
    ISBN 90 272 4121 X (Eur.) / 1 55619 549 4 (US) (Hb; alk. paper)   CIP
    ISBN 90 272 4129 5 (Eur.) / 1 55619 951 1 (US) (Pb; alk. paper)

John Benjamins Publishing Co. • P.O.Box 75577 • 1070 AN Amsterdam • The Netherlands
John Benjamins North America • P.O.Box 27519 • Philadelphia PA 19118-0519 • USA

Helenalle

Contents

Acknowledgements

The ideas presented in this book evolved over many years. Much of the original impetus for this work goes back to the early to late 1970s when I worked as a member of Jürgen Meisel's research team, the ZISA[1] group, which has had a profound influence on my thinking on language acquisition.

Between 1983 and 1987 Malcolm Johnston and I elaborated a model of SLA which I presented at the "International Conference on Explaining Interlanguage Development" at LaTrobe University in August 1987. The manuscript of that presentation (Pienemann and Johnston 1987a) has been cited in various places. But it was never published because not long after that conference I fundamentally reconceptualised that framework. The most notable changes concern the inclusion of a formal grammatical theory and the systematic exclusion of epistemological issues. I summarised this position in another unpublished paper which I presented at the workshop "Philosophy of Science and Language Acquisition Research", organised by Alan Beretta (Michigan State University) in Washington in September 1992. With his thoughtful comments on that paper Henning Wode gave the final impetus to the writing of this book which is based on the 1992 paper. I would like to thank him for inspiring me to undertake this task.

Many people have supported my work most generously through comments and discussion. Peter Petersen assisted me in the process of conceptualising interlanguage development within LFG which was also aided by comments from Avery Andrews and Cindy Allan. I have benefited from many discussions with Malcolm Johnston on SLA processes and explanatory approaches to SLA. My understanding of the latter area has also been facilitated by interacting with Mike Long, Patsy Lightbown, Kevin Gregg, Cathy Doughty and Alan Beretta. Gisela Håkansson kindly and patiently collaborated with me on the application of the theory proposed in this book to Swedish as a second language. This process greatly facilitated my own conceptualisation of the theory and motivated my continued work on this book.

Robert Bley-Vroman, Deborah Masterson and Lynn Eubank were extremely helpful and supportive in making their own software programs and test sentences for the on-line experiments accessible to me. I also benefited from their comments on my adaptations of their work to my purposes.

I also want to thank Avery Andrews, Kees de Bot, Bruno Di Biase, Theo Bongaerts, Helen Charters, Michael Clyne, Bronwen Dyson, Lynn Eubank, Esther Glahn, Kevin Gregg, Björn Hammarberg, Michael Harrington, Jan Hulstijn, Margriet Jagtman, Malcolm Johnston, Gabi Kasper, Doug Kennedy, Toni Liddicoat, Pieta Littleton, Dean Mellow, Susanne Schlyter, Liz Temple, Russell Tomlin, Lydia White and two anonymous reviewers for their multifaceted input into this manuscript. My thanks also go to Michael Dunn and Pieta Littleton for their careful editorial work on the manuscript and to Tracy Wood who patiently worked on many charts and tables in the book. And finally I would like to thank Jürgen Meisel for invaluable comments he made on various sections of this book from an inter-continental distance, particularly in relation to the comparison of first and second language acquisition.

I would like to gratefully acknowledge the financial assistance provided for parts of this research by the Australian Research Council and the Australian National University.

Naturally, the writing of books takes place in a social context that interlaces with the author's private life, and one person's stamina may be the other person's obsession. I would like to thank my family, especially my wife, Helena, for enduring those inevitable pressures. Their presence and support has been a great source of strength.

Manfred Pienemann
Canberra, February 1997

Preface

A brief overview

The objective of this book is to provide a systematic perspective on some central psychological mechanisms underlying the spontaneous production of interlanguage (IL) speech. This perspective rests on the incorporation of a number of key cognitive factors into a psychologically plausible grammatical system. The resulting framework is a theory of processability of grammatical structures which I will refer to as Processability Theory.

This theory formally predicts which structures can be processed by the learner at a given level of development. This capacity to predict which formal hypotheses are processable at which point in development provides the basis for a unified explanatory framework which can account for a diverse range of phenomena related to language development.

Whether a theory can be considered as supported by observation often depends on the capacity of the theory to make inter-subjectively observable predictions. Therefore, in this book, great emphasis is placed on a principled relationship between theory and data analysis.

The starting point for the exposition of the proposed theoretical framework, beginning in Chapter 2, is a review of the so-called 'strategies approach to SLA'. This approach formed the basis of an explanation of sequences in the acquisition of German word order found in studies by Meisel, Clahsen & Pienemann (1981), Clahsen, Meisel & Pienemann (1983), Meisel (1983) and Pienemann (1981, 1984). Clahsen later utilised this approach in his contrastive work on first and second language acquisition, and I utilised it in my work on what became known as the 'teachability hypothesis' (Pienemann 1984, 1987).

These three authors have since developed in their theoretical outlook, and some readers have expressed the view that there is some lack of continuity in the published documentation of these developments. In Chapter 2 the original proposal is therefore summarised together with its application to SLA sequences. My review then goes on to critically evaluate the proposal in relation to the role of grammar, its restriction to 'movement operations', the role of comprehension and production, and the problem of extendibility. Some of these points were raised earlier by other researchers and had not been responded to by the proponents of the 'strategies approach' because their own theoretical perspective had developed beyond the points being critically evaluated.

In a way, this chapter restores the continuity of conceptual development by summarising the above 'historical' facts and by adding to it a perspective on language processing that overcomes the shortcomings of earlier approaches. Much of this perspective is based on Levelt's (1989) work on language production which is utilised to hypothesise a hierarchy of processing procedures for second language acquisition.

In Chapter 3 this hierarchy is implemented into a theory of grammar, namely Lexical-Functional Grammar (LFG) (Kaplan and Bresnan 1982). This move guarantees the applicability of the hierarchy to typologically different languages and to different areas of grammar. It also ensures the internal consistency of a processing-based approach to SLA. We will refer to the implementation of the above hierarchy of processing procedures into LFG as Processability Theory. The syntactic aspects of mechanics of Processability Theory will be demonstrated on the basis of a re-analysis of the well-known German word order sequences in the new framework.

It will then be demonstrated that Processability Theory also applies to a range of morphological phenomena, and theoretically motivated predictions will be derived from Processability Theory for the acquisition of German morphology. This step is crucial for the explanatory power of the theory which, in this way, is widened by one further domain (Long 1993).

Chapter 4 deals with several aspects of testing these predictions in empirical observations. I will argue that the nature of the theory to be tested requires the data to relate to the learners' capacity to utilise their interlanguage (IL) grammar under the time constraints of spontaneous oral language production. This excludes a whole range of data types as relevant to testing the predictions made by the proposed theory. I will make the point that corpora of spontaneous oral language production constitute a rich source of insight for an inquiry into the processability of interlanguage grammars. It is for this reason that the first empirical test of the proposed theory will be based on a longitudinal corpus of the acquisition of German as a second language (GSL).

Leaving the theoretical issues aside, this empirical test raises a number of issues concerning the relationship between theory and data. I will outline a dynamic system for the description of IL development which will be finely tuned with the requirements of the proposed theory.

The predictions made by Processability Theory are entirely formal in nature; i.e. they are related to structural properties only. However, the learnability of such properties is also dependent on the complexity of the form-function relationship which varies between specific structures and individual languages. I will outline ways in which these two sources of complexity can be kept apart for the purpose of analysis.

In Chapter 5 the cross-linguistic validity of processability will be tested further by deriving from it predictions for developmental paths for languages other than German. The particular test cases will be English, Swedish and Japanese as second languages. This application of the theory further demonstrates its explanatory value and it illustrates the procedure of applying the theory to 'uncharted languages'. From a more descriptive point of view this application has the side-effect of unifying extensive descriptions of developmental paths for the languages in question.

Chapter 5 also reports on a set of reaction time experiments where the underlying hypothesis is tested that language acquisition can be understood as the acquisition of the procedural skills needed to produce the second language. The empirical evidence for Processability Theory thus includes on-line data as well as corpus data.

A further extension of the explanatory power of Processability Theory is presented in Chapter 6 where the theory is used to formally define the "hypothesis space" of the learner. This concept refers to the delineation of those structural hypotheses which are processable at a given point in development. The range of these hypotheses will be formally defined. I will demonstrate that the leeway of processability available at a given point in development can account for the possible range of IL variation. In effect this amounts to a theoretically motivated re-conceptualisation of interlanguage variation which is fundamentally different from mainstream accounts of IL variation.

I will further apply the concept of Hypothesis Space to the teachability of languages. In this context I will demonstrate that Hypothesis Space defines the range within which interlanguage systems can develop under the influence of formal instruction. In other words, the 'teachability hypothesis' (Pienemann 1984) can now be understood as a special case of Hypothesis Space. To illustrate this claim I will analyse several cases of change from one type of IL variety to another which occurred under the influence of formal instruction.

Processability Theory assumes a certain degree of steadiness in the dynamic IL system. This assumption is crucial to the theory and to a number of practical applications deriving from it such as second language screening procedures. I will therefore demonstrate in a large set of data the empirical validity of this steadiness assumption. In particular I will demonstrate that learners' stages of development are steady across different communicative tasks/situations.

Finally, the concept of Hypothesis Space will be utilised for the comparison of first and second language acquisition. I will show that the differences in developmental patterns found in the two 'types' of acquisition fall well within the domain of Hypothesis Space and that therefore the assumption has to be rejected that the architecture of the language processor is fundamentally different in L1 and L2. Instead, I attribute the developmental differences to the dynamics inherent in the developmental process. Those dynamics derive from different initial hypotheses and the way these propagate (via *generative entrenchment*) throughout the developmental process.

Explanatory issues in SLA

1.1 Introduction: The thematic focus

Learnability is defined as a purely logico-mathematical problem (e.g. Berwick and Weinberg 1984). Such a perspective ignores the fact that this problem has to be solved, not by an unconstrained computational device, but by a mind that operates within human psychological constraints.

In this book I propose a theory which adds to learnability theory the perspective of processability; i.e. "processability theory". In my view, the logico-mathematical hypothesis space in which the learner operates is further constrained by the architecture of human language processing. Structural options that may be formally possible, will be produced by the language learner only if the necessary processing procedures are available that are needed to carry out, within the given minimal time frame, those computations required for the processing of the structure in question. Once we can spell out the sequence in which language processing routines develop in the learner, we can delineate those grammars that are processable at different points of development.

The architecture of human language processing therefore forms the basis for Processability Theory. It will be argued that language acquisition incorporates as one essential component the gradual acquisition of those very computational routines. In other words, the task of acquiring a language includes the acquisition of the *procedural skills* needed for the processing of the language. It follows from this that the sequence in which the target language[2] (TL) unfolds in the learner is determined by the sequence in which processing routines develop which are needed to handle the TL's components.

This implies a processing-oriented version of Pinker's (1984) *continuity hypothesis*: in the same way as Pinker argued that the basic fabric of grammar does not change at any given stage in the acquisition process it is reasonable to assume that the basic architecture of the language processor doesn't change. Such basic parameters as word access or the linearisation problem (Levelt 1981) are imposed on the human mind in a very general way. What changes in development is the language-specific way of handling these general constraints: I will therefore assume different sets of computational mechanisms for L1 and L2 learners or for adults or children only if there are compelling reasons to do so.

Hence, the above-mentioned continuity hypothesis implies that the basic non language-specific parameters of the language processor are the same across all learners. In other words, the nature of the computational mechanisms employed by native and non-native speakers is substantially the same. If this assumption can be supported by empirical evidence then observational differences are attributable only to different maturational states and to non-processing variables.

Assuming the continuity of processing mechanisms in language acquisition does not imply an opposition to the 'Fundamental Difference Hypothesis' (Bley-Vroman 1990), because the latter assumes general, non-explicit differences between child and adult language acquisition in the acquisition process *per se*. In contrast, the processing-based continuity hypothesis refers to the nature of language processing only and leaves it open as to whether non-processing parameters may be fundamentally different.[3]

In other words, while I propose a constraining effect of linguistic information processing on the genesis of linguistic knowledge, I do not imply that processing constraints describe *sufficient* conditions for the genesis of linguistic knowledge. Even in the debate between Piaget and Chomsky (Piatelli-Palmarini 1981) it became obvious that in both schools of thought a universal basis has to be assumed for the epistemological process to be possible. In this book I do not want to speculate on the nature of the universal basis of language acquisition; neither will I speculate on the inferential mechanisms which allow the learner to construct linguistic knowledge on the basis of a universal core and linguistic observations. Instead, I will explore the universal constraints which the language processing mechanisms of the human mind impose on the discovery process.

In the rationalist tradition learnability analyses have in the past been based on four components that must be specified in any learnability theory (e.g. Wexler and Culicover 1980, Pinker 1979):

(1)   the target grammar,
(2)   the data input to the learner,
(3)   the learning device that must acquire that grammar, and
(4)   the initial state.

The idea behind this is that a learnability theory must specify how a learner develops from an initial state to the target grammar with the available input and the given learning device.

The rationale for assuming these components, is rooted in the way in which learnability theory has been formulated in response to the 'logical problem' in language acquisition (cf. Wexler 1982). The logical problem basically describes the following paradox: children acquire in a relatively short period of time and on the basis of limited linguistic input the basic principles of their native language, and many of these principles are said to be impossible to be inferred from the observations made by the learner.

In other words, the rationalist approach proposed by Wexler (1982) characterises a theory of language learnability as a solely linguistic problem of the relationship between the representation of linguistic knowledge and the acquisition of that knowledge. This is why the four components of such a theory are described as (1) *the target grammar* which describes linguistic knowledge, (2) *linguistic input*, and (3) *the learning device* the interaction of which have to acquire the target grammar given a certain set of knowledge contained in the (4) *initial state*.

These assumptions go hand in hand with the assumed *autonomy of syntax*. Chomsky (1990) claims that natural languages display properties which are learnable only if the principles underlying these properties do not have to be explicitly acquired but can be inferred from the structure of an innate cognitive system. Fodor (1981) argues that such principles cannot be reduced to principles of other domains of cognition and that one therefore has to assume that they are specific to the linguistic domain of cognition which is similar in its specificity to the visual domain of cognition. This assumption is known as the *modularity hypothesis* and forms the basis for limiting the components of a theory of language learnability to the above four components: if there is an independent linguistic module of cognition, then it is possible to study it in isolation. This does not exclude interaction with other cognitive systems but it justifies the reductionism present in Wexler's assumption.

As long as learnability theory is limited to the objective of explaining the acquisition of the *linguistic knowledge* present in the final state of the learner this strategy may be possible. However, it has been noted by several GB-oriented researchers (e.g. Felix 1984, 199; Clahsen 1992; Gregg 1992; 1996) that there are at least two observable sets of phenomena that a theory of language acquisition must explain:

(1)   What enables the learner to attain linguistic competence?
(2)   What causes the development of this competence to follow a describable route?

Question (1) is, of course, the classical basis for Chomsky's assumption of a Universal Grammar, while (2) has only more recently been recognised as part of the learnability problem. I will refer to it as the 'developmental problem' (cf. Gregg 1996).

My fundamental point is this: to account for the developmental problem, recourse needs to be made to some of the key psychological aspects of human language processing because describable developmental routes are, at least in part, caused by the architecture of the human language processor. For linguistic hypotheses to transform into executable procedural knowledge the processor needs to have the capacity of processing those hypotheses.

In this book, I will demonstrate that indeed a wide array of developmental phenomena can be accounted for by the architecture of the language processor and its adaptation to the L2. Given that the language processor plays a key role in the transformation of structural hypotheses into procedural knowledge, language processing mechanisms constitute, in my view, a key component of a theory of language learnability.

1.2 An outline of the proposed theory

The wider context

The details of Processability Theory will be laid out over several chapters, and it may be useful to provide a brief and informal overview of the main concepts entailed in the theory. However, the reader should be mindful of the fact that such a summary is bound to be a sketch only.

As I mentioned above, the basic logic underlying Processability Theory is this: Structural options that may be formally possible, will be produced by the language learner only if the necessary processing procedures are available. In this perspective the language processor is seen with Bresnan and Kaplan (1982) as the computational mechanisms that operate on (but are separate from) the native speaker's linguistic knowledge. Processability Theory primarily deals with the nature of those computational mechanisms and the way in which they are acquired.

My fundamental point is that recourse needs to be made to key psychological aspects of human language processing in order to account for the developmental problem, because describable developmental routes are, at least in part, caused by the architecture of the human language processor. For linguistic hypotheses to transform into executable *procedural knowledge* (i.e. a certain processing skill), the processor needs to have the capacity of processing the structures relating to those hypotheses.

In other words, Processability Theory focuses solely on the developmental problem (cf. section 1.3) as an explanatory issue; it is not designed to contribute anything to the question of the innate or learnt *origin* of linguistic knowledge or the inferential processes by which linguistic input is converted into linguistic knowledge. Instead, it is the sole objective of Processability Theory to determine the sequence in which procedural skills develop in the learner.

The point of viewing language acquisition as the acquisition of procedural skills has been made by several authors (Levelt 1978; McLaughlin et al. 1983; McLaughlin 1987; Hulstijn 1990; Schmidt 1992). One might characterise the perspective of the above authors as the "procedural skill approach" to language acquisition.

The basic logic of this approach goes as follows: the real-time production of language can only be accounted for in a system in which word retrieval is very fast and in which the production of linguistic structures is possible without any conscious or non-conscious attention, because the locus of attentive processes is short-term (or immediate) memory, and its capacity is limited to fewer operations than are required for most of the simplest utterances. Such language production mechanisms therefore have to be assumed as being highly automatised. Given these psychological constraints on language production, acquisition has to be viewed as the process of automatisation of linguistic operations.

This view incorporates a number of basic assumptions about language processing, including the following:

- The dichotomy of *procedural knowledge* and *declarative knowledge* (Anderson 1983);
- The dichotomy of *controlled* and *automatic processing* (Posner and Snyder 1975; Schneider and Shiffrin 1977; Shiffrin and Schneider 1977; McLaughlin 1987);
- The *limitation of Immediate Memory* as the locus of language processing (Levelt 1978, 1989);
- The role of *automatisation* in linguistic skill formation (Levelt 1978).

These assumptions are well summarised in McLaughlin (1987) and in Schmidt (1992) and will be expanded on in Chapter 2.

The core of Processability Theory

In order to leave this brief summary manageable in size, I will not lay out the mechanics of processability theory in detail. Instead, I will summarise the outcome of those mechanics, which is a hierarchy of language processing procedures. That hierarchy, in turn, can produce predictions for the processability of linguistic structures when it is implemented into an LFG treatment of the target language grammar.

The point of departure for the above-mentioned hierarchy of processability is Kempen and Hoenkamp's (1987) Incremental Procedural Grammar (IPG) which incorporates many key features of psychologically plausible language processing. IPG forms an integral part of Levelt's (1989) overall model of lexically driven language generation. IPG provides a formal framework for the description of the grammatical encoding process. It involves a time-constrained set of mechanisms for the translation of conceptualisations into lexico-grammatical forms. In other words, these mechanisms are the procedures for the generation of lexico-grammatical forms.

In Processability Theory a set of key grammatical encoding procedures are arranged according to their sequence of activation in the language generation process, and it is demonstrated that this sequence follows an implicational pattern in which each procedure is a necessary prerequisite for the following procedure. The basic thesis of Processability Theory is that in the acquisition of language processing procedures the assembly of the component parts will follow the above implicational sequence.

The following processing procedures and routines form the hierarchy that underlies Processability Theory:

1. lemma access,
2. the category procedure,
3. the phrasal procedure,
4. the S-procedure,
5. the subordinate clause procedure — if applicable.

These processing procedures and routines are activated — amongst other things — in the above sequence. I hypothesise that this set of key grammatical encoding procedures are arranged according to their sequence of activation in the language generation process, and this sequence follows an implicational pattern in which each procedure is a necessary prerequisite for the following procedures. The basic thesis of Processability Theory is that in the acquisition of language processing procedures the assembly of the component parts will follow the above-mentioned implicational sequence. The hierarchical nature of this list arises from the fact that the procedure of each lower level is a prerequisite for the functioning of the higher level. A word[4] needs to be added to the target language lexicon before its grammatical category can be assigned. The grammatical category of a lemma (i.e. certain semantic and grammatical aspects of a word) is needed before a category procedure can be called. Only if the grammatical category of the head of a phrase is assigned can the phrasal procedure be called[5]. Only if a phrasal procedure has been completed and its value is returned can the function of the phrase (subject, object etc.) be determined. Only if the function of the phrase has been determined can it be attached to the S-node and sentential information be stored in the sentence procedure.

What happens when an element is missing in this implicational hierarchy? My hypothesis is that the hierarchy will be cut off in the learner grammar at the point of the missing processing procedures and the rest of the hierarchy will be replaced by a direct mapping of conceptual structures onto surface form as long as there are lemmata that match the conceptually instigated searches of the lexicon.

In other words, it is hypothesised that processing procedures will be acquired in their implicational sequence as depicted below:

	t_1	t_2	t_3	t_4	t_5
5 • Sub.-clause procedure ↑	−	−	−	−	+
4 • S-procedure ↑	−	−	−	+	+
3 • Phrasal procedure ↑	−	−	+	+	+
2 • Category procedure ↑	−	+	+	+	+
1 • Word/ lemma access	+	+	+	+	+

In this context it is important to note that Levelt's model can, in principle, account for language processing in bilinguals, since second language acquisition will lead to a bilingual language processor. De Bot (1992) adapted Levelt's model to language production in bilinguals. He demonstrated that the extended version of Levelt's model accounts for the majority of the additional requirements a language production model has to meet in a in a bilingual context, including the simultaneous use of two languages, cross-linguistic influences and differing degrees of fluency or proficiency in the languages concerned.

It may be useful, at this point, to briefly illustrate the predictive power of the above hierarchy by highlighting a basic distinction of three types of morphemes which can be inferred from the above implicational relationship of processing procedures.

A *lexical morpheme* minimally requires the corresponding diacritic feature (such a 'person', 'number' etc.) to be part of the lemma and for the lexical category to be listed in the lemma. This will allow the category procedure to be called for the corresponding lexical item.

For *phrasal agreement* to occur, phrasal procedures have to be in place, so that the diacritic and other features of the head can be exchanged with the modifier. And for *inter-phrasal agreement*, (e.g. subject-verb agreement) to be processable two other processing procedures also have to be in place: grammatical functions need to be identified through Appointment Rules and the S-procedure has to be in place to store the relevant phrasal information needed for the agreement process.

The above hierarchy of processing procedures thus predicts the following structural target language outcomes:

Processing procedures	structural outcome
5 • Sub.-clause procedure	main and sub clause
4 • S-procedure	inter-phrasal info. exchange
3 • Phrasal procedure	phrasal info. exchange
2 • Category procedure	lexical morphemes
1 • Word/ lemma access	"words"

If the above hierarchy is to be universally applicable to language acquisition, then it needs to be interpretable in relation to grammatical structures in individual languages. This is achieved by interpreting the processability hierarchy through a theory of grammar which is typologically and psychologically plausible. The theory of grammar I chose for this purpose is LFG which shares two key features with Kempen and Hoenkamp's (1987) procedural account of language generation, namely (1) the assumption that grammars are lexically driven and (2) the functional annotations of phrases (e.g. "subject of") which assume the status of primitives.

Similarly with Pinker (1984) and Levelt (1989), I use LFG as a convenient reference point which has been demonstrated to be psychologically and typologically plausible. I utilise in particular the process of lexical feature unification (cf. Sections 3.1 and 3.2) which captures the essence of the IPG mechanisms relating to the processability hierarchy. In other words, key aspects of LFG are used as a short hand description of key IPG mechanisms.

The scope of Processability Theory — 'hypothesis space'

Once the processability hierarchy is expressed in terms of a theory of grammar, it can be applied to any L2 in an array of structural domains to predict the course of grammar development.[6] However, it also acts a set of constraints that operate on a number of other processes related to acquisition. This set of constraints can be viewed as defining a space within which formal grammatical hypotheses can be entertained. Hypothesis Space is not merely a metaphor, but it is constrained by the application of the processability hierarchy to the grammar of a given L2. This application process results in the delineation of those grammars which are processable at different stages of acquisition.

This is where the concept of interlanguage variation as conceptualised by Meisel, Clahsen and Pienemann (1981) is productive: at every level of the hierarchy a well-defined range of grammars is processable. Different grammars at the same level represent different interlanguage varieties. Differences in learner varieties can therefore be understood as the learner's utilisation of a limited number of structural options. It can further be demonstrated that early structural options have repercussions for the range of options which are available later. In this way early structural choices are determining factors for later development. The latter concept is known as 'generative entrenchment' (Wimsatt 1986; 1991). In other words, Processability Theory, amongst other things, delineates the scope within which interlanguage variation can occur. However, it does *not* attempt to define the set of conditions which determines the individual form of variation; e.g. 'why does learner x use form y in situation z?'.

Dynamic systems

Processability Theory with its delineation of Hypothesis Space represents a linguistic framework for the description of dynamic systems. This it shares with the 'multi-dimensional model' (Meisel et al. 1981) which utilises aspects of implicational scaling (Bickerton 1971; DeCamp 1973; Guttmann 1944) of Labov's (1972a, b) probabilistically weighted rules and of Bailey's (1973) wave model. The purpose of this framework is to enable the researcher to represent grammatical development within a variable system and to represent development and learner variation as two distinct phenomena.

Processability Theory adds a set of consistent language processing procedures to the descriptive framework of the 'multi-dimensional model'. In this context, acquisition criteria for morphological and syntactic structures are integrated into a dynamic description of the acquisition process from emergence to mastery. These acquisition criteria are related to the psychological dimension of the acquisition process and thus provide a valid tool for the testing of hypotheses that can be derived from Processability Theory.

Form-function relationships

Processability Theory makes predictions about the emergence of grammatical forms in relation to the processing procedures needed to produce these forms. However, this does not mean that these forms will emerge under all circumstances. There are several intervening sets of circumstances. One is developmental gaps which correlate with certain well defined aspects of interlanguage variation. The other set of circumstances can be described as form-function relationships. As Andersen (1984) pointed out, form-function relationships can have different degrees of complexity, and these may interact with processability.

One example of the interplay between processability and functional complexity is German morphological markers in the noun phrase where nouns, adjectives and determiners can all be marked for number, case and gender. The marking of number and gender in N and Det requires similar processing procedures, including the NP-procedure to hold the diacritic features 'number' and 'gender'. In terms of processability both processes produce phrasal morphemes. Nevertheless, gender agreement marking is acquired later than "plural agreement". This is because the diacritic feature 'number' can be read off the conceptual structure while the feature 'gender' has to be introduced one by one into the lexicon, and this process is complicated by the fact that there is no simple one-to-one relationship between the three classes of gender and certain classes of nouns. On the contrary, German gender assignment is highly arbitrary. To test Processability Theory it is therefore advisable to construct the distributional analysis in such a way that predictions can be tested on the emergence of forms, i.e. without functional accuracy.

Interlanguage variation and the steadiness hypothesis

The above theoretical constructs have an important implication for the steadiness of an interlanguage system. At the level of processing procedures, an interlanguage has to be assumed to be steady at any one point in development. Unless one makes this assumption, Processability Theory and the constructs that follow from it will not be falsifiable and thus not be theoretically interesting. Without the steadiness assumption one could always explain level-differences in samples of IL speech as learner variation, no matter whether it occurs in different situations or between different learners. In other words, the steadiness hypothesis is formed in opposition to Tarone's (1988) and Ellis' (1985b) unconstrained models of interlanguage variation.

Because of its falsifiability the 'steadiness hypothesis' is more 'daring' than the position that there is unconstrained variation in interlanguages. The empirical problem posed by the steadiness hypothesis is the following: One has to use a method of testing the hypothesis which is delicate enough to allow for the degree of variation that is predicted by Processability Theory while at the same time detecting violations of a degree of steadiness. For this purpose the latter concept is operationalised through the emergence of key processing indicators. These instruments were used in a large sample of IL speech involving different communicative contexts and different learners and no indicators of unsteadiness were found. These findings support the notion that interlanguage variability is constrained by Processability Theory.

Age differences

The constraints imposed on Hypothesis Space by Processability Theory also shed light on the question of age-related differences in SLA. At the level of accuracy, ultimate attainment and route of acquisition such differences are well documented (cf. Long 1990; Bley-Vroman 1990; Clahsen 1985). The fundamental question is what causes these differences and if they are caused by two fundamentally different processes of acquisition, exactly what is the nature of those processes. The most productive and explicit proposal in this area is Clahsen's who suggests that child language learners have access to UG, while L2 learners do not. According to Clahsen, the latter group uses processing strategies instead.

In other words, Clahsen proposes two sets of procedures for two types of learners. He has been blamed (e.g. du Plessis et al. 1987) for not properly testing the null-hypothesis by applying the opposite sets of procedures to the two groups. Processability Theory puts us in the position to do exactly that for the processing components for Clahsen's explanation. The result of this exercise is that the route of acquisition described by Clahsen for child language data is fully explicable within Processability Theory.

However, my point is that this does not refute Clahsen's hypotheses. Instead, it re-focuses the debate. One is not really surprised to find that child language grammars are processable and definable within Processability Theory. The architecture of the Grammatical Encoder has to be constructed by child and L2 learners alike. There is no reason to believe that fundamentally different processing procedures have to be developed by the two types of learners. If this were the case one would have to explain how, when and why the one set of procedures will be translated into the second in the course of maturation.

Nevertheless, the finding that Processability Theory can account for the route of acquisition in child and adult language acquisition leaves a number of phenomena unexplained, namely (1) what is the basis of hypothesis generation in L1 and L2 and (2) which mechanisms orchestrate the development of structural properties in the learner's language? These questions relate to the observation made by Clahsen and also by Meisel (1991) that L1 learners generate more effective hypotheses than L2 learners and that they orchestrate them more efficiently. To tackle these questions explanatory modules other than processability have to be introduced into the debate.

Teachability

Processability Theory provides a wider theoretical context for the "teachability hypothesis" (Pienemann 1984, 1987, 1988) which predicts that stages of acquisition cannot be skipped through formal instruction and that instruction will be beneficial if it focuses on structures from 'the next stage'.

This hypothesis can now be understood as a subset of Processability Theory. The latter is the formal basis for the definition of Hypothesis Space which delineates orderly sequences in the acquisition of morpho-syntactic rules as well as the formal margin for variation. Within this overall concept it is logical to hypothesise that 'stages cannot be skipped' (cf. Long 1988) through formal intervention, because each stage requires processing procedures which are developed at the previous stage. 'Skipping stages' in formal instruction would imply that there would be a gap in the processing procedures needed for the learner's language. Since *all* processing procedures underlying a structure are required for the processing of the structure, the learner would simply be unable to produce the structure.

Processability and strategies

In developing Processability Theory in Chapter 2, care will be taken to present the new theory in the context of the 'historical' development of ideas, starting from the strategies approach. The change in the shape of the theories from the strategies approach to Processability Theory may be confusing since both theories were designed to explain a single set of facts about language acquisition. When characterising Processability Theory it may therefore be tempting to focus merely on the descriptive facts about IL development which the theory is designed to explain, rather than on the underlying mechanics of language production.

It may therefore be helpful to very briefly compare two prominent manifestations of psycholinguistic approaches to explaining language acquisition, namely the strategies approach and Processability Theory. In section 2.3 this comparison will be made in its proper historical context.

Basically, the strategies approach dates back to psycholinguistic concepts of the 1970s which are based, amongst other things, on 'transformations', a psychologically implausible concept which is also no longer relevant in linguistic theory. Processability Theory, in contrast, is based on a core hierarchy of grammatical processing procedures which is inferred from a psychologically and computationally plausible theory of language production which is supported by strong empirical evidence. This hierarchy spells out, in abstract terms, how grammatical information can flow at various points in L2 development.

To apply processability to a specific L2, the information distribution involved in producing grammatical structures has to be determined. This can be done within LFG. The key notion in analysing information distribution is that of feature unification. In other words, Processability Theory employs a typologically and psychologically plausible metric for the analysis of grammatical information distribution.

1.3 Three competing approaches

In this section I will give a brief overview of some of the key issues of learnability theories in order to put into perspective the contribution a theory of processability can make to a theory of language acquisition. This will be no more than a rough sketch, the main purpose of which is to take a step back from discussions of detail within any one school of thought and to categorise the main philosophical issues of language learnability so that the contribution of processability to this debate can be evaluated.

I will organise this overview in form of an 'unfair' comparison by sketching out what three key explanatory approaches have to say about each of the above four issues in learnability. During this comparison it will become clear that the unfairness of the comparison lies in the choice of the four components of learnability theory which I will initially adopt from the rationalist position.

Table 1.3-1. *Three key explanatory approaches*

	Parametrisation	*Functionalism*	*Constructivism*
target grammar	described by GB	only fragments of descriptive framework	theory not applied to language
input	unsystematic	aided by speech-adjustments of caretaker	'assimilation' into 'schemata'
learning device	triggering of parameters	complex system: Competition Model	complex system of self-organisation
initial state	very rich =UG, linguistic universals	no innate linguistic knowledge, basis = conceptual/ semantic	contains basic learning principles

The choice of the three approaches is motivated by their foundation in the philosophy of science. One of them is rationalist and one empiricist in orientation, while the third, Piaget's 'genetic epistemology' (Rotman 1978), is neither of the two. The fundamental philosophical orientation of these approaches covers a wide range of possible explanatory approaches to language acquisition.

Table 1.3-1 summarises what these three approaches to the explanation of language acquisition have to say about the four components of a theory of learnability discussed by Wexler and Culicover (1980) and Pinker (1979).

Parametrisation

At the time of writing this book, *parametrisation* is the most widely used explanatory approach to SLA. The philosophical orientation of this approach is rationalist. Two highly accessible introductions to this school may have contributed to its wide acceptance, namely Cook (1988) and White (1989). The strength of the argument in favour of this school derives from the solution it has to offer to the 'logical problem' (Wexler & Culicover 1980).

The utilisation of the parameter setting framework in SLA occurs at a time when the underlying generative theory of grammar has undergone radical changes which materialise in the Minimalist program of Chomsky (1993) (cf. also Cook and Newson 1996, Chapter 9 and Radford 1996). I will briefly deal with this new development below after sketching out the rationalist debate in SLA of the past ten or fifteen years.

Several researchers have argued that the logical problem also applies to second language acquisition. One of the strongest cases is White and Genesee's (1996) study which identifies groups of adult learners whose ultimate attainment is indistinguishable from that of native speakers. If such L2 speakers, so the argument goes, are indistinguishable from native speakers, then they must have access to the same epistemological principles as native speakers.

The solution of the logical problem which the parametrisation approach has to offer is nativist in nature: if those principles of language cannot be inferred from observation then they must be innate. The parametrisation approach is based on a theory which spells out a set of universal principles and parameters of language and ways in which the latter can be set for specific languages (Chomsky 1981b). In this framework the concept of 'universal grammar' (UG) is attributed a very specific meaning. UG refers to those principles and parameters which all languages have in common and which are part of the genetically endowed knowledge of humans.

Principles and parameters are abstract notions which are specific to the formal aspect of language. Often a parameters applies to several structural domains. An example is the 'headedness parameter' (utilised, for instance by Schwartz & Tomaselli 1992) which determines the headedness of a language in all types of phrases, i.e. NPs, VPs, PPs etc. A parameter has different settings (e.g. 'left' or 'right' in the case of the headedness parameter). Another example is the pro-drop parameter which relates to a cluster of superficially unrelated phenomena, such as overt subjects, inversion and agreement (cf. Meisel 1995, 12).

In other words, every parameter has a limited number of settings (two or more), and it is the particular setting of all the parameters that apply to a given language that determines its structure. In this perspective, the language learner knows from the outset such things as that language has phrase structure and that certain principles apply to phrase structure, and he or she needs to discover from the input which phrase structures are part of the target language. The linguistic input serves to trigger the language-specific setting of a given parameter.

This scenario produces a very powerful learning device. After minimal contact with the language to be acquired, the system can set a parameter in a way which is consistent with the language. In addition, contact with one domain (e.g. headedness of NPs) automatically sets the parameter correctly in all the other domains. In this way the learner doesn't have to rely on negative evidence (i.e. to be 'told' that a possible structure is inconsistent with the language to be learned) to rule out formally possible but ungrammatical structures.

The parametrisation approach utilises a powerful theory of grammar, 'government and binding theory' (GB) (Chomsky 1981a) which is a variety of Generative Grammar (cf. Horrocks 1987). This formal theory makes it possible to apply the parametrisation approach to any human language. In other words, the approach is well-equipped to produce a formal account of the target grammar (cf. point (1) above). It also contains an account of the initial state through the concept of UG (cf. point (4) above) which formally spells out the content of the initial state. In other words, the question of the origin of linguistic knowledge which is at the heart of epistemology is addressed with great care and in the rationalist tradition.

Scholars who accept that UG plays a role in SLA attribute different roles to it. These roles vary according to the degree to which L2 learners are thought to have access to UG and according to the degree to which L1 knowledge is transferred to the L2.

The most radical position is that of Schwartz & Sprouse (1994; 1996) who propose the "Full Transfer/ Full Access model". These authors assume that "... the initial state of L2 acquisition is the final state of L1 acquisition." Schwartz & Sprouse (1996, 40f.). In other words, L2 learners have full access to UG. However, parameters are already set as in the L1. In this perspective, L2 acquisition is seen as the process of restructuring of the existing system of grammatical knowledge. This implies that when positive evidence in the input is needed to restructure aspects L1 knowledge and this evidence is not available or 'obscure', then this can lead to fossilisation. The latter process is thought to explain why, contrary to child language, in L2 acquisition "... convergence with the TL grammar is not guaranteed." Schwartz & Sprouse (1996, 42). At this point, I do not intend to evaluate the different approaches. I merely want to characterise them in order to lay out the 'terrain' of recent UG-based research on SLA. However, I do want to indicate here that in section 2.5 I will present empirical evidence that contradicts Schwartz &

Sprouse's model in rather strong terms.

The position of Vainikka & Young-Scholten (1994; 1996) might be labelled "Full Access/Minimal Transfer". In other words, it differs from that of Schwartz & Sprouse's Full Access/Full Transfer position in the amount of transfer that is assumed to occur form the L1 to the L2 setting of parameters. For Vainikka & Young-Scholten (1994; 1996) transfer is limited to lexical categories; they assume that there are no functional projections in the L2 initial state. They therefore describe their position as the 'minimal tree' position.

A further position is proposed by Eubank (1993) who hypothesises that lexical and functional categories can be transferred to the L2, but the strength of inflection associated with functional categories is not transferred. Eubank argues that the strength of the inflection will not be transferred because the affixes themselves may be fundamentally different from language to language. Meisel (1995) gives a detailed review of the positions summarised above.

The above views all have in common that L2 learners do have full access to UG. However, several scholars hold different views. Felix (1984), Clahsen (1986) and Meisel (1983; 1991) have all developed models in which L2 learners have limited access to UG (cf. also Bley-Vroman's 'Fundamental Difference hypothesis'). This assumption is congruent with the observation that L2 acquirers do not necessarily become native speakers of the L2. Given that the limited availability of UG creates an explanatory void, these authors all make proposals for a more general cognitive substitute that can account for the somewhat deficient process that is present in second language acquisition. Most of these substitute proposals are related to early precursors of the theory developed in this book. They will be dealt with in section 2.1 and 2.2 below.

As Gregg (1992; 1996) notes, the developmental problem in SLA (cf. section 1.1) has been somewhat neglected in UG-based research. Nevertheless, proposals have been made as to how to deal with this aspect of language acquisition. In principle there are two positions: (a) a maturational schedule and (b) an ordering of parameters (cf. Meisel 1995).

The choice between the two positions depends on the researcher's commitment to Pinker's (1984) continuity assumption; i.e. the assumption that the basic building blocks of grammar are the same in the learner and the fully developed user of the language. The maturational position (Felix 1984; White 1982) contradicts the continuity assumption. It claims that UG principles evolve according to an innately specified maturational schedule.

Meisel (1995, 23 ff.) illustrates the explanatory power of parameter ordering with an example from Roeper and Weissenborn (1990) who suggest that the pro-drop parameter can only be set after the parameter determining wh-movement has been set because the latter provides crucial grammatical knowledge that is a prerequisite for the pro-drop parameter (Meisel 1995, 24). Such an intrinsically defined ordering of parameters would account for the fact that not all parameters are set once the appropriate input is received. As Meisel (1995, 24) puts it, "... the learner is 'blind' towards what the input offers ..." unless the prerequisite features for a parameter have been integrated into the developing linguistic system.

The exact description of the principles and parameters contained in UG is the subject of a great deal of theorising with proposals being conceptualised and revised constantly. As Bechtel (1988) remarks, it is not unusual for a cognitive science to be in a state in which not all parts of the theory are sufficiently accepted and precise to be empirically testable. One has to accept that the incompleteness of a theory does not prove it wrong. However, given the far-reaching demands that the above principles (1) and (4) put on a theory one has to bear in mind that parametrisation is currently an in-principle solution only.

There is a further restriction of the explanatory power of the parametrisation approach: this approach does not provide very explicit principles which would explain the *route* of the gradual unfolding of the language being learned; i.e. the developmental problem.

Some researchers operating within the parametrisation paradigm appeal to concepts external to its own set of assumptions to be able to address the question of developmental schedules. Felix (1984), for instance, tackled the developmental problem by introducing a set of developmental parameters which orchestrate the setting of morphogenic parameters. However, it is not very economical to assume a set of parameters for every phenomenon that needs to be explained and runs counter to presently available insight into development in biology (Coen & Carpenter 1992).

Tomaselli & Schwartz (1990) and Du Plessis et al. (1987) show that the acquisition of word order rules found by Clahsen, Meisel and Pienemann (1983) can be explained by the setting of a small number of parameters. While their proposals do indeed provide one possible account of the origin of the linguistic knowledge developed in the described sequence, they do not contain a theoretical motivation for the order in which the parameters are set.

Tomasello (1995) gives an overview of a whole range of counter-arguments to the basic philosophy of the parameter setting perspective. Amongst other things, he quotes sources which indicate that postulated universals contained in UG are typologically implausible. He further argues with Bates (1984) that "... the fact that all cultures have a language does not mean that the basic structure of language is innate." (Tomasello 1995; 137) He goes on to reason that the species universality of language "... does not imply specifically linguistic genes." (Tomasello 1995; 137). Tomasello's position, like that of Bates, is, of course, that of a cognitive functionalist. I will characterise the functionalist outlook on SLA in some more detail and in contrast to the parameter setting perspective in a separate section later in this chapter.

The 'minimalist program' and other generative approaches

I noted above that a post-script is needed for the previous section. There are two reasons for this. One is the fact that the theoretical basis for 'principles and parameters' has fundamentally changed. The second reason is the fact that other types of generative grammar can also provide a strong formal framework for theory-based SLA research within a rationalist tradition even though they have not received the same amount of attention.

In their overview of the 'minimalist program', Cook and Newson (1996, 312) insist that "[d]espite its radically different analysis, the Minimalist Program is a progression rather than a complete U-turn." They further assert that "[t]he majority of the innovations ... do not depart from the basic concept of principles and parameters, only from the particular version of these proposed by Chomsky (1981a). ... [B]oth approaches can be called principles and parameters theory ..." Cook and Newson (1996, 312).

The paradigmatic change from the 80s version of Chomsky's theory to the 'minimalist program' was motivated, at least in part, by internal problems within GB, amongst other things, the assignment of grammatical roles to constituent structure positions. Another problem arose from the concept of 'government'. Both of these critical notions are crucial to the whole theory. As a consequence many of the key concepts of GB were abolished in the minimalist program. These include the following:

D-structure and S-Structure
Government
X-bar.

All of the above notions were essential to the mechanics of the previous version of the theory. For instance, the relationship between D-structure and S-Structure was regulated through movement operations. Neither level of representation is present in the new theory.

Naturally, all of these conceptual changes mean that each relevant linguistic phenomenon has to be re-interpreted in terms of the new theory. For instance, most of the parameters discussed in White's (1989) overview of parameters in SLA would have to be fundamentally reconceptualised because they utilise one or several of the abolished concepts. This reconceptualisation is evident in some recent work in first language acquisition (e.g. Paradis and Genesee 1996). The need for reconceptualisation does not invalidate GB-based SLA research, but it removes a minimalist version of UG one level from access to empirical scrutiny: before the applicability of the new paradigm to SLA can be demonstrated, linguistic phenomena have to be captured with the new machinery, and those theoretical treatments can only then be subjected to empirical tests. In other words, UG-based SLA research (carried out from a Chomskyan perspective) would have to restructure fundamentally if it was to be continued in the minimalist framework.

There are few scholars who have pursued this line of research in the SLA context at the time of writing this book, i.e. three years after the appearance of the first 'minimalist' publication. One example of a minimalist treatment of SLA is that of Platzack's (1994) work who applies the revised notion of parameters to first and second language acquisition, language attrition and specific language impairment. Platzack (1994, 63) notes that:

> "... the parameter concept itself was rather fuzzy [in pre-minimalist theory, MP], and most attempts to find constructions in different languages correlated by a particular value of a single parameter can be severely doubted. In a minimalist grammar, on the other hand, there is no confusion regarding parameters. The range of possible differences is laid down within the system as the dichotomy ±PF-visible, i.e. strong features versus weak features on functional categories."

Platzack's study focuses on the acquisition of Swedish word order, and he demonstrates that word order constellations can be captured by the weak/ strong distinction in functional heads.[7] He assumes that the default value of functional heads is 'weak'. If all functional heads are weak in a sentence, a universal default word order 'Subject-Verb-Complement' will be generated (Platzack 1994, 65). Only if a functional head is strong, can the position of grammatical functions change. Platzack therefore states that "... to master the word order of a particular language, you must know where the strong features are." Platzack (1994, 62)

Platzack (1994, 64) claims that "... the initial syntactic hypothesis of the child must be that all syntactic features are weak." He further claims that "... the child has access to the full range of functional categories already at the time of first sentence-like utterances ..." (Platzack 1994, 65). In other words, he claims that "... *every human child is expected to start using the word order Subject-Verb-Complement, regardless of what language he* [sic] *is exposed to* ..." [emphasis added, MP] Platzack (1994, 65-66). About second language acquisition he claims that "... we will initially go back to IHS [the initial hypothesis of syntax, i.e. SVO, MP] when trying to come to grips with a second language (Platzack 1994, 68)."

Platzack summarises some empirical evidence in support of his "initial hypothesis of syntax". He quotes cases such as the acquisition of Irish, a VSO language, in which children start with an SVO word order. He also quotes the cases of two Swedish aphasic patients who have lost the verb-second constraint and reverted to an SVO pattern. He further quotes Håkansson's (in press) study of five expatriate Swedes, none of whom lost the verb-second constraint even though their L1 grammar had been simplified in other ways. Further support is quoted from Swedish SLA which starts with an SVO pattern (cf. section 4. 3) and the case of special language impairment in Swedish which is characterised, amongst other things, by the absence of the verb-second constraint.

However, Platzack's 'initial hypothesis of syntax' is at odds with findings from German child language and the acquisition of typologically different second languages. Clahsen (1982) found that the first discernible word order constellation in German child language is SOV and not SVO, as predicted by Platzack. Huter (1996) found that English learners of Japanese, an SOV language, start with SOV as the initial word order even though English is an SVO language. Both these sets of findings strongly contradict Platzack's hypothesis which is also typologically implausible. Why should the initial, "... genetically determined language system (Platzack 1994, 59)" be constructed as a configurational system with an English-like pattern, while the languages of the world rarely display this pattern and instead contain large groups of non-configurational languages?

Nevertheless, the implausibility of Platzack's hypothesis and the empirical counter evidence to it do not demonstrate that the 'minimalist program' as such is unproductive for SLA research. It may be possible that the child and/ or the L2 learner does initially not have access to the full range of functional categories or that lexical categories do not contain only weak features or that the default word order in UG is not SVO. In other words, many other ways of applying the new framework can be hypothesised. However, Platzack's attempted application of the new framework to SLA and child language does amplify the point I made above, namely that much work needs to be done before the new framework can be applied to SLA research with the same degree of productivity as the GB framework.

Finally it needs to be noted that the notion of 'universal grammar' is one that derives quite logically from the rationalist basis of generative schools of grammatical theory (Horrocks 1987). In a less technical form this notion has been part of rationalist approaches to the philosophy of language for centuries (Chomsky 1990, Bresnan 1988). However, this does not mean that all rationalist approaches to grammatical theory or all Generative Grammars are committed to the same architecture of UG as the theory of Government and Binding or later the 'minimalist program'. One has to remember that the historical commitment to some universal and presumably innate core of language which Chomsky (1990) refers to is in itself rather vague, and even though these ideas can be found in von Humboldt's (1836) famous typological observations, von Humboldt's concept of universality would be an unsuitable component for a theory of learnability if for no other reason than its lack of explicitness.

The reason for highlighting the significance of the architecture of UG for a theory of language learning is that later in this book I will utilise a generative theory of grammar other than GB, namely LFG, to describe L2 developmental grammars. I want to point out early on that the substance and nature of UG is radically different in LFG. While Chomsky's principles and parameters are based primarily on constituent structure configurations, Bresnan's (1988, 1993) conceptualisation of UG as part of Lexical-Functional Grammar (Kaplan and Bresnan 1982) is concerned with the relationship between semantic predicate argument structure and constituent structure. This relationship is regulated by a system of functional structures. Bresnan's version of UG

therefore does not contain 'formal parameters' but a hierarchy of semantic roles
which the theory formalism can relate to one single level of grammatical
representation using lexical and syntactic principles. The consequence of this
difference in the design of UG is pointedly summarised by Bresnan (1988, 18):

> "These differences in design give rise to different computational and psycho-
> linguistic models of how language is processed, and to potentially very different
> views of the natural processes by which children learn languages.*"

---

* See Pinker 1984, Ford (1982), and Ford, Bresnan, and Kaplan (1982)

In other words, the rationalist tradition in no way demands a commitment to
the specific architecture of UG as proposed by Chomsky in the GB framework and later. The commitment in-principle to some form of universal
grammar reflects no more than a general rationalist stance. However, to be
productive in the discussion sketched out here, the mechanics or actual
substance of universal grammar has to be spelt out in detail.

Functionalism

Functionalism is not one homogeneous theory, but the label for a general
approach to linguistics which aims at the description and explanation of
language use through an understanding of the communicative conditions
which lead to the use of one form over another. Tomlin (1990) identifies four
major schools of functionalist linguistics: (1) The Prague School (Daneš,
1974), (2) the European School (Dik 1987), (3) Systemic Grammar (Halliday
1985) and (4) North American functionalism which subsumes a whole range
of research efforts some of which include work on language acquisition.

Those functionalists who address language acquisition share one concern, namely the relationship of linguistic form and its function. While the
Chomskyan framework sees form and function as largely independent and
autonomous, functionalists seek to explain the use of alternative forms
through their functions. In the context of language acquisition, form-function
relationships can be seen as a heuristic basis for learning and also as its
motivational basis. However, there is a great deal of variation in the way in
which this general tenet is translated into functionalist approaches to language
acquisition.

As Bates and MacWhinney (1982, 177) point out, one "... can find both nativists and empiricists within the functionalist camp." However, it is important to remember that the type of nativism found here is mediated via an indirect causal route. The example Bates and MacWhinney (1982, 177) give is the innateness of hand-feeding as a human characteristic: "... it is the most efficient and probable solution to the particular problem." In other words, the universal hand-feeding behaviour is not directly genetically encoded but mediated by the general bodily architecture of the organism.

In his discussion of nativism Wimsatt (1986) identifies many, mostly biological, examples of this type of nativism which is mediated by the environment. Let me give a relatively recent example, namely the development of the fruit fly (Wolpert 1992) which is illustrated in Figure 1.3-1. At a certain early stage of development in the larvae the organism needs to identify the relative position of its segments so that the appropriate organs can grow in the right place. It has been demonstrated that this process of self-organisation depends on the level of acidity in the immediate environment of the organism (i.e. the embryo). Genetic information is used to create an environment for the egg which contains a concentration gradient of the protein bicoid, and this gradient is used to mark out the space inside the egg as shown in Figure 1.3-1 (Wolpert 1992, 40). In other words, while the bioprogram for the development of organs is part of the genetic code, the location problem is solved dependent on the environment, and no genetic code is necessary to co-ordinate the relative location of parts of the body in the developing organism.

It is important to remember that the key issue in characterising functionalism is not to determine the exact percentage ratio in the *nature-nurture* debate. What differentiates nativism in GB and in functionalism is its philosophical program. GB is committed to the modularity of mind. This means that in order to explain the origin of linguistic knowledge, specifically linguistic parameters are assumed to be innate, while in functionalism innate ideas are not assumed to be specifically linguistic. Instead they are seen to be general to all domains of the developing individual. The functionalist can therefore derive linguistic phenomena from factors of general cognition.

Most functionalists would therefore not be able to accept the validity of the logical problem because the latter is built on premises which they do not share.

The logical problem is based on the assertion that the target language grammar is extremely complex and that part of its complexity is caused by the fact that it contains many formal categories such as 'noun' or 'subject' which do not relate in a simple way to the experiential world of the learner.

Figure 1.3-1. Development of the fruit fly

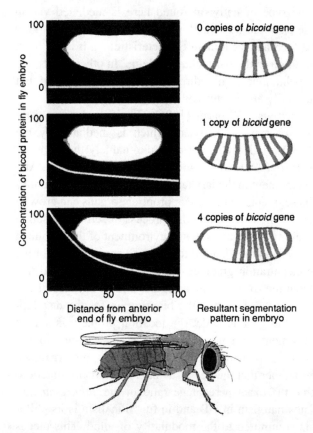

From: Wolpert (1992, 40)

Functionalists such as Bates and MacWhinney point out, however, that the degree of complexity very much depends on the theory of grammar chosen to represent the final state of the learning process. Bates and Elman (1992) present a general framework for the representation of language learning processes which in their view would make the final state appear much less complex.

Functionalists have pointed out that many formal categories do indeed have correlates in the experiential world of the learner (e.g. Bates & MacWhinney 1982): for instance, in child language early nouns mostly refer to objects, and grammatical subjects coincide with agents. However, the crux of the matter is to demonstrate how the learner manages, without recourse to innate linguistic knowledge, to construct a formal category on the basis of this tentative relationship which will soon be falsified once exposed to adult linguistic data. Bates and Elman (1992) contend that the connectionist network describing the learner's use of linguistic categories is sufficient to model their linguistic behaviour. In connectionist networks[8] learning is a matter of strengthening and weakening neural connections in response to statistical frequency patterns in the input. In other words, in this context the notion of the impoverished state of the input is completely reversed: the input contains all the clues, and these can be modelled by the network.

The basic assumption of connectionism that language use does not require mentally-represented rules, runs counter to fundamental assumptions of rationalist linguists. Pinker and Prince (1988), for instance, have argued that certain networks which they tested cannot produce all linguistic forms in a specific domain that are contained in the target language, but they do produce non-forms and have other 'learning problems'. They conclude that therefore the dispensability of rules in the psychology of language must be rejected. In my opinion this epistemological riddle is yet to be solved. One has to ask oneself if one can conclude that it is *in principle* impossible to produce an inferential mechanism which is able to infer formal classes on the basis of conceptual classes just because functionalists have so far had limited success.

J. Fodor (1981) makes exactly the point that this *is* an impossibility. He does this not on the basis of the functionalists' assumed lack of success but from a radical rationalist philosophical perspective. In his paper "On the Impossibility of Acquiring 'More Powerful' Structures" he asserts that new concepts cannot be acquired solely on the basis of existing concepts because otherwise the new concept would have been part of the existing concept in the first place. Fodor contends that there is no theory of learning that can generate new conceptual structures on the basis of existing structures and by inferencing. Therefore all concepts must be innate.

This point was directed against Piaget who believes that more complex structures are constructed by the child on the basis of less complex structures through certain adaptation processes. At the same time Fodor's point also affects the basis of functionalist theories of language acquisition which make an even greater use of the inferencing component in the acquisition process. I will return to this point in the context of Piaget's genetic epistemology.

The question, why the learner moves on in the acquisition process appears to be naturally answerable from a functional perspective, since form-function relationships can be seen as a moving force behind the acquisition process (e.g. Bates and MacWhinney 1982). However, the very logic of Bates & MacWhinney's approach has been questioned by Roeper (1982) and Maratsos (1982) who point out that the languages of the world contain some linguistic forms which are not related to any function. This obviously creates a serious problem for a form-function based discovery process: How, in such a system, can forms be discovered if they do not relate to any function? If one were to shift the question back to some historical time when a presently absent form-function relationship did indeed exist (cf. Roeper 1982) one would only add an unrealistically massive module to the functionalist explanation. Considering the many thousand years of human language development, where would all this information about previous historical form-function relationships be stored?

The 'logical problem' is partly based on the alleged poverty of the linguistic input the learner receives. Non-rationalist scholars of language acquisition, however, do not agree with the assumption that the linguistic input received by the learner is impoverished. They point out that there are many aspects in the input itself that will aid the acquisition process. In the context of first language acquisition this hypothesis was advanced, amongst others, by Charles Ferguson and Catherine Snow (e.g. in Snow and Ferguson 1977). These authors suggested that the linguistic adjustment of the 'caregiver' (i.e. mother, father etc.) to the level of the child's language and cognitive development acted as a natural language learning program. This is quite a different perspective from that of the 'logical problem' which abstracts away from interactional circumstances and treats input merely as the set of sentences received by the learner. This is where functionalists may see an 'unfairness' in my comparison of three schools of thought on the basis of the components of learnability theory as defined in a rationalist framework. Functionalists will maintain to varying degrees that speech and interactional adjustments are essential to language learning and should therefore form a component of a theory of learnability.

The speech adjustment ('motherese') hypothesis was followed by extensive empirical research on speech adjustments in the areas of morphosyntax, semantics, discourse and interaction. On the one hand, Newport, Gleitman and Gleitman (1977) found little evidence for adjustments with morphosyntactic precision. This finding weakens the role of speech adjustments in facilitating the acquisition of linguistic form. On the other hand, the same authors did find evidence that 'caregivers' adjust their speech semantically to the level of the child, for instance in the use of deixis. The general trend in studies on L1 input modification was that caretaker talk conforms more closely to grammatical norms than speech addressed to mature native speakers and that it is simpler and more redundant.

Input modification also received a great deal of attention in the second language context. It formed part of Krashen's (1980) 'input hypothesis' according to which L2 learners progress in the acquisition process because of 'comprehensible input', i.e. semantically simplified and contextually enriched input. Long's (1985) position focuses on a different aspect of the input, namely interaction. Long claims that acquisition is promoted when interactional adjustments occur and that these are more beneficial for L2 comprehension than adjustments at the level of linguistic form. There is a great deal of empirical evidence in support of Long's hypothesis. There is not the space to review all of these studies here; a few examples will have to suffice. Issidorides and Hulstijn (1992) demonstrated that syntactic simplifications in areas that are known to cause learning problems in language production do not have an effect on comprehension. Pica, Doughty and Young (1986) demonstrated that interactionally modified input resulted in better L2 comprehension than any other type of input.

In the context of this chapter, which is aimed at providing an overview of issues in different approaches to learnability, one has to consider how the concept of input modification contributes to an understanding of learnability. Faerch and Kasper (1986) pointed out that acquisition will only take place if the learner notices the gap between the input and his or her current grammar. In a similar vein Gass (1988), points out that research on the facilitating role of modified input on comprehension does not show how comprehension results in acquisition. In other words, Faerch and Kasper's and Gass' critique is supportive of the general idea and advocates a further conceptual refinement of the original hypotheses.

Researchers working in the parametrisation paradigm have criticised more the substance of input research. For instance, White (1987) claims that certain overgeneralisations made by the learner cannot be rectified merely by comprehending input. Instead, what would be required is negative feedback. If one accepts White's argument then one would have to conclude that the comprehensible input hypothesis makes empirically incorrect predictions

about overgeneralisations. The only way to maintain the comprehensible
input position would be to assume that comprehensible input is only a necessary but not a sufficient condition of L2 acquisition. With this position in mind
one would have to make provisions for other explanatory components to
interact with the input component.

Constructivism: Genetic epistemology

Piaget's approach to the development of conceptual structures is neither
rationalist nor empiricist. Piaget's approach is deeply anti-empiricist; this it
shares with Chomsky. Piaget's anti-empiricism grew out of his opposition to the
work of Spencer (1864-7) who saw the growth of knowledge as a cumulative
process of habit formation transmitted through generations. Spencer's perspective was a mixture of associationist psychology and the empiricist view of
science as an accumulation of facts (Rotman 1978).

    Piaget developed a brand of philosophy that is referred to as 'constructiv-
ism'. This philosophical framework is derived from the Kantian idea that the
human mind *actively constructs* its knowledge of the world, rather than
passively records data as the empiricists saw it. Piaget designed his theory
with this Kantian connection in mind (cf. the Piaget-Chomsky debate in
Piatelli-Palmarini 1981). However, as Rotman (1978) points out, Piaget had a
number of reservations about Kant's position, particularly in relation to
Kant's introspective method and his concept of fixed rather than developing
mental structures. With these modifications Piaget adds to the concept of
mental construction a *physiological* sense: knowledge derives from the movement of the individual in the world.

    For his theory of the development of mental structures Piaget assumes a
very small set of innate ideas which equip the individual to acquire concepts
in all cognitive domains. These biologically innate ideas consist mainly of
two core functions: assimilation and accommodation. By acting in their
natural environment, children assimilate new objects into existing schemata
as long as the existing knowledge system is compatible with the new objects.
When new objects disturb the equilibrium of the knowledge system by
highlighting an inconsistency, the whole system can be revamped (accommodation). This is the mechanism by which new concepts arise.

    Boden (1979) criticised Piaget for a lack of explicitness about the details
of this mechanism:

> "... Piaget's theory lacks specification of detailed procedural mechanisms competent to generate the phenomena it describes."
> (Boden 1979, 23)

However, she hastens to add that most other psychological theories are guilty of the same omission.

Piaget's cognitive system is intended to explain the development of knowledge as an active process of mental construction. This process has its origin in sensorimotor activity and develops from there, through a self-regulated process, in necessary and therefore universal stages to a mature level of knowledge representation. The necessity of this process of construction is seen to be inherent in the implicational relationship of the mental processes involved. Those developed at the higher level build on those at the previous levels and so on.

It is therefore inherent in Piaget's approach that he cannot accept rationalist nativism. As Rotman (1978, 47) puts it, "Piaget ... rejects any preformationist solutions (in which he includes Husserlian essences, Platonic forms and Kantian *a priori* forms) as avoiding the question of genesis altogether." According to Piaget, every structure has a genesis.

As I remarked earlier, this clashes sharply with the radical rationalism of J. Fodor who claims that it is impossible to acquire 'more powerful' structures merely on the basis of simpler structures and inferencing. While Piaget cannot offer a detailed and formalised theory which can generate new and more powerful concepts through learning, he counters that Fodor's conclusion that all concepts are innate, is implausible both developmentally and phylogenetically. In Piaget's words:

> "... this innateness of mathematics is for me a real problem: at what age are we going to discover the appearance of innateness of negative numbers, of complex numbers, and so forth — at age 2, 7, 20? And most of all why on earth would this be special to the human species if we have here necessary innate structures? For my part, I have a difficult time believing that Cantor's theories or today's theories of categories are already preformed in bacteria or viruses ..."
> (Piaget in Piatelli-Palmarini 1981, 149ff)

In this attempted *constructio ad absurdum* of Fodor's position one sees the literal biological dimension of the origin of knowledge that Piaget assumes and that is absent from Fodor's purely logical perspective. In response to Piaget's objection, Fodor (1981, 151) points out that "... the nativist isn't committed to saying that viruses know about set theory ...". Instead, he

describes a theory of modification of concepts which excludes the invention
of new concepts as follows:

> "... a theory of the conceptual plasticity of organisms must be a theory of
> how the environment selects among the innately specified concepts. It is not
> a theory of how you acquire concepts, but a theory of how the environment
> determines which parts of the conceptual mechanism in principle available
> to you are in fact exploited."
> (Fodor in Piatelli-Palmarini 1981, 151)

This, however, does not satisfy Piaget's desire to know, in a biological sense,
where innate structures originate. This raises the question of the evolutionary
plausibility of the Fodor/ Chomsky position. More recently, several authors
(e.g. R.-A. Müller 1995) have argued that for complex mental structures such
as language to exist, they must consist of component parts which can be
traced in evolution. However, despite their biological metaphors, for Fodor
and Chomsky the question of the origin of knowledge does not need to be
translated into genetic code and is dealt with purely on logical grounds.

A modular approach towards a theory of SLA

Obviously, the two positions are, at least currently, not reconcilable, and I will
leave the debate here, even though there would be a wide array of arguments
that could illuminate the discussion further. However, I hope that this discussion has served the purpose of illustrating that the key issues in language
learnability are far from being resolved, and that every one of the major
schools of thought has a number of shortcomings.

These shortcomings do not invalidate any of the frameworks *per se*, but
they illustrate the fact that, currently there is no one framework which can
provide satisfactory answers to all of the above explananda in language
acquisition. Already in this brief discussion we noted that parametrisation is
good at explaining the *origin* of linguistic knowledge and poor at explaining
developmental schedules. This is supported by the evaluation of Gregg (1992;
1996) who finds that the GB framework has made major contributions in the
area of 'property theory' while it is lacking in well-designed 'transition
theories'. In the traditional functionalist perspective the origin of knowledge
is not really an issue, since it is derived from the individual's interaction with
the fully structured environment. These theories therefore capitalise on the
way in which the individual relates to the environment. It has been stated by

Tomlin (1990) that there is a lack of well-defined formalisms for this undertaking. This is also true for genetic epistemology (cf. Boden 1979), which has never been seriously applied to the cognitive domain of language.

My point is not to demonstrate a lack of validity for these explanatory approaches. My concern is rather that they attempted to explain too much. If one accepts the above explanatory issues, one does not necessarily have to develop all from within one theory package. This was quite obvious in genetic epistemology, the major strength of which was a deep insight into the *development* of mental structures and a major problem of which was the *genesis* of those structures. Of course, it was the ambition of Piaget and his co-workers to solve both of these problems in one unified approach, and one would distort their work if one was to look at the above issues separately. On the other hand, the unified approach was not achieved with the necessary procedural precision even within the long lifetime of Jean Piaget.

Naturally, one has to ensure that a modular approach to language learnability does not lead to theoretical incompatibilities of the component parts (e.g. empiricist functionalism and UG). However, I see no reason why, for instance, some form of genetically specified knowledge could not interact with processing factors. In this way, one theoretical module would contribute to a property theory which can interact with another module that contributes to a transition theory.

In other words, I want to make the case that it is a worthwhile research strategy to reduce the task of explaining SLA to discrete subtasks, and to employ different theoretical modules for each of those tasks as long as the different modules are able to communicate with each other and are theoretically consistent. In this approach a certain degree of executive control in the division of labour between the different components is also needed because the design of one component influences the design of the others.

The explanatory module I develop in this book concerns the question of processability. Obviously, any structural hypothesis entertained by the learner must be "humanly processable". Since the class of grammars which are humanly processable at any one given stage is smaller than the class of grammars which are logically possible, a formal account of processability will reduce the formal Hypothesis Space of the learnability problem.

While the proposed module is a specialist theory restricted to the domain of processability of linguistic structures, I will apply it to a range of contexts which span from interlanguage variation to age differences. In other words:

rather than developing an all-encompassing theory for one domain of SLA, I develop a special theory which is capable of unifying a whole range of domains and thereby solidifies its explanatory value (Gregg 1993, Long 1993). Obviously, the processability module will say nothing about the genesis of mental structures and a range of other issues in learnability. This should not be construed as a flaw, instead the focus on only one explanatory issue is the specific point of a modular theory and will not serve to falsify it.

Some distant relatives

The processability module which will be laid out in this book focuses on the issue of development in SLA. It treats interlanguage as a dynamic linguistic system that spreads in several dimensions. The dynamics of the interlanguage are related to the way in which the learner develops language-specific processing procedures. These concepts will be applied to a whole range of dynamic phenomena in the interlanguage, such as IL variation, typological differences, age differences etc.

My focus on the developmental problem in language acquisition is shared by two well-known researchers: Jean Piaget and Roman Jakobson. I discussed Piaget's "genetic epistemology" above and pointed out that it has a much wider scope than the proposed modular theory. At this point it would be easy to dismiss the Piaget-connection as irrelevant because of all the opposition that his work has experienced (1) because of the lack of precision in his description of the development of 'intelligence, (2) because of its mathematical imprecision and (3) because of its epistemological problems. Nevertheless, what remains, is Piaget's deep insight into the implicational nature of development. This design feature is one which the processability account proposed here, shares with Piaget's perspective — as well as the desire to connect mental development to the constraints of the developing organism.

Roman Jakobson's (1941/69/86) famous book *Kindersprache, Aphasie und allgemeine Lautgesetze*[9] sets out a general framework of structural prerequisites for the production of phonemic distinctions. In this framework basic phonemic oppositions form the basis of the hierarchical system of distinctive features that constitutes the set of phonemes of any given language. The hierarchy is linguistic in nature, and Jakobson traces it in predicted patterns of child language acquisition, in the reduced linguistic systems of aphasic patients, in people with a hearing deficit, and in linguistic typology.

What is of interest here is not the reliability of the predictions made in Jakobson's theory, but its overall design. The basis of this theory is purely linguistic in nature. The novelty of Jakobson's approach was to test the validity of his theory in developmental phenomena in acquisition and aphasia as well as cross-linguistically. Jakobson's point was that a valid hierarchical system of phonemic distinctions (or more generally: any hierarchical linguistic system) ought to materialise in the developing linguistic system of language learners, and in the "decayed" linguistic system of aphasic patients, as well as in linguistic patterns found in the languages of the world.

The reader will notice below that some of these basic assumptions are also present in my own theory. At this fundamental level the main difference between the two approaches is that I add a psychological dimension to the explanatory formula.

The cognitive connection

In the context of this introductory chapter which traces some of the general trends in developmental linguistic issues, a statement on the nature of the philosophical position taken in this book may be in order. In this book I treat language acquisition as a cognitive process by identifying mental states of the learner in terms of their causal interactions with other mental states. This is part of the overall aim of cognitive science (Bechtel 1988) which is based on the assumption that the basic architecture of cognitive processes is comparable between individuals and that the acquisition of skill and knowledge can be understood through the discovery of their constituent cognitive processes.

This stance does not imply a denial of the social dimension of learning; it merely separates the cognitive from the social aspect. In this view the two aspects of learning have a degree of autonomy, each following its own internal logic. While the two aspects of learning doubtless interact with each other, my assumptions imply the view that the internal logic of cognitive processes, such as the basic structure of 'temporary memory' (Baddeley 1990), cannot be altered by social dynamics and vice versa.

Once one views language learning in terms of cognitive processes, this position has powerful implications: one can no longer assume that the state of the learner's linguistic system can suddenly change fundamentally under the influence of social variables such as interactional parameters or formal learning environments. In other words, one does not expect phenomena such as a new situation or new learning environment to cause a low-level learner suddenly to turn into a high-level learner. At the same time it is quite consistent with this cognitivist position to assume that social parameters may cause a sequence of changes in the learner's processing of the language which leads to the gradual attainment of a high-level skill. However, these changes of cognitive processes would always occur within the overall architecture of the cognitive system.

The position assumed in this book

As noted above, in this book I will focus on one aspect of language learnability, namely on the constraints imposed on the learning process by the architecture of the human language processor. This explanatory module makes a contribution to solving the developmental problem, and no explicit proposals for other components will be made.

The modular approach of Processability Theory contrasts with that taken by Towell and Hawkins (1994) who attempt to integrate all major explanatory issues into one model of SLA that accounts for epistemological, inferential and processing aspects of the acquisition process. This is not the place for a detailed review of the work by Towell and Hawkins. It will have to suffice to say that, in my view, the issues tackled by these authors are currently too large to permit a testable synthesis of all those issues. Towell and Hawkins use the parametrisation approach for epistemological and developmental issues and use J. R. Anderson's (1982) model of "adaptive control of thought" as a basis for inferential (or 'learning') issues. While Towell and Hawkins name many of the relevant issues in constructing a theory of second language acquisition, it has yet to be demonstrated how this mix of models and theories can produce internally coherent and empirically falsifiable predictions.

Processability Theory brings the language processor into the focus of the study of language development, and this constitutes an overlap with Jean Piaget's approach to the development of cognitive structures, namely their dependence on the architecture of the living body in which they develop. However, this is where the overlap ends. I noted above that Piaget was fundamentally opposed to the notion of any innate *a priori* forms. In the context of a modular approach to the explanation of language acquisition, I feel that it would be premature to exclude innate *a priori* forms from the possible range of epistemological processes. One reason for this is that at present one cannot be confident that principles of self-organisation are sufficient to account for the epistemological issues involved in language acquisition. Piaget certainly has not presented a formally explicit and empirically testable constructivist paradigm in which new forms emerge out of less developed forms on the basis of self-organisation.

While the explanatory module developed in this book systematically excludes specific contributions to other explanatory modules, I nevertheless attempted to design it in such a way that it can interface with other potential or existing modules. The epistemological process is therefore not totally irrelevant to the design of the processing component. The reader will note that I chose a mildly adapted version of Lexical-Functional Grammar as the theoretical linguistic point of reference to formalise the psychological processes developed in this module. This was done because of the high degree of psychological plausibility present in LFG and because of its ability to model most of the key psychological features of the language processor which are relevant here. I noted above that the notion of 'universal grammar' is quite compatible with LFG and the processing approach taken here. However, this does not imply a commitment to a specific formalisation of UG as, for instance, within Chomsky's framework of GB or the 'minimalist program'.

Given that Wexler and Culicover's four parameters of their learnability analysis compete with each other, assumptions on the linguistic information that is genetically encoded will depend on the strength of the other parameters. In addition, I will show that there are at least two other factors that potentially have a bearing on innate and genetically fully specified linguistic information, namely processability and 'generative entrenchment'. The first relates to constraints imposed on the learning process by the learning organism; the second relates to the dynamics of the developmental process itself.

In other words, I prefer to develop a testable account of processability and generative entrenchment before attempting to hypothesise exactly which bits of linguistic knowledge are genetically specified. Towards the end of this book I will engage in some speculation on the interaction between these three elements: UG, processability and generative entrenchment.

Chapter 2

Language processing
and language acquisition

2.1 Introduction: The wider context

The main line of argument pursued in this book is the following: the task of acquiring a second language implies the acquisition of the *skills* needed for the processing of the language. This approach which focuses solely on the transitional aspect of SLA derives its explanatory power from the fact that a set of observations, developmental patterns, can be reduced to a more basic set of operations, processing procedures.

A number of scholars have pointed out the interrelationship between SLA and language processing (e.g.. Hulstijn 1990, Hulstijn & Hulstijn 1984; Dechert et al. 1984; Schmidt 1992; Faerch & Kasper 1983a; Levelt 1978; Clahsen 1979, 1984). McLaughlin's work (1978; 1980; 1987) is often seen as one key points of reference which opened up the processing perspective for second language acquisition.

In his approach, McLaughlin utilises two major concepts, namely (1) *automaticity* and (2) *restructuring*. Automaticity makes recourse to the dichotomy of *controlled* and *automatic processing* (Posner and Snyder 1975; Schneider and Shiffrin 1977; Shiffrin and Schneider 1977). Restructuring refers to the replacement of existing procedures by more efficient ones. McLaughlin (1987, 138) believes that "... once the procedures at any phase become automatised ... learners step up to a 'metaprocedural' level, which generates representational change and restructuring".

In other words, McLaughlin's approach is aimed at the skills that underlie L2 processing as well as at the acquisition of these skills. In fact, the very term 'automatisation' which is used by McLaughlin and others with related views refers to the process of skill acquisition.

Several authors working in this perspective (e.g. Dechert, Möhle & Raupach 1984; Towell and Hawkins 1994; cf. also Schmidt 1992) build upon J.R. Anderson's (1982, 1983) original approach to the acquisition of cognitive skills. In this approach the assumption is made that knowledge in a new domain starts out in declarative form and is then *converted* into procedural knowledge. In the first edition of Anderson's (1980) "Cognitive Psychology and its Implications", child language acquisition was indeed mentioned to illustrate a number of concepts involved in skill acquisition, in particular 'generalisation' and 'discrimination' (Anderson 1980, 247f.). It is therefore not surprising to find Anderson's model in SLA research. However, fifteen years later Anderson (1995) appears to have revised this position. He states:

> "With very little and often no deliberate instruction, children by the time they reach age 10 have accomplished *implicitly* what generations of Ph.D. linguists have not accomplished *explicitly* [emphasis added]. They have internalised all the major rules of a language ... " Anderson (1995, 364)

In other words, Anderson no longer sees language acquisition as an instance of the conversion of declarative into procedural knowledge. This revised view is indeed much more compatible with Paradis' (1994) survey of the neuropsychological basis for the dissociation of (implicit) procedural and (explicit) declarative knowledge. In a section entitled "Metalinguistic Knowledge Does Not Become Procedural" Paradis (1994, 401) states the following:

> "It appears that what has been acquired incidentally is stored implicitly and can only be evidenced through behaviour (performance). On the other hand, some deliberately learned tasks seem to gradually become automatic through prolonged practice ...".

It seems that the majority of examples of learning quoted in Anderson (1980) and in later applications to SLA research refer to such things as letter recognition (cf. also Shiffrin and Schneider 1977), arithmetic operations or skilled typing. These are examples of deliberately learned tasks where it is indeed plausible that declarative knowledge is converted into procedural knowledge. However, it is questionable if the acquisition of second (or first) languages can *generally* be characterised in this way. For instance, one has to assume that the procedures that underlie the production of morphosyntactic structures are quite different and independent from the rules of grammar which were consciously learned. Recently, SLA researchers such as Hulstijn and de Graaff (1994) have adopted Anderson's modified position.

Bialystok (1978) was one of the first to utilise the dichotomy of procedural and declarative knowledge in the SLA context. In her more recent work (Bialystok 1991) she follows Karmiloff-Smith (1986) in assuming that the acquisition of linguistic skills moves from 'implicit' to 'explicit' with the proviso that explicit linguistic knowledge does not have to be conscious. In other words, the process of skill development is seen here as the reverse of Anderson's original proposal. This position is supported by Paradis (1994) who sums up the case of 'grammar learning' as follows:

> "What is automatised is not the explicit knowledge of the rule, ... but its application. ... What is automatised is the ability to produce the correct sequence of words in their proper inflectional from, whatever the processes have been used to reach this result. These remain in fact for ever opaque to introspection." Paradis (1994, 401-2)

This is quite consistent with the view and empirical evidence presented by Levelt (1989) upon which some of my own proposals rely. In addition, in experiments on the non-conscious acquisition of knowledge (e.g. Ling and Marinov 1994) it is well-documented that procedural knowledge does NOT have to progress through a declarative phase. In fact, human participants in experiments on non-conscious learning were not only not aware of the rules they acquired, they were not even aware that they had acquired any knowledge in the first place.

The reason for this detour on Anderson's model is that in my own approach to SLA theory which will be set out in the chapters below, I will exclude the process of automatisation from the focus of this book. Instead I will concentrate on the *architecture* of the automatic procedures which produce fluent language use. I will then form hypotheses about the acquisition of this architecture while excluding, for the time being, questions about its origin, i.e. the process generally referred to as automatisation.

After this detour let us return briefly to McLaughlin's (1987) approach. In his 1987 overview, McLaughlin quotes a number of empirical studies which operate productively in his framework. These are studies of bilingual word retrieval, lexical, syntactic and semantic encoding and decoding. In these studies a range of differential effects of automaticity were identified in comparing the performance of L1 and L2 speakers. In other words, McLaughlin was able to demonstrate the productivity of his approach to SLA theory.

While this work was influential for development of a cognitive perspective on SLA, McLaughlin himself points out (1987, 148-53) that his outline of

Completes in verbal processing of
input + processing
as part of long-term
acquisition of experience

a cognitive theory of SLA does not contain sufficient detail for specific predictions about such things as sequences of acquisition. He proposes a modular approach to a theory of SLA in which a linguistic theory and processing theory take on complementary roles. This is precisely the position I argued for above and which I will try to implement in the following chapters.

While many authors working in the 'cognitive skill tradition' in SLA did not explicitly construct their theoretical self-image in opposition to a parametrisation perspective and some authors (e.g. Meisel and Clahsen) have felt at home in both 'camps', the two perspectives have also been perceived to be in opposition to each other. An example of this is the paper by White (1991) "Second Language Competence versus Second Language Performance: UG or Processing Strategies". White perceives this contrast because she supports the perspective that L2 learners have access to UG and several of the authors who believe that UG is not accessible to L2 learners devised alternative explanations to UG for L2 acquisition which are based on general cognitive concepts. From her perspective, it is logical to ask if these alternatives are as powerful as UG, and it is also understandable that she perceives an opposition between UG and the 'strategies approach'.

In contrast, Towell and Hawkins (1994) attempt to integrate the two perspectives into one. However, their model is, at this stage, merely a sketch, the mechanics of which needs to be worked out before one can decide on its internal coherence and its capacity to produce empirically testable predictions.

In the context of language processing and first language acquisition a general cognitive perspective has been developed which bears some resemblance to the above information-processing perspective. The logic of the general cognitive perspective is similar to the one applied in this book: what is easy to process is easy to acquire. The "classic" proponents of this approach are Dan Slobin and Thomas Bever.

Bever's original work (Bever 1970) focused on language processing. Bever demonstrated that the shape of linguistic forms depends on the cognitive basis for the processing of those forms. What is relevant in the current context is that Bever identified a number of "processing strategies" which can better account for the way native speakers process language in real time than the procedural version of linguistic theories. His strategies were therefore conceived of as the performance counterparts to linguistic theories. This discussion has to be placed in the historic context of the debate on the psychological reality of linguistic structures. The idea of processing strategies as a systematic account of the cognitive basis of linguistic performance was developed further by Kimball (1973) who developed a set of processing strategies all of which were directed at economically utilising surface structure cues to discover the semantic-conceptual structure being communicated.

By the late 1970s to early 1980s it became clear that this line of thought would ultimately not be productive because (1) there was no way to construct processing strategies in an *a priori* and theoretically coherent manner. (2) This lack of theoretical constraints left open a potentially unlimited number of strategies and (3) these would not be able to be related in a principled way to the representation of linguistic knowledge.

Slobin's (e.g. Slobin 1973, 1977, 1985) framework for first language acquisition consists of a number of 'operating principles' which concern two aspects of the acquisition process: the processing of language and the discovery of its formal and functional properties. In other words, his framework reaches beyond language processing to incorporate also learning mechanism. Andersen (1988) applied Slobin's approach to SLA and was able to make relatively specific predictions for sequences of acquisition.

However, operating principles share a limitation with language processing strategies: they do not contain procedural information to implement the micro-structure of language processing. For instance, to make the operating principle 'be semantically expressive' productive for the speaker, one needs to specify the exact procedures needed to generate the surface structures which best express the semantic structures intended by the speaker. In other words, operating principles, like processing strategies, lack linguistic or procedural explicitness. In addition, Bowerman (1985) points out relation to Slobin's approach, that operating principles are not falsifiable because evidence against existing principles can be countered by the introduction of ever new principles.

At this point a potential source for terminological confusion is worth looking at: at the time when language processing strategies were being explored, the SLA field developed research efforts which were labelled with headings which also contained the word 'strategies' (e.g. Tarone 1981; Faerch and Kasper 1984; Bialystok 1981). Much of this work is reviewed in O'Malley & Chamot (1990). It covers the area of 'learning strategies' as well as 'communication strategies'. Only a small number of studies in these areas have expressed a psycholinguistic perspective (especially Faerch and Kasper

1983b). I will return to these studies briefly in section 6.2.

The development of Augmented Transition Networks (Kaplan 1972) marked a turning point in the formation of psycholinguistic theory. Given that, on the one hand, a lack of psychological plausibility was identified in early versions of Generative Grammars, especially Transformational Grammar (TG) (Chomsky 1965) and that, on the other hand, the strategy 'short-cuts' of the derivational process lacked linguistic or procedural explicitness, the search was on for an algorithm which was sufficiently explicit, and at the same time, computationally economical enough to have a degree of psychological plausibility. One step in this direction was the development of Augmented Transition Networks (ATNs). ATNs rely on surface structure cues in a way similar to Kimball's (1973) strategies and do this in a formal and finite, yet generative system. In fact, ATNs are relatively easy to program and were quite popular in computational linguistics for some time. They are also procedurally explicit. However, their psychological plausibility is somewhat reduced because they assume a high degree of back-tracking for which there is no empirical evidence in natural language processing (Kempen and Hoenkamp 1987).

Lexical-Functional Grammar (LFG) (Kaplan & Bresnan 1982; Bresnan 1982) marks a further turning point in psycholinguistic theory formation: rather than developing a theory of linguistic knowledge separately from a theory of language processing, LFG is a deliberate attempt at designing a theory of grammar that represents linguistic knowledge AND is in line with cognitive features of language processing. In other words, LFG brings linguistic theory and psycholinguistics closer to each other. It is not surprising that several major works in psycholinguistics utilised LFG, most notably Pinker (1984) in the context of language acquisition and Levelt (1989) in the context of language processing.

Kempen and Hoenkamp's (1987) Incremental Procedural Grammar (IPG) shares a number of basic assumptions with LFG, particularly the assumption that grammars are lexically driven. In addition, the architecture of IPG was designed to also model grammatical procedures as they are produced in real time. It is for these reasons that Levelt (1989) sees IPG as the performance companion of LFG.

However, I am now getting ahead of my story, and for the following section we will have to return to the time when language processing strategies were seen to be conceptually attractive.

2.2 Explaining SLA through processing strategies

Clahsen's strategies

One very fine elaboration of processing principles in the context of SLA is Clahsen's (1979, 1984) set of processing strategies which follows from the line of thought expressed by Bever (1970). In order to demonstrate not only the design of Clahsen's approach but also its empirical validity, I will briefly summarise the gist of the findings that emerged from the ZISA study. These findings concern the acquisitional sequence of German word order rules and were obtained from a series of longitudinal and cross-sectional studies by the ZISA research group (Clahsen 1980, Clahsen, Meisel and Pienemann 1983, Meisel, Clahsen and Pienemann 1981, Pienemann 1980, 1981). Similar findings have emerged in studies of the acquisition of German in formal contexts (Jansen 1991, Pienemann 1987, Westmoreland 1983). In all cases, the basic sequence of acquisition can be summarised as follows:

> Stage x = Canonical Order
> > die kinder spielen mim ball (Concetta)
> > 'the children play with the ball'
>
> Stage x + 1 = Adverb Preposing (ADV)
> > da kinder spielen (Concetta)
> > 'there children play'
>
> Stage x + 2 = Verb Separation (SEP)
> > alle kinder muß die pause machen (Concetta)
> > 'all children must the break have'
>
> Stage x + 3 = INVERSION (INV)
> > dann hat sie wieder die knoch gebringt (Eva)
> > 'then has she again the bone bringed'
>
> Stage x + 4 = Verb Final (V-END)
> > er sagt, daß er nach hause kommt
> > 'he said that he home comes'

It should be noted that, in the process of L2 acquisition, the learner accumulates these rules. This means that the structure of a given IL can be described as the sum of all the rules the learner has acquired up to a certain point.

The sequence outlined above was explained by Clahsen (1984) with reference to "speech processing strategies". The basis of Clahsen's explanation is the assumption that the psychological complexity of a structure is dependent on the degree of re-ordering and rearrangement of linguistic material involved in the process of mapping underlying semantics onto surface forms.

Clahsen (1984) assumes a set of speech processing strategies which constrain the otherwise overly powerful grammar of the learner. These strategies are stated below because they are essential to the unfolding of the argument:

1 - Canonical Order Strategy (COS)

"In underlying sequences [x1 + x2...Xn]Cx [ ] Cx + 1 [ ] Cx + m, in which each of the subconstituents contributes information to the internal structure of the constituent Cx, no subconstituent is moved out of Cx, and no material from the subsequent constituents Cx+ 1, Cx + 2, Cx +n is moved into Cx".

2 - Initialisation-Finalisation Strategy (IFS)

"In underlying sequences, [X Y Z]s permutations are blocked which move X between Y and Z or Z between X and Y".

3 - Subordinate Clause Strategy (SCS)

"In subordinate clauses permutations are avoided (Clahsen, 1984)".

Clahsen based these strategies on research into speech processing and language acquisition. COS was based on Bever's (1970) experiments on comprehension. IFS was based on findings from memory research. Lastly, SCS is based on the finding that subordinate clauses are processed in a different mode than main clauses.

Table 2.2-1 shows schematically how the above strategies explain the observed order of acquisition.

Table 2.2-1. German word order rules and associated strategies

Stage	Rule	Strategies		
x	canonical order		+COS	+SCS
x+1	adverb preposing	+IFS	+COS	+SCS
x+2	verb separation	+IFS	–COS	+SCS
x+3	inversion	–IFS	–COS	+SCS
x+4	verb final	–IFS	–COS	–SCS

In principle, the above strategies are understood as heuristic principles which allow the learner to short-cut the comprehension-production process. For instance, the COS, which is based on Bever's (1970) postulation of an NVN strategy permits direct mapping of semantic structure onto syntactic forms. This in turn allows the sentence to be processed in an extremely "flat" manner. By "flat", I mean that constituents in the sentence can be identified and processed in a manner that attributes to them a minimum of hierarchical constituent structure. In the above cases, with the exception of Stage x + 4, this would appear to involve no hierarchical structure at all. Such "flat" processing is convenient when no grammatical information needs to be transferred from one constituent to another.

As Table 2.2-1 illustrates, learners gradually divest themselves of one strategy after another as they produce more complex structures. Readers can verify this for themselves by perusing the word order examples above.

Although Table 2.2-1 does describe a very well attested acquisitional sequence, the sequence itself could be more appropriately described as devolutional, because the "acquisition" it describes is a process of constraint shedding. I will have more to say about the implications of this below.

Explanatory scope

The "strategies approach" does not only correctly apply to the original word order rules investigated by the ZISA project, but also to a range of further word order structures. Table 2.2-2 summarises further word order rules of German and the way in which they fall into Clahsen's paradigm. All predictions about orders of acquisition and the interlocking stages of development in the acquisition of structures from different domains of German grammar have been borne out by later analyses of the ZISA data base. Therefore, this strategies paradigm can be said to have predictive power.

Table 2.2-2. Stages and German word order rules

Stage	V	PP	NP	neg
x	SVO	—	—	neg+V
x+1	—	adv-front	—	—
x+2	SEP	—	Topi	neg-End
x+3	inversion	adv-VP	—	—
x+4	verb-final	—	—	—

Application to teachability

Pienemann (1984, 1987, 1989) has applied Clahsen's paradigm to the question of whether or not formal interventions (such as "teaching") can alter acquisition. Pienemann claims that the different levels of complexity as described by Clahsen's paradigm are related in an implicational way: processing strategies for a given stage of development are built up on the strategies developed at the immediately preceding stage. The assumption behind Pienemann's position is that formal interventions cannot alter a sequence of acquisition postulated in this way, since the learner needs to build up all processing strategies in a lockstep fashion. This prediction has been fully supported by a series of experiments and longitudinal and cross-sectional studies (Pienemann 1987, 1989).

Pienemann's teachability hypothesis is in fact important for a characteristic of the ZISA framework I have not so far touched on. This is the so-called "two dimensional" aspect of the framework, in which the "developmental" dimension — the dimension that has been under consideration in the preceding paragraphs — is complemented by a "variational" dimension, along which learners are essentially located according to their degree of linguistic norm-orientedness, as evidenced by percentages of production of redundant items or structures within the developmental processing capacities of the learner.

The variational dimension is an important construct because it captures the fact that there are phenomena in ILs which are independent of stages of acquisition. However, one side effect of a postulated variational dimension is that "gaps" in developmental data can be explained as variation. To a degree this reduces the falsifiability of the ZISA framework, since the "gaps" in question can be developmental structures themselves. This reduction in falsifiability is limited since a given learner will behave in a predictable way in relationship to a relatively wide range of variational features, and can therefore be located at a fixed point on the variational dimension. The significance of the "teachability" hypothesis is that it predicts that variational "gaps" can be filled, and in so doing it relaxes the constraining effect on falsifiability that the construct of the variational dimension introduced.

2.3 Limitations of the strategies approach

The role of grammar

One of the shortcomings of the processing approach is that the status of grammar in language acquisition remains unclear. If the strategies constrain grammar for reasons of limited processing capacity in the learner, then the role of the strategies cannot be that of a "grammar substitute". First, this would contradict the function of speech processing strategies as performance devices. Second, the strategies would not provide sufficient information for the production of the structures described, for instance, in the above developmental sequence.

Consider the following example. The strategy description for Stage x + 1 is -COS, +IFS, +SCS. It is possible to produce a number of structures within these constraints, and Clahsen (1984) has in fact shown that the rules "Object-Topicalisation", "Neg-End" and "Verb-Separation" are all within the range of strategy description of this stage, and are, indeed, all acquired at the same relative point in time. It is this general level of defining processing complexity which makes the strategies approach predictive. The other side of the coin, however, is that the abstractness of the strategies themselves also renders them insufficient as rules of production or comprehension. The specification -COS, +IFS, +SCS needs to be complemented by an explicit grammatical rule or system of rules.

Underlying Clahsen's strategies approach is the necessity that the L2 learner already "has" fully developed components of a grammar which need to be constrained for the L2. This view is quite common in L2 research: it has frequently been assumed that categories and phrase structure are transferred from the L1 to the L2 because they are so general in nature (Clahsen, Meisel and Pienemann 1983, Dato 1970, Felix 1982). Felix (1982) even went so far as to suggest that this type of transfer of abstract knowledge from L1 to L2 explains the greater grammatical systematicity of early L2 acquisition compared to L1 acquisition.

Clahsen, Meisel and Pienemann (1983) also assume that categories and phrase structure do not have to be acquired but are already present in the learner's competence, and it is only their production that is suppressed by the learner's limited processing capacity. What remains to be accounted for, given this assumption, is the highly regular way in which phrase-structure rules are gradually expanded in an on-going way. This is assumed by the ZISA researchers to be the result of a gradual automatisation of lower level plans.

A similar, though implicit assumption is to be found in Slobin's (1973, 1977) "operating principles", which have been used to explain both L1 and L2 acquisition. For instance, the principle of not disrupting associated elements definitely requires the existence of specific hierarchically related categories because the learner is assumed to be able to identify respective elements which themselves are firmly established in a hierarchical organisation. On this basis, Slobin posits, a "perceptual gestalt" (Slobin 1977). In the case of INVERSION, for example, the learner has to identify verb and NP as well as the object NP: none of the foregoing can occur in the absence of a hierarchical constituent structure.

I believe that assumptions of this kind about the role of categories and constituent structure in L2 acquisition are incorrect. First, at the outset of the acquisition process the learner acquires lexical items that cannot be shown to be indexed to particular syntactic categories. Consequently, syntactic indexation has to be accomplished during the acquisition process. Thus, at an early stage of acquisition the learner cannot rely on the identification of grammatical categories as a formal cue for the location of various syntactic and morphological elements.

In both the German and the English L2 data discussed in this book there are a number of cases where categories have been incorrectly assigned — for instance, nouns are treated as verbs, adjectives treated as nouns, and so forth. Early L2 acquisition is characterised by such explicit "squishiness".

Furthermore, the psychological nature of phrase structure cannot be captured by simple phrase structure expansion rules of the type that can be found in the work of Klein and Dittmar (1979), Dato (1970) or Clahsen, Meisel and Pienemann (1983). Such rules are far too inexplicit descriptions of the corresponding TLs. The following rule

Det → Num + Quant + Art

does not capture (or even hint at) the intricate constraints which operate on the German determiner system. Numerals, to take one case, cannot be combined with every conceivable type of article or quantifier although the rule above would generate all such combinations.

Another point is that the learner has to do much more than expand simple phrase structure rules. He or she has to be able to determine the beginning and end of a constituent in the context of an actually occurring utterance, and given this, must be able to build up a hierarchical phrase structure from a linear input. Levelt (1981) has named this process as the speaker's *linearisation problem*. Problems of this kind of identification within the constituent structure have been simulated in ATN networks (Kaplan 1972), and are dealt with in highly developed theories of grammar, such as Lexical Functional Grammar (Bresnan 1982). As regards the present argument, one important point is that recognition and/or production of the constituent structure of a sentence relies crucially on the syntactic sub-categorisation of lexical material. For instance, the constituent boundaries of an NP depend on the sub-categorisation of the noun itself.

(1)   He bought [his shoes]NP [in Italy]PP
(2)   She praised [[his belief]NP [in humanity]PP]NP

In short, the recognition or production of constituent structure is dependent on lexical learning and is thus specific to the language being learnt.

Restriction to movement

As can be seen from the above quotations, Clahsen's strategies are stated in such a way that they are constraints on movement transformations as these were conceptualised in TG. German word order can be neatly described by a small set of movement transformations: this, in a nutshell, is the "transformational connection". Theoretical considerations apart, however, it is now accepted that transformations are psychologically implausible concepts (Altmann 1990, Horrocks 1987, Levelt 1989, cf. also Ingram, 1971). As a result of this, it is illogical to assume that processing constraints can operate on linguistic structures which have no psychological plausibility.

The fact that the processing strategies are interpreted in terms of transformational grammar has a rather important side effect: it is set up to prevent the movement of "materialised" subconstituents across the boundaries of major constituents. This view automatically limits the strategies approach to the domain of word order. I will show below that this limitation can be overcome if processing constraints are interpreted in terms of transfer of abstract grammatical information across constituent boundaries.

Comprehension and Production

A further problem with the "strategies" approach has been pinpointed by
White (1991). This is that the strategies outlined above are based on compre-
hension-related phenomena and formulated through the interpretation of
empirical findings on comprehension, although it is clear that comprehension
and production are not mirror images of each other. The NVN strategy, in
particular, accounts for observational facts in speech comprehension.

To expand on this point: White (1991) points out, for instance, that while
GSL learners produce SauxVO structures exclusively when the interlanguage
strategy is +COS and IFS has not yet "appeared" they doubtlessly comprehend sentences with SauxOV structures. These latter structures are normal
input structures, even though learners at the stage in question may not be able
to utilise productively the information encoded in their particular word order
configuration. Since SauxOV is not permitted by the COS, they must rely on
more than the COS in comprehension. Most probably, in my view, the learner
relies on something like the theme-rheme structure. Such an assumption,
however, adds a whole new "strategy" to the processing system which is thus
in competition with the rest of the "strategies". This, put bluntly, vitiates the
whole "strategy approach": how do learners know when to use, say, theme-
rheme and not the COS? And why is the COS used in production but never
theme-rheme, if the latter is also part of the processing system?

Obviously, the set of strategies proposed by Clahsen are not powerful
enough to handle these problems and should be viewed in the context of a
more comprehensive view of language processing in order to retain explanatory power.

Extendibility

A final problem with the processing approach is its relation to learnability and
extendibility (see Pinker 1984). I have noted above that the set of strategies
given in Clahsen's framework are not sufficient prerequisites for the learnability of the structures in question. At the same time they serve to predict the
order of complexity once the structures are described with recourse to an
additional paradigm, namely, aspects of a grammatical formalism. Only in
this latter sense is the processing approach predictive.

It is important to understand that the limited validity of the processing approach does not invalidate it completely. Its predictive power is an important contribution to an understanding of language acquisition. Problems only arise when the processing approach is taken a step further to explain why and how L2s are learnable (see Clahsen and Muysken 1989). It is with this step that a new dimension is added to the *explanandum* the processing approach is intended to address. Now the explanatory domain of the approach is no longer limited to the chronology of syntactic patterns, but the question of "where do they come from?" is added to the formula.

Eubank (1990), who tried to apply the processing approach to data on German negation collected in a formal context, further noted that the strategies do not give the learner any clue in which direction to extend the interlanguage system. Again, this would not create any problems if the processing approach was used for the limited domain of predicting hierarchies of psychological complexity. As a theoretical account of extendibility in L2 acquisition, however, it must be discarded because it does not meet two crucial criteria of a learnable theory.

Positive points

Despite all the criticism directed against the "strategies" approach, and the way strategies have been applied to explaining language acquisition, it remains a fact that all their predictions about word order have turned out to be rock solid. One is therefore entitled to ask whether this is merely a coincidence or whether some part of the approach generated these successful predictions.

The kernel of the strategies approach is the concept of linearity of the constituent configurations. Any discontinuity or rearrangement was treated as a predictor of increased processing complexity. This concept does have psychological plausibility, because constituent boundaries have been shown to be psychologically plausible constructs in both comprehension and production (cf. Levelt 1989). I believe that one does not need to take the additional step and assign the COS a role in mediating between underlying predicate-argument structures and constituent configurations. This mediation can be carried out quite logically by a grammatical theory aiming at psychological plausibility.

2.4   Grammatical encoding

We have now reached the point where the foundations of a new psychological approach to SLA have to be laid. In this section I will outline a number of key psychological factors in language processing to characterise the cognitive environment in which language development takes place. In section 2.5 below language production mechanisms will be looked at from the perspective of language acquisition. There the question will be the following: how do processing procedures develop? In response to this question I will develop a hypothetical hierarchy of processing procedures which will, in later chapters, be put to use in a theory of grammar.

Levelt's model

My point of departure is Levelt's (1989) model of language production the rough outlines of which are sketched out in Figure 2.4-1 below which is taken from Levelt (1989,9).

In his 1989 book Levelt presents a coherent view of language production from intention to articulation, a glimpse of which is given in Figure 2.4-1. The focus of this book is quite different. It concentrates on the acquisition of morpho-syntax and the lexicon. I will therefore confine my sketch of Levelt's model to the production of morpho-syntax which takes place in the "Formulator". In other words, we step into the language production process at the point where the speaker has conceptualised what he or she intends to say by "... conceiving an intention, selecting the relevant information ..., ordering this information for expression, keeping track of what has been said before, and so on." (Levelt 1989,9). At this point the speaker has created a "preverbal message" which forms the input to the Formulator.

To sketch out the procedures for grammatical processing one will have to focus on the structure of the Formulator. Levelt (1989,11) summarises the role of the Formulator as follows: It "... accepts fragments of messages as characteristic input and produces as output a *phonetic* or *articulatory plan*. In other words, the Formulator translates conceptual structures into a linguistic structure." This translation process proceeds in two steps: (1) the grammatical encoding and (2) the phonological encoding. It is the first step, the grammatical encoding of the preverbal message, which is relevant to the objectives of this book.

The Speaker as Information Processor

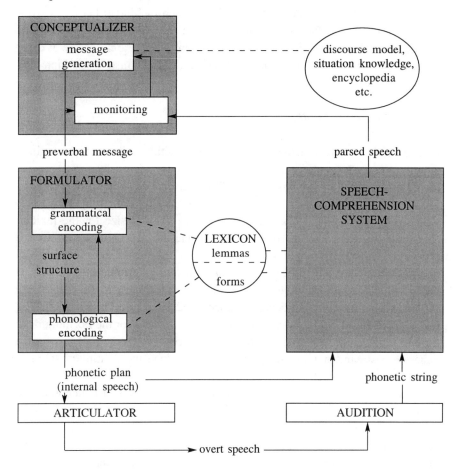

Figure 2.4-1. Levelt's model of language generation (Levelt 1989, 9)

This particular portion of Levelt's model which I have identified amounts to a theory of the production of grammatical structures; i.e. the performance counterpart to a theory of grammar. Below I will look at the two main aspects of the production of grammatical structures, (1) the role of the lexicon and (2) the nature of syntactic procedures. For the first part I will outline a theory of the mental lexicon and for the second part I will summarise some key aspects of a procedural grammar for sentence production, in particular Kempen and Hoenkamp's (1987) theory, which emulates much of Merrill Garrett's work (e.g. Garrett 1976; 1980; 1982) and on which the corresponding section of Levelt's model is based. However, before I summarise the architecture of these procedures I will briefly characterise the psychological constraints which they attempt to satisfy.

Psychological constraints

One of the key characteristics of language production is its time-constrained nature. We produce one word every 400 milliseconds on average and can increase this speed to one word every 200 milliseconds (Maclay and Osgood 1959) and yet we produce no more than about one slip of the tongue in 1,000 words (Garnham et al. 1982), and this with an average size for the lexicon 'database' of some 30,000 records. However, the aspect of speed in the process of language production goes far beyond mere retrieval times for items in a static database. The processes of conceptualising, formulating and articulating, which are all quite separate from each other, have to be *temporally aligned* to produce fluent speech (Kempen and Hoenkamp 1987, 202). The material produced by the Conceptualiser has to be ready for the Formulator in time to build grammatical structures and to access words, and all this has to generate a stream of phonetic plans which produce the continuous signals known as fluent speech.

To complicate things, the relationship between events or conceptualised material and surface structures is not linear. One case of non-linearity is the relationship between the natural sequence of events and the order of clauses. As Levelt (1983) points out, propositions do not necessarily have to be produced in language in the natural order of events. Consider the following example:

Before the man rode off, he mounted his horse.

In this example the event described in the second clause happens before the one described in the first clause. In order to produce such sentences then, the speaker has to store one proposition in memory.

There are similar *linearisation problems* (Levelt 1981, 1983) in matching conceptualised propositions onto possible word orders of a language. In other words, syntactic constraints impose a degree of discontinuity on the relationship between conceptualising and articulation. Given the non-linear nature of spoken language, the temporal alignment of the sub-process of language production is not a trivial problem: what kind of procedures can account for the fast, temporally well-aligned production of linear strings representing non-linearly related concepts?

Kempen and Hoenkamp (1987) point out that "The traditional view, implicitly held by many students of sentence production, is that they are ordered strictly serially in time. First, the conceptual context is fully specified by the conceptualisation process. Next the syntactic structure is built for the whole utterance. Finally, this structure is realised phonetically" (Kempen and Hoenkamp 1987, 202). The serial processing view (e.g. Forster 1979) is depicted in part a of Figure 2.4-2 below.

Kempen and Hoenkamp put up a strong argument against this view. They point out that the "... serial model implies that hesitations *within* sentences cannot have a conceptual or syntactic origin. This is ... empirically wrong (cf. Goldman-Eisler, 1968) ... " (Kempen and Hoenkamp 1987, 203). They further point out that a serial model of language production would not be able to explain the introspective observation that speakers can start producing

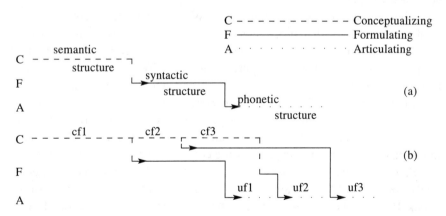

Two theoretically possible alignments of conceptualizing, formulating and articulating processing (cf = conceptual fragment, uf = utterance fragment).

From: Kempen and Hoenkamp (1987, 203)

Figure 2.4-2. Serial versus incremental processing

a sentence after having worked out only a fragment of what they want to say. In addition, Kempen and Hoenkamp argue that for a serial model of language production to be able to map conceptual structures onto linguistic forms in a non-linear fashion, the system would have to engage in back-tracking even for sentences which do not contain 'garden path' (Kimball 1973) constructions. No evidence for this can be found in the production of natural language (Kempen and Hoenkamp 1987, 205).

Kempen and Hoenkamp (1987) and also Levelt (1989) therefore assume that sentence production is *incremental* or *piecemeal*. This means that "...the next processor can start working on the still-incomplete output of the current processor..." Levelt (1989, 24). The idea is that the surface lexico-grammatical form is gradually being constructed while conceptualisation is still ongoing. This feature was highlighted for the comprehension system by Marslen-Wilson and Tyler's (1980) studies which demonstrated that in on-line processing, semantic representations are constructed by the comprehension system before grammatical structures have been entirely processed.

Also note that incremental processing necessitates the use of *storage facilities* to allow for non-linearity in the matching of underlying meaning onto surface form. Below I will take a closer look at the interrelation between non-linearity and memory.

The assumption that language processing is non-serial has a further implication, namely that processing sub-components operate automatically and in parallel. In other words, processing components are relatively autonomous specialists which largely operate automatically. Levelt (1989) shows that the opposite assumption to autonomous and automatic components leads to serious problems: if the processing components were not autonomous, exchange of information between all processing components (or levels of processing) would have to be co-ordinated by a central control. This would imply that the operation of the processing components is consciously attended to, while empirical studies have shown that grammatical information is normally not attended to and can only be memorised if attention is focused on it (Bock 1978, Kintsch 1974, Garman 1990). On the other hand, parallel processing is supported by evidence which shows that different processing components exchange information in a parallel manner (Engelkamp and Zimmer 1983, Sridhar 1988).

Autonomous specialist processing components can further be characterised as processing procedures which are able to accept and pass on only information of a highly specific nature, for instance, only information concerning NPs. The advantage of such task-specificity is a gain in processing speed, since non-attended processes can be executed in parallel. Thus the notion of task-specificity is in line with the observation that grammatical information can only be memorised if it is attended to.

Levelt (1989, 259) points out that the automatic nature of grammatical processing can also be inferred from the fact that "... the complexity of ... syntactic operations is not reflected in measures of mental load, such as reaction times and hesitation pauses." This is supported by Goldman-Eisler's (1968), Taylor's (1969) and Rochester and Gill's (1973) studies in which no effects of complexity on hesitations, speech latencies or disruptions were found. The logic of the argument is this: If syntactic processing components operate automatically, i.e. without any attention, and if they are further task-specific and run in parallel, then they do not take up any of the capacity of the general processor because parallel processors can handle great numbers of operations at the same time and automatic processes do not deposit information into short-term memory, the locus of the general processor (Levelt 1989).

As with other motor and cognitive skills, automatic processes in language production utilise what is known as "procedural knowledge" or "procedural memory", which is contrasted with "declarative knowledge/ memory". The latter "... concerns everything that can be represented at a conscious level, and which groups together what Tulving (1983) called 'episodic' memory, and Penfield termed 'experiential' memory (Penfield and Roberts 1959)" (Paradis 1994, 395). There is ample empirical evidence for the dissociation of procedural and declarative memory (Paradis 1994) from studies of amnesia and aphasia, based on the patients' loss of ability to perform or to learn to perform certain tasks which can be defined according to the procedural-declarative distinction.

Grammatical information storage

In characterising some of the key psychological constraints on language production in the last few pages, I repeatedly made reference to the storage of linguistic information. It will therefore be useful to clarify to some extent the role of the storage of grammatical information in the process of language production.[10] At this stage this will be a preliminary exercise which will be updated after the lexicon and syntactic procedures have been described, i.e. at the end of this section (2.4).

There are several factors that necessitate the storage of linguistic information in language production. At various points in the production process, propositional or grammatical information has to be held in memory. One factor was mentioned above, namely the linearisation problem (Levelt 1983): when conceptualisation and articulation are not temporally aligned, processed material has to be held in memory until it can be used by the Articulator. What is needed here is a store with fast access time.

Often researchers in SLA assume that this job can be carried out by Working Memory (e.g. Towell and Hawkins 1994). However, this assumption is inconsistent with the known properties of Working Memory which is the locus of *attended processing* (Baddeley 1990, Levelt 1989) whereas the Formulator operates automatically, i.e. without attention. The information generated by the Formulator is specifically syntactic in nature and therefore has to be deposited in a store which is suited to handle this type of information, and attention to it (conscious or non-conscious) is not necessary for this operation. For instance, one does not need to be aware of, or control, the fact that the information concerning "person" and "number" matches the lexical entries of the verb and the grammatical subject. In fact, it is possible to attend to only a small number of such processes. Otherwise , with the normal speed of language generation, Working Memory would get "clogged up". On the other hand, attention must be focused on the propositional content, because it reflects the conceptualisation the speaker wants to express.

Propositional information is therefore temporarily stored in Working Memory which, as I mentioned, is the resource for temporary attentive processes that include conceptualising and monitoring (Baddeley 1990, Broadbent 1975). It has a highly limited capacity, and is therefore not suitable to process great amounts of grammatical information at high speed.

Levelt (1989) and other authors (e.g. Engelkamp 1974) assume that grammatical information is held temporarily in the Syntactic Buffer, a memory store which is highly task-specific and in which specialised grammatical processors can deposit information of a specific nature. Such a buffer is needed to synchronise the availability of surface structure fragments for phonological encoding, because surface structure fragments may be available before they need to be produced. The Syntactic Buffer is mirrored in the Articulator, which has access to the Articulatory Buffer (Levelt 1989, 26) which holds bits of the phonetic plan. In the discussion of syntactic procedures later in this chapter, I will demonstrate that syntactic procedures themselves also store a subset of pieces of grammatical information in interaction with other procedures.

Specialised 'ultra-short-term' stores are also known in other cognitive fields, for instance in vision where Gough (1972) argues on the basis of experimental evidence that letters are taken out of the 'visual buffer' at the rate of about 15 milliseconds per letter.

The lexicon is stored in Permanent Memory and is at least partly open to conscious processing. It is therefore a store of declarative knowledge which can be activated for language production.

In other words, there is a fundamental division between procedural (implicit) and declarative (explicit) memory stores which is crucial to the architecture of the Formulator. Overwhelming empirical evidence supporting the dissociation of procedural and declarative knowledge has been amassed by Paradis (1994). He summarises the available clinical evidence as follows:

> Lesions in the hippocampal and amygdalar system as well as in parietal-temporal-occipital and frontal association cortices compromise recognition and recall, and cause selective anterograde impairment of declarative memory while preserving procedural memory such as the acquisition and execution of complex skills. On the other hand, lesions of the basic ganglia, cerebellum, and other non-limbic-diencephalic sites, as well as circumscribed neocortical lesions, selectively affect learning and memory for skilled, automatised functions (Mayes 1988) such as language (aphasia) and well practised voluntary movements (apraxia). (Paradis 1994, 396)

Paradis goes on to cite a wealth of studies demonstrating the dissociation of procedural and declarative knowledge in patients with Alzheimer's Disease, alcoholic Korsakoff's syndrome, anterograde amnesia, Parkinson's Disease, as well as in aphasia, apraxia and in relation to anaesthetic techniques. He summarises these findings as follows:

> Patients with Alzheimer's Disease, Korsakoff's syndrome, or amnesia have impaired explicit memory but intact implicit memory; patients with Parkinson's Disease demonstrate a selective impairment of procedural memory.... Anaesthesia with isoflorane/ oxygen spares implicit memory ..., but not with sufentanil/ nitrous oxide ..." (Paradis 1994, 396)

Paradis quotes Cohen (1984, 1991), according to whom procedural and declarative memory "... are subserved by neuroanatomically distinct systems. While declarative memory depends on the integrity of the hippocampal system and is stored over large areas of tertiary cortex, procedural memory is linked to the cortical processors through which it was acquired." (Paradis 1994, 396).

Other psychological aspects of language processing are also supported by neurophysiological evidence. In particular, Levelt's model represents the Conceptualiser and the Formulator as two entirely distinct components — to the extent that the Conceptualiser is not capable of processing the type of information contained in the Formulator. Empirical evidence for the different nature of the processing of propositional content and grammatical information comes, amongst other things, from the study of aphasia and amnesia. Cooper and Zurif (1983), for instance, showed that in Broca's and, to a lesser extent, in Wernicke's aphasia, lexical retrieval and semantic representation are functional, while grammatical information cannot be processed. This is true for production as well as for comprehension. Tests carried out by the authors showed that patients suffering from Broca's aphasia are able to construct semantic relations on the basis of pragmatic principles, while the same is not possible using only grammatical markers. This means that the capacity to use grammatical markers can be located in the region which is affected in Broca's patients, but not in Wernicke's.

In a recent study Zurif, Swinney, Prather and Love (1994) went a step further and linked a specific set of syntactic procedures to changes in cortically localised processing procedures. They demonstrated that Wernicke's patients can link the elements of dependency relations in the same way as neurologically intact subjects, while Broca's patients cannot.

I will return to these studies briefly at the end of this section, in order to view some findings from research on aphasia, in the light of an outline of the mental lexicon and of syntactic procedures.

The lexicon

The Grammatical Encoder contains procedures for lemma access and syntactic building procedures. Lemmata contain the meaning of lexical items and the syntax of each word. For instance, the parameters of the lemma for "give" are as shown in Figure 2.4-3.

The conceptual specification defines the meaning of the word. The exact nature of this definition is not relevant to the focus of this book. Levelt uses a set of conventions that roughly follow Jackendoff (1983). What does matter in this context is that the conceptual arguments are well defined, and that in

give: conceptual specification:
CAUSE (X, (GOposs (Y, (FROM/TO (X,Z)))))
conceptual arguments: (X, Y, Z)
syntactic category: V
grammatical functions: (SUBJ, DO, IO)
relations to COMP: none
lexical pointer: 713
diacritic features: tense
                        aspect
                        mood
                        person
                        number
                        pitch accent

From: (Levelt 1989, 191)
Figure 2.4-3. Lemma for 'give'

the process of language production these have to be mapped onto grammatical categories. This, by the way, is what Kaplan and Bresnan (1982) identify as the main objective of a psychologically plausible theory of grammar. The conceptual arguments fulfil certain thematic roles in the message. They can be identified as "agent", "theme" and "goal". These thematic roles have to be mapped onto the grammatical functions, which are also listed in the lemma. One possible mapping for 'give' is the following:

$$
\begin{array}{ccc}
\text{X (agent),} & \text{Y (theme),} & \text{Z (goal)} \\
| & | & | \\
\text{SUBJ} & \text{DO} & \text{IO.}
\end{array}
$$

One crucial insight can be gained from this already: the lexical information stored with the entry for the verb has to 'communicate' with other constituents in the sentence. The verb "knows" that it has three arguments; it also "knows" what their grammatical roles are. This is brought about by the fact that Levelt conceptualises the Formulator in such a way that "... the lexicon is an essential mediator between conceptualisation and grammatical ... encoding ..." (Levelt 1989, 181). Levelt calls this assumption the *lexical hypothesis*, an assumption which is also made in Lexical-Functional Grammar (Bresnan 1982). Following Kempen and Hoenkamp (1987), Levelt views language production as being driven on the one hand by conceptualisation and on the other by the lexicon.

Returning to the lemma for 'give', there are two further aspects that need to be looked at: (1) the *lexical pointer:* a pointer (which is relevant for lemma access) links all the word forms with the same conceptual specifications which are differentiated only by diacritic variables; (2) *diacritic variables*: in many languages these are related to the morphological forms of the lexical entry *(look-s, look-ing, look-ed* etc.).

A *lexical entry* contains all the different morphological variants that relate to the same conceptual specification. Hence not all *lexical items* are lexical entries. Sets of meaning-related items are grouped into *semantic fields*. Speech errors may reveal such connections. The mental lexicon is seen as a "... passive store of declarative knowledge about words." Levelt (1989, 185). One of the main issues in a theory of language production is how speakers access lemmas at high speed.

To account for the extreme time constraints found in lexical access a theory of lexical access should be based on parallel (rather than serial) processing. To account for the high degree of accuracy in lexical access, such a theory would also have to include convergence principles which ensure that intended concepts will not be expressed by their hyponyms. Levelt discusses several models of lexical access, including Logogen Theory (Morton 1969, 1979) which satisfies the 'speed criterion'. In this theory lexical items are represented as *logogens* which are devices that collect evidence for the appropriateness of a word. Each logogen is sensitive to information that relates to the word it represents. All logogens are active simultaneously. This is where parallel processing comes in. Logogens have their individual information threshold and will 'fire' when the information collected has reached the threshold. This is when the phonological code will be made available to the Response Buffer, which can use the phonological code for a vocal response. When the phonological code is deposited in the Response Buffer, the logogen's activation level drops back and its threshold decreases temporarily. Rather than using the phonological code, the Response Buffer can also return it to the Logogen System. The logogen will then be reactivated and because of its lowered threshold it is likely to fire again. This to-and-fro-ing between the Logogen System and the Response Buffer can theoretically continue *ad infinitum*, and this is a way of keeping the phonological code available for use since the Response Buffer has to be cleared in short intervals in order to interact properly with the parallel processing of great numbers of logogens.

Logogen Theory is consistent with findings on pre-lexical pauses. It was found that transitional probability, as defined by the contextual information present for word choice, is a predictor of pre-lexical pauses: the more likely a word is in the context provided by the preceding words, the fewer pre-lexical pauses (Butterworth 1983). There is also evidence that pre-lexical pauses can be predicted by the frequency of words (e.g. Maclay and Osgood 1959). This finding relates to the threshold of logogens, which decreases with frequency.

However, Levelt cautions that while findings on speech pauses provide general support for Logogen Theory, they are open to multiple interpretations. The most attractive property of the theory for fluent language production identified by Levelt (1989, 204) "... is its distributional control structure" which satisfies the speed condition for lexical access. However, Levelt adds that Logogen Theory has no solution to offer to the convergence condition. What prevents the logogen of a hyponym firing instead of, or together with, that logogen which fits all of the conceptual features intended by the speaker? In the case of the hyponym, all of its conceptual features map onto the ones activated by the cognitive system, whereas the reverse is not true. A speaker intending to say *collie* may therefore access *dog*. Levelt (1989) proposes a set of three principles which overcome this problem.

Despite our relatively limited knowledge of lexical access a number of its key architectural features became apparent in the above discussion:
- Lemmata are activated conceptually.
- Lemma access must be a parallel process.
- Lemmata 'communicate' with syntactic structures.

Syntactic procedures

Let us return to syntactic procedures. The architecture of the Grammatical Encoder envisaged in Levelt (1989) is described in Kempen and Hoenkamp's (1987) "Incremental Procedural Grammar". I will summarise the main features of this approach below.

It was pointed out above that one of the main features of natural language production is its incremental nature. Kempen and Hoenkamp (1987) demonstrate that incrementality can be implemented into a time-constrained grammar only if syntactic procedures are *both conceptually and lexically guided*. The Conceptualiser delivers conceptual structures to the Formulator which then has to build syntactic structures that dovetail into conceptual structures.

This interaction is facilitated by the mental lexicon. Once a lemma is (conceptually) activated, it instigates a range of syntactic procedures to construct a proper syntactic environment.

Kempen and Hoenkamp follow to some extent Garrett's (1975) 'functional' and 'positional' levels of processing which were inferred from observations on speech errors. "The Functional Stage works on all constituents more or less simultaneously. The Positional Stage assigns the constituents a left-to-right order ... traversing the sequence of constituents from left to right." (Kempen and Hoenkamp 1987, 208)

Syntactic procedures are experts in the building of constituent structures. They are instigated by the activation of a lemma which contains categorial information. Category N builds NPs, V builds VPs etc. for the categories N, V, A, and P where these categories can take on the function of head of a phrase. These syntactic procedures can all run in parallel once they have been called by an activated lemma.

The categorial procedure looks for conceptual material modifying the conceptual structure of the lemma. In this way, it matches parts of the conceptual structure with syntactic forms and functions as defined in lemmas. The outcome of such a process is the hierarchical constituent structure of the phrase concerned.

Figure 2.4-4 below illustrates the process of incremental language generation. Special emphasis is placed on the temporal aspects of this process. Figure 2.4-4 depicts the three main components of Levelt's model, which constitute the focus of this chapter: the Conceptualiser, the Grammatical Encoder and the lexicon. The process of language production is initiated by the output of the Conceptualiser (preverbal message) which is depicted in Figure 2.4-4 in two different notations.

It is important to keep in mind that in either notation, the sequence in which the conceptual material is described does not have to coincide with the actual sequence of temporal evolution. Kempen and Hoenkamp (1987) assume that conceptual material is delivered to the Grammatical Encoder in small chunks. Each delivery is called an 'iteration'. This refers to the temporal structure of the encoding process.

In Figure 2.4-4, I assumed that the concept denoted as 'CHILD' is the first to be delivered to the Grammatical Encoder. The sequence in which concepts are generated is crucial for the syntactic structures that follow. For instance, if the sentence "a child gave the mother a cat" (which is adapted from Levelt's example) started with one of the object noun phrases, then this would likely lead to the use of a passive structure.

In the example chosen in Figure 2.4-4, the conceptual material produced first activates the lemma CHILD in the lexicon. The lemma contains the category information N which calls the categorial procedure NP. This procedure can build the phrasal category in which N is head, i.e. NP. The categorial procedure inspects the conceptual material of the current iteration for possible complements and specifiers and provides values for diacritic features, including those from the head of phrase.

In discussing a similar example sentence to the one in Figure 2.4-4, Levelt makes an additional assumption about the three referents. I will assume that the first referent is marked "- accessible". This feature was not captured by the simplified account of the conceptual structure that represents the pre-verbal message. It would form part of Kempen and Hoenkamp's (1987) 'Functorisation' rules which would read as follows:

NP, N, < Ref-indefinite, Number - singular >

This rule ensures that the branch Det is attached to NP, the lemma for 'A' is activated, and that the lexeme 'a' is inserted.

Functorisation Rules instigate the activation of free grammatical morphemes and the insertion of bound grammatical morphemes. Naturally, Functorisation Rules are language-specific and thus have to be acquired for every language.

In the above attachment of Det to the NP-node, one notices a key feature of the language production process, which I will later focus on in the context of language acquisition: the selection of the lemma for "A" partly depends on the value of a diacritic feature ('singular') of the head being checked against that of the targeted lemma. The value of the diacritic feature is 'stored' by the categorial procedure until it is 'delivered' to the modifier. A similar phenomenon occurs in subject-verb agreement marking, where the value of diacritic features 'person' and 'number' of the SUBJECT-NP are held by the S-procedure. In Kempen and Hoenkamp's (1987, 224) words: "Subj's output is finally delivered at the holder created by S and thus made accessible to VFin: Subject-verb agreement."

In other words, Kempen and Hoenkamp conceptualise the matching of diacritic features as a process of 'feature-copying' where features have a source and a destination. Vigliocco, Butterworth and Garrett (1996) demon-

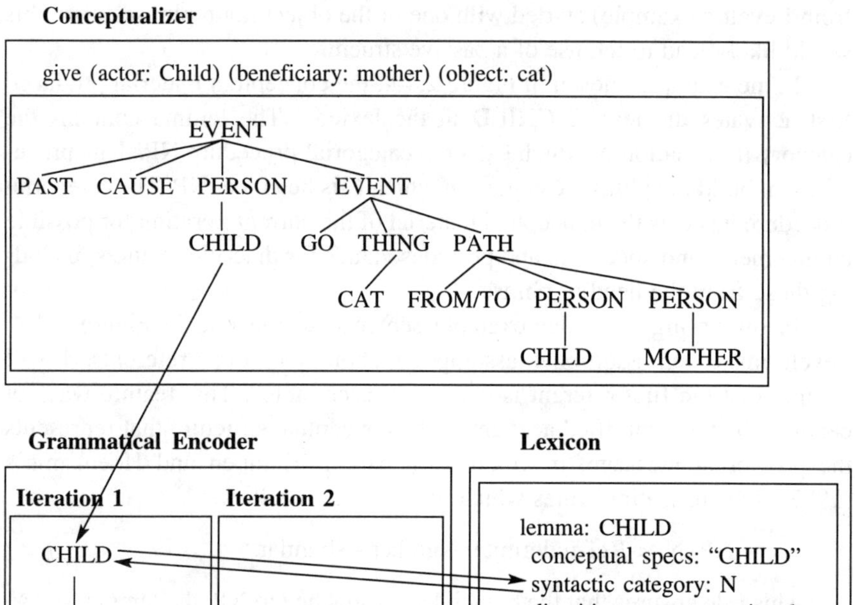

Conceptualizer

give (actor: Child) (beneficiary: mother) (object: cat)

EVENT

PAST CAUSE PERSON   EVENT

CHILD   GO THING PATH

CAT FROM/TO PERSON PERSON

CHILD   MOTHER

Grammatical Encoder   **Lexicon**

Iteration 1   Iteration 2

CHILD

lemma: CHILD
conceptual specs: "CHILD"
syntactic category: N
diacritic parameters: singular
...

S

NPsubj

lemma: A
conceptual specs: "A"
syntactic category: Det
diacritic parameters: singular
...

NP

DET

N

a   child   ....

Figure 2.4-4. Incremental language generation

strate in cross-linguistic experiments on subject-verb agreement in Spanish and English that it is psychologically more plausible to view the matching of diacritic features as a process of 'feature-merging' (or unification) in which both constituents involved in the matching process can derive features independently from conceptual structure. They show that the advantage of the merging process is that it can account for null-subject languages such as Spanish and for certain distributivity effects of conceptual structure on agreement phenomena. Vigliocco, Butterworth and Garrett (1996) therefore modify Incremental Procedural Grammar replacing the feature copying mechanisms by feature merging mechanisms. In Lexical Functional Grammar this feature merging process is managed through the 'unification' of features found in lexical entries. I will adapt Vigliocco, Butterworth and Garrett's modification because of its psychological plausibility and because this creates a tighter fit with LFG.

Our production process has proceeded to the point where the structure of a phrase has been created and the associated lemmata are activated. What is missing to make this the beginning of a continuous and fluent utterance is the establishment of a relation between the phrase and the rest of the intended message. This is accomplished by assigning a grammatical function to the newly created phrase. In fact, it is the categorial procedure itself that chooses its functional destination. This highlights the active nature of syntactic procedures.

Possible functional destinations are defined in a set of Appointment Rules which are also language-specific. The default for NP procedures is 'subject of S'. In languages where Det and N are marked for case the destination 'subject' would also provide NP with the value 'nominative' for the diacritic feature 'case'.

However, this does not quite solve the problem of allowing the tree created so far to grow further, i.e.. to make the production of the sentence continuous. What is missing is the attachment of the NP to a higher node. This occurs as follows: "The preferential higher-order categorial procedure is activated by receiving the output of a lower-order procedure." Levelt (1989, 240) In the above example NPsubj calls the procedure S which accepts the calling NP as its subject and stores the diacritic features deposited in the NP, namely the values for 'person' and 'number'.

The outcome of all of this is depicted by a tree structure in Figure 2.4-4 above. And while this structure was produced and the associated lemmata were activated, the next conceptual fragment would have been processed in parallel and the output of the Formulator would have been delivered to the Articulator, which will set the articulatory plans in action. This means that new conceptualisation occurs while the conceptual structure of the previous iteration is being produced. The whole process then moves on from iteration to iteration. This is what Kempen and Hoenkamp (1987) and Levelt (1989) mean by incremental production.

In the above summary of the process of grammatical encoding one aspect was left aside, namely word order. I mentioned in passing that the sequence in which grammatical material is activated and delivered to the Formulator determines the choice between active and passive. I also mentioned the role of Appointment Rules in defining the functional destinations of phrases.

The definition of the acceptable set of word order constellations for configurational languages is carried out by Word Order Rules, which co-ordinate the assembly of phrasal subprocedures. I assume that for non-configurational languages grammatical roles can be specified directly from the semantic roles specified in the conceptual structure.

The assembly of phrasal subprocedures in Incremental Procedural Grammar proceeds roughly as follows: "apart from assembling a list of zero or more subprocedure calls and putting them to work simultaneously, a syntactic procedure also has the duty of processing the subtrees they return as their *values*" (Kempen and Hoenkamp 1987, 220). These subtrees are then combined into a single grammatical clause by subprocedures depositing their information into a data structure, called a 'holder', which is created by a higher procedure. The holder contains a sequence of positions chosen on the basis of the set of word order rules for the given language. The possible sequences of constituents is defined for every language, and the sequence is free for non-configurational languages.

In the case of German or Dutch subject-verb inversion in interrogatives (cf. Section 2.2 above), for instance the presence of a conceptual structure relating to a question, puts 'query' or a wh-word into position 1 of S-holder. Position 1 is now occupied and cannot receive any output values by procedures lower in hierarchy. The information relating to 'query' is deposited in S-holder and utilised in conjunction with Word Order Rules when the V-branch and the NPsubj branch are created, thus yielding the required word order with V-NPsubj. In other words, the production of the correct word order that deviates from a linear mapping of conceptual structures through either canonical order or free word order requires the use of a highly specific syntactic store similar to the process that operates in subject-verb agreement marking.

Earlier in this chapter I discussed the role of memory in language processing and indicated that I would briefly return to this issue. The point that needed to be added concerns the ability of syntactic procedures to store syntactic information. I illustrated this for the storage of diacritic features in categorial procedures. In IPG this store is the relevant syntactic procedure. For instance, in the case of English subject-verb agreement the values for PERSON and NUMBER will be held in the S-procedure. I noted above that Vigliocco, Butterworth and Garrett (1996) modified the specific type of operation that matches these values to a feature-merging process. However, the directionality of the matching process has no bearing on the memory requirements. Given that language is produced in a linear manner, the features created earlier have to be stored until the second set of features has been created. The merging (or unification) of the relevant features guarantees the production of the correct morphological markers.

My second example of unification and the need for a specific syntactic store which I gave above was related to word order. I showed that the syntactic information 'query' is stored in a procedure for producing the correct word order. It is important to note that the need for these stores arises from the time-constrained nature and the automaticity of grammatical encoding. These stores are extremely specific in what they can hold and completely stupid. They will hold only grammatical information of a specific kind and pass it on to its destination no matter if the overall result makes sense or not. In fact, these stores have no access to a view on the overall result. That is what makes them stupid and efficient specialists. This can be evidenced when something goes wrong in the overall planning of a sentence resulting in speech errors. Levelt (1989) demonstrates that even in these circumstances the grammatical procedures deliver 'their' information to the predicted destination.

It may be precisely the syntactic store that is defunct in patients suffering from Broca's aphasia. Zurif, Swinney, Prather and Love (1994) report that these patients can carry out complex judgements on syntactic structures, while they fail to comprehend sentences with the same structures. In particular, these patients cannot assign grammatical functions to constituents in non-canonical order (or in GB terminology 'assign thematic roles to moved constituents'; cf. also Grodzinsky, 1986). Zurif et al. conclude that the patients' failure to comprehend these structures is based on a lack of temporal alignment of the different subprocedures, rather than a loss of grammatical knowledge. This is supported by their observation that lexical access in these patients is slower than in neurologically intact persons. The unavailability of the syntactic store to these patients would have exactly the consequence that information on the functional destination of phrases would not be retained by the holder, thus leading to a reduced ability of the patient to assign grammatical functions to constituents, especially in cases where syntactic function and semantic role do not match in a linear fashion. In other words, the above findings on Broca's aphasia are consistent with the assumptions made form a computational and psychological point of view on the specifically syntactic storage capacity of syntactic procedures.

In the course of this section, I mentioned repeatedly a connection between Incremental Processing Grammar (IPG) and LFG. I also mentioned that I will utilise LFG to set out a framework for L2 processability. As I stated above, Lexical-Functional Grammar (LFG) (Kaplan & Bresnan 1982; Bresnan 1982) is a deliberate attempt at designing a theory of grammar that represents linguistic knowledge AND is in line with cognitive features of language processing. Several major works in psycholinguistics have utilised LFG, most notably Pinker (1984,) in the context of language acquisition, and Levelt (1989) in the context of language processing.

Two of the key features which LFG shares with IPG are (1) the assumption that grammars are lexically driven and (2) the functional annotations of phrases (e.g. 'subject of') assuming the status of primitives. The second feature marks a major difference from Government and Binding (Chomsky 1981a; cf. also Horrocks 1987) where the GB counterpart to grammatical functions, thematic roles, are assigned to constituents by way of projection from the lexicon. The above architectural similarities between LFG and IPG are explicitly noted in Kempen and Hoenkamp (1987).

As I demonstrated in this section, IPG was designed to also model grammatical procedures as they are produced in real time. It is for these reasons that Levelt (1989) sees IPG as the performance companion of LFG. The modification of the feature matching process into a unification process, as proposed by Vigliocco, Butterworth and Garrett (1996), adds another key similarity to the two frameworks. With this modification, both rely on the unification of lexical features for inflectional morphological processes and in the production of word order.

In other words, the unification of lexical features, which is one of the main characteristics of LFG, captures a psychologically plausible process that involves (1) the identification of grammatical information in the lexical entry, (2) the temporary storage of that information and (3) its utilisation at another point in the constituent structure. The word order example (inversion) which I discussed above involves a similar process. In that case, the presence of a conceptual structure relating to a question deposits linguistic information into position 1 of S-holder, where it is utilised in conjunction with Word Order Rules when certain branches of the constituent structure are assembled, thus yielding the required word order. I will return to the relationship between IPG and LFG at the beginning of Chapter 3.

2.5 Processing procedures for the acquisition of L2 grammar

The account of grammatical processing presented in the previous section applies only to a fully operational language production system, i.e. to mature language users, not to language learners. In this section I will put forward a set of hypotheses on the sequence in which processing components become available to the second language learner. These hypotheses will be based mainly on the internal architecture of the Formulator, as discussed in the previous section. In other words, my hypotheses will not be concerned with the question as to how the architecture of the Formulator is acquired through practice, inferencing etc. Following the overall approach chosen for this book (cf. Chapter 1) the hypotheses will focus on the internal implicational relationship of the components of the Formulator.

Language-specific processing procedures

While even beginning second language learners can make recourse to the same *general* cognitive resources as mature native language users, they have to create language-specific processing procedures. In this context it is important to ensure that Levelt's model can, in principle, account for language processing in bilinguals, since second language acquisition will lead to a bilingual language processor.

De Bot (1992) adapted Levelt's model to language production in bilinguals. Based on work by Paradis (1987) he shows that information about the specific language to be used is present in each part of the preverbal message and this subsequently informs the selection of language-specific lexical items and of the language-specific routines in the Formulator. Drawing from Paradis's (1987) research, De Bot concludes that "... the speaker who speaks two closely related languages will for most part use the same procedural and lexical knowledge when speaking either of the two languages, while in the case of languages which are not related an appeal is made to much more language-specific knowledge." (De Bot 1992, 9). De Bot further shows that Paradis' (1987) 'Subset hypothesis' about the bilingual lexicon is in line with the overall design of Levelt's model. According to the subset hypothesis, the bilingual lexicon is a single storage system in which links between elements are enforced through continued use. This has the effect that links will be stronger between elements from one language. However, in the case of bilingual communities with a tendency for code-switching, links between elements from different languages may be similar to those in a monolingual lexicon.

De Bot (1992) demonstrates that the extended version of Levelt's model accounts for the majority of the additional requirements a language production model has to meet in a in a bilingual context. These include the following requirements: The two language systems concerned may be used quite separately from each other or in varying degrees of mixes (code-switching). The two systems may influence each other. Neither system will necessarily slow down in speech rate in comparison with a monolingual speaker, and the bilingual speaker may master the two (or more) systems to differing degrees.

Given the focus of Processability Theory on the Formulator, the key assumption from De Bot's work for the present context is that in all cases where the L2 is not closely related to the L1, different (language-specific) procedures have to be assumed. In section 2.4 I pointed out a number of components of the Formulator and the lexicon which are language-specific and which therefore have to be acquired. These include the following:

- Word order rules,
- Syntactic procedures and their specific stores,
- Diacritic parameters in the lexicon,
- The lexical category of lemmata,
- Functorisation rules.

Obviously, word order rules are language-specific, even though genetically related languages (such as the Germanic languages) share certain characteristics (in the case of Germanic languages the verb-second position in main clauses). Despite such relationships there is no *a priori* way of knowing for the language learner how closely related L1 and L2 are. Learners therefore have to be equipped to bridge maximal typological gaps in their L2 acquisition, for instance from English to Walpiri, a central Australian indigenous language (Simpson 1991) which is non-configurational and agglutinative.

There is no guarantee that the learner will not attempt to transfer L1 word order onto L2, but it is equally likely that he or she will initially express the relationship between conceptual structures and surface form in a computationally simpler way. After all, the L1 word order rules may rely on categories of phrasal descriptions which do not exist in the L2, and this would interfere with the application of L1 word order. In any case, there is no way around acquiring the unique set of word order rules for the L2 if acquisition is to progress.

Diacritic features of lemmata contain items such as 'tense', 'number', 'gender', 'case' etc. Again it is obvious that the list of diacritic features varies from language to language. For instance, the parameter 'gender' does not exist in English nouns but it does in German, Dutch, Swedish etc.

I noted above that syntactic procedures build constituent structures and temporarily store specific grammatical information such as diacritic features of lemmata for the language production process and that this storage capacity can be disturbed in aphasia. Phrasal categories do not have to be the same across languages. For instance, the category VP is assumed for some languages, but not for others. Even the distributional behaviour of nouns and verbs varies across languages. Secondly, given that diacritic features are language-specific and that these are stored in syntactic procedures, L1 procedures are not equipped to handle the specific storage task required by the L2.

The lexical category of lemmata may also vary from language to language. For instance English 'house' and German 'Haus' can either be a noun ('This is my house', 'Das ist mein Haus') or a verb (English example 'We housed the whole party'; German example 'Die hausten wie die Wilden': 'They *lived* like savages'). In contrast, the Finnish equivalent to 'house' (talo) can only act as a noun. Again, the language learner is only fit to acquire any of the world's languages if he or she tests the lexical category for every new lexical item.

The reader will recall that Functorisation Rules instigate the activation of free and bound grammatical morphemes. And the same is true for grammatical morphemes as for word order rules: these are language-specific and therefore have to be acquired with the L2.

Exchange of grammatical information

One can conclude from the above that the L2 learner is initially unable to deposit information into syntactic procedures, because (1) the lexicon is not fully annotated and more importantly (2) because even if the L1 annotation was transferred, the syntactic procedures have not specialised to hold the specific L2 syntactic information. For this reason one can predict that the beginning learner is unable to produce any structures which rely on the exchange of specific L2 grammatical information using syntactic procedures, or in LFG terms 'feature unification'.

This prediction serves as the first anchor point of my approach to predicting L2 processability: structures involving no exchange of grammatical information between constituents can be processed before structures that do require such information exchanges. Note that this prediction is based solely on the acquisition of *processing procedures*: no syntactic store — no syntactic non-linearity; it does not, at this stage, make recourse to the notion of processing complexity, which may indeed be different for the same structure at different points in language development.

It is now possible to expand on the principle of grammatical information exchange in line with the architecture of the Formulator. In Figure 2.4-4 above I illustrated different sources of grammatical information that result in the production of grammatical morphemes. One source is the conceptual structure itself. An example is reference to time in Figure 2.4-4 which is conceptualised as 'PAST'. This conceptual information will contribute to the activation of the correct lemma with the value 'past' for the diacritic parameter 'tense'. In other words, the concepts related to time reference and 'EVENT' are activated in the same iteration, and together they activate the lemma search. This means that the diacritic feature in question is available in the same location where the morpheme for the marking of past has to occur and no information has to be deposited into any syntactic procedure to achieve this process.

A second type of source of grammatical information is the lemma of the head of a phrase. Again, an example was given in Figure 2.4-4 above, namely the NP 'a child'. Amongst other things, the lemma CHILD is marked 'singular', and the value of this diacritic feature has to match that of the determiner. To achieve this, the lemma information for CHILD has to be deposited in the NP-procedure and kept there for the activation of the lemma 'A'. In other words, this second type of morpheme is linguistically characterised as agreement between the head of phrase and another phrasal constituent. Its processing characteristic is that of the storage of diacritic features in phrasal procedures. We can infer that this type of process will become available to the language learner once phrasal procedures have been developed for the L2.

There is one further type of process which involves the exchange of grammatical information. It has much in common with the previous type since it is also an agreement phenomenon, only this time the agreement occurs between heads of different phrases as in subject-verb agreement. If the time reference chosen for the example in Figure 2.4-4 above had been 'PRESENT' and 'IMPERFECTIVE', this would have resulted in the marking of 'third person singular' on the verb.

Let us consider the differences in the processing of phrasal and inter-phrasal agreement. First of all, the phrase 'a child' was produced in one and the same iteration. This is unlikely to apply to inter-phrasal agreement due to the incremental nature of language production. In other words, while the one phrase is being produced the head of the agreeing phrase has not been conceptualised. This means that the relevant diacritic information cannot be stored in the phrasal procedure. Instead it has to be stored in the S-procedure. However, in order to arrive there the functional destination of the phrase from which it originates has to be determined. This is carried out by a language-specific set of Appointment Rules as discussed above.

In other words, in comparison with the exchange of grammatical information within phrases, there are two additional processing procedures which have to develop before grammatical information can be exchanged between phrases: (1) a language-specific S-procedure and (2) language-specific Appointment Rules.

Given the key role of the S-procedure in co-ordinating phrasal information, it is worth noting that clause boundaries have been found to be psychologically plausible units of language processing (Ford and Holmes 1978; Levelt 1989; Ford 1982). Evidence in support of this is based on the analysis of pauses in speech, sentence completion experiments and dual task experiments. It is important to keep the psychological plausibility of constituent structure separate from the falsification of the derivational complexity hypothesis (Slobin 1966, Kintsch 1974, Engelkamp 1974), as well as from the search for units of conceptualisation (cf. Engelkamp 1974, Bock 1978). The notion of c-structure as a unit of language processing is part of Levelt's approach to language production which I follow in my approach to second language acquisition.

The first principle for establishing an accessibility hierarchy of processing procedures was that of grammatical information exchange. This can be complemented by a second principle, namely *perceptual salience*. Murdock (1962) (cf. also Sridhar 1988, Kintsch 1974) established this principle through a number of studies which found persistent primacy and recency effects on the memorisation of any sequence of stimuli. The first and the last stimulus is more marked than the other stimuli and is persistently remembered better (cf. Kintsch 1970). The reader will recall that Clahsen (1984) made recourse to the same principle in his strategies approach.

It is important to appreciate that perceptual salience is a general cognitive principle which is available to the beginning L2 learner as a processing procedure. It allows learners to identify sentence initial and final positions merely through their salience. A range of linguistic forms can rely on this cognitive principle alone. For instance a strictly serial word order (e.g. SVO or SOV) can be modified without invoking any language-specific procedures (e.g. XSVO). This simple device can extend the range of functions expressible through the learner's grammar. As the interlanguage develops, other linguistic forms may rely on a mix of salience and language-specific procedures.

A hierarchy of processing procedures

Table 2.5-1 affords us a summary of the proposed hierarchy of processing procedures. This table also contains a brief characteristic of the interlanguage grammar which results from the gradual availability of these processing procedures. The characterisation of developing grammars has been applied to configurational and non-configurational languages.

Table 2.5-1. Hypothetical hierarchy of processing procedures

	t_1	t_2	t_3	t_4	t_5
S'-procedure (Embedded S)	–	–	–	–	+
S-procedure	–	simplified	simplified Topic - Subj	+ inter-phrasal morphemes	+
Phrasal procedure (head)	–	–	+ phrasal morphemes	+	+
category procedure (lex. categ.)	–	+ lexical morphemes	+	+	+
word/ lemma	+	+	+	+	+
inter-language grammar of configurational languages	single words and 'phrases'	canonical order; morphemes: lexical	canonical order - TOPI; morphemes: lexical, phrasal	L2 word order in main clauses; morphemes: lexical, phrasal, inter-phrasal	L2 word order in main + subordinate clauses; morphemes: lexical, phrasal, inter-phrasal
inter-language grammar of non-configurational languages	single words and 'phrases'	free or canonical order morphemes: lexical morphological marking of semantic roles	free or canonical order-TOPI; morphemes: lexical and phrasal morphological marking of semantic roles	L2 word order in main clauses; morphemes: lexical, phrasal, inter-phrasal	L2 word order in main + subordinate clauses morphemes: lexical, phrasal, inter-phrasal

The first column of Table 2.5-1 contains a list of processing procedures which is implicationally ordered. This list consists of the following elements:
- subordinate clause procedure,
- S-procedure,
- phrasal procedures,
- category procedures,
- lemma access,

This hierarchy reflects the temporal alignment of procedures and rules in IPG which starts with the activation of the lemma. The latter contains information about lexical category membership which calls the category procedure. The head of the phrase calls the phrasal procedure, based on the category information in the lemma. The phrasal procedure also acts as a repository for phrasal information. The grammatical function of the phrase is decided by language-specific Appointment Rules. Once the grammatical function of a phrase is determined it can be attached to the S-node and the S holder can store sentential information.

The hierarchical nature of this list arises from the fact that the procedure of each lower level is a prerequisite for the functioning of the higher level: A word needs to be added to the L2 lexicon before its grammatical category can be assigned. The grammatical category of a lemma is needed before a category procedure can be called. Only if the grammatical category of the head of phrase is assigned can the phrasal procedure be called. Only if a phrasal procedure has been completed and its value is returned can Appointment Rules determine the function of the phrase. And only if the function of the phrase has been determined can it be attached to the S-node and sentential information be stored in the S-holder.

One might wonder if it should not be possible to utilise a subset of procedures from the L1, at least those that overlap to some extent with the L2. However, it needs to be pointed out that this would lead to internal problems, because all of the above processing procedures need to be orchestrated in a language-specific way. If any one of them is missing or incompatible with the rest, the Formulator is inoperable. If, for instance, the lexical category information is missing, category and phrasal procedures cannot be called. If diacritic features are missing or have no values or values which are not compatible with those listed in agreeing phrases or if they are incompatible with the Functorisation Rules, then the processor will be inoperable.

Table 2.5-2. The German definite article

| | masculine | | feminine | | neuter | |
	sgl	pl	sgl	pl	sgl	pl
nominative	der	die	die	die	das	die
genitive	des	der	der	der	des	der
dative	dem	den	der	den	dem	den
accusative	den	die	die	die	das	die

This does not mean that the learner will never attempt to form diacritic features and Functorisation Rules that reflect L1 regularities. However, a "bulk-transfer" of the L1 Formulator would lead to very unwieldy hypotheses. German learners of English, for instance, would have to invent large sets of diacritic features for nouns, verbs and adjectives without any evidence of their existence in the L2, since German definite determiners express a complex set of diacritic features of the noun (three genders, four cases and two numbers). Since English nouns do not contain these diacritic features the complex system of definite determiners presented in Table 2.5-2 corresponds to merely one English grammatical morpheme ('the').

In this case the simplest structural solution would be to abandon the L1 diacritic features altogether. This would in fact reproduce a situation which is close to the English determiner system. However, the relationship between L1 and L2 diacritic features may be more complex than in the above example, with two intersecting sets of diacritic features and different form-function relationships in L1 and L2. In other words, there is potentially a multitude of L1 features only some of which are applicable to the L2. While it may be clear to the linguistic analyst, which of the diacritic features of the L1 apply to the L2, there is no obvious *a priori* way for the learner to know this. A random choice of features could well generate procedures which are incompatible with the rest of the Formulator. Unless the learner simply limits herself or himself to the L1 Formulator, thus not acquiring the L2, there is no other obvious choice than to re-construct the set of diacritic features specific to the L2.

In other words, I hypothesise that the L1 Formulator will not be 'bulk-transferred'. Instead, the learner will re-construct the Formulator of the L2. This would not exclude that in the course of this process L1 procedures be utilised. However, I hypothesise that such L1 transfer always occur as part of

the overall reconstruction process. Any other type of transfer of L1 procedures would not be in tune with the intermediate L2 procedures constructed at
that point and would therefore be unable to feed into the processor.

There is ample empirical support for the "no bulk transfer hypothesis".
One strong piece of evidence is the rather surprising outcome of a study on
the acquisition of verb placement by Swedes learning German (Håkansson
1996a). One has to remember that both, German and Swedish place the finite
verb in second position even after non-subjects in sentence-initial position.
One might therefore assume that verb position constraints could simply be
transferred from the L1, Swedish. However, Håkansson's study shows that
that is not the case. By comparing the description of German and Swedish
syntax in sections 3.3 and 5.2, the reader can see that the rules involved are
almost identical in the two languages. Nevertheless, Håkansson's subjects
had to learn it and continued to have problems with it for a long time.

There is a wealth of additional empirical evidence for the "no bulk transfer
hypothesis", including the observation that Italian learners of German have
to acquire subject-verb agreement even though such an agreement system
exists in both languages (Pienemann 1981). Those studies and particularly
Håkansson's study boldly falsify the so-called "full transfer/ full access model"
by Schwartz and Sprouse (1994; 1996) who claim that "... the entirety of the L1
grammar (excluding the phonetic matrices of lexical/ morphological items) is
the L2 initial state ... " Schwartz and Sprouse (1996, 41). Håkansson's study
demonstrates particularly clearly that the Schwartz and Sprouse hypothesis
makes the wrong prediction.

However, it is important to note that rejecting the "no bulk transfer"
hypothesis does not exclude transfer altogether. In particular, I hypothesise
that L1 procedures may be transferred when they are processable within the
overall interlanguage system, i.e. as soon as the necessary processing prerequisites have been developed. This hypothesis is compatible with findings
from studies on second language speech processing; for instance with
Harrington's (1987) study who found evidence of the transfer of processing
strategies from Japanese to English in Japanese ESL learners in the assignment
of grammatical subject and agency. In this case, the learners had already
developed procedures to process the competing linguistic means (cues in the
terminology of Bates and MacWhinney, 1982) such as animacy, stress and
word order, and they showed a preference for the L1-like cues.

Assuming the "no bulk transfer" hypothesis, the hierarchy of processing procedures spelt out above allows one to differentiate five major stages in the development of the L2 processor.

(1) The first stage in this hierarchy is characterised by the complete absence of any language-specific procedures. New words have to be entered into the lexicon. De Bot (1992) assumes that this can initially be accommodated by the one L1 lexicon. However, he is aware that one large store for two linguistic systems does lead to problems because the one-store assumption "... does not explain how the two systems are separated in bilinguals ..." (De Bot 1992, 9).

Also, it is unclear how L2 items would be annotated in the L1 lexicon at this early stage. If the L2 word is simply attached to the L1 lemma as an alternative morpho-phonological form, then the complete L1 syntactic information would be available upon accessing the lemma. For the purpose of L2 processing this would be irrelevant because the L1 lemma would either not contain relevant information or it would be unclear which of the information it does contain is applicable to the L2. Sooner or later a language-specific structure has to be created for the L2 lexicon, possibly with different lexical categories and different diacritic features, depending on the structure of the L2.

What is relevant for the structure of the interlanguage is the fact that the lack of access to syntactic information about the L2 lexical item blocks the language production process off, since no phrasal and other procedures can be called, no grammatical information can be exchanged, and phrases cannot be assigned functions. This means that all that can happen at this stage is the mapping of conceptual structures onto individual words and fixed phrases.

(2) Once L2 lexical items have been assigned a grammatical category, lexical morphological markers can be produced. Lexical morphemes can be activated by the conceptual structure or be retrieved from the lexicon and do not rely on the exchange of any grammatical information which is still blocked at this stage. This is because the L2 phrasal procedure which carries the information has not been automatised.

Unlike L1 learners, L2 learners do have access to a more or less (depending on age) developed conceptual system and the acquisition of the Formulator is independent of the development of conceptual structures. In other words, L2 learners have a set of well-defined semantic roles which they will attempt to map onto L2 forms. Since this mapping is not possible using L2 procedures the only solution is to use simplified procedures. Since no grammatical information can be exchanged, the learner will be confined to procedures which do not require information exchange.

One such procedure for the mapping of semantic roles onto surface form is a strictly serial word order — similar to the NVN sequence discussed by Bever (1970). This makes it possible to match semantics directly onto linguistic form without any arbitrariness. In its simplest form, all this procedure requires is the identification of lexical categories. This circumvents all intervening procedures, the appointment rules, the L2 S-procedure etc. On the other hand, the output of the grammar that results from this is unlikely to meet the requirements of the target language.

This intermediate solution applies to configurational languages. For non-configurational languages a marking of semantic roles through lexical morphemes will yield a similar result. A hypothetical example illustrates the case:

'CHASE' action   'CAT' agent   'DOG' patient

Since the morphological markers of semantic roles are activated directly by the conceptual structure they do not require any information exchange and can be produced at this stage and the morphemes clearly mark the semantic roles. This is the case, for instance, in Turkish (cf. Aksu 1978). Again, any other L2 constraints will not be able to be observed by the learner.

(3) Once phrasal procedures have been developed for the L2 (as automatic processes), diacritic features can be stored and unified between the head of a phrase and its modifiers. This enables the learner to produce phrasal morphemes.

Since Appointment Rules and S-procedures rely on the input from phrasal procedures, the first can only develop once the latter have emerged. In the absence of Appointment Rules and S-procedures, interphrasal agreement and non-serial word order is still blocked at this stage. These procedural gaps are circumnavigated by using a serial order strategy to map semantics onto linguistic form:

agent   action   patient
N   V   N.

However, there is a path for further development while certain procedures are blocked: the strict seriality of word order can be maintained while the learner utilises general cognitive principle in conjunction with canonical word order. The positions external to the NVN sequence can be identified on the basis of the non-linguistic principle of salience, and the canonical schema would be active after the salient position has been processed.

$$
\left.\begin{array}{l} \text{INITIAL} \\ \text{PP/Wh} \end{array}\right] \quad \begin{array}{cccc} \text{agent} & \text{action} & \text{patient} \\ \text{NP} & \text{V} & \text{NP} \end{array} \quad \left[\begin{array}{l} \text{FINAL} \\ \\ \end{array}\right.
$$

In practical terms, these additional 'pragmatic' word order options (cf. Rutherford 1988) allow the learner to imitate a range of L2 syntactic phenomena without full access to L2 procedures. Note that in the above representation of the canonical schema the component parts of the canonical sequence are described as phrases because phrasal procedures are operational at this stage. This makes it possible for the canonical schema to allow a definition of 'position' in terms of phrases rather than words.

(4) Once phrasal procedures are present, Appointment Rules and the S-procedure can be developed. This means that the functional destination of phrases can be determined and phrases can be assembled into sentences. I noted above that in this book I will not focus on the acquisition of these processing procedures itself. For that purpose one would need to make explicit, amongst other things, the inferential mechanisms that lead to the construction of the newly acquired rules and procedures.

What is of interest in the context of this book are the repercussions that the availability of new types of procedures have for the interlanguage grammar, and those are quite clear. Once the Appointment Rules are present and the S-procedures are complete interphrasal morphemes can be produced and word order can be structured syntactically according to L2 constraints; i.e. the pragmatic word order principles can be replaced by syntactic ones.

Utilising the above salience principle one can predict that in the process of acquiring L2 word order constellations, the salience principle will support those constellations where information has to be brought into a salient position. This marks an intermediate stage which has not been separately identified in Table 2.3. As proposed by Clahsen (1984), target positions can be identified more readily if they are perceptually salient (as discussed above; cf. Murdock 1962). It is therefore hypothesised that the exchange of grammatical information between constituents will first occur when one position is salient.

(5) The fifth stage concerns subordinate clauses, or more precisely the distinction between main and subordinate clauses. At level 4 Appointment Rules and the S-procedure are developed which allow a syntactic formation of sentences with L2 word order. However, at stage 4 one major limitation

exists, namely that "... standard Appointment Rules ... fail to apply [to allow sentential complements] since they only provide for NP-shaped object constituents." (Kempen and Hoenkamp 1987, 225). In other words, with the given machinery sentential complements cannot call S as a subprocedure. Therefore complement clauses cannot be constructed. This applies to object complement clauses (e.g. *'he wants to drink some juice'*, *'she sees him eat an apple'*, *'they noticed that he left'*), adverbial complement clauses (e.g. *'I'll see you when you get back'*) and relative clauses (e.g. *'the things you want are never cheap'*).

To enable the processor to call S as a subprocedure new elements need to be introduced to the lemma of verbs, so-called 'Lemma Functions' which serve the purpose of refining the list of procedure calls contained in the lemma. These 'Lemma Functions' are therefore at the top of our list of processing procedures. For these reasons I hypothesise that the distinctive syntactic features of subordinate clauses will be acquired after interphrasal exchange of grammatical information.

The reader will remember that in his strategies approach Clahsen (1984) arrived at a very similar conclusion with his more specific claim that word order 'permutations' will be blocked in subordinate clauses until the distinction between main and subordinate clauses is acquired. Clahsen (1984) claimed that "... subordinate clauses are processed differently to main clauses." He based his claim on evidence from Bever and Townsend's (1979) experiments on sentence comprehension and cited Givon's (1979) typological arguments. Our understanding of syntactic processing has changed since Bever and Townsend's (1979) work appeared, in particular the psychological interpretation of the 'autonomy of syntax' assumption. Nevertheless, the empirical evidence presented in their study supports the thesis of a basic processing difference between the two types of clauses.

Summary and evaluation

At this stage it may be useful to summarise the implicational hierarchy of processing procedures developed above. This summary is provided in form of Table 2.5-3. Note that in Table 2.5-3 a level has been added to the hierarchy by use of the saliency principle ('exchange of information from internal to salient constituent').

Table 2.5-3. Hierarchy of processing procedures - summary

- Subordinate clause procedure;
- S-procedure; inter-phrasal morphemes; exchange of information between internal constituents;
- Simplified S-procedure; exchange of information from internal to salient constituent;
- Phrasal procedures; phrasal morphemes;
- Category procedure; lexical morphemes; no exchange of information - canonical word order;
- Lemma access; words; no sequence of constituents.

This hierarchy represents a set of hypotheses about the implicational order in the development of L2 processing procedures. The implicational nature of the hierarchy derives from the fact that the processing procedures developed at one stage are a necessary prerequisite for the following stage: A *word* needs to be added to the L2 lexicon before its *grammatical category* can be assigned. The grammatical category of a *lemma* is needed before a *category procedure* can be called. Only if the grammatical category of the head of phrase is assigned can the *phrasal procedure* be called. Only if the latter has been completed and its value is returned can *Appointment Rules* determine the *function* of the phrase after which it be attached to the *S-node*. Only after appointment Rules are refined by *'Lemma Functions'* can subordinate clauses be formed — with their own structural properties.

The predictions about acquisition that can be derived from this hierarchy are based on the following logic: the learner cannot acquire what he/she cannot process. It should be noted that this proposition is different from the notion of *processing complexity* which assumes that an increased number of processes increases the complexity of a structure. In relation to acquisition, several authors (e.g. Slobin 1977, Clahsen 1984) have argued that less complex structures can be acquired earlier than more complex structures. While the logic behind this prediction is intuitively appealing, it is dissonant with the concept of automatic processing. For automated procedures, linguistic complexity is not a predictor of processing speed. Automated procedures are complex coding mechanisms which make recall and production more efficient and faster than less complex coding mechanisms. This is evident from studies of word, sentence and text recall (e.g. Bock 1978) as well as from the more general literature on storage and production (e.g. Baddeley 1990).

The crux of the matter is that it is not the difficulty of processing as such that makes complex structures impossible for the learner to process, but the lack of the appropriate processing procedures. This view is more consistent with empirical findings about language processing, for instance with the fact that mature native speakers can recall grammatical texts more rapidly than ungrammatical texts (Bock 1978).

Also note that the proposed implicational hierarchy of processing procedures is no longer restricted to "movement" as Clahsen's framework was, since the concept of information exchange is applicable to morphological as well as to syntactic phenomena. It is easy to see that these principles will generate predictions for developmental paths for any language with mildly differentiated syntax and/or morphology. At the present stage this is all I am aiming at. In other words, I believe that languages which do not employ a differentiated syntax or morphology do not invalidate Processability Theory. One can only conclude that Processability Theory has nothing to say about such languages.

Chapter 3

Processing procedures and the development of grammar

In this chapter the hierarchy of processing procedures developed in Chapter 2 will be implemented into a psychologically plausible theory of grammar. This will make it possible to predict grammatical development in different languages.

3.1 Reasons for implementing processability into a theory of grammar

I would like to make it clear that the "news value" of this book is not that a theory of grammar *other than GB* has been found to make predictions for language acquisition or that LFG is superior to GB because of its greater psychological plausibility. The discussion of this book concentrates on psychological issues in language acquisition, and many of the arguments for and against different schools of Generative Grammar are not psychological or epistemological in nature (cf. Horrocks 1987 for a formal evaluation of the main theories). Similarly with Pinker (1984) and Levelt (1989), I merely use LFG as a convenient reference point which has been formalised and tested sufficiently to be practical for this purpose. The architecture of LFG coincides with most of the key points I made in the previous section in relation to language processing. This does not mean, however, that I want to argue the case for LFG as the optimal theory in relation to language processing.

Interfaces between explanatory modules

Let us start with the more general question: why implement processability into a theory of grammar? To put this question into context one has to remember the key issues in the explanation of language acquisition. In Chapter 1 I discussed the following four components which a theory of language learnability must specify:

(1) the target language,
(2) the data input to the learner,
(3) the learning device that must acquire that grammar,
(4) the initial state.

It was also noted that the psychological constraints on the processing of grammar which this book focuses on are related to two of these components: the learning device and the target language. The relationship to the learning device is based on my proposition that the learner can produce only those structures which he/she can process at any given point in time. This then limits the hypothesis space by a further dimension which would not exist if one permitted the set of all logically possible hypotheses without further restrictions. The connection to the target language is the following: the Hypothesis Space defined by Processability Theory ultimately has to allow for those structures found in the target language; i.e. it must not unduly constrain structures which do indeed occur in the target language. It must also allow for intermediate versions of the L2 to be able to develop in the finite state of that language.

Even though I wish to confine the present book to the problem of processability, this module of a theory of L2 acquisition nevertheless has to be compatible with other potential modules. Otherwise the processability component would be unable to communicate with the other modules, and the abstraction one makes by focusing on only one aspect of a theory of learnability would become illegitimate, because one would have no way of knowing that the information provided by this module can be fed into other modules or vice versa.

Another logical limitation in formulating processing constraints for a theory of learnability is the fact that the predictions derivable from such constraints need to be applicable to a wide range of phenomena and a range of languages. They also need to be testable with ease.

The most economical way to accommodate these logical limitations on the shape of the theory of processability is to implement processing constraints into a theory of grammar. This ensures that the target language can be represented. In fact, if the theory is valid any target language ought to be able to be represented. This step also ensures that any intermediate version of the interlanguage is a possible grammar as defined by the theory used so that it can be extended to the TL. This step further ensures maximal generalisability of predictions that can be derived from processability.

We have seen in the case of the strategies approach that psychological constraints on language production cannot, on their own, make predictions that are powerful enough to describe exact linguistic structures. Such constraints are only useful if they are complemented by a theory of grammar. Otherwise the question will always be: what do the constraints act on, what do they constrain? The only alternative would be to make the constraints so powerful that they act as a theory of grammar.

Psychological and typological plausibility

In this context the reader may wonder what motivated the author to implement the above hierarchy of processing procedures into a theory of grammar rather than directly into IPG which *is* a processing grammar. I decided against this option for several reasons. I demonstrated in Chapter 2 that feature unification, which is one of the main characteristics of LFG, captures a psychologically plausible process that involves (1) the identification of grammatical information in the lexical entry, (2) the temporary storage of that information and (3) its utilisation at another point in the constituent structure. I also demonstrated that feature unification is one of the key processes in morphology and word order, the two areas to be studied in the empirical sections of this book. Every level of the hierarchy of processing procedures can be represented through feature unification. In other words, the essence of that hierarchy can be captured through feature unification in LFG.[11]

The only proviso on this is that the procedures that underlie LFG cannot be understood to represent psychological procedures themselves. Instead, they can be considered a short-hand notation which contains all the necessary elements to relate structures to a hierarchy of processability. The LFG formalism is designed to be highly noncommittal as to when unifications are performed. They can be done incrementally, as each phrase is built, or at the end, when an entire c-structure has been constructed (see Maxwell and Kaplan 1995 for some discussion). Since Processability Theory assumes strict limits on grammatical memory, it would follow that unifications ought to be done as soon as possible.

The limitations on memory are relevant to a further feature of LFG, which is that the theory in its present form imposes no limitations on the amount or nature of information that can be transferred between constituents by unification. For example, arbitrarily complex substructures can be built in different constituents, and checked for consistency. This possibility has been shown to lead to the possibility of writing LFG grammars for highly unnatural kinds of languages (Berwick and Weinberg 1984, 107-114;), and to computational intractability (Barton, Berwick and Ristad 1987, 103-114). In Processability Theory, rather than having an unlimited and unconstrained ability to unify information from different constituents, learners are assumed to have no such ability, which is then gradually acquired. This argues that the LFG theory should be modified so that information flow between constituents is inherently restricted. I will use the LFG system with the informal assumption that unification occurs at lowest node which the 'source' and the 'destination' of the unification share.

A theory of second language acquisition has to be typologically plausible since it has to apply to any pair of L1 and L2 from amongst the languages of the world. One of the great strengths of LFG is its proven typological plausibility. In this respect, LFG is a 'tried and tested' framework with extensive studies on typologically diverse languages (e.g. Simpson 1991; Bresnan and Kanerva 1989). IPG may have this capacity as well. However, it has not yet been demonstrated, and my own resources are too limited to undertake this task.

A further reason for the suitability of LFG in defining processability in the context of language acquisition is the fact that the acquisition process itself can most plausibly be viewed as a lexically driven process. The main reason for this assumption is an epistemological one: the inferential process is more powerful if it is based on lexical learning, because the learner can assimilate grammatical features with lexical items on the basis of positive evidence. Roeper, Lapointe, Bing and Tavakolian (1981) point out that a lexical acquisition theory has two advantages: (1) it eliminates many potential grammars which would be logically possible if acquisition was based on the generation of structural hypotheses only, and (2) it provides a solution for the learning of optional rules which cannot otherwise be inferred from positive evidence (Roeper et al. 1981, 38).

In short, LFG promises to afford a valid application of my hierarchy of processing procedures; it is readily available, compatible with Levelt's model and attractive from a typological point of view.

3.2 A sketch of Lexical-Functional Grammar

LFG belongs to the "family" of unification grammars, the most prominent characteristic of which is — as the name suggests — that of the unification of features. Put simply, the process of feature unification ensures that the different parts that constitute a sentence do actually fit together. I pointed out above that one of the main reasons why I opted for LFG in the construction of the present SLA framework is that the process of feature unification is one that is attributed psychological plausibility in current work on speech processing.

LFG consists of three parts: (1) a constituent structure (= c-structure) component that generates "surface structure" constituents and c-structure relationships, (2) a lexicon, whose entries contain syntactic and other information relevant to the generation of sentences, and (3) a functional component which compiles for every sentence all the grammatical information needed to interpret the sentence semantically .

The interaction of these three components is subject to a set of well-formedness conditions, which are basically very general rules constraining the process of feature unification, ensuring that all properties of an f-structure are compatible with each other. We will see that many types of ungrammaticality in SLA can be explained on the basis of functional ill-formedness.

Constituent structures

The c-structure component of LFG is similar to the phrase-structure component of the Standard Theory of transformational grammar (Chomsky 1965). The similarity is, however, only superficial.

In contrast to the Standard Theory, all c-structures are generated directly by phrase structure rules without any intervening transformations. Hence the mapping of predicate-argument structures onto surface forms is achieved without any intervening levels of representation. Another major difference is that in c-structure rules, grammatical functions (such as "subject") are not represented by the "geometry" of phrase structure as is the case in the Standard Theory. Instead, grammatical functions assume the role of grammatical primitives, and major constituents are annotated for their grammatical function. The sentence "Peter owns a dog", for instance has the c-structure shown in Figure 3.2-1 which can be generated by the following annotated phrase structure rules:

$$
\begin{aligned}
S &\rightarrow NP_{subj} \; VP \\
NP &\rightarrow (det) \; N \\
VP &\rightarrow V \; (NP_{obj}).
\end{aligned}
$$

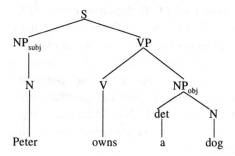

Figure 3.2-1. Constituent structure - example

Lexical entries

A simplified account of the lexical entries relating to Figure 3.2-1 is given in Figure 3.2-2.

As is obvious from these simplified examples, lexical entries specify a number of syntactic and other properties of lexical items by assigning values to features (e.g. NUM = SG). In most cases such equations *define* the value of features. In some cases they may also "demand" certain values elsewhere in

Figure 3.2-2. Lexical entries

Peter:	N,	PRED	=	"Peter"
owns:	V,	PRED	=	"own" (SUBJ, OBJ)
		TENSE	=	present
		SUBJ PERSON	=	3
		SUBJ NUM	=	SG
a:	DET,	SPEC	=	"a"
		NUM	=	SG
dog:	N,	PRED	=	"dog"
		NUM	=	SG

the functional description of a sentence. One example for such a constraining equation would be

$$\text{V-COMP INF} =_c \text{ge.}$$

This equation applies to some German auxiliaries which require the lexical verb to form a particular infinitive with the prefix 'ge-' as in 'ge-gangen' (gone).

Functional structures

The functional structure or "f-structure" of a sentence is a list of those pieces of grammatical information needed to semantically interpret the sentence. It is generated by the interaction between c-structure and the lexicon. The f-structure of the sentence in Figure 3.2-1 is given in Figure 3.2-3.

The predicate entry [PRED "own" (SUBJ, OBJ)] is taken from the lexical entry of the verb. Listing the stem of the verb in quotation marks ("own") is simply a short-hand convention for a semantic representation of the word. The slots to the right of the verb which are filled by SUBJ and OBJ in Figure 3.2-3 list the arguments of the predicate: first the *owner*, then the *item owned*. In Figure 3.2-3, these slots are occupied by grammatical functions. This means that the functions listed in those places mark the semantic relations associated with the slots they occupy.

The PRED entry of the f-structure therefore makes it possible to relate the different constituents to the "players" described by the sentence (actor, patient, etc.). This forms the link between the syntactic form and its underlying predicate-argument relations.

Figure 3.2-3. Functional structure

PRED	"own" (SUBJ, OBJ)	
TENSE	present	
SUBJ	PRED	"Peter"
OBJ	SPEC	"a"
	NUM	SG
	PRED	"dog"

Well-formedness conditions

LFG contains a number of functional well-formedness conditions which ensure that the different interacting components, particularly c-structure and the lexicon, generate sentences which are consistent in the assignment of functions and feature values. These conditions guarantee for instance that all constituents listed in the lexical entry of the verb are actually generated, so that sentences such as (3) are rejected.

(3)   * The real estate agent bought.

One well-formedness condition which is of particular interest in the present context is the *uniqueness condition* (henceforth UC), according to which the values attributed to a constituent must be compatible. Otherwise the sentence would be rejected. The example given in Kaplan and Bresnan (1982, 204) is

(4)   * A girl handed the baby a toys.

In this case the lexical specifications of two constituents of the NP "a toys" are in conflict. "a" specifies "singular" for the feature NUM while "toys" specifies "plural". Obviously, the NP cannot be both singular and plural.

The Uniqueness Condition thus filters out a whole range of ungrammatical sentences. It is worth noting here that the ungrammatical sentences screened out by the UC have in common the fact that they contain conflicting lexical specifications, as in (5)-(7).

(5)   * they will went   (future - past)
(6)   * they goes   (plural - singular)
(7)   * the man ... she   (masculine - feminine).

All of these cases involve the grammatical encoding of semantic features or relations. The UC itself is not the mechanism for the instantiation of these grammatical encodings, but it is the formal guarantee that the informational prerequisites for the grammatical encoding process exist.

It is this grammatical encoding that SL learners have to acquire. Below I will show that the application of the UC poses different degrees of complexity to the learner in different linguistic contexts and that the degrees of complexity determine which semantic features/functions can be encoded at what relative point in time.

Obviously, many interlanguage forms result from what appear to be violations of the UC. One has to remember, however, that they are only violations of the UC from the perspective of the target language. In interlanguage grammar it is possible that only the determiner or only the noun or neither of the two is annotated for NUM(BER). In language acquisition, new lexical items are often integrated into the lexicon as a unitary morpho-phonological shape and only later are they broken down into their constituent units.

If lexical entries are not annotated for certain features, the UC logically does not apply to the constituent containing that lexical item.

It may seem as if it did not matter very much whether phrases like "a toys" are ungrammatical because of a violation of the UC or because of immature lexical entries. My point, however, is that the UC is an absolutely necessary condition for any grammar to exist. It holds the fabric of the LFG components together. Without it no language or interlanguage containing grammatical encodings of semantic features could be represented. In other words, such grammatical encodings cannot be learnt without the UC. And it is the learning of grammatical encodings which a theory of language acquisition seeks to explain.

Unification

I mentioned above that the process of feature unification is one that is shared by LFG and Incremental Procedural Grammar (Kempen and Hoenkamp 1987) and that this is one reason for choosing LFG as the grammatical formalism for Processability Theory. The process of feature unification was described for the language generation process in Section 2.4 (Grammatical encoding) above. One example of feature unification is the assembly of the noun phrase 'a dog'. As one can see in Figure 3.2-2, the lexical entries 'a' and 'dog' are both annotated with the feature NUM(MBER), and in both cases this feature has the value 'singular'. For the noun phrase to be grammatically acceptable the two features have to be matched. This matching process is called 'unification'.

In section 2.4 I noted that Kempen and Hoenkamp (1987) conceptualise this process as 'feature copying' where features have a source and a destination. I further noted that Vigliocco et al (1996) propose a psychologically and typologically more plausible view according to which features are merged. In this view both constituents involved in the merging process can derive features independently form conceptual structure or from the lexicon. In other words, I made a number of assumptions about how the unification process needs to be modified within LFG to account for additional psycholinguistic factors. One such assumption was mentioned in the previous section where I argued that LFG should be modified so that information flow between constituents is restricted and that unification should occur at the lowest node that is shared by the affected constituents.

3.3 Word order revisited

The first step in my revision and extension of the original processing explanation of orders of acquisition is to show that the observed German word order phenomena can be explained in an LFG framework. This does not, however, falsify any other analyses, it merely prepares the way for the further unfolding of our argument which is aimed at a unified explanation of a wider range of phenomena. I will then demonstrate that this account of German word order is in line with the processability hierarchy developed in Chapter 2.

It will be useful to bear in mind that the LFG formalism employed for this exercise is somewhat simplified. I pointed out above that I will use the LFG system with the informal assumption that unification occurs at lowest node which the 'source' and the 'destination' of the unification share. This is done to capture a key feature in the incrementality of language production. I will therefore not use the ↑ = ↓ annotation as a means of formally linking c-structure and f-structure. I pointed out above that this assumption is in line with the procedural aspects of IPG.

In the 'strategies approach', processing strategies were conceptualised as constraints on transformations. In my approach, they are viewed as constraints on unification, which is the central psychologically plausible operation in LFG. This allows us to predict the same range of phenomena in syntax as the TG-based approach. However, it also allows the integration of morphological phenomena.

Basic word order patterns

In LFG possible word orders of languages are defined through c-structure rules (Bresnan and Kaplan 1982, 175ff.), since there is only one level of c-structure.

(R1) $S \rightarrow NP_{subj}$ V (NP_{obj1}) (NP_{obj2})

(R1) allows for a basic SVO order (i.e. NP_{subj} V NP_{obj1} NP_{obj2}), as it occurs at stage x (cf. section 2.1).

The occurrence of wh-words, PPs and NPs in focus position, the characteristic of stage x+1, can be accounted for by (R2) which is adapted from Pinker (1984, 278):

(R2) $S' \rightarrow (XP)$ S

$$\left\{ \begin{array}{l} \text{wh} =_c + \\ \text{adv} =_c + \\ \text{NP} =_c + \\ \text{PP} =_c + \end{array} \right\}$$

The control equations in (R2) ensure that only wh-words, adverbs, NPs and PPs can occur in focus position. Standard German also allows lexical verbs to occur in this position, but such structures appear later than at x+1. In a more explicit treatment of these facts one would have to append a further equation to the XP position which shows that XP controls the gap created by topicalisation (e.g. in "was er hat gegessen (gap)?" as compared with "er hat gegessen ein Kuchen" (both examples in x+1 interlanguage). For the purpose of this book I will not include this aspect of the description. Also, note that at stage x+1 structures like "hat-ge-sag-en" (have-past-say-infinitive) may occur. I analyse this as "PAST-PAST-V" and thus as a single verb entry, which can be inserted into the V-slot in (R1).

Hence (R2) allows for the possibility that the topic position becomes available separately to wh-words, adverbs, etc., because each of these categories requires separate control equations, which may be acquired individually. Empirical studies (e.g. Clahsen, Meisel and Pienemann 1983, and Pienemann 1981) show that this is exactly what happens in GSL acquisition.

'Split verbs'

The German "split verb" position (i.e. stage x+2 or "SEP" in section 2.1) can be described as a gradual lexical acquisition process which is based on a number of alterations of the existing c-structure rule as shown in (R3). One alteration concerns the introduction of VP as a constituent, which is necessary to account for a range of phenomena in German, as we will see below. The other alteration is concerned with the position of the verb. VP rewrites alternatively into the structure known from R1, or as V-COMP, and the latter constituent rewrites as $(NP_{obj1})(NP_{obj2})$ V. This ensures that V will only occur in second position unless "licensed" by a V that takes V-COMP.

$$(R3) \quad S \quad \rightarrow NP_{subj} \; VP$$

$$VP \rightarrow V \quad \begin{Bmatrix} (NP_{obj1})(NP_{obj2}) \\ V\text{-COMP} \end{Bmatrix}$$

$$V\text{-COMP} \rightarrow (NP_{obj1})(NP_{obj2}) \; V$$

Apart from this change in c-structure rules, I assume that the learner gradually re-analyses the verbs of his/her interlanguage, by analysing AUX and V as two separate entries and by adding the feature AUX to the lexical features of V.

To achieve the split verb effect, the newly created auxiliaries and modals are treated as main verbs (with the feature AUX that takes the value' +'), which take VP complements (as in Kaplan and Bresnan 1982, Netter 1987). Let us take sentence (8) as an example:

(8)   er *hat* ein Bier *getrunken*
      he has a   beer drunk
      "he has drunk/drank a beer".

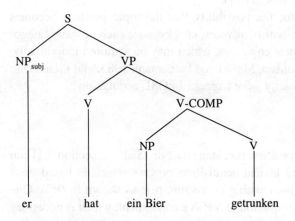

Figure 3.3-1. C-structure of sentence (8)

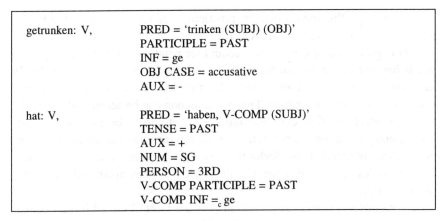

| getrunken: V, | PRED = 'trinken (SUBJ) (OBJ)'
PARTICIPLE = PAST
INF = ge
OBJ CASE = accusative
AUX = - |
| hat: V, | PRED = 'haben, V-COMP (SUBJ)'
TENSE = PAST
AUX = +
NUM = SG
PERSON = 3RD
V-COMP PARTICIPLE = PAST
V-COMP INF =$_c$ ge |

Figure 3.3-2. Lexical entries for sentence (8)

The c-structure of (8) is represented in the form of a simplified tree diagram in Figure 3.3-1. The simplified lexical entries for the verbs in (9) are as shown in Figure 3.3-2.

This set of entries and rules, etc., ensure two things which are of relevance here: (1) that a particular (at this stage not necessarily the correct) morphological form of the main verb is used with the auxiliary to express the intended grammatical function. This is achieved by the functional well-formedness conditions mentioned above which ensure that functional annotations match across related constituents. In this case it is the value PAST in (PARTICIPLE) = PAST and (V-Comp PARTICIPLE) = PAST which allows a unification of these two functions and thus legitimates these two constituents in this particular sentence.

(2) The second point is that the c-structure rules, in conjunction with the unification processes mentioned under (1), ensure that the two verbs appear in a split position and that only the lexical verb can appear in final position. Figure 3.3-2 illustrates why, according to the rule system developed above, only lexical verbs can occur in final position: the PRED value for 'hat' contains V-COMP and SUBJ, while that of 'getrunken' contains SUBJ and OBJ. The SUBJ of 'getrunken' needs to be unified with the SUBJ of 'hat' since it is not directly linked to any argument. Because of these differences in the lexical entries of the verbs, and the way they interact with c-structure, 'hat' cannot be inserted under that V that is dominated by V-COMP, i.e. 'hat' in final position is excluded.

In essence, this means that the positioning of verbs is controlled by the unification of the feature PARTICIPLE.

This grammatical system can account for what seems to be an unsystematic behaviour on the part of the learner, who applies SEP (= split verb) only in a certain percentage of all contexts. In other words, the rule is applied with some verbs but not with others. This phenomenon can be accounted for by the fact that some AUX-V combinations can continue to be analysed as one lexical entry while others are not. What determines this variational phenomenon, then, is whether the verbs in question have been analysed as single lexical entries and whether the feature AUX has been appended and annotated correctly.

Note that while these rules account for the facts observed in L2 acquisition, the reality of German word order is far more complex.

Verb-second

To account for German Subject-Verb INVERSION, c-structure has to be modified further. The modifications suggested here are adaptations from Bresnan and Kaplan's (1982) and Pinker's (1984) treatment of inversion in English, which assumes that there is an optional Verb to the left of S as illustrated below:

$$S' \rightarrow (V)\ S$$

Pinker adds the constraining equation $ROOT =_c +$ to the verb position in this rule to ensure that inversion only applies to matrix (i.e. "root") sentences (i.e. the feature ROOT is constrained to be + in matrix and — in embedded clauses). This distinction is also relevant to the analysis of Standard German, where INVERSION is blocked in embedded questions. I will return to this point below.

Pinker (1984) further adds the constraining equation $SENT\ MOOD =_c INV$ to the verb position in order to be able to allow the rule to constrain INVERSION *lexically* in elements which can occur in topicalised position (cf. (R2) above). The resulting rule is given in (R4).

$$(R4)\ S' \rightarrow (V) \qquad S$$
$$\left\{ \begin{array}{l} ROOT =_c + \\ SENT\ MOOD =_c Inv \end{array} \right\}$$

In Pinker's treatment of inversion it is not quite clear what information the equation *SENT MOOD* $=_c$ *Inv* is checked against. I suggest appending the equation *SENT MOOD* = *Inv* to XP in (R2) so that INVERSION can be triggered by the application of R2.

(R2) S' → (XP)   S

$$\left\{ \begin{array}{l} \text{wh} =_c + \\ \text{adv} =_c + \\ \text{N} =_c + \\ \text{SENT MOOD} = \text{Inv} \end{array} \right\}$$

In effect, the elements listed in the constraining equation now ensure that the equation SENT MOOD = Inv feeds into the constraining equation SENT MOOD $=_c$ Inv, appended to V in R3. In English the elements which trigger inversion include wh-words and adverbs (cf. Steele 1981), while in German the class of these words is much larger. R4 now allows INVERSION to occur with topicalised wh-words, adverbs, PPs and NPs.

When applying this treatment of INVERSION to German interlanguage one first needs to re-consider topicalisation in German. As mentioned above, the class of elements triggering INVERSION is much larger in German than it is in English. German allows wh-words, objects, adjuncts, lexical verbs and subordinate clauses to be placed in topic position. In standard German, all of these phenomena obligatory trigger INVERSION. In the present account of German interlanguage, (R2) already allows wh-words, adverbs, objects and adjuncts containing N as a head in topic position.

For the sake of simplicity, I will exclude verbs in topic position from these considerations, although they would formally fall into the same category as other topicalised elements as can be seen from examples (9) and (10).

(9)   Gekauft habe ich den Wagen, nicht geliehen
      Bought have I the car, not borrowed.

(10) Essen tat er das Brot nicht
      Eat did he the bread not.

Note that to handle sentences like (10), additional rules would be required which never materialise in the acquisition processes described in this book.

Back to INVERSION: there is only one further change to Pinker's "inversion rule", (R4) that I want to suggest. This change is motivated by the way (R4) can account for developmental data. Basically, I suggest that the feature ROOT is not present in the interlanguage from the beginning and that its acquisition is, naturally, linked to the distinction between matrix and embedded clauses. Pinker's reason for introducing the feature ROOT was to account for the fact that English "inversion" only occurs in matrix clauses, but never in embedded clauses.

While this observation is true for the target language it is not true for the learner's language, in which, at certain stages, "inversion" is produced indiscriminately in matrix and subordinate clauses — once the latter have been acquired, as shown in (11) and (12).

(11)   * I wonder what does he want.
(12)   * I asked her when would Peter come.

The same phenomenon can also be observed in German, (13):

(13)   * Die Mutter fragt ihn, was ißt du.

It can, of course, be argued that sentences like (12) and (13) are direct questions that appear in "quotation form". However, examples like (11) would still remain, and they cannot be explained in the same way. In addition, there would still be no positive evidence to the effect that the feature ROOT is productive at this stage.

The assumption that the learner does not distinguish between matrix and subordinate clause does not imply, however, that the learner has to produce only matrix clauses. All this assumption would mean is that both types of clauses are — at this stage — generated by the same rules and display the same syntactic characteristics.

I have shown above that acquisition data do contain initialised wh-words and subsequent INVERSION in subordinate clauses. The existing rule system can handle the initialisation of complementisers in subordinate clauses in the same way as wh-words: the learner would simply have to add a further equation to (R2) that permits complementisers in topic position. The verb position in subordinate clauses would then depend on the annotation of complementisers for the feature SENT MOOD. If the feature does not exist, the verb remains in its position right adjacent to NP_{subj}. If it does exist, (R4) applies, and the verb would occur to the left of NP_{subj}.

To illustrate how the unification of the feature SENT MOOD brings the verb into second position in German consider sentence (14)

(14) Jetzt sieht der Mann ein Kind
     Now   sees   the man a   child

A simplified account of the f-structure of (15) is given in Figure 3.3-3.

SUBJ	SPEC	=	'DER'
	NUM	=	SG
	PRED	=	'MANN'
TENSE	PRESENT		
PRED	'SEHEN' (SUBJ)(OBJ1)		
	SPEC	=	'EIN'
OBJ	NUM	=	SG
	PRED	=	'KIND'
ADJ	{'JETZT'}		

Figure 3.3-3. F-structure of sentence (14)

der: DET,	SPEC = DER
	NUM = SG
	GENDER = MASC
Mann: N:	PRED = 'MANN'
	NUM = SG
	PERS = 3
	GENDER = MASC
sieht: V	PRED = 'SIEHT' <SUBJ OBJ>
	NUM = SG
	PERS = 3
	TENSE = PRESENT
ein: DET,	SPEC = "EIN"
	NUM = SG
Kind: N,	PRE = 'KIND'
	NUM = SG
	PERS = 3
jetzt: Adv	"jetzt"

Figure 3.3-4. Lexical entries for sentene (14)

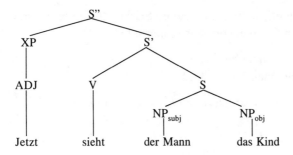

Figure 3.3-5. C-structure of sentence (14)

The lexical entries contain further schemata which guarantee the functional well-formedness of (14) and these features have a bearing on the position of the verb.

Applying (R2) and (R4), sentence (14) has the c-structure shown in Figure 3.3-5.

This account of German INVERSION (which again simplifies matters somewhat but is sufficient for the given set of observations) explains a number of facts which are relevant to the description of language acquisition:

(1) The acquisition of INVERSION hinges crucially on the lexical annotations of elements which can be topicalised. This explains why initially INVERSION is applied after topicalisation of some wh-words, but not after others.

(2) The class of elements that can be topicalised depends on the appropriate constraint equation being appended to the topicalised position. Viewing these equations as being acquired successively would account for a successive acquisition of topicalisation (from wh-word to adverb, etc.) and a successive acquisition of INVERSION in these contexts.

(3) Nevertheless, topicalisation may occur with all elements permissible in the target language, while all or some elements in topicalised position may not be annotated for the feature SENT MOOD, so that — in the interlanguage — INVERSION does not have to co-occur

with topicalisation. This explains the time gap that occurs in the acquisition of ADV and INVERSION.

Verb-final

On the basis of the picture that has emerged so far, word order in subordinate clauses has been treated in exactly the same way as in matrix clauses. However, at stage x+5 the learner starts to distinguish between matrix and subordinate clauses. This is evidenced by the final positioning of verbs:

$$[XV_{INF=-} \quad V_{INF=+}]_S,$$

where *INF* = - refers to verbs not marked for person or number and *INF* = + refers to verbs which are marked for those features.

At the same time, INVERSION disappears (sometimes gradually) from subordinate clauses.

At first glance there seems to be an obvious way to account for these facts, namely, by introducing the feature ROOT: i.e. by introducing — at this point in time — the distinction between matrix and subordinate clause. This would have two effects on the grammar developed so far:

(1)   INVERSION would be ruled out in subordinate clauses, assuming that Pinker's constraining equation *ROOT =c* + is appended to V in (R4).

(2)   This would block off the generation of all subordinate clauses through (R2).

However, there are a number of reasons why this account of V-END is not plausible.

The first problem is of an empirical nature: according to the above account of V-END, the rule would have to be learned simultaneously in all types of subordinate clauses and with all complementisers, because the development of the rule depends entirely on the acquisition of the one feature, ROOT. It is known, however, that the V-END is first learned in a restricted range of subordinate clauses, even though there does not seem to be a fixed order of acquisition. Also, INVERSION would have to disappear very suddenly from subordinate clauses, which is not what is found in the data (this point will be discussed in more detail below).

The second problem is related to the rule formalism: Pinker does not specify which lexical element the feature ROOT resides with so that it can be utilised in the c-structure rule. COMP seems to be the obvious option, but many subordinate clauses do not require complementisers. In addition, some elements that fulfil the COMP function can also fulfil other functions such as Q-Focus. Therefore annotating the complementiser with the feature ROOT would entirely erode the reason for the introduction of the feature ROOT, since wh-words could then introduce matrix clauses *and* subordinate clauses. The same problem would occur if the verb was annotated with ROOT.

The treatment of V-Final that would be most consistent with the rest of my analysis of German word order is a separate c-structure rule for subordinate clauses, as in (R5).

(R5) $S \rightarrow (COMP)_{ROOT=-} \ NP_{subj} \ (NP_{obj1}) \ (NP_{obj2}) \ (ADJ) \ (V)_{INF=-} \ (V)_{INF=+}$

(R5) would explain the developmental facts observed above, particularly the gradual acquisition of V-Final and the possibility of a gradual shedding of INVERSION in subordinate clauses. To be able to unfold this explanation more easily, all rules introduced so far are listed below:

(1) $S' \rightarrow \ NP_{subj} \ V \ (NP_{obj}) \ (ADJ) \ (S)$

(2) $S' \rightarrow \ (XP)$ S

$$\left\{ \begin{array}{l} wh =_c + \\ adv =_c + \\ N =_c + \\ SENT \ MOOD = Inv \end{array} \right\}$$

(3) $S \ \rightarrow NP_{subj} \ VP$

$VP \rightarrow V \left\{ \begin{array}{l} (NP_{obj1})(NP_{obj2}) \\ V\text{-}COMP \end{array} \right\}$

$V\text{-}COMP \rightarrow (NP_{obj1})(NP_{obj2}) \ V$

(4) $S' \rightarrow (V)$ S

$$\left\{ \begin{array}{l} ROOT =_c + \\ SENT \ MOOD =_c Inv \end{array} \right\}$$

(5) $S \rightarrow (COMP)_{ROOT=-} \ NP_{subj} \ (NP_{obj1}) \ (NP_{obj2}) \ (ADJ) \ (V)_{INF=-} \ (V)_{INF=+}$

The rule system now contains a clear point from which the learner can infer whether a sentence is a matrix clause or a subordinate clause, namely the feature ROOT which I suggest should be appended to complementisers as in R5 and to be listed in the lexical entry of complementisers.

Learners would now be able to annotate complementisers gradually for the feature ROOT. This would allow for a gradual acquisition of V-Final. At the same time the learner could continue to incorrectly treat S' as S; i.e. to treat for instance, interrogative complement clauses as main clauses. This would explain, why V-Final and INVERSION may occur simultaneously in subordinate clauses. The target word order in interrogative complement clauses can only be achieved if the learner observes the hierarchical constituent structure, i.e. the bar-level of S.

So much for the formal solution. The reader might wonder why I dismissed the feature ROOT for main clauses but accept it in subordinate clauses. The reason against appending the equation ROOT=+ to the verb position in (R4) was that, in matrix clauses, the clause level cannot be inferred (in German or English) from any lexical annotation. In subordinate clauses, however this is possible, since *some* complementisers will *always* be followed by subordinate clauses (ROOT=-); e.g. "weil" (because), "als" (while). Such complementisers could be marked ROOT=-, while other complementisers may be marked ROOT=+ , for instance, "when", which can introduce interrogative clauses (matrix or subordinate) and adverbial subordinate clauses ("I'll give it to you when you arrive").

The learner would therefore be in a position to first apply (R4) only if the sentence contains a complementiser with the equation ROOT=-, thereby relying exclusively on the lexical clue. The acquisition process would be completed when the learner observes the constituency hierarchy for all S and therefore applies (R4) to all subordinate clauses. With this treatment of V-Final in mind one could predict a number of intermediate stages within this acquisition process. For the time being, however, I will not consider such conclusions.

Once again, my account of German word order greatly simplifies the situation that exists in the standard language but the present account is sufficient for the range of observations discussed in the present context. [12]

Word order and processing procedures

If one accepts this rough proposal for the treatment of German interlanguage word order, then the next point in my argument will be to show that the hierarchy of processing procedures developed in Chapter 2 can be incorporated into this description and that the combination of the two elements is capable of predicting the orders of acquisition discussed above.

My account of German word order development started with phase 2 of the acquisition process which is characterised by a strict SVO word order. Since grammatical functions are assigned at the level of c-structure, a strict canonical order does not involve any feature unification and therefore corresponds to level 2 of the hierarchy of processing procedures developed in Chapter 2. In other words, the LFG account of this structure positions it correctly in the hierarchy of processability and its actual phase of acquisition.

An equally simple way of marking grammatical functions would be affixation on the head of the phrases to be marked. Such affixes could be inferred directly from c-structure and would not involve any agreement marking. Slobin (1982) supplied evidence in support of this prediction. His data show that in the acquisition of Turkish, a non-configurational language, i.e. a language with no fixed word order, children acquire morphological markers of grammatical functions at the same developmental point in time as fixed word order is acquired in configurational languages.

German stage 3 syntax was accounted for by a modification of the stage 2 c-structure rule. This modified rule also does not involve any exchange of grammatical information and at the same time accounts for the learner's use of the saliency principle.

From a processing point of view, the difference between SVO and ADV is the following: while SVO is a completely linear structure with the NPsubj in a predictable and invariable position, there is a degree of non-linearity in ADV where the sequence of conceptualisation may deviate somewhat from a strictly canonical sequence. In the latter case, the canonical sequence starts after the topicalised phrase. However, in contrast to structures which are acquired later, with ADV grammatical functions can be read directly off c-structure and no cross-constituent unification is required.

For the German split-verb construction to occur, the PARTICIPLE value of the main verb and that of V-COMP in the auxiliary entry have to be unified. This exchange of information occurs across constituent boundaries. However, the only non-canonical position involved in this process is one that is perceptually salient (namely the lexical verb in final position). Therefore SEP requires processing procedures which are located higher on the implicational hierarchy than SVO and ADV, i.e. level 4 of the processability hierarchy.

One might argue against this proposal that, according to the above account of SEP, a non-final position of the verb would appear to require more advanced processing procedures than a final one, since a string of the type *NPsubj Aux V X* would seem to involve feature unification across constituent boundaries without the aid of perceptual salience, while the developmentally later string *NPsubj Aux X V* does utilise the perceptual aid.

One has to remember, however, that these processing procedures are only ever involved in the production of these structures if the corresponding features are indeed unified. This is true only for the mature target language. Learners, on the other hand, may at this stage choose to interpret the auxiliary as a second tense marker, which can be read off the lexical entry in the same way as the affix. As mentioned above, "**hat gesagen*" (has PARTICIPLE-say-INFINITIVE) may then be analysed as (PAST-PAST-say) in which case the insertion of the morpheme *ge-* would be formed only for the tense-entry.

German V-2nd position, then, involves a process that depends on the unification of the feature SENT MOOD across XP and V. This process cannot rely on any saliency principles. Therefore this structure is positioned at level 5 of the processability hierarchy.

The German structure V-Final is one of the features distinguishing embedded from matrix clauses in the target language. In the above LFG description this structure is accounted for by the introduction of the feature ROOT into the IL grammar and a separate c-structure for embedded sentences. This description accounts for the fact that in the processability hierarchy, features of embedded clauses which distinguish those from matrix clauses are acquired after word order constraints in the matrix clause have been acquired. In other words, the above account of V-Final is in line with the processability hierarchy which predicts that V-Final occurs at level 6.

3.4 Lexical, phrasal and inter-phrasal morphemes

The next step in our argument is to show that the implementation of processing constraints in LFG opens up a wider area of analysis by making the basic line of argument accessible also to morphology.

Phrasal morphemes

In LFG, the morphological component operates on the basis of a functional description of the sentence. Sentence (15) may illustrate this.

(15) This man owns many dogs.

Note that lexical entries contain schemata which are relevant here. These are shown in Figure 3.4-1.

The well-formedness of sentences is guaranteed, amongst other things, by ensuring that functional descriptions of the sentence and lexical entries match, i.e. the phrase "this man" is functionally well-formed because — amongst other things — the value for NUM is 'SG' in the subsidiary function NUM = SG under SUBJ of as well as in the lexical entry for "man". In the same way "many dogs" is well-formed because of a match of the feature 'NUM'.

The actual structure of the morphological component is not crucial to the present line of argument. The central point here is that morphological processes are informed by feature unification. One can now see that the unification of the NUM value in noun phrases is an operation which is restricted entirely to the NP. I call this type of affixation *phrasal*, because it occurs inside phase boundaries.

This: DET,	(SPEC) = THIS
	(NUM) = SG
man: N,	(PRED) = 'MAN'
	(NUM) = SG
	(PERS) = 3
owns: V	(PRED) = 'OWN' (SUBJ) (OBJ)
	(SUBJ NUM) = SG
	(SUBJ PERS) = 3
	(TENSE) = PRESENT
many: DET,	(SPEC) = MANY
	(NUM) = PL
dogs: N,	(PRED) = DOG
	(NUM) = PL

Figure 3.4-1. Lexical entries for sentence (15)

The following is an example of phrasal morphology in German:

- plural   [die Hund-e]$_{NP}$
         pl   pl

Note that the actual form of the morphological marker is not of interest here. That is, while native German distinguishes a wide range of noun classes with different paradigms for plural formation and different verb classes with different paradigms for tense marking, I am interested only in the basic process of affixation and information distribution here. The crucial point is that in phrasal morphology grammatical information is exchanged between two constituents within a phrase. What matters here is the information exchange, not the shape of the affix. For affixation to be phrasal according to the above definition, the affix has to be used systematically for the marking of grammatical or semantic information and has to involve transfer of information between phrasal constituents.

The learning of the morphological form of the affix constitutes an additional task. Some morphemes have a one-to-one relationship between form and function (e.g. the Finnish genitive marker on nouns '-n', <*talo* - talon>; house - houseGEN), while other morphemes may express a multitude of functions (e.g. German 's' on nouns for plural, possessive etc.).

To account for the learning task which is entailed in unlocking such form-function relationships, one would need to develop a theory module which can interact with the one being developed here. I will refrain from making such an attempt in this book in order to focus on the task at hand, namely to systematically relate different types of affixation processes to the hierarchy of processing procedures developed above. Nevertheless, the issue of form-function relationships raises the question as to how hypotheses on information distribution and affixation can be tested in an L2 context. I will deal with this issue in section 4.3. At this point I merely want to foreshadow that the most straight-forward way to test the hypotheses developed here is to use affixes with a one-to-one form-function relationship or to construct the distributional analysis on this basis.

Inter-phrasal morphemes

In contrast to phrasal affixation, SV-agreement involves the matching of features in two distinct constituents, namely NPsubj, and VP. The insertion of the -s-affix for SV-agreement marking requires the following syntactic information:

S -V affix   TENSE   =   present
                 SUBJ NUMBER   =   sg
                 SUBJ PERSON   =   3

While the value of the first two equations is read off the functional description of sentences as illustrated in (x), the values for NUMBER and PERSON must be identical in the f-structure of SUBJ and the lexical entry of V. Hence this information has to be matched across constituent boundaries from inside both constituents. One may informally describe this process as follows:

[A man]$_{NPsubj}$ [{holds} ...]$_{VP}$ (Present, imperfective)

PERSON = 3   PERSON   = 3
NUM   = sg   NUM   = sg

One can now see that — from a processing point of view — the two morphological processes, plural agreement in NPs and SV-agreement have a different status: while the first occurs exclusively inside one major constituent, the second requires that grammatical information be exchanged across constituent boundaries. I term the latter type of morphological process *interphrasal affixation*.

Lexical morphemes

In a third and developmentally earlier type of morpheme no features have to be unified at all, neither within the phrase nor between phrases. An example of this is the German marker for 'past' (-te):

• past   [such-te]$_V$
              past

The lexical entry for the example "suchte" (searched, looked for) is as follows:

suchte: V   (PRED) = 'suchte' (SUBJ) (OBJ)
             (SUBJ NUM) = SG
             (SUBJ PERS) = 3
             (TENSE) = PAST

In other words, the information on tense is part of the lexical entry and does not have to be exchanged with any other constituent. The reader will recall that in Levelt's model the search for this lexical item is instigated by the conceptual structure which would have specified "past" as a time reference. Hence, the information for the morphological marker is part of the lexical entry. For this reason I will call this type of morpheme *lexical*.

The information structure of the LFG account of IL morphology matches that of the processability hierarchy. Lexical morphemes rely on diacritic features which are contained in the lexical entry. Phrasal morphemes require the unification of diacritic features in the head of a phrase and the modifier, while inter-phrasal morphemes rely on the unification of diacritic features between phrases. According to this hierarchy morphemes will be acquired in the following sequence:

lexical < phrasal < inter-phrasal.

The LFG account of IL morphology is compatible with the architecture of the Grammatical Encoder since lexical morphemes receive their essential information from f-structure, while phrasal morphemes require the unification of features between the head of a phrase and its modifier. In the case of a morphological marker for English past tense ('-ed') the verb receives information from f-structure where TENSE has the value PAST. Similarly to Kempen and Hoenkamp (1987) I assume that this information is available to the speaker in the same iteration of the production process when the verb is conceptualised. Basically, this is conceptual information. All grammatical information relating to the morphological tense marker '-ed' is located in the lexical entry of the verb.

Given their status concerning information transfer, the two rules, SV-agreement and V-2nd, form a junction point between morphology and syntax, since both rules are located at the same point in the processing hierarchy (unification across constituent boundaries, i.e. level 5). At first glance one might therefore expect these rules to be acquired simultaneously. However, one has to bear in mind that the levels of processability are characterised by those processing procedures which same-level structures have in common. In addition to this, the procedures for each of the structures also have to be acquired. There is no reason why a learner would necessarily acquire all same-level structures simultaneously as soon as the processing procedures have developed. I will demonstrate below that strategic advantages can be gained from delaying the acquisition of some structures in relation to others. I will examine this point in more detail in section 4.1, section 4.2 and section 6.3 in the context of empirical evidence.

Summing up sections 3.3 and 3.4

In the preceding two sections I mapped the linguistic analysis of German word order and morphology onto a hierarchy of linguistic processing procedures. This mapping process results in predictions of orders of acquisition. The overall picture which derives from Processability Theory is illustrated in Table 3.4-2.

Table 3.4-2 illustrates, in summary, developmental inferences that have been drawn from the hierarchy of processing procedures described in section 2.1 when implemented into a grammatical theory. These inferences are all based on the German grammatical system — as were sections 3.3 and 3.4 of this book. The reader will recall that the word order stages were validated by large empirical studies of the acquisition of German as a second language.

The first real validity test of these predictions will consist of a study of GSL morphology presented in Section 4.1 below. This will be the first test of structurally new developmental predictions which were derived from Processability Theory. In Chapter 5 I will present similar developmental predictions for the morphosyntax of English, Swedish and Japanese as second languages and I will review the empirical basis for these predictions.

Table 3.4-2. The general picture for German

stage	exchange of information	procedures	word order	morphology
6		sub. cl. plrocedure	V-End	
5	inter-phrasal no saliency	S-procedure	INV	SV-agreement
4	inter-phrasal with saliency	simpl. S-procedure	SEP	
3	phrasal	phrasal procedure	ADV	plural agreement
2	none	lex. categories	SVO	past-te etc.
1	none		words	—

Chapter 4

Empirical and theoretical issues in processability theory

In the previous chapters I presented a principled approach to the development of processing procedures for second languages. This approach was made explicit for major syntactic and morphological aspects of German. While the acquisition of German word order is well documented in the literature, the acquisition of morphology has received far less attention. It is important to note that, in terms of theory development, the first crucial test of the validity of the proposed theory is to see whether its predictions for GSL morphology are borne out by empirical data.

In this chapter I will test the theoretically motivated predictions for the development of GSL morphology which are mentioned above. If it can be demonstrated that the actual course of morpheme acquisition follows the route predicted by Processability Theory, then one can argue that the latter goes beyond a mere generalisation of observations about syntactic development. In other words, this empirical test completes the extension of the original processing explanation of orders of acquisition to morphology.

The demonstration of the validity of Processability Theory for German L2 morphology will proceed as follows: first I will examine longitudinal data of GSL acquisition. The analyses of these data will highlight a crucial methodological problem, namely the definition of acquisition criteria which are meaningful for the emergence of morphology and which, at the same time, allow a comparison of syntactic and morphological developmental dynamics for a single learner. This problem will be examined in a separate section (4.2) which will give an overview of the research methodology employed in this book. In Section 4.3 I will reflect on the relationship between form and function in the analysis of IL data.

This chapter therefore not only serves the purpose of providing a first validity test for the proposed theory, but it also exemplifies within an empirical context the methodological principles on which the theory is based.

4.1 A test case: German morphology

In this section I will lay out a one-year longitudinal study of the acquisition of German as a second language in a formal environment. I will focus on the interlanguage of one learner, Guy, who was a student at the University of Sydney. The informant began learning German without any prior exposure to the language. He was interviewed at fortnightly intervals. The language course consisted of six hours per week. It was taught with the textbook "Sprachkurs Deutsch" and supplementary material on German grammar. The textbook follows a communicative approach from which the tutor deviated when he/she felt it necessary (especially for the formal teaching of grammar).

Since some of the predictions of Processability Theory relate to the interplay between syntactic and morphological development, it will be useful to trace the learner's development in the area of syntax. This will enable us to relate his morphological development to syntactic points of reference.

Word order

Table 4.1-1 displays the learning objectives as they were structured over the first nineteen weeks of the course (i.e. two trimesters). The table lists those structures in the domain of word order which were contained in the syllabus (i.e. a conscious attempt was made to teach them through intensive exercises). The most important observation to be gleaned from Table 4.3-1 is that all major word order rules (except V-END) are introduced as early as the fifth and seventh week, within a short period of time, even though the different syntactic contexts in which these rules apply are spread over a more extensive time frame.

Table 4.1-2 provides an analysis of 19 weeks of Guy's interlanguage development. The occurrence of optional rules is marked with an "X", while for obligatory rules the relative frequency is given. The symbol "/" is used in order to stress that in the given interlanguage the structural description of the rule given on the left hand side of the table is not met in a single case. If this fact was not to be stressed, the appropriate cell of the table was simply left blank.

Let me also draw the reader's attention to the line "SEP with V-Complement" in Table 4.1-2. In many cases a sentence will only consist of NP+AUX+V. In such cases one cannot decide whether the learner applied SEP or whether the structure was simply left in the same order as it would appear at the stage preceding SEP. This question can only be answered if AUX and V are separated by a verbal complement. In this line I therefore noted the relative frequency of SEP application in sentences with verbal complements. There is a similar phenomenon with the other obligatory word order rules. If one finds a structure like PP+V+NPsubj one cannot decide whether the learner has simply applied a subject-final strategy requiring the same processing procedures as SEP (cf. Clahsen 1984, Pienemann 1984) or whether he can in fact apply INV. Again, the test case is a sentence with a verbal complement. Therefore, I included the line "INV with V-Complement" which gives the relative frequency of INV application for sentences with verbal complements. A similar line is also included for V-END, because without a verbal complement the word order of German subordinate clauses is simply SV, which does not give us a basis to decide about the application of V-END.

If one now compares the input the learner received, with the output he produced, one is not surprised to find that he acquired SVO first, because this structure was also contained in the input from the first week on. Similarly, TOPI is present in the input as well as in the early interlanguage of the learner.

The interesting structures are SEP, INV and V-END. SEP was an explicit learning objective from the seventh week on and INV from the first week on, while V-END was not included as a formal learning objective. Table 4.1-2 shows that Guy does produce the linguistic contexts for SEP from as early as the 5th week. Applications of SEP, however, only occur from week 15 onwards — as can be seen from the line "SEP with V-Complement". (The figure for week 9 is based on just one sentence with a verbal complement). In week 15 the frequency of SEP application in sentences with complements rises from 0. to 0.75. That is to say: over a period of 10 weeks, Guy's interlanguage structure contrasted sharply with the input and the learning objectives of his German course.

The contrast between input and output continues with the learning/ acquisition of INV. As can be seen from Table 4.1-2, Guy produces INV-like structures in questions (yes/no-questions and WH-questions), but never applies INV after preposed PPs. Most of these INV-like structures, however, do not contain a verbal complement (compare the figures in the line "INV with V-complement" in Table 4.1-2), i.e. they can be accounted for by a subject-final strategy. Thus the frequency of INV application for sentences with verbal complements is close to zero. The first exception to this is Guy's interlanguage in week 19, when INV is applied in 36% of all sentences with verbal complements, which meet the structural description of INV. Therefore, this marks the beginning of Guy's acquisition of INV.

Table 4.1-1. Learning objectives

Weeks →		1	3	5	7	9	10	11	12	13	14	15	16	17	18	19
SVO	COP	X	X	X	X	X	X	X	X	X	X	X	X	X	X	X
	AUX	X	X	X	X	X	X	X	X	X	X	X	X	X	X	X
	V	X	X	X	X	X	X	X	X	X	X	X	X	X	X	X
	Question	X	X	X	X	X	X	X	X	X	–	X	X	X	X	X
TOPI	PP					(X)	(X)	X	X	X	X	X	X	X	X	X
	Object			X	X	X	X	X	X	X	X	X	X	X	X	X
	Q-Pro	X	X	X	X	X	X	X	X	X	X	X	X	X	X	X
SEP	AUX+V													X	X	X
	MOD+NV			(X)	X	X	X	X	X	X	X	X	X	X	X	X
	P+FV				(X)							X	X	X	X	X
	SEP with V-Complement															
INV	PP					(X)	(X)	(X)	X	X	X	X	X	X	X	X
	TOPI 2															
	TOPI 1			X	X	X	X	(X)	(X)	X	X	X	X	X	X	X
	WH-Q	X	X	X	X	X	X	X	X	X	X	X	X	X	X	X
	YES/NO	X	X	X	X	X	X	X	X	X	X	X	X	X	X	X
	INV with V-Complement															
	TOTAL															
V-END	V-End with V-Complement															
	TOTAL															

Table 4.1-2. Guy's development of German word order rules

Weeks	1	3	5	7	9	11	13	15	17	19
COP		X	X	X	X	X	X	X	X	X
AUX			X	X	X	X	X	X	X	X
V	X	X	X	X	X	X	X	X	X	X
QUESTION	X			X	X		X	X	X	X
PP				X		X	X	X	X	X
OBJECT							X			
Q-PRO		X	X	X	X	X	X	X	X	X
AUX+V								1.	.37	1.
MOD+V			(0.)	(1.)	(.4)	.25	0.	.66	.75	.26
Particle+V						0.	0.		0.	
SEP WITH V-COMPLEMENT			/	(0.)	(.5)	0.	/	.75	.46	.41
PP				0.		0.	0.	0.	0.	0.
TOPI 2										
TOPI 1						0.	0.			
WH-Q				1.	1.	1.	1.	1.	1.	1.
YES/NO				1.	1.	.8	.88	1.	1.	1.
INV WITH V-COMPLEMENT				0.	0.	(.22)	0.	0.	.1	.36
V-END WITH V-COMPLEMENT					(0.)		(0.)	(0.)	(0.)	(0.)
TOTAL					(.5)		(0.)	(0.)	(0.)	(0.)

The rule V-END was not a formal learning objective. It was, however, included in the linguistic input from week 7 on. Guy in fact produced a small number of subordinate clauses from week 7 on, but never applied V-END.

The following is a schematic overview of the schedule of Guy's GSL development:

Week	1	7	15	19	--
rule	SVO	ADV	SEP	INV	(V-END)

Looking at Guy's interlanguage development as a whole, there are two general findings which are important in the present context:

(1)   the formal learner developed his language stepwise, despite the scheduling of the teaching;

(2)   the sequence of development is the same as in the natural acquisition of German as a second language.

From a theoretical point of view one would have expected this result, because the structures involved are based on specific processing procedures; each structure requires a processing procedure developed at the preceding stage. Because of this there is no way for the learner to gradually develop the processing procedures other than in the order observed. The fact that the sequence of acquisition observed in the natural context was not able to be altered through formal instruction provides general support for the hierarchical nature of the hypothesised processing procedures. This then is the case for syntax. However, the real test case I want to examine in this section is the development of morphology.

Morphology

Processability Theory makes a distinction between phrasal and inter-phrasal morphemes and the points in time when these can be acquired. I demonstrated in Chapter 2 that phrasal morphemes are characteristic for levels 3 and 4 of the processability hierarchy and that inter-phrasal morphemes appear at level 5. This prediction is based on the fact that the processability hierarchy is based on a set of processing procedures which are utilised for syntactic and morphological structures — while the actual procedures are, of course, different. For instance, INVERSION and subject verb-agreement utilise a number of the same processing procedures, namely lemma access, category procedures, phrasal procedures, appointment rules and the S-procedure. However, the procedures involved in executing INV and SV-agreement also contain components which are specific to the two rules. Therefore the presence of one does not guarantee the presence of the other.

Nevertheless, Processability Theory predicts that morphemes are acquired in the following sequence: (1) lexical morphemes, (2) phrasal morphemes and (3) inter-phrasal morphemes. We are now in the position to test these predictions in Guy's interlanguage development.

There is one example of a lexical morpheme in Guy's interlanguage for the domain of verbal morphology, namely the German tense marker "ge-", a verbal prefix. In fact, this is a 'type 1' morpheme which does not require any feature unification. The first occurrence of this morpheme in Guy's interlanguage is in week 15 (i.e. three weeks later than it was set as a learning objective) with the following examples:

> ge-denk-t
> ge-fäll-t
> ge-hör-t
> ge-komm-t.

This is also the point in time when Guy acquires SEP. In this case the two acquisition processes appear to be simultaneous. According to Processability Theory this does not necessarily need to be the case, because this morpheme is located at level 2 of the processability hierarchy while SEP is at level 4. In contrast to this I found in a separate study on child natural GSL acquisition (Pienemann 1981) a considerable temporal gap between the acquisition of the "ge-" marker and SEP. In other words, the presence of all processing procedures for a structure does not imply that the learner will indeed exploit all available structural possibilities. I will return to this phenomenon of 'developmental gaps' in section 4.2.

The example of an inter-phrasal morpheme I want to analyse here is the morphological marking of person and number agreement in the verb. For reasons of simplicity the analysis will be restricted to grammatical subjects which are marked as "singular". I will analyse subject-verb agreement with lexical verbs and the copula in present tense only, since the very limited number of occurrences of other verbal elements and tense markings would not permit a meaningful distributional analysis of other linguistic contexts.

In German, the marking of person agreement in the verb is very similar to

English subject-verb agreement:

Copula

1st person	ich *bin*	I am
2nd person	du *bist* or *bis*	you are
3rd person	er, sie, es	he, she, it
	singular-NP*ist* or *is*	singular-NP*is*

Lexical verb

1st person	ich V-e or V-Ø	I V
2nd person	du V-st or V-s	I V
3rd person	er, sie, es	he, she, it
	singular-NP V-t	Singular NP V-s

(Note: V signifies "verb stem")

The results of a distributional analysis of the marking of person agreement in Guy's interlanguage are displayed in Tables 4.1-3 and 4.1-4. The left-hand side of Tables 4.1-3 and 4.1-4 lists the different linguistic contexts which were analysed. In the line "ich-cop1" in Tables 4.1-3, the relative frequency is listed with which the correct form of the copula was supplied in sentences with a first person subject (= "ich").

The line "x - cop1" reverses the analysis of the previous line. It displays the relative frequency with which the same form of the copula was used in other contexts (thus the number of cases with cop1 and a subject other than "ich" divided by total of cases with cop1). The line below gives the relative frequency of sentences in each interview in which either the subject or the copula was missing.

The same basic set-up is repeated for the marking of second and third person in the lines below. The bottom line of Table 4.1-3 gives the type/token ratio for the NPs used in equational sentences, provided that the number of cases was greater than five. In the other cases the corresponding field was left blank. The label "pro3" stands for "third person singular pronoun".

The design of Table 4.1-4 is similar to that of Table 4.1-3 with the exception that the rate for the omission of subjects and verbs and the type/token ratio are not given. The reason for this is that both omission rates were close to zero for the entire observation period and that for all interviews the number of sentences in which the subject was a "full" NP and the verb was marked for person agreement was too small to permit a meaningful calculation of a type/token ratio for NPs.

Looking at Table 4.1-3 one can see that in Guy's interlanguage, the rate of SV-agreement in equational sentences is close to the standard norm right from the beginning of the observational period. The figures in the line "x-cop1" show that the form of "cop1" was exclusively used for grammatical subjects with first person marking and never with grammatical subjects marked in any other way. One can therefore conclude that SV-agreement in the copula is not random, but it is brought about by a highly regular use of the target-form of the copula.

Obviously, the number of cases with "second person subjects" in equational sentences is too small to draw any conclusions from, apart from the fact that the cop2 form is used very rarely. This implies that it is also rarely used in contexts other than for the marking of second person.

For third person pronominal subjects one finds a repetition of the pattern seen with first person marking, i.e. right from the beginning of the observational period, cop3 is almost exclusively used with pro3 or non-pronominal subjects. The picture is unclear with NP-subjects though, because apart from three interviews, the number of equational sentences with a non-pronominal subject is smaller than five and thus does not permit us to draw any conclusions from the corresponding figures given in Table 4.1-3.

Table 4.1-3. Guy: SV-agreement with copula

	3	5	7	9	11	13	15	17	19
ich - cop1	(0.33)	0.83	(1.)	1.	(0.)	(1.)	(1.)	0.67	0.88
x - cop1	(0.)	0.	(0.)	0.	(0.)	(0.)	0.	0.	0.
omission of subj or cop	(0.67)	0.17	(0.)	0.	(1.)	(0.)	(0.)	0.17	0.12
du - cop2	(0.)	/	/	(1.)	/	(0.)	/	(1.)	/
x - cop2	(0.)	/	/	(0.)	(1.)	(1.)	/	(0.)	/
omission of subj or cop	(1.)	(1.)	/	(0.)	/	0.	/	(0.)	/
pro3 cop3	0.75	1.	(1.)	1.	0.75	1.	0.80	1.	1.
NP - cop3	(1.)	(1.)	1.	(1.)	1.	(0.67)	(1.)	0.67	(1.)
x - cop3	(0.)	(0.)	0.	0.	0.	0.	0.	0.	0.
omission of subj or cop	(0.25)	0.	0.	0.	0.25	0.	0.2	0.	0.
typ/token - ratio: NP		0.55		0.53			1.		

Table 4.1-4. Guy: SV-agreement with lexical verbs

	3	5	7	9	11	13	15	17	19
ich - v-e	0.78	0.80	0.63	0.81	0.63	0.82	0.67	0.56	0.74
x - V-e	0.67	0.59	0.51	0.73	0.80	0.79	0.69	0.73	0.47
ich - V-o	/	/	/	/	/	(0.5)	/	(0.5)	1.
x - V-o	/	/	/	/	/	(0.5)	/	(0.5)	0.
du - V-s,st	(0.)	(0.)	(0.67)	(0.67)	/	(0.)	/	0.	0.
x - V-s,st	/	/	/	/	/	/	/	/	/
pro3 - V-t	(0.67)	(0.67)	(1.)	0.33	0.33	0.59	0.57	0.48	0.46
NP - V-t	(0.25)	(0.50)	(0.67)	(0.)	0.17	0.10	0.22	0.33	0.25
x - V-t	0.33	0.25	0.63	0.60	0.33	0.31	0.23	0.30	0.45

These findings for SV-agreement seem, at first glance, to contradict my hypotheses, because — as I showed above — the first phrasal morpheme appears in week 15, while SV-agreement marking which was predicted to develop later, appears to be present at a much earlier point.

However, one must ask oneself whether agreement between pronominal NPs and the copula can indeed be accepted as an instance of non-phrasal morphology. I will demonstrate below that these apparent agreement phenomena can be accounted for by the learning of lexically invariant material. To illustrate this point we first need to look at the development of SV-agreement with lexical verbs.

As Table 4.1-4 shows, the picture is rather different for agreement marking with lexical verbs. The figures for first person agreement varies between 0.56 and 0.82. One might at first glance conclude that this reflects a regular morphological agreement marking. However, the use of the same morpheme with grammatical subjects other than first person varies within the same range of frequency (0.47 to 0.80). Therefore, one must conclude that the formative -e does not mark SV-agreement in Guy's interlanguage.

I will leave the zero morpheme for agreement marking aside for the moment. The marking of second person in verbs is similar to the marking of the copula in one respect, namely that only very few second person subjects occur in any event. The morphological marking for second person in verbs (s/ -st) is virtually never used by Guy, either correctly or incorrectly.

The main tendency found in the marking of first person in verbs repeats itself in the marking of third person. If one excludes the values given in brackets in Table 4.1-4 for reasons of limited reliability, the frequency for the affixation of -t varies between 0.33 and 0.59 with pronominal subjects and between 0.10 and 0.33 with non-pronominal subjects while the frequency of random t-affixation varies between 0.23 and 0.63. Thus the random occurrence of the verbal inflectional morpheme -t varies within the same range as the occurrence of the same morpheme in contexts where it marks SV-agreement. In other words, those cases of apparent SV-agreement can be accounted for simply by "random hits". It is interesting to note that the rate of random hits is markedly lower for "NP-subjects" than for pronominal subjects.

The interpretation that random usage of verb forms is occurring in Guy's interlanguage is supported by a brief look at the morphological variation within the lexical material. If one excludes the prefix 'ge-' [a past marker], only 18% of all verbs alter in their morphological form, thus whatever the subject, the form of the verb is always

helf-e	(help)
leb-e	(live)
les-e	(read)
schlaf-e	(sleep)
fähr-t	(go, drive)
gib-t	(give)
*lauf-t	(go, run)
etc.	

Thus the underlying pattern of morphological person marking in main verbs produces figures for apparent SV-agreement which are in fact brought about by a low degree of morphological variance and not by a morphological affixation rule. The only exception to this appears in the 19th week of observation with the use of zero morphemes for the marking of first person. Table 4.1-4 shows clearly that zero morphemes occurred very rarely before week 19 and that in week 19 they occur exclusively to mark first person. And it comes as no surprise that 75% of the verbs which are marked with a zero morpheme at this point in time belong to the small group of verbs in Guy's interlanguage which vary morphologically.

Therefore, as far as main verbs are concerned, zero marking of first person is the only rule for SV-agreement in Guy's interlanguage. Note that this rule emerges four weeks later than the past marker (ge-). This supports my hypothesis about the order in which phrasal and non-phrasal morphemes are acquired.

The question which remains, however, is why there is such a difference between the acquisition of SV-agreement with main verbs and the copula. I indicated above that I believe the seeming mastery of SV-agreement in equational sentences can be accounted for by the learning of lexically invariant material. To illustrate this point one needs to consider the processes involved in SV-agreement marking.

Typically, SV-agreement marking is based on (1) the recognition of the grammatical subject of the sentence, (2) the recognition of the values of its diacritic features for 'number' and 'person', (3) the recognition of the verbal element which carries the agreement marking and (4) affixation of the correct morpheme to the verb — on the basis of accessibility of (2) in the S-procedure.

However, these procedures apply only if subject and verb vary lexically and morphologically in the given (inter)language, because if they do not vary, they can simply be learned as one block. Looked at from this perspective, a major difference between the copula and lexical verbs is that the latter vary lexically while the former does not. Similarly, pronominal subjects do not vary lexically (except for gender marking in third person), while non-pronominal subjects do.

Thus, since both the subject and the verb do not vary lexically and the position of the two remains fixed in the interlanguage, they can be learned as one block (e.g. *I am* x). This would account for the fact that for pronominal subjects the equational sentences in Guy's interlanguage seem to conform to SV-agreement from as early as the 5th week, while at the same time there is no agreement marking with lexical verbs.

The situation is different for lexical subjects, because here the subject can vary lexically, which makes it impossible for the learner to acquire such SV-structures as unanalysed chunks. Unfortunately there are only very few occurrences of equational sentences with "NP-subjects" in Guy's interlanguage, hence so many figures in brackets in the corresponding line of Table 4.1-3. But there is an important observation concerning this type of structure: The type/token ratio for the use of NPs in these structures increases from 0.55 / 0.53 in the early interviews to 1.00 in interview 17.

This shows that there is a low degree of lexical variation of NPs in this structure in weeks 7 and 11, a condition which facilitates "chunk learning". In week 17, however, these facilitating circumstances have disappeared. Since there is also a high rate of SV-agreement in Guy's interlanguage at this stage one can no longer assume that these structures are unanalysed chunks.

To sum up, we found that the seeming SV-agreement with the copula is not a reflection of the type of morphological process which is characterised by a sentence-internal transfer of grammatical information. The only point in time when there is evidence for such a process is interview 17, and this occurs later than the emergence of lexical morphemes in Guy's interlanguage (i.e. interview 15).

The development of morphological and word order rules in Guy's interlanguage can be summarised as follows:

week	1	7	15	19
word order	SVO	ADV	SEP	INV
morphology	--	--	ge-V	SV agreement

As this overview shows, my main hypothesis about the sequence in the acquisition of lexical and inter-phrasal morphemes can be confirmed by the above analysis of Guy's interlanguage development. It must be borne in mind that these learning processes occurred in a formal learning context where the grading of the teaching objectives and the linguistic input contrast sharply with the linguistic output. In other words, the learning which occurred is not merely a product of the formal learning environment. In fact, in a study of the natural acquisition of German as a second language I found structurally similar learning patterns (Pienemann 1981).

Summary and reflection

The late development of SV agreement marking in SLA is not immediately obvious, because the data contain a high proportion of inflected verb forms. In the above analysis I showed that in equational sentences with pronominal subjects SV-agreement can be accounted for by the rote memorisation of the SV-block in a similar way to the memorisation of a single lexical item. Because it remains lexically and morphologically invariant, no grammatical information needs to be transferred from one constituent to another to produce this structure.

For lexical verbs I showed that the high rate of "correct" usage of the formatives "-e" and "-t" is due to the low rate of morphological variation of the verbs used. This allows the learner to make "random hits". I showed that the random usage of the above formatives varied in the same range of frequency as the apparent marking of SV-agreement.

Thus, what at first glance seemed to be evidence for the presence of agreement marking in Guy's interlanguage before week 17, is only a reflection of Guy's use of lexically and morphologically invariable material. Since the first real case of SV-agreement appeared with those verbs which did vary lexically as well as morphologically, variability in these two dimensions appears to be a key to the development of formatives.

In Guy's interlanguage development one can distinguish three stages of variability in the development of formatives:

variability

	lexical	*morphological*
1	-	-
2	+	-
3	+	+

Stage 1 represents cases such as equational sentences with pronominal subjects or invariable lexical subjects. Because of the invariability the two constituents can be memorised as one unit. Stage 2 represents morphologically invariable verbs which are used with different grammatical subjects. In terms of the target language these verbs contain a formative, but since the same formative does not change for the individual verb, the learner treats the particular form of the verb as one unanalysed unit. At stage three morphologically variable verbs are used in different contexts. This enables the learner to do two things: (1) he/she can recognise the formative as one morphological unit, and (2) this allows him/her to discover the root of the verb. This does not guarantee that the agreement marking will be correct, but it is a necessary prerequisite for morphological affixation.

Thus lexical and morphological variation is one source for the learner to develop formatives. This is further supported by the fact that the first instances of the marking of SV-agreement occurred with those verbs which had previously varied morphologically in the learner's language.

These data lend strong support to the hypothesis I intended to test and they therefore provide support for the validity of the proposed theory which has now been applied successfully to German morphology. In other words, the theory has been demonstrated to make correct predictions for areas which were not part of the observations on which the theory was built.

4.2 Dynamic systems and acquisition criteria

Overview

The above discussion of the acquisition of German morphology raises several issues in descriptive linguistics which will prove highly relevant to the way in which Processability Theory can unfold in the chapters that follow. It will therefore be useful to clarify these issues before I go on to applying Processability Theory to other languages. Because of the wide range of issues related to the descriptive and empirical foundation of the proposed theory it may be useful to start with an overview of these issues.

Since Processability Theory aims at explaining developmental and variational phenomena in interlanguage dynamics, this chapter deals with methods of capturing the dynamics of language acquisition. First, implicational analysis will be presented as a method of representing developmental grammars. Further I will demonstrate that rank orders of accuracy are not valid measures of development. Instead, I will show that distributional analyses can be designed to capture the dynamic nature of interlanguages.

One major issue in determining the nature of interlanguage dynamics is to establish a principled approach to distinguishing between development and variation. I will therefore contrast other researchers' conceptualisation of this dichotomy with the conceptualisation used in this book. Another key concept that is related to the development-variation dichotomy is the acquisition criterion. Below I will make a case for the emergence criterion because it can be related to the emergence of linguistic skills which, in turn, is a key concept in Processability Theory.

The remainder of this chapter deals with the logic of applying the emergence criterion to morphology and syntax and with methods of operationalising the criterion in the spirit of the above theory-data interface.

The theory-data interface

Before I proceed with discussing the descriptive framework used in this book it should be stressed that descriptive issues will not be discussed for their own sake. Instead, the objective of this chapter is to clarify what constitutes evidence for and against the proposed theory. In other words, the treatment of descriptive issues will be guided by their relevance for an empirical validation of the proposed theory.

To some readers 'empirical validation' might have connotations of Logical Positivism (e.g. Popper 1959). This is certainly not the orientation in the philosophy of mind that underlies the theory-data interface proposed here. While Popper's Falsificationism has been demonstrated to be insufficient as a mechanism of theory development (Bechtel 1988), it is nevertheless a common assumption in post-positivist philosophy of science and in current practice of cognitive science research that there be a clear relationship between *explanation* and *explanans*. Below I will try to operationalise this relationship wherever possible, i.e. to spell out how theoretical propositions relate to observations within the domain of the theory.

It is also important to remember that the proposed theory is based on a cognitive science perspective on language acquisition. As I pointed out earlier, Processability Theory treats language acquisition as a cognitive process by identifying mental states of the learner in terms of their causal interactions with other mental states. This is part of the overall aim of cognitive science (Bechtel 1988) which is based on the assumption that the basic architecture of cognitive processes is comparable between individuals and that the acquisition of skill and knowledge can be understood through the discovery of their constituent cognitive processes.

Viewing language learning in terms of cognitive processes has powerful implications: one can no longer assume that the fundamental nature of the learner's linguistic system can suddenly change under the influence of non-cognitive variables such as interactional parameters or formal learning environments. At the same time it is quite consistent with this cognitivist position to assume that social parameters may cause a sequence of changes in the learner's processing of the language which leads to the gradual attainment of a high-level skill. However, these changes of cognitive processes would always occur within the overall architecture of the cognitive system.

I pointed out above that the assumption of an overall cognitive architecture in the gradual acquisition of computational mechanisms implies a psychological version of Pinker's (1984) *continuity hypothesis*: in the same way as Pinker argued that the basic fabric of grammar does not change at any given stage in the acquisition process, it is reasonable to assume that the basic fabric of linguistic computational mechanisms does not change. Such basic parameters as word access or the linearisation problem (Levelt 1981) are imposed on the human mind in a very general way. What changes in development is the language-specific way of handling these general constraints: I will therefore not assume different sets of computational mechanisms for L1 and L2 learners or for adults or children unless there are compelling reasons to do so.

The problem

In the preceding section (4.1) we found that the use of emergence criteria, which I applied to the analysis of L2 syntax, can produce misleading results in the study of L2 morphology. The simple problem is this: the distributional evidence that is needed to decide whether a structure is productive in interlanguage *syntax* is quite different from the evidence needed for interlanguage *morphology*. In other words, sentence (16) can be identified as a genuine instance of auxiliary-second placement unless identical copies of the same sentence appear elsewhere in the same sample and these are the only examples of aux-second placement.

(16)　Why didn't he buy the car?

In contrast, the situation is quite different when it comes to judging the productive use of morphological processes. To be sure that "he goes" is a genuine case of productive SV-agreement one has to ascertain that both, subject and verb vary morphologically and lexically: unless "he *goes*" co-occurs with "I *go*" etc. there is no reason why "he-goes" may not be a single lexical item in the learner's lexicon. This means that the simple occurrence of "he goes" alone is not a sufficient indicator of the emergence of SV agreement. Therefore it makes sense to apply emergence criteria to syntactic development on the basis of (minimally) one occurrence in a sample while the same criterion may generate misleading results for the analysis of morphological development.

　　To explore this point further it will be useful to review some of the basic concepts that underlie the dynamic analysis of interlanguage samples used in the SLA research I refer to in this book.

Implicational analysis

The most general objective of SLA research is undoubtedly to describe and explain how a learner moves from not knowing a language to near target-like use of the language (or any other endpoint of the learning process). Therefore most SLA research is based on some notion of a *transitional paradigm*. I do not intend to trace the history of various transitional paradigms at this stage. Instead, I will outline some of the basic principles of the transitional paradigm used in this book.

The reader will not be surprised to note that the basis of this paradigm is the multi-dimensional model of SLA, developed by Meisel, Clahsen and Pienemann (1981). This model offers a highly refined framework for the description of dynamic processes in language acquisition and has since been utilised for a wide range of empirical studies of SLA. The multi-dimensional model of SLA incorporates aspects of Bailey's (1973) wave model, implicational scaling (Guttman 1944, DeCamp 1973) and the concept of variable rules (Labov, 1972a, b).

Implicational scaling has long been recognised as highly productive in representing dynamic aspects of the interlanguage (e.g. Hyltenstam 1978). The basic point is this: cumulative learning processes can be represented by successive additions of linguistic rules to the interlanguage system: rule 1 + rule 2 + rule 3 etc. In this way changes in the interlanguage system can be accounted for by the addition of rules. Of course, this is only one aspect of the dynamics of interlanguage systems; but let us stay with this aspect for a moment.

When analysing interlanguage corpora one can apply the following logic of implicational scales to individual interlanguage samples. For any set of rules that is learnt in a cumulative fashion the following is true: if sample A contains rule 3, then it will also contain rule 2 and rule 1. This fact is usually expressed in tables of the following kind.

Table 4.2-1. Implicational scale

	time 1	time 2	time 3	time 4
rule 1	−	+	+	+
rule 2	−	−	+	+
rule 3	−	−	−	+

In other words, rules which are learned later imply the presence of rules which are learned earlier:

$$\text{rule } 3 \supset \text{rule } 2 \supset \text{rule } 1.$$

This notation has a number of advantages for the description of linguistic dynamics. Implicational scales make it possible to describe complex acquisition processes on a continuum such as the one in Table 4.2-1. The rules of the interlanguage system are listed on one axis while the samples (here identical with points in time) are listed on the other axis. This presentation amounts to a systematic account of a linguistic system (grammar axis) in relation to developmental time. In other words, this system is a non-static grammar which describes many aspects of the learning process.

When it comes to accounting for cross-sectional data, implicational scaling has a further advantage. As long as one limits oneself to cumulative learning processes, interlanguage samples from different speakers can be represented on what is the time axis in Table 4.2-1. If such an exercise produces a valid implicational relationship of individual interlanguage rules, then the chronological development of these rules can be hypothesised to follow the implicational pattern.

Rank order of accuracy

It may be obvious that this type of dynamic descriptions of interlanguage development goes far beyond a mere description of orders of accuracy such as the ones found in the "morpheme order studies" (e.g. Dulay & Burt 1973; 1974; Rosansky 1976) where linguistic development is expressed in one numeric value, namely the suppliance of morphemes in obligatory contexts. This point becomes more obvious when one looks at scoring methods used in morpheme order studies (Dulay & Burt 1973; 1974):

no functor supplied	=	0 (she's dance)
misformed functor supplied	=	0.5 (she's dances)
correct functor supplied	=	1 (she's dancing)

The fact that 'misformed functors' are included in this type of analysis is obviously an attempt to capture emerging interlanguage forms. However, these analyses are expressed entirely in relation to 'obligatory contexts' as defined in the target language, and the scoring is carried out over large samples in which individual learners are not separated.

The data analysis usually took the from shown in Table 4.2-2.

Table 4.2-2. Rank orders of morphemes - a morpheme order study

Study Summary: Dulay & Burt (1973)
Comparison of Acquisition Sequences for 8 English Grammatical Morphemes for 3
Groups of Spanish-Speaking Children

SAMPLE:			
N:	*151*	Research	
Age:	*6-8 years old*	Design:	*Cross-sectional*
L₁:	*Spanish*	Elicitation	
		Technique:	*Structured conversation*
L₂:	*English*	L2 Environment:	*Host*

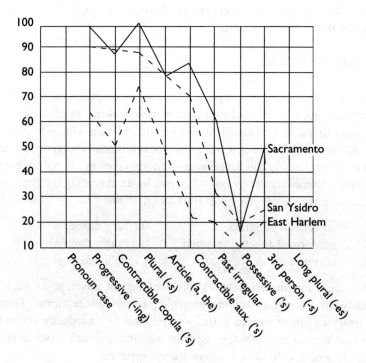

From Dulay, Burt and Krashen 1982, 205

This analysis does not have the potential of describing the dynamics of interlanguage development even though it produces a neat rank order of accuracy of morpheme insertion. However, as several authors have pointed out (e.g.. Larsen-Freeman and Long 1991; Meisel, Clahsen, Pienemann 1981) this rank order is based on the amalgamated sample of a large population. There is no guarantee that the accuracy of morpheme insertion will increase steadily in relation to any two morphemes or in relation to any two learners. On the contrary, it is quite likely and well attested in empirical studies that accuracy rates develop with highly variable gradients in relation to grammatical items and individual learners (Meisel, Clahsen, Pienemann 1981). These observations are represented in Figure 4.2-1.

Figure 4.2-1 illustrates the point that for any given learner and for any given structure, suppliance in obligatory contexts may develop in quite different patterns. A, B and C represent three different structures. The rate of suppliance increases in different ways for A, B and C. Structure B increases in a linear way; C increases exponentially with a step gradient; A has a flat gradient. The interesting point is that cross-sections at different rates of suppliance would result in different accuracy orders:

1%	a - b - c
50%	c - b - a
90%	c - a - b

Figure 4.2-1. Accuracy and development

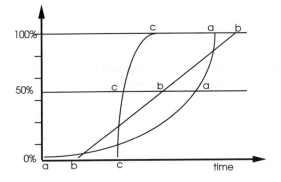

The problem is that it is impossible to predict how suppliance in obligatory contexts will develop in any given structure and learner. There are two important things that follow from this:

(1)   A quantitative acquisition criterion may produce arbitrary orders of accuracy (and acquisition);
(2)   Chronologies of acquisition cannot be established on the basis of "amalgamated" corpora.

The one cut-off point which remains constant, however, is the point of *emergence*, which is also relevant for other reasons. From a speech processing point of view, emergence can be understood as the point in time at which certain skills have, in principle, been attained or at which certain operations can, in principle, be carried out. From a descriptive viewpoint one can say that this is the beginning of an acquisition process, and focusing on the start of this process will allow the researcher to reveal more about the rest of the process.

Distributional analysis

Another important consideration is that obligatory contexts of the target language are not necessarily relevant to the interlanguage. An example is third-person s-marking in English. The target language is sensitive to the following categories, features etc.:

tense
number
person
auxiliary
verb
modal
subject.

The interlanguage may operate on a subset of these categories and features as evidenced in the following hypothetical interlanguage examples:

(17)   *he is goes
(18)   *he musts go
(19)   *he needs help
(20)   *he needs help me
(21)   *he oughts to go.

Therefore, it is more informative to atomise linguistic contexts as much as possible in distributional analyses to determine which contexts or even which lexical items are related to which particular interlanguage rules. In other words, a dynamic description of interlanguage development should be based on a finely-grained distributional analysis (Harris, 1954), a procedure which would be normal practice in linguistic field methods.

The logic of interlanguage forms can be captured in an explicit distributional analysis, which defines the functional and structural context for morpheme insertion. For the above example for instance, I would suggest the following modification, covering a whole interlanguage sample:

time reference	=	present
aspect	=	progressive
subject's person	=	3rd
subject number	=	singular
auxiliary	=	+
lexical verb + O	=	a%
lexical verb + S	=	b%
lexical verb + ing	=	c%

This type of distributional analysis which I use throughout this book can include contexts which are valid for the target language or which are completely idiosyncratic. It can also cover cases which Pica (1984) covered in her target-like use formula to incorporate over-suppliance. One example of over-suppliance is in fact, contained in the above idealised distributional analysis, namely *verb + S* as defined there.

Development can be readily represented in this analytical approach, since rule systems can be generated for different points in time along a time axis. An idealised example is given in Table 4.2-3.

Table 4.2-3. Development of the marking of past in different environments

time	t1	t2	t3
time reference, past	+	+	+
time reference, present	+	−	−
aspect, progressive	+/−	+/−	−
(weak) lexical verb +ed	57	59	65
modal	+/−	+/−	−
(strong) lexical verb +ed	51	21	10
irregular past	49	79	90

Table 4.2-3 illustrates the fictitious acquisition of the past marker *-ed*. It lists a number of functional and structural contexts and notes their presence or absence at different times. It also lists the percentage of suppliance of *-ed* in those contexts. This is nothing more than a refined analysis of suppliance in predefined contexts, except that the definition of all contexts is clearly spelled out and does not have to coincide with the target language.

Table 4.2-3 describes a complex set of information. Between 57% and 65% of all lexical verbs contain the suffix *-ed* at the three points in time. This does not, however, guarantee that the *-ed* actually marks reference to the past. Indeed, one can see that in time 1 the verbs with *-ed* occur in past and in present time references. It is only in time 2 that verbs with the *-ed* affix are confined to past time reference.

The table reveals another interesting fact: although *-ed*-verbs are limited to past time reference in time 2, they still co-occur with auxiliaries, as in

(22)   *he had to walked home.

This shows that at this stage the learner's rule for *-ed*-insertion is sensitive to only some of the contexts defined for the target language, and that fact can be captured very pointedly in this analysis. The linguistic contexts can, of course, be defined in any desired way as dictated by the hypotheses one wants to test.

It is now easy to see that this distributional analysis is far more meaningful than the formation of a single figure to measure the learner's distance form the target language in the use of *-ed* as a past marker. The single figure analysis would, for instance, bring the accuracy level down at t_2 in Table 4.2-2, because the use of *-ed* as a tense marker in the presence of a modal generated a "misformed functor". But it should be noted that this modified accuracy level only disguises the exact linguistic rule which could otherwise be spelt out so distinctly. The same is true for the calculation of over-suppliance in Pica's (1984) formula.

Variable rules, interlanguage variation and the Multi-dimensional Model

Time to re-focus: above I described the transitional paradigm used in this book as resting on two major concepts in linguistic theory: implicational distributional analysis and variable rules (Labov, 1972a, b). It is now time to move on to the latter component and its status in the descriptive paradigm used in this book.

The reader will recall that variable rules are designed to capture three different things:

- the social context in which linguistic forms are being used,
- the linguistic context (e.g.. INVERSION in questions or statements),
- the probability of rule application.

A variable rule typically makes the following kind of statements: rule x (e.g. contraction of the copula) is used with probability X in social context Y given that the linguistic context is Z. The reader will see below that Meisel, Clahsen and Pienemann (1981) reconceptualised this sociolinguistic paradigm in a way substantially different from Tarone's (1979, 1982, 1988) and Ellis's (1985b, 1987) variationist accounts of SLA.

Meisel, Clahsen and Pienemann accommodated two of Labov's descriptive parameters directly in their descriptive framework: linguistic contexts form an essential part of their descriptive approach, and the percentage values given for each rule can be seen as corresponding to Labov's probability of application.

This led Meisel et al. to modify implicational analysis by replacing the original either-or values of implicational scales by percentage values calculated for specified linguistic environments. This addition would also permit a finer description of transitions in the rule system than would have been possible with either-or values only. It is at this point in particular where the emergence criterion becomes relevant, since this criterion adds to the previously qualitative nature of implicational analysis a quantitative dimension.

Meisel et al. did not see the role of the social context in terms of social rules which change from one situation to another. Rather, emphasis was placed on an overall evaluation of the social identity of the individual SL acquirer, since previous studies had shown that natural SL acquirers use different degrees of restrictive simplification (Meisel 1983) depending on the type of their integration into the host society. This proposition appeared to coincide with Schumann's (1976) notion of *social distance* and Gardner & Lambert's (1972) distinction between *integrative and instrumental motivation*.

It is crucial to note, however, that Meisel, Clahsen and Pienemann hypothesised that these social variables interact not with L2 development, but with variation. In other words, these authors proposed that the way in which variable features materialise in a given interlanguage would determine some sort of interlanguage dialect for individual speakers which would have some degree of stability and that these dialects could be plotted along a continuum of restrictive simplification. They further hypothesised that the type of dialect developed by the learner would correlate with his or her social identity.

In other words, the explanatory module advanced for those variational interlanguage dialects (i.e., variational features) is based on the concept of social identity. Clahsen, Meisel and Pienemann (1983) did in fact demonstrate through cluster and discriminant analyses of a large set of socio-psychological variables that these variables correlate with the variational features displayed in the interlanguages of the same speakers (cf. also Pienemann, Johnston and Meisel 1993).

What such a correlation cannot achieve, however, even if the attempted factor analysis had been more successful, is to *predict* which set of socio-psychological factors produces which variational features in a given learner (Pienemann and Johnston 1987b). On the other hand, conceding a lack of predictive power in the socio-psychological explanation of variable features does not amount to a dismissal of the explanation. It merely states the nature of the explanation and of the concepts used in it. The notion of social identity is simply not explicit enough to make such predictions possible.

What is more relevant in the context of the research presented in this book is the notion of interlanguage variation itself which Meisel et al. understand as the learner's linguistic variants at any one stage of development. The main point about interlanguage variation in relation to the dynamic interlanguage paradigm is the following: not every difference that can be found when comparing two interlanguage samples has to be understood as an instance of maturation in the interlanguage system. To allow for the possibility that some such differences are of the 'dialectal' nature described above, Meisel et al. assumed that L2 acquisition can best be described as a two-dimensional process with development and variation as related but distinguishable dimensions.

The assumption of two dimensions is a logical and simple adaptation to the observation that not every difference between two given sets of data can be interpreted as a maturational difference. There are many parallels with other developing systems. If, for instance, one examined two sister-seedlings of a plant and found that the shape of each plant was different in some way, then one would have to allow for the following possibilities:

(1)   the differences are specific to the plant's individual features that differentiate it from its sister, or to its environment;

(2)   the differences are specific to the plant's developmental state.

The purpose of the multidimensional model is to enable the researcher to represent grammatical development within a variable system in which development and learner variation are distinct phenomena.

Meisel et al. (1983) found that using this development-variation distinction, accuracy rates distribute in large sets of SLA data as shown in Figure 4.2-2.

This finding empirically underpins the point that accuracy measures lack validity as measures of development. Apart from this side-effect, the multidimensional model provides a convenient descriptive framework in which development and variation can be separated for the purpose of analysis.

A final point on development and variation: in the original work on the multidimensional model, development was defined in an *a priori* manner through a set of processing strategies which I critically reviewed in Chapter 2. Larsen-Freeman and Long (1991, 285) pointed out that this type of *a priori* definition was missing from the model for the variational dimension and thus limited the falsifiability of some of its components. The theory proposed in this book attempts to overcome this limitation. Its purpose is to provide an *a priori* definition of possible interlanguage grammars; i.e. for both dimensions: development and variation. In the preceding chapters I demonstrated how development can be predicted by hierarchies of processability, and more evidence for a number of L2s will be presented in Chapter 5.

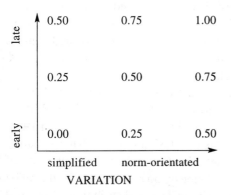

Figure 4.2-2. Variation, development and accuracy

The transition to variable features will be made in Chapter 6 where I will demonstrate that the range of variable features can be predicted from the same hierarchy of processability. Note that this last point is different from predicting which factors trigger which variable features in an individual learner. Instead, the aim of Processability Theory is to give a formal and *a priori* definition of the range of variable features which are possible at any one stage of development.

The emergence criterion and morphology

The story thus far describes the general philosophy behind emergence criteria in syntactic and morphological interlanguage development. In effect, I proposed that it is possible to apply the concept of emergence to morphological development, albeit filtered through more refined analyses which 'neutralise' the effect of unanalysed entries into the learner's lexicon. The analysis of SV agreement marking in Section 4.1 illustrates this point. In that analysis, one would get a false impression of the 'emergence' of many morphological agreement markers if the analysis were based solely on the suppliance of morphemes in their target language contexts. However, I contrasted my analysis of target language environments with a simple test of the 'null hypothesis'; in other words, I analysed the use of agreement markers in non-target language contexts and found a similarly high percentage of suppliance as in the target language contexts.

It turned out that it was impossible to predict morpheme insertion by target language contexts and that there was only one point in time and one morpheme for which the null hypothesis had to be rejected, namely in the case of first person marking in week 19 (cf. Table 4.1-4). This is the only case in which the rate of suppliance is markedly different in TL contexts and non-TL contexts. In fact, in that case the difference turned out to be categorial: 100% suppliance in contexts and no suppliance in non-contexts.

On the basis of this observation Jansen (1994) concluded that "... [Pienemann] is applying a mastery criterion here [with morphology, MP] as against the emergence criterion he formulated for word order." (Jansen 1994, 4). However, I have to point out that this conclusion is somewhat premature. It so happened that in the particular set of data I looked at that the rate of suppliance was indeed 100%. There is obviously no requirement for this to be the case when testing the null-hypothesis. In fact, a distribution of 60 to 0 would have been just as much grounds for rejecting the null-hypothesis.

In other words, the way in which the emergence criterion can be applied to morphology is by laying the distributional analysis out in such a way that the null-hypothesis can be tested for any hypothesised morphological rule. The linguistic context can then be refined down to the level of individual lexical entries. This methodology allows us to implement the basic elements of the emergence criterion into the analysis of morphological development.

Applying the emergence criterion

The above approach to interlanguage analysis raises several further issues some of which are methodological in nature, and some of which relate to acquisition theory. At the methodological level one needs to clarify what type of observation constitutes evidence for which linguistic rule. This is a highly relevant aspect of the process of second language acquisition research, since it is these principles of data interpretation which decide on how the researcher represents the learner's current state of linguistic rule system.

To illustrate this issue with actual data I would like to direct the reader's attention to Table 4.1-2 in Section 4.1. Below I reproduce two essential lines from that table which contains key information on the level of rule application for SEP and INV.

When I interpreted this part of Table 4.1-2 above I stated that in weeks 1-5 there is no evidence of SEP because the learner does not produce the linguistic context for this rule. This is represented by dashes in Table 4.2-4. In weeks 7-9 the figures appear in brackets. This signifies that the total number of contexts is smaller than four. In week 7 this would produce a zero level of rule application, while in week 9 there is one case out of a total number of two contexts in which the rule is formally applied. I decided that this does not constitute a sufficient sample to apply the emergence criterion and to draw the

Table 4.2-4. Guy's development of SEP and INV

Weeks	1	3	5	7	9	11	13	15	17	19
SEP with V-complements	-	-	-	(0)	(0.5)	0.	-	0.75	0.46	0.41
INV with V-complements	-	-	-	0.	0.	(.22)	0.	0.	0.1	0.36

conclusion that SEP has emerged in Guy's interlanguage. In other words, up to and including week 13 there are either no contexts or no rule applications or insufficient data. It is only in week 15 that one finds sufficient contexts and at least one rule application.

I therefore concluded that this is the point at which SEP emerges. The situation for INV is very similar, and I concluded that the emergence criterion was met for INV two weeks later.

This example illustrates that quantitative observations of rule application fall into the following four categories:

(1) no evidence; i.e. no linguistic contexts;
(2) insufficient evidence; i.e. very small number of contexts;
(3) evidence for non-application; i.e. non-application in the presence of contexts for rule x;
(4) evidence for rule application; i.e. examples of rule application in the presence of contexts.

It is easy to see that one obtains the most reliable picture of the state of an interlanguage grammar if the sample contains as many of type (3) and (4) observations as possible. Type (1) and (2) observations are usually inconclusive. Quite often these situations arise when the interlanguage sample is very small or when the communicative situation is such that the situation does not give rise to the use of the linguistic contexts in focus. Such samples will simply remain inconclusive.

In the case of the longitudinal study represented in Table 4.2-4, however, the data are reasonably conclusive, because it is logical to expect that at the very beginning of the acquisition process the learner will not have acquired the context for the rule in question. That is exactly what one finds in weeks 1 to 5 for SEP and INV. One can also see that once the linguistic context is acquired for these rules, the learner uses the context continuously until the rule itself is acquired. In other words, the succession of "no evidence" to "evidence for non-application" to "evidence for rule application" occurs as part of a steady development.

Some degree of ambiguity remains in this analysis when it comes to judging if the number of linguistic contexts is sufficient for a given rule to decide if the rule has been applied or not. An example for this case can be found in table X in line SEP in week 9 when SEP occurs once in the presence of two contexts. A strict application of the emergence criterion would lead one to conclude that SEP emerges in this sample. However, it may be the case that this one and only example of SEP is part of a monomorphemic chunk, i.e. one single lexical element. The only way to test this hypothesis would be to see if SEP also occurs with different lexical elements. To make this possible one would need at least one other instance of SEP.

Testing the opposite hypothesis — that SEP has not emerged at this point — is equally difficult, since again there is only one example of non-application. Both hypotheses would therefore be able to be tested unambiguously if the sample of contexts were larger. However, it is now impossible to collect any additional data.

To resolve this situation one can resort to a version of the continuity assumption that also underlies Brown's (1973) acquisition criterion: If a structure has been acquired it will be a constant part of the interlanguage system at later levels of development. In this way one discounts the single and isolated occurrence of seeming rule application as an aberration in the data.

There is, of course, a degree of circularity in this argument when one wants to empirically demonstrate the continuity of interlanguage development. But I believe that this risk is quite calculable, because the ambiguity under discussion is not such that type 4 evidence precedes type 3 evidence followed by type 4 evidence; in other words the ambiguity does not arise from a situation where rule application alters with non-application in consecutive interviews in the presence of ample contexts for the rule. In fact, no such cases occur in the data discussed in this book. It is the latter finding which gives me the confidence that the above version of the continuity assumption can be supported empirically.

A further principle implied in the above approach to interlanguage analysis is that of converting "quantitative" data into qualitative data. This is the very point of an acquisition criterion. The essence of my interpretation of Table 4.2-4 can be summarised as in Table 4.2-5 below.

Table 4.2-5. Application of the emergence criterion to the development of SEP and INV in Guy's interlanguage

Weeks	1	3	5	7	9	11	13	15	17	19
SEP	–	–	–	–	–	–	–	+	+	+
INV	–	–	–	–	–	–	–	–	+	+

Table 4.2-5 is based on a systematic application to Table 4.2-4 of the emergence criterion for acquisition as just discussed. In other words, the raw data from the interlanguage corpus undergo several stages of interpretation: the quantitative distributional analysis from Section 4.1 was designed to test certain structural hypotheses, e.g. the proximity of verb and complement. These hypotheses were derived from the proposed overall theory of interlanguage processing. One then applies the emergence criterion to the distributional analysis. This is the point at which quantitative data are interpreted on a qualitative basis. By stating that rule X has emerged in interlanguage Y one makes a qualitative assertion about the structure of that interlanguage.

Operationalisation of the emergence criterion

This is a suitable moment to clarify a misunderstanding of the *emergence criterion* which crystallises in Ellis' (1994, 387) summary of the 'multi-dimensional model'. As stated above, the emergence criterion was developed by Meisel, Clahsen and Pienemann (1981) as part of their multi-dimensional model of SLA. The rationale and the historical context for this criterion is summarised pointedly by Larsen-Freeman and Long (1991, 283):

> "... the ZISA project was one of the first to relinquish the prevailing target-language orientation of the 1970s, thereby avoiding what Bley-Vroman has called the 'comparative fallacy in IL [interlanguage, MP] studies'. ... in most SLA research of the 1960s and 1970s, the focus was either on errors defined in terms of the mature L2 system, or alternatively, on items held to be acquired when they were supplied 80 or 90 percent accurately... Studying 'acquisition', in other words, mostly meant [to 1970s researchers, MP] assessing how far learners were from the finishing line or studying them as they crossed it. The ZISA group explicitly rejected this approach, redefining acquisition (of a form) as the first appearance of a form in an IL, this and the subsequent evolution of form-function relationships being treated from the same learner-oriented perspective that had long been taken for granted by creolists..."

The reader will recall that the emergence criterion was introduced not only to allow corpus-based SLA research to be based on the type of distributional analysis carried out as a matter of course in field linguistics, but also because this criterion is ideally suited for a theory which is directed mainly at capturing the systematicity of spontaneous oral production.

Unfortunately, Ellis in his 1994 introduction to SLA research, despite his generally positive review of the multi-dimensional model, misunderstands the status of the emergence criterion. He asserts the following:

> "Another problem concerns the operational definition of 'acquisition'. Whereas the original research on which the Multidimensional Model was based quantified all the features examined by indicating their overall proportion of suppliance in obligatory contexts ... , Pienemann and his co-workers have subsequently redefined acquisition in terms of 'onset' (i.e. the first appearance of a grammatical feature). Hulstijn (1987), while accepting that the study of 'onset' is legitimate in a model that emphasises the importance of processing operations, nevertheless feels that ... the work lacks rigour because Pienemann 'does not set quantitative or qualitative criteria to be met by the learner's production, in order to be considered as evidence for the operation of the predicted processing strategy' (1987,14)."
> (Ellis 1994, 387)

Firstly, the approach to corpus-based SLA studies advocated in this book and previously by Meisel, Clahsen and Pienemann (1981) always includes a quantitative distributional analysis as a first step. This is also what was presented in the 1981 paper, and it was in the very paper where the 'onset' (i.e. emergence) criterion was proposed, and not — as Ellis believes — in a subsequent redefinition of the term acquisition.

Secondly, it would be incorrect to say that no quantitative or qualitative criteria for acquisition are given. This whole chapter deals with the way in which the 1981 emergence criterion can be applied to actual sets of data and to syntax and morphology. The reader will recall that sufficiently large and linguistically varied data sets allow the identification of the point of emergence.

The very point of the 1981 paper (Meisel, Clahsen and Pienemann 1981) was to overcome the **limitations** of quantitative criteria which were demonstrated to be arbitrary and target-language oriented. A return to quantitative criteria would be a retrograde step.

And another point needs to be made: focusing on the point of emergence in data analysis in no way precludes a detailed analysis of the further course of acquisition. On the contrary, that is exactly what distributional analyses are designed to produce. The above example of interlanguage tense marking illustrates this clearly: the proposed type of analysis allows the researcher to trace every step in the development of the relationship between grammatical forms and their functions from the first emergence of the most modest (non-standard) systematicity to the full use of the target language system.

In summary, there are specific conditions that data sets must fulfil before the emergence criterion can be applied with success. Larsen-Freeman and

Long, amongst many other researchers, found that data sets may be too small and linguistically not sufficiently varied to carry out the type of distributional analysis developed in this chapter. However, one has to remember that this observation does not limit the **validity** of the analysis while it may limit what is **practical** for some researchers.

Naturally, I was not spared numerous encounters with these methodological limitations, and I will report on some of them in chapters below. At this stage I would like to briefly point at ways of overcoming these limitations. In Section 6.4 I will report on a study on task variation which was carried out in order to test to what extent interlanguage forms can be triggered by communicative tasks. That research demonstrates that linguistically monotonous samples are often produced in data collection sessions in which communicative demands do not vary and it further demonstrates that linguistically varied data sets can be obtained by employing a variety of communicative tasks.

The size of a sample is another potential limitation which, no doubt, many researchers have experienced. As I illustrated above, to decide on the emergence of a form, the presence of alternate forms and linguistic environments is required. It is therefore impossible to determine in advance how large the sample has to be before inferences can be made about the underlying rule system. For the purpose of distributional analysis, sample size and range of linguistic forms interact, and the reliability of a distributional analysis increases with an increase of linguistic forms in a sample.

Let me return to the practicability of the proposed analysis: there may well be research contexts in which a distributional analysis would be too specific and detailed for the objective of the research. One example may be a project that is designed to monitor the rate of acquisition in a group of learners in relation to the teaching input they receive. What is required in this case is to establish the stage of acquisition for these learners at various points in time. There are methods that can be applied in order to achieve this goal that are more effective than carrying out what amounts to very work-intensive profile studies, for a very large body of data. This task can be achieved by mapping out learner profiles for all informants and points in time using an observation-based profiling procedure (Pienemann, Johnston and Brindley 1988; Pienemann 1992a; Pienemann, Mackey and Thornton 1991). In this way, the research effort can be reduced very substantially without compromising the nature of the measurement; i.e. without replacing a measure of acquisition by a less interesting accuracy measure.

Larsen-Freeman and Long (1991, 286) point out a further complication in applying the proposed analytical approach and its interpretation:

> "... in an unpublished pilot study of ESL and JSL at the University of Hawaii in 1984 testing the predictive framework [a precursor to Processability Theory, MP], it was found that the general IL profile for some learners might place them, say, at stage X+4 in ESL ..., but still show them producing stage X+3 structures in one or more domains and X+5 structures in one or more domains. While some 'trailing' and 'scouting' in particular structural domains is to be expected, the question arises as to how many developmental levels can separate the least and the most advanced structures before the model can be said to have been falsified."

Larsen-Freeman and Long are quite aware that the presence or absence of specific structures may be due to structural 'gaps' which may arise from the nature of the data elicitation session. I mentioned this problem above and will deal with it in more detail in section 6.4 below. As the reader will see, such gaps exist quite naturally also in native speakers who will use grammatical structures according to functional appropriateness, not according to level of acquisition. This is so because interlanguage structures accumulate in the learner in the process of acquisition, and the vast majority of them are also used by native speakers. In other words, native speakers will use low-level structures if required by the context.

What is important here is to determine how the concept of stages in language development can be falsified. Larsen-Freeman and Long seem to suggest that there ought to be some degree of uniformity of level across the different structural domains and that if this is not to be found the concept of stages is falsified. However, such a procedure would mean not to focus on the key features of an implicational hierarchy of stages of acquisition.

What ought to be tested is not the uniformity of levels, but the hierarchical nature of stages. Such a test would have to be based on several interlanguage samples in order to capture the concept of implicational or hierarchical levels; in other words, what is needed is at least one sample each of at least two distinct levels of development. Ideally these samples should be taken in a longitudinal manner to avoid confusion between variational and developmental features and one would also have to be sure that the samples are linguistically sufficiently varied to contain all the linguistic contexts needed to produce the rules to be tested (i.e. type (3) or (4) evidence as discussed above). If 'a' is the context for rule 'A' and 'b' the context for rule 'B' etc.

Table 4.2-6. Identifying hierarchies of rules in linguistic samples

	Sample 1	Sample 2
a	+	+
A	+	+
b	+	+
B	−	+
c	+	+
C	−	+

then the pattern shown in Table 4.2-6 is to be expected for a valid implicational relationship.

This would mean that the environments for rules A,B, and C are present in both samples and rule A is also present in sample 1 and 2, but rules B and C are present in sample 2 and absent in sample 1. These samples would provide evidence for the following implicational relationship:

$$B, C \supset A$$

which is identical with the sequence

A before B and C.

It is important to note that in this example the environments for rules A,B and C do exist. This means that the quality of the data does in fact allow the implicational relationship of these rules to be tested.

To falsify the hypothesised implicational pattern (i.e. B, C … A) a structure positioned at the lower end of the implicational hierarchy would have to be absent in the presence of the required environment and in the

Table 4.2-7. Falsifying hierarchies of rules in linguistic samples

	Sample 1	Sample 2
a	+	+
A	+	−
b	+	+
B	−	+
c	+	+
C	−	+

presence of a 'higher' rule as illustrated below where A is absent from sample 2 in the presence of B and C. This is illustrated in Table 4.2-7.

This clarifies how hierarchical sequences can be falsified, but it still leaves the question of 'trailing' and 'scouting' unanswered. I will provide a brief answer here and deal with this issue in more detail in Section 6.2. The situation Larsen-Freeman and Long have in mind can be sketched as in Table 4.2-8.

The first thing to note is that there is yet another issue involved in determining stages of development once one deals with several structural domains. Larsen-Freeman and Long obviously assume that the overall level of development in this type of analysis is determined by identifying the highest level for which the majority of domains have a plus for 'acquired'. In the above table this would be level 4.

However, throughout this book I make a different assumption. Since the emergence criterion is used to describe the beginning of an acquisition process I apply the same principle to the emergence of evidence for the learner's capacity to process linguistic material at a higher level. With this criterion in mind one would have to conclude that the fictitious learner described in Table 4.2-8 is at stage 5. In other words, the emergence criterion eliminates the 'scouting' phenomenon.

What remains is 'trailing'. In Section 6.2 I will demonstrate that 'trailing' is a variational phenomenon. The existence of gaps in some structural domains characterises the nature of specific interlanguage dialects and correlates with other variational features.

Table 4.2-8. Development in different structural domains

Level	domain 1	domain 2	domain 3	domain 4
6	–	–	–	–
5	–	+	–	+
4	+	+	–	+
3	+	+	–	+
2	+	+	+	+
1	+	+	+	+

4.3 Form-function relationships and processability

The reader will recall that in section 3.4 I distinguished between two discrete aspects in the acquisition of L2 morphology. One aspect concerns the core of processability, namely the processing procedures needed for different kinds of affixation. The other concerns the learning of morphological forms in relation to their functions. In this section I will discuss ways in which these two aspects can be kept apart in testing Processability Theory.

Processability and morphology

Let me first remind the reader of what Processability Theory has to say about the acquisition of L2 morphology. The basic points are summarised in Table 4.3-1.

Processability Theory makes a basic distinction between lexical, phrasal and interphrasal morphology. The distinction is based on the processing procedures involved in each of these types. The hierarchy of processing procedures determines the sequence in which these types of affixation processes evolve.

I pointed out above that the learning of the morphological form of the affix constitutes a task that is different from managing the information distribution in the affixation process where diacritic features have to be exchanged within different grammatical structures.

Table 4.3-1. Summary: acquisition of morphology

stage	exchange of information	procedures	morphology (German examples)	
6		subord. cl. procedure		
5	inter-phrasal	S-Procedure	SV-agreement	**"inter-phrasal morphemes"**
4	inter-phrasal	S-Procedure saliency		
3	phrasal	phrasal procedures	plural agreement	**"phrasal morphemes"**
2	none	lex. categories	past-te etc.	**"lexical morphemes"**
1	none		words	

Form-function relationships

Some morphemes have a one-to-one relationship between form and function (e.g. the Finnish genitive marker '-n', <*talo* - talo-n>; house - of the house), while other morphemes may express a multitude of functions (e.g. English '-s' for plural, possessive, third person etc. or German '-en' for infinitive, plural, dative etc.). Morphemes may also fall into several formal classes which do not necessarily express functions which can be derived from conceptual structure. German, for instance, uses a wide range of different classes of plural marking on nouns (e.g. *Haus - Häus-er; Frau - Frau-en; Auto - Auto-s* etc.). These form-function relationships constitute a learning task which is quite different from the principle of sharing the diacritic features on which all of these affixation processes are based.

When the relationship between morpheme and diacritic feature is "one-to-many", diacitic features are bundled. For instance, in German the affix '-es' marks genitive on nouns if they are singular and masculine or neuter. In other words, the diacritic features 'genitive', 'singular', 'masculine' and 'neuter' are fused into one bundle of features which correlates to the morpheme '-es'. To account for German nominal affixes a complex system of such bundles of features has to be constructed as small portion of which is depicted in Table 4.3-2.

Table 4.3-2. German nominal affixes

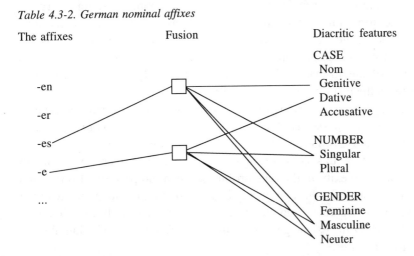

The affixes	Fusion	Diacritic features
		CASE
		Nom
-en		Genitive
		Dative
-er		Accusative
-es		
		NUMBER
		Singular
-e		Plural
...		
		GENDER
		Feminine
		Masculine
		Neuter

Table 4.3-3. Finnish nominal affixes

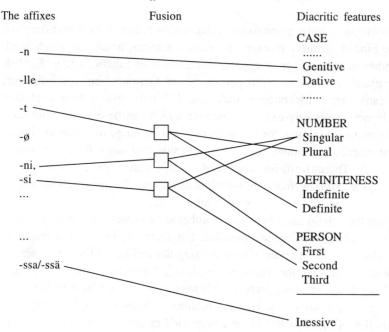

This complex system of form-function relationships contrasts with that of Finnish nominal morphology which contains a number of straight-forward one-to-one form function relationships, such as the marking of genitive, dative, inessive etc. A small section of Finnish nominal morphology is depicted in Table 4.3-3. As can be seen from that table, Finnish also contains a number of one-to-many relationships, most notably the possessive affix which fuses the marking of number and person.

In Finnish most affixes agglutinate and follow a specific order, for instance "inessive before possessive" as is exemplified in *"talo-ssa-ni"* (house-INESSIVE-POSSESSIVE{-1st pers, sg} = "in my house") (cf. Karlson 1987).

The point of this comparison is to illustrate that there are different degrees of complexity in the relationship between morphological forms and their function and that this complexity adds another dimension to the learning task which is separate from the task on which Processability Theory is focused, namely the exchange of grammatical information, including the use of diacritic features.

Testing the processability hierarchy

The most straight-forward way of testing the hypotheses derived from the processability hierarchy is to use affixes with a one-to-one form-function relationship if they occur in the target language. This avoids the issue of intervening variables entirely. When the target language does not include such affixes one can nevertheless construct a distributional analysis which will reveal if a relationship exists between a diacritic feature and a certain affix. When designing such a distributional analysis one has to be mindful of the nature of the one-to-many relationships which can go in two directions: either one morpheme marks a bundle of diacritic features, such as the German morpheme '-e' on nouns[13] which marks dative if the noun is neuter or masculine and singular. This is illustrated in Table 4.3-4.

Table 4.3-4. Marking of dative on German nouns

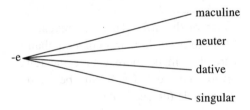

Another scenario is one in which several morphemes mark the same feature. This is exemplified below with German plural marking where the choice of the morpheme depends on the class of the noun. This is illustrated in Table 4.3-5.

Table 4.3-5. Plural marking in German nouns

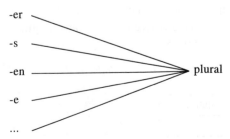

A third scenario is one with many-to-many relationships. The reader will notice that this is in fact the case for the German affix '-e' since for some noun classes it marks dative as well as the plural.

In all of these scenarios there is a relationship between affix and diacritic feature, however complex the relationship. This is what the distributional analysis can focus on. If we take German plural marking as an example, the first step in the analysis would be to test if there is any morphological plural marking at all in a given sample. To test this one would have to check if the presence of any affix correlates with the presence of a plural context. This is illustrated in the Table 4.3-6 where all occurrences of nouns in the sample would be quantified:

Table 4.3-6. Matrix for distributional analysis

	singular	plural
N+affix		
Nø		

The next step is to specify the form of the affix. This will reveal if a particular form of the affix is more likely to occur in plural contexts than in non-plural contexts. Naturally, such trends will be more visible the fewer forms and diacritic features are involved, and the test will only be valid if plural and singular contexts exist in the sample (cf. section 4.2).

The same principle can be applied to the one-to-many relationship which is present in the example of the German dative '-e'. The distributional analysis sketched out in Table 4.3-7 will differentiate between the following minimal oppositions: nouns with the affix '-e' versus nouns without affix and non-dative contexts versus dative contexts.

In this way, the gender distinction in nouns and the marking of number will initially be left out of the analysis. Each of these sets of diacritic features can be added to the analysis. But since it is not known how the learner unlocks the complex form-function relationship, provisions have to be made to test every logical possibility, for instance '-e' marks dative or dative and singular or dative and singular in masculine nouns only etc.

Table 4.3-7. Distributional analysis for the use of the affix -e in dative and non-dative contexts

	non-dative	dative
N-e		
Nø		

One has to remember that the acquisition of the diacritic features themselves constitutes varying degrees of difficulty. For instance, the concept of 'number' can be inferred from conceptual structure and applies to most items of the lexical class 'noun'. In contrast, 'gender' is an idiosyncratic diacritic feature of German nouns, the value of which has to be acquired individually for every lexical entry. It is therefore possible that the notion of 'dative' is acquired before all nouns of the interlanguage are correctly marked for gender in the learner's lexicon. In this case, it will be impossible for the learner to mark German dative correctly.

Factorising diacritic features

Nevertheless, the insertion of '-e' may be sensitive to the context 'dative'. If this is the case, then the learner has acquired a simplified version of the target language system of case marking. If indeed the marking of dative singular is overgeneralised to all nouns, or even to a subclass of nouns, then this will show in the distributional analysis. In other words, what I will call *factorising* the diacritic features and the linguistic environment will allow one to trace the learner's own system of form-function mapping which may be closer to one-to-one relationships earlier on in the acquisition process (cf. also Andersen's (1984) 'one-to-one principle).

A brief example from the acquisition of Swedish as a second language by children will illustrate the significance of factorising diacritic features. The example is merely one sample from one learner which was supplied by Håkansson (1996b). In this sample adjectival endings will be examined which relate to a set of diacritic features in a many-to-many relationship.

I will deal with the acquisition of Swedish morpho-syntax in more detail in section 5.3 below. At this point, a brief summary of the adjectival system will suffice: In its attributive function the adjective agrees with the head noun of the noun phrase. In its predicative function the adjective agrees with the subject. The diacritic features 'gender', 'number' and definiteness' are simultaneously marked by one affix which can take three forms: a zero morpheme, the suffix *t,* and the suffix *a.* The contexts for these markings are given in Table 4.3-8.[14]

In Håkansson's sample we will only consider the predicative and indefinite context. The diacitic features that remain are gender (uter and neuter) and number (singular and plural). The distributional analysis is set up as in Table 4.3-9.

Table 4.3-8. Adjectival affixes in Swedish

	attributive			
	indefinite		definite	
	sing	pl	sing	pl
uter	Ø	a	a	a
neuter	t	a	a	a

	predicative			
	indefinite		definite	
	sing	pl	sing	pl
uter	Ø	a	Ø	a
neuter	t	a	t	a

Table 4.3-9. Analysis of form-function relationship in Swedish interlanguage plural marking

	Function		
Form	plural uter/neuter	singular uter	singular neuter
-a	7/9	*0/7	*0/7
zero	*2/9	7/7	*7/7
-t	*0/9	*0/7	0/7

In the above analysis, the two sets of diacritic features have been separated and each bundle of features has been related to the three possible morphemes allowing for a total of nine logical form-function relationships. For ease of comparison, the ungrammatical form-function relationships have been marked with an asterix.

As can be seen from the above distributional analysis, only four of the possible nine form-function relationships are being used in this sample. Two of those are ungrammatical, and one grammatical option, the -t-marker for singular neuter, does not occur. What's important in the context of factorising diacritic features, is the morphological paradigm that emerges from this analysis.

One can see clearly, that gender marking which, in Swedish, is productive only in the singular, does not materialise in this sample. The learner uses
the zero morpheme consistently in all singular contexts and in only 22% of the
plural contexts. The morpheme '-a' is used in 78% of all plural contexts and
never in any singular context. This shows quite clearly that the learner has
created a zero/-a opposition to mark singular and plural. The complete lack of
gender marking is evident from the fact that the marker of neuter (in the
singular) is missing from the sample although there are seven contexts for it.
In other words, the learner created a simplified, though highly systematic
paradigm of adjectival morphology in which the set of diacritic features is
reduced to one, namely the one that can be inferred directly from conceptual
structure.

One can now see that for the purpose of testing Processability Theory,
one can rely on the learner's own linguistic paradigm rather than on the
emergence of the full target language paradigm. In the case discussed above,
the full paradigm can be expected to develop much later because of the
complex form-function relationships involved in the morphological marking
of gender on adjectives. Factorising the diacritic features makes it possible to
isolate those morphological markers for which no complex form-function
relationships intervene in the distribution of grammatical information, the key
metric of Processability Theory.

A non-factorised analysis would not have revealed the striking regularity
underlying this sample. A linear analysis of target use would have revealed
the percentages shown in Table 4.3-10.

Obviously, none of these percentages can reveal the actual grammatical
system that underlies the interlanguage sample, and one might incorrectly

Table 4.3-10. Results of a non-factorised analysis of plural marking with the same informant as in Table 4.3-9

• correctness of function:

plural uter/neuter	singular uter	singular neuter
78%	100%	0%

• correctness of morpheme insertion:

-a 78%
zero 69,6%
-t 0%

assume that the sample does not contain any adjectival agreement phenomena. Instead, the learner's agreement system operates only on a sub-set of diacritic features and morphemes.

In conclusion, without factorisation it will be difficult to keep aspects of processability and aspects of form-function relationships apart.

A post script on the perceived target-language orientation of Processability Theory

This may be a suitable point at which to bring to the reader's attention a comment that was made by one of the colleagues who I asked for feedback on the manuscript of this book.[15] The comment was as follows:

> "In your model you seem to start from the full language system as the point of reference for learners. Learning is seen as not having acquired full mastery of rules. ... Form a processing perspective that is a problematic stance. What counts is what learners have and how they use that information, not what they are lacking."

I was rather surprised by this comment. Isn't the theme of the whole book to look at what learners have, not what they lack? On reflection, I believe it might be useful to make my response to this perception accessible to the reader of this book. This might provide a broader basis for discussion.

The reader will recall that the very theme of this chapter was to develop descriptive methods which allow the analyst to avoid any target language bias. One example that was given in section 4.2 was the case of verbal morphology. There I showed that a straight comparison with the target language structure would be quite misleading, and I made a case for inflectional morphemes to be subjected to a careful distributional analysis which is not guided by the target language system but by the internal mechanics of the interlanguage system.

The same motive underlies the emergence criterion and my critical view on target-language accuracy as a measure of acquisition or development. And it is this motive that is the driving force behind this very section (4.3) where the message is that in interlanguages, forms may emerge in the same shape as in the target language. However, they may relate to different functions. Again, the genuine systematicity of the interlanguage can be found only through a careful unbiased distributional analysis. The example of Swedish interlanguage plural marking highlights this point most clearly. I demonstrated that a careful distributional analysis which treats the interlanguage as a system entirely in its own right can reveal a kind of systematicity which is not accessible through a simple target language accuracy count. This point is also made by Klein and Perdue (1992).[16]

The analysis of interlanguage morphology and syntax of all second languages presented in this book (German, English, Swedish and Japanese) was carried out on this basis. For instance, in the analysis of English 'do support' morphological phenomena were systematically separated from syntactic phenomena. This made it possible to show that the position of the auxiliary is acquired separately from its morphological form. In fact, the reader will see in section 5.2 that the initial position of 'do' is acquired at level 3, while the marking of third person singular on 'do' occurs only two stages later. These developmental phenomena would not have been visible by looking through target language glasses.

I believe that all of this shows a very stringent commitment to the concept of the interlanguage as a system in its own right and that the methods developed in this book are designed exactly to show "what learners have and how they use that information, not what they are lacking".

The perception that Processability Theory is target-language oriented could hardly have arisen from Chapter 4. A more likely possibility is Chapter 2 where I detailed the components of the processability hierarchy. This assumption is based on another statement made by my critic who states that to the learner "there is no end-point in the acquisition process, but merely changes in what he or she knows". The reader will recall that the processability hierarchy was based on an implicational sequence of processing procedures. It might have been here that my critic had the impression that an end-point was firmly implanted in Processability Theory because the latter spells out those processing procedures.

However, it has to be pointed out that there was no suggestion that the learner would at any time "see" the highest-order or any intermediate procedure or the associated structures as a target. In fact, in Processability Theory the question of epistemology was explicitly excluded. This means that I did not set out to say anything about the origin of structures or by what means the learner moves on to new levels or structures.

The point that I do make is that the target language consists of a number of processing procedures and that the sequence of acquisition of the target language can be accounted for by a piece-meal emergence of those procedures. In other words, possible developmental paths are constrained by what is processable by the pieces compiled so far. However, this does not imply that the learner can at any time "see" the pieces that are ahead of them or the whole that the pieces form. None of these things are of any concern to Processability Theory. In fact, it is implied in Processability Theory that there is very little need for the learner to keep sight of the whole or pieces of the target language and that the highly regular course that the learner appears to "steer" towards the target language is mainly a reflection of the hierarchy of processability itself.

Chapter 5

Cross-linguistic validity and on-line evidence

What I presented in the previous sections is a principled approach to the interface between linguistic theory and the acquisition of language processing procedures. This approach was exemplified on the basis of one language. The goal of an explanatory theory of SLA must, of course, be to provide a mechanism which has the capacity of making predictions for ANY human language. It would therefore be desirable to demonstrate the applicability of the proposed theory for a range of typologically different languages.

In this section I will make two steps towards this goal. First I will sketch out in general terms how Processability Theory can be applied to typologically different languages. The major part of this section will then, in a second step, deal with the application of the theory to particular second languages, namely English, Swedish and Japanese. In other words, predictions will be derived from Processability Theory for the SL development of these languages. These theoretical predictions will then be tested in empirical studies.

The logic of this test is as follows: if it can be demonstrated that the actual course of SL development follows the route predicted by the theory, then the status of that theory must be beyond a mere generalisation of observational facts for the language (German) in the context of which the theory was first developed.

Another empirical validation of Processability Theory will be based on data from on-line experiments which are presented in section 5.6. The logic behind presenting this empirical evidence is straightforward: The objective of Processability Theory is to model the development of the language processor in a second language. Therefore a direct test of the functioning of the processor in real time will provide valid empirical evidence relating to the assumed architecture of the processor.

5.1 Typological plausibility

It may be useful to recall the general nature of the mechanisms contained in the proposed theory: the analysis of the acquisition of German word order and morphology has shown that the concept of "exchange of grammatical information" within a theory of grammar captures the essence of an implicational hierarchy of processing procedures. What one would have to demonstrate now are two points:

(1) that "exchange of grammatical information" is a productive concept for typologically different languages, and

(2) that predictions that can be derived from the general architecture of the theory for specific languages will be borne out by empirical observations.

In this section I will restrict myself to the first point for the purpose of a brief sketch of my argument. The second point will be taken up in the sections that follow.

I noted earlier in this book that, according to the theory I developed here, there are several computationally simple ways of marking grammatical relations. I found that in English and German second language acquisition, the marking chosen by all learners is canonical word order. The computational simplicity of this solution lies in the fact that grammatical functions can be read off the positions of elements: in English the first NP is the subject, the second NP is the object etc. No grammatical information has to be exchanged for this marker to be effective.

This is exactly what Bever (1970) was aiming at with his NVN-strategy. However, the difference between Bever's strategies (cf. also Kimball 1973) and the proposed theory is that the latter is embedded in a theory of grammar rather than being a grammar substitute. This makes it possible to relate the canonical order phenomenon in acquisition to other word order phenomena and to morphological marking. These relationships establish an overall framework for the processability of syntactic and morphological structures.

In an extension of Bever's approach, Slobin and Bever (1982) claim that children use canonical sentence schemata to discover grammar. The problem with this claim is that for such a discovery process to have explanatory power it would have to be universal, while for non-configurational languages such as Walpiri (Simpson 1991) it would be utterly unproductive, because in these languages word order plays no role at all in the marking of grammatical relations. It is not plausible to assume universal discovery procedures which are ineffective for a whole class of languages, because, for those languages, procedures would have to be assumed which would be ineffective for the first set of languages. With this approach one would find oneself in a situation where for every new typological feature one would have to assume a new universal procedure.

In contrast, the proposed theory is not a discovery procedure; it is simply an *a priori* definition of constraints on processability. One possible outcome of these constraints is defined in terms of word order. However, the very same constraints can also define constraints on morphological marking in the presence or absence of word order constraints.

Processability Theory predicts that morphological marking allows for a solution of the initial hypothesis which is equally complex as canonical word order, namely the marking of grammatical functions by phrasal morphemes. Note that not *all* morphological markers of grammatical functions are phrasal morphemes. However, Turkish is a language in which grammatical functions can be directly read off c-structure: e.g. Turkish has a regular and obligatory direct object marker which does not exchange information with any other constituent. In this case, the affix can be inserted on the basis of the functional annotation that comes with every constituent, and no exchange of information is necessary between constituents.

Processability Theory predicts that in a language with regular and unambiguous morphological marking of grammatical functions these markers will be acquired at a similar developmental point to that at which word order is acquired as a marker of grammatical functions in configurational languages. Indeed there is empirical evidence in support of this view. Aksu (1978) found that children acquiring Turkish as L1 master the case marking system before the age of two: i.e. at a point in development when learners of English acquire basic canonical word order. Slobin and Bever (1982) derived the same findings from comprehension experiments with learners of English, Italian, Serbo-Croatian and Turkish.

Given that German uses word order *and* morphological marking for the marking of grammatical functions, one has to ask oneself why GSL learners opt for the canonical solution. To answer this question one has to remember that German case markers are different from Turkish ones for two reasons.

First, in German, one morphological form can denote several functions. This makes it harder to learn than morphemes with a one-to-one form-function relationship.

Table 5.1-1. Examples of morphological case marking in German

	masculine	feminine
nominative	der Baum	die Blume
genitive	des Baumes	der Blume
dative	dem Baum	der Blume
accusative	den Baum	die Blume
Translation:	*'Baum' - tree*	*'Blume' - flower*

In the example given in Table 5.1-1 it is easy to see that the forms "der" and "die" denote several functions.

Secondly, German case markers have to exchange information with the verb which licenses certain types of core arguments. The contrast between sentences (23) and (24) illustrates this point: German direct objects can be marked "dative" or "accusative" depending on the verb.

(23)   ich kaufe [*einem Freund*]$_{dirObj}$ ein Buch
    I   buy   a   friend   a   book

(24)   es   kostet [*einen Freund*]$_{dirObj}$-50 Dollar
    it   costs   a   friend   50 dollars

This means that for the morphological marking of grammatical objects to be produced, information has to be exchanged between the verb and the object. This exchange of grammatical information places object marking at a higher level in the hierarchy of processing procedures than canonical word order. Therefore, morphological object marking is not available in German as an initial hypothesis for the organisation of the sentence. The only option that is open to GSL learners for the initial marking of grammatical relations is canonical word order.

Neither do ESL learners have any other option than using canonical order marking. The reason for this, however, is simply because English does not mark grammatical function through affixation. In other words, this option is *structurally* not available.

5.2 English as L2

The previous section was merely a rough sketch of the typological validity of the proposed theory which was intended to illustrate the nature of the theory's predictive power: the availability of structural options to the learner is constrained by processing procedures on the one hand and the architecture of the target language on the other.

In this section Processability Theory will be applied to a range of morphological and syntactic structures in the acquisition of English as a second language. I will proceed as follows: First I will list a number of frequent inflectional morphemes and word order regularities which the learner has to acquire. I then characterise these rules within LFG. This characterisation serves as a basis for the analysis for transfer of grammatical information required for the production of these rules. The analysis of information transfer allows a prediction of the processability of these structures by L2 learners. Finally, these predictions will be tested empirically using results from Johnston's (1985) extensive study on adult ESL and a study of my own on child ESL.

The structures

Before I list the morphological structures which form part of the test it will be useful to remember that it is not the morphological process itself that my predictions are concerned with but certain pieces of grammatical information that the morphological process has to rely on.

The following morphological structures form part of the test:

- *Plural marking* on nouns (e.g. two dog-*s*),
- *possessive pronoun* (e.g. *my* house...),
- *S-V-agreement marking* (e.g. He eat-*s* at home)

In the area of syntax I will concentrate on word order. Generally speaking, word order is more constrained in English than in German. However, there are quite a number of structural similarities. The phenomena I will to look at in this section are the following:

- canonical order
- adverb fronting (ADV)
- Do-Fronting

- WH-Fronting
- yes-no inversion
- Do/Aux 2nd
- Cancel inversion

Canonical word order (SVO) can be found in most affirmative sentences in English. ADV refers to the occurrence of adverbs and adverbials in initial position of sentences.

By 'DO-Fronting' I do *not* refer to what is traditionally described as 'do-support'. While the latter implies one type of SV-agreement and is operational in negation and direct questions without auxiliary, 'do-fronting' isolates only one single aspect of this amalgamation of rules, namely the appearance of 'do' in initial position in the sentence for the purpose of marking direct questions. 'Do-fronting' therefore covers (25) as well as (26) and (27):

(25) do you like it?
(26) do he like it?
(27) do he have lunch yesterday?

WH-Fronting refers to the position of question words in sentence initial position. Note that in learner language the structure that follows can be canonical word order as in (28):

(28) Where you have been?

Yes/no-inversion refers to the syntactic pattern found in 'direct yes/no-question' in which the subject and the auxiliary are inverted as in (29).

(29) has he seen you?

"Do/Aux2nd" refers to inversion in WH-questions as in (30) to (32):

(30) Why did he sell that car?
(31) Where has he gone?
(32) What is she eating?

"Cancel inversion" describes the fact that the word order phenomena observed in direct questions do not apply in the context of indirect questions. This phenomenon is illustrated by adding a matrix clause to examples (28) - (32). The resulting sentences are given in (33) - (37).

(33) I wonder whether *he had lunch yesterday*.

(34) I wonder whether *he has seen you.*
(35) I wonder *why he sold that car.*
(36) I wonder *where he has gone.*
(37) I wonder *what she is eating.*

A processability hierarchy for English

Table 5.2-1 gives an overview of how these morphological[17] and syntactic structures can be accounted for in the proposed processability framework.

One thing is very obvious in Table 5.2-1, namely the similarity of the German hierarchy presented in Chapter 3 and the English hierarchy. This is not surprising, given that these languages are closely related. The reader will notice that this similarity continues when we turn to Swedish as a second language in section 5.3.

The morphological forms of English included in this hierarchy relate to processing procedures in a straight-forward manner. Diacritic features such as 'possessive' and 'number' are listed in the lexical entries of words. They can therefore be matched directly from conceptual structure and no exchange of grammatical information is required for this process as long as the diacritic feature is to be marked in one constituent only. This process can therefore occur at level 2.

Once diacritic features are to be marked in several constituents their value information has to be matched between constituents, grammatical

Table 5.2-1. Processing procedures applied to English

Processing procedure		L2 process	morphology syntax
6 • subord. cl. procedure		main and sub cl	Cancel INV
5 • S-procedure/ WO Rules -saliency	inter-phr info	SV agreement (= 3sg-s)	Do2nd, Aux2nd
4 • S-procedure/ WO Rules +saliency	inter-phr info		Y/N inv, PS inv
3 • phrasal procedure	phrasal info.	NP agr	ADV, Do-Front, Topi Neg+V
2 • category procedure	lex morph	plural possessive pro	canonical order
1 • word/ lemma	'words'	invariant forms	single constituent

information needs to be exchanged requiring phrasal or other procedures as repositories. Therefore phrasal agreement, such as plural agreement is predicted to occur at level 3. For instance, the relevant lexical entries for the phrase "many dogs" are as follows:

many: DET,   (SPEC)   =   MANY
             (NUM)   =   PL

dogs: N,   (PRED)   =   DOG
             (NUM)   =   PL

To achieve agreement marking, the value for the diacritic feature 'number' has to be unified between Det and N.

The situation is rather different with Subject-Verb *agreement* marking (i.e. "third-person singular-s"). As illustrated in section 3.5 above, the features for Number and Person have to be unified across constituent boundaries and the grammatical information consisting of the values of the diacritic features 'person' and 'number' have to be deposited in the S-procedure to be placed in the specified constituent of S. This is illustrated below:

[This man] $_{\text{NP}_{\text{subj}}}$ [owns] $_{\text{V}}$... (Present)
           | |
      Person = 3   Person = 3
      NUM = SG   NUM = SG

Word order

We will now look at how the syntactic phenomena contained in the ESL processability hierarchy can be accounted for by LFG and how this treatment justifies the position of the individual rules in the hierarchy. The general line of argument followed here is very similar to the analysis of German word order in section 3.3. In most points I will follow Kaplan and Bresnan (1982) and Pinker (1984).

Since there is only one level of c-structure in LFG, the canonical SVO order follows directly from c-structure rules such as R7 below:

(R7)   S → NP$_{\text{subj}}$ V (NP$_{\text{obj}}$) (ADJ) (S)

In other words, no exchange of grammatical information is needed here which places this rule at level 2 of the hierarchy. Note that no S-procedure has been developed at this point, and the learner can be expected to use a simplified version of that procedure which, in Chapter 3 and in Section 5.3 are argued to be based on a direct mapping of conceptual structures onto linguistic form.

ADV and WH-Front can also be derived from c-structure by allowing wh-words and adverbs to appear in focused positions (i.e. in XP position) — as shown in R8 below:

$$(\text{R8}) \quad S' \to (XP) \qquad\qquad S$$
$$\begin{Bmatrix} \text{wh} =_c + \\ \text{adv} =_c + \end{Bmatrix}$$

Comparing (R8) with its German counterpart (i.e. (R2) in section 3.3 above) one can see that the elements which are permitted in XP position are more constrained in English than in German.

Note that (R8), together with (R7), allows for sentences such as (38).

(38)   Where you have been?

We will see below that this type of sentence structure does indeed occur in the data.

The constraint equations in (R8) ensure that the XP position can only be filled by lexical material which is either a member of the class "*wh*-word" or "adverb". This notation further allows the researcher to trace the lexical nature of the acquisition process by describing the transition from a lexically to a categorially defined rule system. This would be possible by annotating the lexical elements permitted by the equation (e.g. $\text{wh} =_c$ '*who*'). This annotation will then at some stage become categorical (i.e. $\text{wh} =_c +$).

In terms of processability, the structures ADV and WH-Front are a modification of the serial order principle which allows the learner to map conceptual structures directly onto linguistic form:

agent action patient
N   V   N

The new structure (ADV S) modifies the seriality principle utilising the general cognitive principle of saliency which identifies initial and final positions and allows the canonical order principle to apply once the salient position have been processed:

INITIAL] agent   action   patient [FINAL
PP/wh/adv NP   V   NP

These additional word order options allow the learner to produce a range of L2 syntactic phenomena without acquiring the full range of L2 word order.

Also note that in the above representation of the canonical schema the constituents of the canonical sequence are described as phrases. This is so, because phrasal procedures are operational at this stage. This makes it possible for the canonical schema to allow a definition of 'position' in terms of phrases rather than words.

Do-FRONT can be generated if one assumes the following modification of (R7):

$$(\text{R 9}) \ S \rightarrow (V_{aux =_c \ 'do'}) \ NP_{subj} \ V \ (NP_{obj}) \ (ADJ) \ (S)$$

The constraint equation $aux =_c \ 'do'$ ensures that only the auxiliary 'do' can appear in the position of the first V. This treatment of Do-FRONT is similar to Bresnan's (1982) treatment of Aux-2nd, which is also based on a constraint equation at the level of c-structure. Note that this account of Do-FRONT only deals with the *position* of the aux not with its morphological form or that of the lexical verb. It therefore permits structures as in (39) and (40).

(39) Do she see him?
(40) Do he going home?

As the reader will see below, these are indeed structures that one finds at the same relative point in time as the first occurrences of Do-FRONT.

By generalising the above equation to $aux =_c \ +$ all auxiliaries are possible in initial position. This form of the rule then describes the *positional* facts of yes/no-inversion, while the morphological form of AUX and V are untouched.

To inform the morphological component, the feature values for INF and PARTICIPLE have to be unified between the auxiliary and the lexical verb, before any verb can be selected for the verb positions. The lexical entries for verbs would contain, amongst other things, the following features:

seen: V,   PRED = 'see' (SUBJ, OBJ)
           PARTICIPLE = PAST
           INF = +
           AUX = -

has: V,   PRED = 'have, V-COMP (SUBJ)'

TENSE = PAST

AUX = +

NUM = SG

PERSON = 3RD

V-COMP PARTICIPLE = PAST

V-COMP INF $=_c$ +

In this example the constraint equation V-COMP INF $=_c$ + listed under the entry for 'has' is checked against the INF value in the entry for 'seen'. This ensures that the complement does not define any tense. In other words, this provision rules out sentences such as (41) and (42).

(41) He has sees him.

(42) He has see him.

Such errors do, however, occur in ESL data. This means that not all the necessary features are listed in the entries to the learner's lexicon. In other words the unification of INF values described above accounts for this aspect of the learning process which constitutes phrasal agreement, and the latter occurs at level 3.

To account for auxiliaries in second position (Aux2nd) after preposed question words or preposed adverbs such as "never" (R8) needs to be modified along the lines of Kaplan and Bresnan's (1982) and Pinker's (1984) original proposal:

(R8a)   S' → (XP)   S

$$\left\{ \begin{array}{l} \text{wh} =_c + \\ \text{adv} =_c + \\ \text{SENT MOOD} = \text{INV} \end{array} \right\}$$

(R9) then has to be modified to be similar to (R4) used for the analysis of German above:

(R9a)   S' → (V)   S

$$\left\{ \begin{array}{l} \text{aux} =_c + \\ \text{ROOT} =_c + \\ \text{SENT MOOD} =_c \text{Inv} \end{array} \right\}$$

In this way it is guaranteed that (1) only auxiliaries appear in this position (in contrast to German), that (2) this position is filled only by in matrix sentences and (3) only after the constraints expressed in (R8a), i.e. in the context of preposed question words and some other lexical items.

Again, it is possible to account not only for structures that occur in mature English, but also for the dynamics of the learning process, i.e. for structures created by the learner on the way to acquiring target structures. For instance, it is known that Aux2nd is first acquired in the context of a limited number of preposed question words and certainly not in the context of preposed adverbs like "never". As I indicated above, the formalism used here can express this through an alteration of the constraint equations appended to XP.

In the same way it is possible to account for the application of Aux2nd to a limited set of auxiliaries or the over-application of this position to subordinate clauses (i.e. indirect questions). In the latter case the distinction +/- ROOT has not been appended to (R9a).

In terms of the processability hierarchy Do/Aux2nd occurs at level 5 because grammatical information needs to be exchanged between sentence constituents, namely the equation SENT MOOD $=_c$ Inv.

Cancel Inversion can be accounted for by assuming a linear c-structure for subordinate clauses — similar to that of stage 1 clauses.

(R 10) $S \rightarrow (COMP)_{ROOT=-} NP_{subj} (V)_{INF=+} (V)_{INF=-} (NP_{obj1}) (NP_{obj2}) (ADJ)$

This ensures that Aux2nd, Do-Fronting and ADV are blocked in subordinate clauses.

It is worth noting that this treatment again allows for a gradual acquisition of properties of English subordinate clauses. Learner data are full of seemingly unsystematic examples such as the following:

(x+13)   I asked if could he come home.
(x+14)   I asked when he could come home.

The seeming unsystematicity is nothing but a reflex of the lexical nature of the acquisition of Cancel Inversion. This imaginary learner has not properly classified question words and complementisers. In (X+13) "if" is not classified as complementiser so that the clause "if he could come home" is treated as a main clause, while in (X+14) "when" is classified as a complementiser and consequently the 'when-clause' is treated as being subordinated. The reader will recall that in the processability hierarchy the distinction between main and subordinate clauses occurs at level 6.

Testing the predictions: Johnston (1985)

I mentioned above that I will test the ESL processability hierarchy against two empirical studies. The first study is that by Johnston (1985) which consists of a total of 24 samples from Polish and Vietnamese adult immigrants in Australia. The results of Johnston's study for the 12 grammatical rules listed in Table 5.2-2 which is based on a subset of 16 informants were summarised by Johnston in Pienemann, Johnston and Brindley (1988). This summary is replicated with some amendments by Johnston (personal communication) in Table 5.2-2 below.

The full distributional analysis of this study is available in Johnston (1985). I will therefore focus on the summary of his analysis, i.e. after the application of the emergence-based acquisition criterion. The true size of the corpus may not be obvious from the compact format of Table 5.2-1. I would therefore like to point out that each of the 16 interviews was between 40 and 60 minutes in length, resulting in a 60,000 word corpus.

Table 5.2-2 is laid out as an implicational table (cf. section 4.2). The 12 grammatical rules of English discussed above are listed on the left-hand side in their order of processability. For each learner and rule a '+' marks rules which have been acquired according to our emergence criterion (cf. section 4.2); a '-' marks those rules which have not been acquired, and a '/' marks those rules for which there is no linguistic context in the sample.

They key issue in reading this implicational table is to check to what extent the hypothesised implicational relationships hold, i.e. to check if it is true that for every rule and learner the acquisition of highest rule in the hierarchy implies the acquisition of all lower-level rules. The reader will recall that the implicational relationship is contradicted if there is 'negative evidence' (cf. section 4.2, marked '-' above) for any rule in the hierarchy in the presence of positive evidence (marked '+') for any higher-level rule.

The scalability of Table 5.2-1 is 100%. This means that there is not a single piece of evidence to contradict the hypothesised implicational pattern, and this means that Johnston's study strongly supports the English processability hierarchy.

There are several factors which add to the strength of this support. First of all, five of the six levels of processability are documented in the above analysis. This means that for each of the five levels there is at least one speaker for whom the given level is the highest. This demonstrates that every

Table 5.2-2. Adult learners of ESL

Stage	Structure	van	IS	my	ks	tam	long	vinh	jr	sang	bb	ka	es	ij	ja	dung	phuc
6	Cancel Inversion	−	−	−	−	−	−	−	−	−	−	−	−	−	−	−	−
5	Aux2nd/ Do2nd	−	−	−	−	−	−	−	−	−	−	−	−	−	−	+	+
4	3 sg-s	−	−	−	−	−	−	−	−	−	−	−	−	+	+	+	+
	Y/N Inversion	−	−	−	−	−	−	−	−	+	+	+	+	/	/	+	+
	PS Inversion	−	−	−	−	+	+	+	+	/	+	+	+	+	+	/	/
3	Neg+V	−	−	−	+	+	+	+	+	+	+	+	+	+	+	+	+
	Do Front.	−	−	+	+	+	/	+	+	+	+	+	+	+	+	+	+
	Topi	−	−	+	+	+	+	+	+	+	+	+	+	+	+	+	+
	ADV	−	+	+	+	+	+	+	+	+	+	+	+	+	+	+	+
2	SVO	−	+	+	+	+	+	+	+	+	+	+	+	+	+	+	+
	Plural	−	+	+	+	+	+	+	+	+	+	+	+	+	+	+	+
1	single words	+	/	/	/	/	/	/	/	/	/	/	/	/	/	/	/

Legend: + acquired − not acquired / no context

level is a genuine entity that is separate from the other levels.

The second contributing factor is the richness of the database. This is evident in the small number of slashes ('/') in Table 5.2-2. A slash indicates that there were no contexts for an obligatory rule or, in the case of an optional rule, that there were no instances. Cases marked in this way have to be considered gaps in the corpus (cf. section 4.2). Leaving aside one constituent utterances[18], such gaps occur in merely 3.125% of Johnston's corpus. In other words, in this corpus it hardly ever happens that it provides neither evidence for nor against the hypothesised hierarchy.

Child ESL

The second ESL study is based on samples collected from 13 children aged 8 to 10 years (Pienemann and Mackey 1993)[19]. The samples were collected using the range of communicative tasks described in section 6.5 below. Table 5.2-3 sets out some of the key bio-data of this group of informants.

Table 5.2-4 displays the implicational analysis of this corpus. Table 5.2-4 is set out in the same way as Table 5.2-2 for the Johnston study. The only difference is that in the child ESL study two additional structures were included, namely 'pronoun case' and 'possessive pronouns' which at the time were hypothesised to be located at level 2 of the ESL processability hierarchy.

Table 5.2-3. Bio-data of child learners of ESL

Subject ID	Sex	Age	L1	Length of residence
1.1	F	9	Polish	7 months
1.2	F	8	Hindi	8 months
1.3	F	8	Syrian	11 months
1.4	F	8	Khmer	6 months
1.5	M	9	Spanish	11 months
1.6	M	8	Khmer	8 months
1.7	M	8	Polish	8 months
2.1	M	8	Spanish	9 months
2.2	M	9	Spanish	11 months
2.3	M	8	Spanish	60 months
2.4	F	8	Spanish	22 months
2.5	F	10	Spanish	44 months
2.6	F	9	Spanish	22 months

As in the Johnston study, the scalability of Table 5.2-4 is 100%, i.e. there is no contradictory evidence to the hypothesised hierarchy, and this includes the two additional structures. While this study lends strong additional support to the empirical accuracy of the ESL processability hierarchy, the internal consistency of this study is not quite as strong as that of Johnston's study.

Firstly, the gaps in this corpus amount to some 24%. This means that in about a quarter of all structures per informant there is no evidence for or against the hypothesis to be tested. While this in no way disqualifies the hypothesis it highlights the fact that this corpus is not as rich as that in Johnston's study.

The second limitation is that not all structures are documented by at least one learner who displays evidence that the structure marks a developmental step. Again, this does not falsify the hypothesised sequence, but the data are not sufficiently rich to support all of the structures. One very clear example is that of one constituent utterances. While these do appear in the data, there is no individual learner who produces this structure and no other structures. To prove that one constituent utterances mark a developmental level one would have to 'supply' such an informant. The reader will notice that the Johnston study does indeed discriminate between all the structures of the hierarchy, except for Cancel Inversion. However the latter is documented in the child ESL study.

Summing up, Johnston's (1996) study produces strong evidence in support of the ESL processability hierarchy. Taken with this, the child ESL study (Pienemann and Mackey 1993) strengthens and supports this position.

Table 5.2-4. Child learners of ESL: implicational table

Stage	Structure	1:7	1:4	1:2	1:3	2:3	1:5	2:2	2:1	2:5	2:4	1::6	2.6	1:1
6	Cancel Inversion	/	/	/	/	/	/	/	/	/	/	–	/	+
5	Aux2nd/ Do2nd	/	/	–	/	–	/	+	+	+	+	+	/	/
	3 sg-s	–	–	–	–	+	+	+	+	+	+	+	+	+
4	Y/N Inversion	/	/	/	/	+	/	+	+	+	+	/	+	/
	Particle verbs	/	/	/	+	+	+	+	+	+	+	+	+	+
	Copula Inversion	/	/	/	/	+	/	+	+	+	+	/	+	/
3	Neg+V	+	+	+	+	+	+	+	+	+	+	+	+	+
	Do Front.	/	/	+	/	/	/	+	+	+	+	/	/	/
	Topi	+	+	+	+	+	/	+	+	+	+	+	+	+
	ADV	+	/	+	+	+	+	+	+	+	+	/	+	/
2	SVO	+	+	+	+	+	+	+	+	+	+	+	+	+
	Plural	+	+	+	+	+	+	+	+	+	+	+	+	+
	possessive pronoun	+	+	+	/	+	+	+	+	+	+	/	/	+
1	single words	+	+	/	/	/	+	/	/	/	/	/	+	/

Legend: + *acquired* – *not acquired* / *no context*

5.3 Swedish as L2[20]

This section deals with the application of Processability Theory to Swedish interlanguage (SSL). The reason for applying Processability Theory to Swedish is that a vast amount of data is available on SSL which can serve as a basis for testing the proposed theory. In other words, predictions will be derived from Processability Theory for SSL development, and these theoretical predictions will be tested in empirical studies of SSL acquisition.

Our test of Processability Theory will focus on morphological and syntactic structures in SSL. First a number of frequent inflectional morphemes and word order regularities will be described which the learner has to acquire and these rules will be characterised within LFG. This characterisation then serves as a basis for the analysis of the exchange of grammatical information required for the production of these rules. The analysis of information exchange then allows a prediction of the processability of these structures by L2 learners which will be tested against fourteen empirical studies.

Swedish morphology

Before I list the morphological structures which form part of our test it will be useful to remember that it is not the morphological process itself that our predictions are concerned with but certain pieces of grammatical information that the morphological process has to rely on. Therefore, I will be looking

Table 5.3-1. Swedish morphology and processability

Processing procedures	L2 processes	Swedish morphology
5 • subord. clause procedure	main and sub clause	
4 • S-procedure/ WO Rules	inter-phr info	adjective agreement in predicative constructions
3 • Phrasal procedure	phrasal info	definiteness agreement markings in NPs, compound tense markings in VPs
2 • category procedure	lexical morphemes	plural marking (no agreement), definiteness on nouns, past, present tense on verbs
1 • word/ lemma	'words'	invariant forms

specifically for morphology that can be used to test the predicted differences between lexical, phrasal and inter-phrasal morphology. Table 5.3-1 lists the relevant morphological rules for Swedish in relation to the hierarchy of processing procedures.

The noun phrase

Before I detail the morphological forms in Swedish noun phrases, I would like to point out that the constituent structure of Swedish NPs is similar to English. The major contrast to English NPs is the morphological structure of their constituents. Basically, a full noun phrase may consist of the following constituents:

(Det) (AP) N

This highly simplified account ignores multiple embedding of adjectival phrases, embedded clauses and adverbials and the nature of the optionality of some of the above constituents. Instead, it concentrates on more basic structures which are relevant to the studies discussed below. In Swedish, NPs, articles and adjectives agree with the head noun. There are several dimensions of agreement which involve the diacritic features 'gender', 'number' and 'definiteness'.

There are five different forms of the article: *en, ett* (= a, indefinite, sing), *det, den* (=the, definite, sing) and *de* (=the, plural) The form system is summarised in Figure 5.3-1.

In its attributive function the adjective agrees with the head noun of the noun phrase. In its predicative function the adjective agrees with the subject. The diacritic features 'gender', 'number' and 'definiteness'[21] are simultaneously marked by one affix which can take three forms: a zero morpheme, the suffix *t,* and the suffix *a.* The contexts for these markings are given in Figure 5.3-2.

Figure 5.3-1. Swedish articles

	indefinite		definite	
	sing	pl	sing	pl
uter	en	–	den	de
neuter	ett	–	det	de

Figure 5.3-2. Swedish adjectival affixes

	attributive			
	indefinite		definite	
	sing	pl	sing	pl
uter	Ø	a	a	a
neuter	t	a	a	a

	predicative			
	indefinite		definite	
	sing	pl	sing	pl
uter	Ø	a	Ø	a
neuter	t	a	t	a

Nouns can be morphologically marked for gender, number and definiteness. They can also be marked for genitive. However, the latter will be disregarded for the purpose of this paper because it has not been part of any SLA studies. The suffixes used to mark the above diacritic features agglutinate in some cases:

(43) hund - ar   -   na
      dog - UTER/PLURAL - DEFINITE
      "the dogs"

In many cases two or three diacritic features are expressed by the same suffix:

(44) hund - ar
      dog - UTER/PLURAL/INDEFINITE
      "dogs" (as in "dogs are smart")

Suffixes on nouns agglutinate only if they express the following combination of diacritic features:

(i)   plural + definite (+genitive)
(ii) definite + genitive

The morphemes that mark the different diacritic features possible on nouns are listed in Figure 5.3-3. The reader will notice that in some cases there is a choice of different morphemes, e.g. a zero morpheme or "-or" or "-ar" to mark uter, indefinite and plural. The choice of the form of the marker depends on the declension class of the noun. There are five different classes and a set of irregular nouns.

Figure 5.3-3. Affixes on nouns in Swedish

	indefinite		definite	
	sing	pl	sing	pl
uter	Ø	Ø, or, ar, (e)r	(e)n	na
neuter	Ø	Ø, n, (e)r	(e)t	en, na

Lexical morphemes

We can now proceed to analyse the above morphological structures in terms of their processability. Morphological plural marking in nouns is based on the lexical entry. When no other constituent of the NP has to agree with the head, this is an example of a lexical morpheme. For instance, the relevant lexical entry for the word "hund-ar" (dogs) is as follows:

> hundar: N, PRED = 'HUND' ("dog")
> NUM = PL

Lexical morphemes also occur in the marking of definiteness and gender. As mentioned above, these two diacritic features are marked by one morpheme. There are two different genders, uter and neuter, with different morphemes ((e)n and (e)t) for definite form.

> hunden: N, PRED = 'HUND' ("dog")
> SPEC = DEFINITE
> GENDER = uter
>
> huset: N, PRED = 'HUS' ("house")
> SPEC = DEFINITE
> GENDER = neuter

Again, on its own, this marker is lexical.

Phrasal morphology

A specific feature of Swedish is the simultaneous marking of definiteness on the article and the noun. Unlike in German and in English, definiteness has to

Figure 5.3-4. Lexical entries for the example 'den stora hunden'

den:	DET,	PRED = "den" ("the")
		GENDER = UTER
		SPEC = DEFINITE
		NUM = SING
stora:	ADJ	PRED = "stor" ("big")
		NUM =SING
		SPEC = WEAK
hunden:	N,	PRED = "hund" ("dog)
		GENDER = UTER
		NUM = SING
		SPEC = DEFINITE

be marked on the article and the noun when a noun phrase contains an adjective. In this context the article is obligatory and the adjectival ending is weak. This is illustrated in the following example:

$$[[den] \ [stor\text{-}a]_{Det} \ hund\text{-}en]_{N}]_{NP}$$

UTER	DEF	UTER
DEF		DEF
SING		SING
"the"	"big"	"dog"

The lexical entries for this example are given in Figure 5.3-4.

The above examples illustrate phrasal morphology in Swedish. Here the features for gender, number and definiteness must be unified across constituents within the phrase.

Inter-phrasal morphology

Some of the same morphological markers that are used in phrasal agreement in the NP can also be used inter-phrasally, when the features are unified across phrases with predicative adjectives, i.e. in sentences with copular verbs. This is demonstrated in Figure 5.3-5.

In the examples above, the features "gender" and "number" are unified across the different phrases, and, therefore, they belong to level 4 in the processability hierarchy. Adjectival agreement in predicative adjectives is inter-phrasal only if one can be certain that the learner language has devel-

Figure 5.3-5. Interphrassl agreement in equational sentences

[Hus-et]$_{NP_{subj}}$ [är]$_V$ (Pres) [stor-t]$_{Adj}$	
| |	
GENDER = NEUTER GENDER = NEUTER	
NUM = SING NUM = SING	

oped equational sentences. In simplified interlanguages Noun-Adj sequences may occur which may be structurally ambiguous, e.g.

(45) hund-en stor

which could be analysed as

$[[[hunden]_N]_{NP} [\emptyset] [stor]_A]_S$ or as

$[[hunden]_N [stor]_A]_{NP}$

To assign an inter-phrasal status to Noun-Adj sequences there has to be distributional evidence that equational sentences are part of the interlanguage system. This can be decided on the basis of the presence of the copula and on the basis of the adjectival morphology in definite contexts. In the latter case the distribution of the morphological form of the marker for definiteness, gender and number is complementary in attributive and predicative contexts, i.e.

(46) den *stor-a* hunden (attributive)
(47) hunden är *stor* (predicative)
(48   det *stor-a* hus-et (attributive)
(49) hus-et är *stort* (predicative)

This complementary distribution can be used to test the presence of equational sentences in the interlanguage system in question.

Verbal morphology

Like English, the Swedish verb phrase may consist of one or many verbs. One of the verbs in a clause is marked +FINITE. The others are marked - FINITE. Only one verb can be marked +FINITE. This verb has to be marked for TENSE.[22] The morphological forms of these markers are shown in Figure 5.3-6. They vary according to verb classes. The morphemes that mark the two

Figure 5.3-6. Verbal affixes

	Present	Past
+FIN	r, er	de, dde, te
	Infinitive	Supine
–FIN	Ø, a	t, it

types of infinitives are also shown in Figure 5.3-6. They, too, vary according to verb classes.

Examples (50)-(53) illustrate the use of morphemes displayed in 5.3-6 above.

(50) de prata-r
      (they talk-PRES)

(51) de prata-de
      (they talk-PAST)

(52) de ska prata
      (they will talk-INF)

(53) de har prata-t
      (they have talk-SUPINE)

In examples (50)-(51) the diacritic features PRESENT and PAST can be directly inferred from conceptual structure and are located in the lexical entry. No exchange of grammatical information is needed. This type of tense marking can therefore be classified as lexical morphology.

Examples (52)-(53) show morphological markers of tense for which feature values have to be unified between the auxiliary and the main verb. To inform the morphological component, the feature values for INF and SUPINE have to be unified with an auxiliary, before any verb can be selected for the verb positions. The lexical entries for verbs would contain, amongst other things, the following features:

> pratat: V,   PRED = 'prata' (talk) (SUBJ, OBJ)
>   TENSE = PAST
>   INF = t
>   AUX = -

har: V,   PRED = 'har' (has), V-COMP (SUBJ)'
                     TENSE = PAST
                     AUX = +
                     V-COMP TENSE = PAST
                     V-COMP INF $=_c$ +

In example (53) the constraint equation V-COMP INF $=_c$ + listed under the
entry for 'har' is checked against INF value in the entry for 'pratat'. This
ensures that the complement does not define any tense. In other words, this
provision rules out sentences such as (54) and (55).

(54) *Han har pratar.
      (he has$_{PRES}$ talk$_{PRES}$)

(55) *Han har prata
      (He has$_{PRES}$ talk$_{INF)}$

Such errors do, however, occur in SSL data. When this happens, it means that
not all the necessary features are listed in the entries to the learner's lexicon or
they are not matched. When the features are matched across the two verbs this
feature unification defines the underlying process as phrasal morphology,
located at level 3 of the processability hierarchy. Table 5.3-1 gives an overview of the hierarchy of processability for all Swedish morphological structures discussed above.

Syntax

In the area of syntax I will concentrate on word order in main and subordinate
clauses and on the position of the negator. The following phenomena will be
discussed in this section:

- canonical word order   neg + verb
- adverb fronting (=ADV)   (Aux) neg + verb
- WH-Fronting   Verb + neg
- yes-no inversion   Neg + verb in sub clauses
- INV
- Cancel inversion

Before I go into detail it might be useful to take another look at the schema
presented above and see how Swedish syntactic structures fit into the general

Table 5.3-2. Processing procedures applied to Swedish word order, morphology and negation

Processing procedures	L2 structure	morphology	syntax	negation
5 • subord.clause procedure	main and sub cl	Cancel INV	neg V_f	
4 • S-procedure/ WO Rules	inter-phr info	pred. agr	INV	X V_f NP_s neg
3 • phrasal procedure	phrasal info.	NP agr VPagr	ADV WH fronting	V_f neg
2 • category procedure	lexical morph	pl, def past, pres	canonical order	(Aux) V neg (Aux) neg V neg V
1 • word/ lemma	'words'	invariant forms	single const.	neg+X

pattern. Table 5.3-2 displays these structures in relation to the level of processing procedures by adding two rows to Table 5.3-2.

Word order

Canonical word order can be found in most affirmative sentences in Swedish. In LFG, canonical word order follows directly from c-structure rules such as R3 below:

(R3) S → NP_{subj} V (NP_{obj1}) (NP_{obj2})

In other words, canonical word order requires no exchange of grammatical information. It is therefore positioned at level 2.

"ADV" refers to the occurrence of adverbs and adverbials in initial position of sentences. ADV requires the addition of one constituent to the given set of c-structure rules in initial position:

S' → (ADV) S

Note that in the target grammar this structure must be accompanied by the verb in second (INVERSION) position to be grammatical. Nevertheless, ADV without INVERSION is frequent in interlanguage. An example is given in (56).

(56) *Igår han reste till Stockholm
       adv - NP_{subj} - V - PP
       ('yesterday he went to Stockholm')

In terms of processability this structure is a modification of the serial order principle which allows the learner to map conceptual structures directly onto linguistic form:

> agent action patient
> N   V   N

The new structure (ADV S) modifies the seriality principle utilising the general cognitive principle of saliency which identifies initial and final positions and allows the canonical order principle to apply once the salient position have been processed:

> INITIAL]   agent   action   patient [FINAL
> PP/wh/adv   NP   V   NP

These additional word order options allow the learner to produce a range of L2 syntactic phenomena without acquiring the full range of L2 word order.

Also note that in the above representation of the canonical schema the constituents of the canonical sequence are described as phrases. This is so, because phrasal procedures are operational at this stage. This makes it possible for the canonical schema to allow a definition of 'position' in terms of phrases rather than words.

By "WH-Fronting" I refer to the position of question words in sentence initial position. As in ADV, the structure that follows can be canonical order in learner language (as in (57)) which is ungrammatical in Swedish.

> (57) *Var du bor?
>   WH - NP$_{subj}$- V
>   ('Where you live?')

"INVERSION" refers to subject-verb inversion in declaratives with an adverb or object in initial position and to inversion in interrogatives. This is illustrated by (58).

> (58) Igår *reste han* till Stockholm
>   adv - V- NP$_{subj}$ - PP
>   ('Yesterday *went he* to Stockholm')

English subject-verb inversion was discussed in section 2.3 above where it was noted that (R1) and (R2) can account for this syntactic phenomenon. It was also noted that a lexical redundancy rule for wh-words ensures that the filling of the focus position creates the information "sentence MOOD = inv" and this information then feeds into the equation in (R2) which licences a verb in a position left of NP_{subj}.

Swedish subject-verb INVERSION can be accounted for by some variation on (R1) and (R2). For this purpose, c-structure has to be modified somewhat. The modifications suggested here are adaptations from Bresnan and Kaplan's (1982) and Pinker's (1984) treatment of inversion in English, which assumes that there is an optional verb to the left of S as illustrated below:

(R4) S' → (V) S

Pinker adds the constraining equation $ROOT =_c +$ to the verb position in this rule to ensure that inversion only applies to matrix (i.e. "root") sentences (i.e. the feature ROOT is constrained to be + in matrix and as - in embedded clauses). This distinction is also relevant to the analysis of Swedish, where INVERSION is blocked in embedded clauses.

Pinker (1984) further adds the constraining equation $SENT\ MOOD =_c INV$ to the verb position in order to be able to allow the rule to constrain INVERSION *lexically* in elements which can occur in topicalised position (cf. (R2) above). The resulting rule is given in (R5).

$$(R5)\ \ S' \to (V) \qquad\qquad\qquad S$$
$$\left\{ \begin{array}{l} ROOT =_c + \\ SENT\ MOOD =_c Inv \end{array} \right\}$$

Similar to Pinker I suggest the equation $SENT\ MOOD =_c Inv$ is checked against a set of lexical redundancy rules which operate on (R6) so that INVERSION can be triggered by the application of (R6).

$$(R6)\ \ S' \to (XP) \qquad\qquad S$$
$$\left\{ \begin{array}{l} wh =_c + \\ adv =_c + \\ N =_c + \end{array} \right\}$$

In effect, the elements listed in the constraining equation and the associated lexical redundancy rule now ensure that the equation SENT MOOD = Inv feeds into the constraining equation SENT MOOD $=_c$ Inv, appended to V in (R5). In English the elements which trigger inversion include wh-words and adverbs (cf. Steele 1981), while in Swedish the class of these words is much larger.

(R6) now allows INVERSION to occur with topicalised wh-words, adverbs, PPs and NPs.

Since the process described above for Swedish subject-verb inversion involves the exchange of information across constituent boundaries into sentence-internal position it corresponds to level 4 of the processability hierarchy.

It is possible to account not only for structures that occur in mature Swedish, but also for the dynamics of the learning process, i.e. for structures created by the learner on the way to acquiring target structures. For instance, it is known that INV is first acquired in the context of a limited number of preposed question words and preposed adverbs. The formalism used here can express this through an alteration of the constraint equations appended to XP.

"Yes/no-inversion" refers to the syntactic pattern found in a 'direct yes/no-question' in which the subject and the verb are inverted as in (59).

(59) Bor du här?
      V - NP$_{subj}$ - adv
      ('Live you here?')

This structure can be produced by (R5), and the constraint equation appended to V would be satisfied when one assumes a mechanism which creates the equation SENT MOOD = INV for all questions. Because of the similarity of information distribution this rule is to be positioned at the same level in the hierarchy as INVERSION.

"Cancel inversion" describes the fact that the word order phenomena observed in direct questions do not apply in the context of indirect questions. This phenomenon is illustrated by adding a matrix clause to example (59). The resulting sentence is given in example (60).

(60) Jag undrar om *du bor här*
      NP$_{subj}$ - V - WH -NP$_{subj}$ - V - adv
      ('I wonder *if you live here*')

Cancel Inversion can be accounted for by assuming a linear c-structure for subordinate clauses — similar to that of stage 1 clauses.

(R 7) S' → (COMP)$_{ROOT =-}$ S

(R 3) S → NP$_{subj}$ V (NP$_{obj1}$) (NP$_{obj2}$)

This ensures that ADV and INV are blocked in subordinate clauses. In this way it is also possible to account for the over-application of this position to subordinate clauses (i.e. indirect questions). In the latter case the distinction +/- ROOT has not been appended to (R5).

Placement of negation

To account for the position of the negator (R3) is amended as follows:

   (R4) S → NP$_{subj}$ V$_f$ neg (V$_i$) (NP$_{obj}$) (PP)

In other words, the negator is positioned to the left of the non-finite verb. This also applies in conjunction with subject-verb inversion (cf. above). In the latter case the word order constellation is as follows.

           X V$_f$ NP$_{subj}$ neg (V$_i$) (NP$_{obj}$) (PP)
   or
           X V$_f$ neg NP$_{subj}$ (V$_i$) (NP$_{obj}$) (PP)

As can be seen, in inverted sentences the negator is positioned to the left of the optional non-finite verb. The negator is placed either after or before the subject, depending on how the information is structured.

   In subordinate clauses the negator always occurs in preverbal position:

           NP$_{subj}$ neg V$_f$ (V$_i$) (NP$_{obj}$) (PP)

There are several non-target negation constructions which occur in learner Swedish and which conform to a canonical order pattern. One example is the structure *neg+V*, i.e. preverbal negation which is ungrammatical in Swedish main clauses which is exemplified by (61). This structure can be interpreted as constituent negation and thus be produced at phrasal level. It therefore requires no exchange of grammatical information and can occur at level 2, (category procedure) above. A similar analysis of *neg+V* as constituent negation has also been proposed by Bolander (1988:23) and by Clahsen, Meisel & Pienemann (1983).

   (61) Jag inte bor här
         NP$_{subj}$ - Neg - V - adv
         ('I no live here')

A second learner construction is (Aux) neg + V. In other words, here, neg + V has been complemented by an optional auxiliary. As long as the tense marking is not co-ordinated between Aux and V this structure requires no exchange of information and can occur at level 2. Tense marking that *is* co-ordinated between Aux and V occurs at level 3 (cf. above).

A third interlanguage variant of Swedish negation is quite similar to the previous one. In this case the negator is placed after the lexical verb:

X Aux V neg

This structure is ungrammatical in Swedish. Even this superficial error analysis demonstrates that the main problem of the learner is to differentiate between finite and non-finite verbs. None of the above interlanguage forms is sensitive to finiteness. Once finiteness is acquired the correct position of the negator can be described by one simple c-structure rule (cf. R4 above)

To achieve the correct position of the negator in subordinate clauses the learner has to develop special processing procedures for subordinate clauses and no longer treat subordinate clauses as matrix clauses. This phenomenon is similar to the position of verbs in German subordinate clauses and in English and Swedish indirect questions.

In summary, there are seven structures relating to Swedish negation which occur in interlanguage data. According to the implementation of Processability Theory they are predicted to emerge in the sequence depicted in Table 10. From a processing point of view, the structures listed under level 2 are equivalent to each other. Nevertheless, we will see in the following section that they emerge in two sub-stages.

Testing the predictions

For the purpose of testing the theoretical predictions discussed in section 3, the fourteen major empirical studies on the acquisition of Swedish morpho-syntax will be reviewed. Research on Swedish as L2 has been conducted for about twenty years and there is a large body of studies, longitudinal as well as cross-sectional. They cover topics that go far beyond the focus of this paper, including phonology (Johansson 1973), the lexicon (Kotsinas 1982), lexical semantics (Viberg 1993) code-switching (Andersson and Nauclér 1988) and socio-linguistic variables (Boyd 1985). Most of these studies are descriptive. Within the set of studies that examine morpho-syntactic development we will review only those that are published, and for each researcher his or her main exposition of their work was chosen.

Although these studies represent a very large body of research, they have never been compiled and presented in one unifying framework. The objective of this section is to paste together as much as possible of the picture of developing Swedish as L2. In doing this it will soon become clear that the many studies involved were designed with different research questions in mind. Therefore the empirical methods employed are rather diverse and many authors, although interested in related issues, did not address some of the questions pursued in this section. The overarching organisational principle of this section is, of course, that of developmental grammars.

In other words, I will compile whatever evidence is available to construct as coherent a picture as possible of developmental patterns in the acquisition of SSL morphosyntax. In this context, one will have to be mindful of three things: (1) Different studies may produce contradictory findings. (2) The acquisition criteria are not the same in different studies. There are considerable differences between studies in this respect. Some researchers have applied a target perspective, and used correctness as the criterion; others have used a learner perspective and looked at occurrences of structures. (3) In some studies the structures in question may be absent from the corpus. When this is the case it will be important to establish whether the absence of these data is due to a lack of opportunity to produce the structure or whether the context for the structure is present and the learner failed to produce it. In other words, one has to be mindful of how to falsify the hypothesised developmental patterns of SSL. The issue of falsifiability of processability is discussed in detail in section 4.2. Here I merely want to state the principle I will apply: A hypothesised sequence will be falsified if empirical evidence shows a different sequence containing all the original elements.

Acquisition of morphology

Several studies of SSL deal with the acquisition of morphology, especially the acquisition of noun phrase morphology which is known to present difficulties for L2 learners of Swedish. There are studies focusing on how learners assign gender to the noun (e.g. Andersson 1992), studies on acquisition of definiteness (e.g. Axelsson 1994) and studies on the acquisition of agreement in noun phrases between article, adjective and noun (e.g. Hammarberg 1996, Lahtinen 1993, Salameh et al. forthcoming). These studies provide a rich testing ground for Processability Theory.

Table 5.3-3. Studies of SSL morphology

Study	Design	Period	Data collection	Subjects	L1
Andersson 1992	longi-tudinal	1-3 years	conversations	12 children	8 different
- " -	longi-tudinal	1-2 years	interviews retelling	4 adults	Finnish Spanish
Axelsson 1994	combined longi-tudinal and cross-sectional	5 months	interviews, picture description	60 adults	Finnish Polish Spanish
Hammar-berg 1996	longitudinal	1,5 years	interviews	6 adults	Chinese Greek Portuguese
Lahtinen 1993	cross-sectional		written compositions	342 adults	Finnish
Noyau 1992	longi-tudinal	1-3 years	interview retellings	4 adults	Finnish Spanish
Salameh et al forthc.	cross-sectional		conversation story retelling	18 children	Arabic
Viberg 1991	longi-tudinal	4 years	interviews retellings	30 children	different

Studies on the acquisition of verbal morphology are less pertinent to the issues discussed in this paper since they focus on the acquisition of tense from a semantic/pragmatic aspect, rather than on the form of morphological markers (e.g. Viberg 1991).

Table 5.3-3 summarises the empirical basis of the major studies on the acquisition of Swedish morphology.

The studies listed in Table 5.3-3 vary greatly in design, data collection methods, age and L1 of the learners. These studies also differ with respect to the research questions that are posed and the theoretical framework they are based on. In some studies, L2 acquisition is compared to child L1 acquisition. Other studies are based on L2 error analysis while yet another group of studies is aimed at describing developmental patterns found in interlanguage data.

Acquisition of the noun phrase

Table 5.3-1 displays the predictions of Processability Theory in relation to some morphological structures of Swedish. Lexical morphology is predicted to be acquired before phrasal and inter-phrasal morphology. In the following survey of empirical studies on L2 Swedish, I will therefore specifically look for examples of lexical morphology (i.e. plural and definite suffixes on nouns), phrasal and inter-phrasal morphology (i.e. agreement marking).

Most studies on SSL noun phrases do indeed provide empirical evidence, against which these hypotheses can be tested. The only exception is Axelsson's (1994) study on semantic aspects of definiteness. Because of her focus on semantics, the morphological form of the constituents of the NP was not studied. Nevertheless, this study does show that there is an initial stage devoid of morphological markers. This lends support to Stage 1 in the Swedish processability hierarchy.

Andersson's (1992) study examines the acquisition of gender assignment in L1 children, early L2 children (under three years of age), late L2 children (over three years) and L2 adults. For the purpose of the present discussion, it is important to keep in mind that Andersson is not interested in the morphological process *per se*, but in morphology as a marker of gender. However, in his analysis of gender he also captures aspects of the acquisition of noun morphology. He argues that "... the acquisition of gender is closely linked to the acquisition of the Swedish system of definiteness/indefiniteness, notably the suffixed definite article (...) The learner who acquires nouns with definite suffixes gets an entrance into the Swedish gender system as part and parcel of the bargain" (Andersson 1992, 208).

Apart from his major study of group levels of accuracy in gender assignment, Andersson also describes the development of noun phrase morphology in terms of learner language in an in-depth study of one L2 child, Lien. Andersson observes the development of noun phrase morphology, based on the first emergence of forms. He bases his analysis on clusters of recordings as set out below.

• Recording cluster 3	N (invariant form)	docka (doll)
• Recording cluster 4-5	N+ definite suffix	dockan (doll-the)
• Recording cluster 6-7	N N+ definite suffix	docka (doll) dockan (doll-the)
• Recording cluster 8	Det+N+suffix	den dockan (that doll-the)
• Recording cluster 9	N+ def suffix Indef art + N	dockan (doll-the) en docka (a doll)
• Recording cluster 10	N N+ def suffix Indef art + N	docka (doll) dockan (doll-the) en docka (a doll)

The above summary shows that there is an early stage (recording cluster 3) which contains no morphological marking at all. This is followed by a stage (recording clusters 4-5 and 6-7) when Lien starts using lexical gender marking on the noun, thus differentiating between base form and definite form. Then phrasal marking (agreement), starts to appear. When these markers first appear there is a period of overgeneralisation where the indefinite article is used in combination with definite suffix. Andersson's interpretation is that at this stage Lien uses the noun marked for definiteness as an unanalysed chunk. After this period agreement between article and noun emerges.

Summing up, this study provides strong empirical support for the processability hierarchy as applied to Swedish NPs. The development NP morphology follows exactly the predictions of the theory, starting with no morphology, then lexical morphology and after that phrasal morphology.

Lahtinen's (1993) study is focused on plural and gender agreement marking on determiners, adjectives and nouns by Finnish learners of Swedish in Finnish schools. Lahtinen analyses over fourteen thousand noun phrases in the learner's written production. As the point of departure she chose to compare the number of arithmetically possible combinations of the morphological forms of article, adjective and noun to the realisations in the target language and in interlanguage. There are many combinations that are not used in the target language. However, L2 learners tend to use more combinations than native speakers, see below:

No. of logically possible combinations	90
No. of combinations used by early L2 learners	31
No. of combinations used by late L2 learners	21
No. of combinations used in the target language	8

Thus, the L2 acquisition of Swedish noun phrase morphology seems to proceed from large variation of forms to more and more restrictions on learner hypotheses.

A closer analysis of the errors reveals that it is almost always the articles that violate the noun phrase agreement, whereas the suffixes on the nouns agree with the adjectives to a higher degree. In the example *det vita mössan* ('the-NEUTER white cap-DET-UTER') the definite article (det - NEUTER) does not match the gender of the noun (mössa - UTER). The noun itself has the correct uter suffix. In other words, the lexical morpheme is acquired before phrasal agreement — as predicted by Processability Theory.

Lahtinen explains the difference in error patterns by assuming that the noun has been acquired together with its suffix as an unanalysed chunk. As the reader may recall, this was also the explanation used by Andersson. However, Processability Theory offers an alternative explanation for the same phenomenon by distinguishing between lexical and phrasal morphology. The gender affix is acquired first because it is a lexical morpheme.

Hammarberg's (1996) study was designed to test precisely these predictions of Processability Theory for morphology. He compares the acquisition of adjectival agreement in attributive position within the noun phrase to adjectival agreement in predicatives. In other words, he compares phrasal morphology to inter-phrasal morphology. Interestingly, he finds that in his data, agreement markers for plural (-a) follow the order predicted by Processability Theory, i.e. phrasal markers appear before inter-phrasal markers. However, the markers for neuter appear in a different order.

Hammarberg claims that it is the notion of "Perceived Communicative Value" (PCV) of structural properties that override processability constraints. Neuter is first marked in predicative contexts. However, the examples of PCV given by Hammarberg are not examples of morphological agreement, but of morphological non-agreement or disagreement (cf. Källström 1990). Although the main rule for the Swedish adjective is to agree with its head as in (62) below, there are also instances where there is no agreement but the neuter form is used instead as in (63) below.

(62)   Blommor är vackra
        flower-PL are beautiful-PL

(63)   Blommor är vackert
        flower-PL are beautiful-NEUT.

The meaning of the first example is that each individual flower is beautiful, whereas the meaning of the second example is that each possible group of flowers is beautiful, i.e. in a more general, or circumstantial sense. Källström (1990) describes this difference as follows:

> "When the subject is in itself too delimited to be able to receive a dividuative interpretation, the non-agreeing adjective serves as a marker of the subject's circumstantial reference". Källström (1990:240)

In other words, the reason for the neuter to appear in inter-phrasal contexts before their appearance in phrasal contexts is the fact that it does not agree with any other lexical item in this context. This claim is quite congruent with Processability Theory.

The study by Salameh et al. (forthcoming) deals with morphology and syntax. In this cross-sectional study, 18 Arabic-speaking children with Swedish as L2 are recorded in dyads performing various communicative tasks. The tasks were designed to elicit yes/no questions, topicalised declaratives and agreement in noun phrases.

The distributional analysis of the data revealed that there are intermediate steps in the acquisition of agreement morphology. Instead of looking for error types, Salameh et al. searched for possible instances of agreement morphology. The reader will recall that Swedish definite NPs containing an adjective obligatorily need to contain a definite article *and* a morphological marker of definiteness on the noun. Salameh et al. found that learners sometimes mark definiteness on the noun only.

An implicational analysis of the eighteen learners revealed that the structures in question are acquired in the following sequence:

$$\text{Adj}_{\text{affix}}+\text{N}_{\text{affix}} > \text{Art}+\text{Adj}_{\text{affix}}+\text{N}_{\text{affix}} > \text{y/n Question} > \text{INVERSION.}$$

This sequence accurately follows the prediction of Processability Theory. In the structure $\text{Adj}_{\text{affix}}+\text{N}_{\text{affix}}$ the feature 'definiteness' has to be unified between the head and the adjective (i.e. level 3), while $\text{Art}+\text{Adj}+\text{N}_{\text{affix}}$ the unification of the same feature occurs in three constituents (also level 3). INVERSION in y/n questions and declaratives is located at level 4 according to our analysis in section 3.2. In other words, these data support the Swedish processability hierarchy.[23]

Acquisition of verbal morphology

There are two studies which deal with the development of tense marking in verbs. However, they are not aimed at morphological markers *per se*. Instead, they study the development of reference to time irrespective of the rule system underlying morphological form. While this procedure is perfectly legitimate it limits the usefulness of these studies for the purpose of testing Processability Theory. However, since tense is expressed by morphological marking, one can still gain some information about morphology.

In his study of child SSL acquisition Viberg (1991) quantified the morphological form of verbs and found that his informants first used invariant forms before they systematically used lexical morphemes.

Verbal morphology was also studied in the ESF-project (Noyau 1992). In this study, too, the focus was on reference to time. Viberg and Noyau both seem to focus on the morphology of *single words* to capture the development of tense. This method is suitable when the purpose is to look at verbs with different suffixes, but it does not permit one to differentiate between lexical and phrasal morphology markers. Both authors mention that there are sometimes mismatches between auxiliary and main verb, but they do not discuss the reasons behind this. For this purpose, it would be necessary to analyse the whole verb phrase to gain information about agreement features.

Nevertheless, these studies do provide weak support for the two basic levels of Swedish processability hierarchy in verbal morphology.

Acquisition of syntax

Table 5.3-4 summarises the main studies on the acquisition of Swedish subject-verb word order and negative placement.

The first study on L2 acquisition of Swedish word order was carried out by Hyltenstam (1977, 1978) who identified a universal sequence in the acquisition of word order. The data for this study were collected by means of a cloze test which was designed to elicit a range of contexts for inversion and negation. An implicational analysis of the data revealed a clear pattern in the acquisition of word order:

ADV > y/n questions > INVERSION.

The reader will recall that the last two steps in this sequence were also found

Table 5.3-4. Studies of SSL syntax

Study	Design	Period	Data collection	Subjects	L1
Bolander 1988	longi- tudinal	5 months	interviews, picture description	60 adults	Finnish Polish Spanish
Colliander 1992	longi- tudinal	10 months	interviews, story retelling	30 adults	Persian Polish Spanish
Håkansson & Dooley Collberg 1994	cross- sectional		elicited imitation	19 children	Icelandic Polish
Håkansson & Nettelbladt 1993, 1996	longi- tudinal	5 months	conversation	5 children	Bulgarian Karmandji Romanian Syrian
Hyltenstam 1977, 1978	combined longitudinal and cross- sectional		written elicitation form	160 adults	35 different
Rahkonen 1993	cross- sectional		written composition	999 adults	Finnish
Salameh et al forthc.	cross- sectional		conversation, story retelling	18 children	Arabic

in the study by Salameh et al. (forthcoming) and that this sequence is predicted by Processability Theory. In addition, ADV is located at level 3 of the hierarchy and therefore also follows its predicted location in the sequence. Hyltenstam's study did not show clear results for Cancel Inversion which is located at level 5 of the Swedish hierarchy, and Hyltenstam states: "there are no regular patterns in the way the learners invert or do not invert in embedded clauses when acquiring the inversion rule for the simple clauses" (Hyltenstam 1978:42). Bolander's (1988) extensive analysis of a corpus of spoken data confirms Hyltenstam's sequence.

Håkansson & Nettelbladt (1993, 1996) compare L2 acquisition of subject-verb inversion to normal and impaired L1 acquisition. On the basis of a distributional analysis they find that the sequences are different for L2 children and L1 children with normal language development, while the SLI

(Specific Language Impairment) children follow the same sequence as L2 children. The development of the L2 children is approximately the same as was found in Hyltenstam, with one exception: Håkansson & Nettelbladt found an early stage of canonical word order (stage 2 of the processability hierarchy) which was not captured by Hyltenstam's test. This adds further weight to the empirical support provided by this study for the processability hierarchy.

In other words, Håkansson & Nettelbladt's study confirm most of Hyltenstam's findings, and all three studies (Hyltenstam 1978; Bolander 1988; Håkansson & Nettelbladt 1996) lend further support to the processability hierarchy for L2 acquisition.

Rahkonen's (1993) study is based on written material from 999 Finnish high schools students learning Swedish in their tenth year and from 173 Swedish students acquiring Finnish. The study compares two typological scenarios: (1) the acquisition of Inversion after topicalisation in Swedish by Finns and (2) the acquisition of a canonical order after topicalisation in Finnish by the Swedes. The analysis reveals that the level of accuracy is significantly higher in scenario (2). Rahkonen argues that this is so because in scenario (1) the learner has to move from an unmarked L1 word order to a marked L2 word order, whereas in scenario (2) the learner moves in the opposite direction: from marked to an unmarked word order. Processability Theory offers an alternative explanation: INVERSION is located at level 4 while topicalisation is located at level 3. All learners have to move through the hierarchy irrespective of their native language. Scenario (1) therefore corresponds to the longer stretch on the hierarchy that has to be covered by the learner.

Acquisition of negation placement

In his pioneering work on the L2 acquisition of Swedish word order, Hyltenstam (1977, 1978) also found a universal sequence in the acquisition of negative placement. The developmental pattern consists of five stages and is the same for all learners, irrespective of L1. It is described below. For the sake of comparison, the predictions from processability hierarchy are placed to the right.

Hyltenstam's results	predictions based on the processability hierarchy
5. sub clause: neg AUX V	Level 5 step 2, sub-clause procedure
4. sub clause: neg V	Level 5 step 1, sub-clause procedure
3. V neg	Level 4, inter-phrasal procedure
2. (AUX) neg V	Level 2, category procedure
1. neg V	Level 2, category procedure

1. In an initial stage the learners tend to use preverbal negation ("Han inte kommer" He not comes). This preference has also been found in studies of L2 acquisition of other languages with post-verbal negation, such as English and German, and it is predicted to be the starting point for sentence internal negation in Processability Theory (i.e. level 2).

2. Hyltenstam's next stage in the development shows an auxiliary appearing in front of the negator ("Han vill inte komma" He will not come). This is another structure of level 2 of the processability hierarchy. In terms of processability there is no difference between Neg+V and (Aux) +Neg V as long as one disregards the matching of tense marking in Aux and V.

3. At Hyltenstam's stage 3 the learners master negative placement in main clauses, and place the negator after the finite verb ("Han kommer inte" He comes not). This corresponds to level 3 of the processability hierarchy. Examples of stage 4 of the processability hierarchy were not elicited in Hyltenstam's study.

4. Once the negator is placed to the right of the finite verb in main clauses, the learners differentiate between main and subordinate clauses and place the negator before the verb in the latter type of clauses. This rule first occurs in main verb contexts: "..därför att han inte kommer" ..(because he not comes).

5. The last point in the development is reached when the learners place the negator before the auxiliary verb ("...därför att han inte har kommit " .. because he not has come). The structures at Hyltenstam's stages 4 and 5 are predicted to occur at level 5 in Processability Theory.

Summing up, Hyltenstam's findings support our predictions extremely well. The only proviso on this is that currently the Swedish processability hierarchy does not differentiate between all of the stages he found. Instead it conflates some of them into one.

    The studies by Colliander (1993) and Bolander (1988) replicated Hyltenstam's study and further examined the linguistic contexts for the acquisition of the structures included in Hyltenstam's study. Colliander's

(1993) and Bolander's (1988) studies were based on spontaneous data, and they fully confirm Hyltenstam's findings.

Håkansson & Dooley Collberg (1994) used an L2 perspective to study L1 acquisition of negative placement. Using Hyltenstam's sequences for L2 adults as a starting point, they looked at negative placement in L1 and L2 children. The sequences were found to be exactly the same as Hyltenstam's. All these replication studies lend strong support to Processability Theory.

Summary and conclusion

In this paper Processability Theory was applied to Swedish morphology and syntax. The Swedish processability hierarchy was tested against fourteen empirical studies which constitute an ideal testing ground for the hierarchy. Wherever a study produces findings which relate to the processability hierarchy it confirms the predictions derived from the hierarchy. There is not a single piece of counter-evidence to the predictions. The only limitation is that even though a very extensive database was reviewed, not all structures contained in the Swedish processability hierarchy are covered in empirical studies and conversely, not all structures covered in empirical studies are discriminated with the same resolution as in some of the highly refined implicational analyses.

In other words, the sizeable body of SLA research produced in Sweden over the past two decades lends strong empirical support to Processability Theory which spells out the assumption that second language acquisition can be understood as the gradual construction of the computational mechanisms needed for processing the second language. However, this is by no means 'the last word' on the acquisition of Swedish as a second language or about Processability Theory. The framework presented in this paper raises new questions for both, research on Swedish and Processability Theory generally.

These open questions may act as an incentive for new research directions. In the area of SSL it became obvious that several structural areas are under-researched, that often relatively narrow structural areas are studied without linking them up to the larger picture of the developing grammar. The paper also raised the issue of the interrelation between processing constraints vis a vis functional constraints which was apparent in the study of multifunctional morphemes in the NP. Finally, the study by Håkansson and Nettelbladt (1996) compared the acquisition of L1, L2 and impaired L1. These authors found fundamental similarities between L2 and impaired L1 acquisition. This raises the issue of the applicability of Processability Theory to L1 acquisition (cf. section 6.6). For all of these issues Processability Theory can serve as a point of reference.

5.4 Application to Japanese

I mentioned repeatedly above that a test of the typological validity of Processability Theory optimally ought to involve a range of typologically different languages. Therefore, Japanese is a welcome counterbalance to the Germanic bias of the first three L2s examined above. Fortunately, progress has been made in studying the second language acquisition of Japanese, a non-configurational and agglutinative language. In this section I will test Processability Theory with the studies of two of my graduate students, Kirsten Huter and Satomi Kawaguchi. However, this is merely a first look at the acquisition of Japanese, for which at present the typological test is limited to the first three levels of the processability hierarchy.

Japanese as a second language

Recently, research on JSL has received considerable attention. Doi and Yoshioka (1990) based their study of the acquisition of the particles *'wa'* (topic), *'ga'* (subject) and *'o'* (object) on Pienemann and Johnston's (1987a) model of second language acquisition, a precursor to Processability Theory. They hypothesise that *'wa'* is a continuation of topic and therefore does not require any internal syntactic analysis. They therefore place this structure on level 3 of Pienemann and Johnston's (1987a) hierarchy. In contrast, they hypothesise that the processing of grammatical functions, such as subject and object, require the processor to be developed at level 5. They test this hypothesis in comprehension experiments with JSL learners and are able to confirm that *'wa'* is acquired before *'ga'* and *'o'* .

Kanagy (1994), studied the acquisition of negation in spoken Japanese. Her database is a longitudinal study of 34 JSL learners in the US who were followed over one academic year. Kanagy modelled her study on the basis of Clancy's (1986) research on Japanese first language acquisition. Her study revealed that morphological markers of negation which, in Japanese, vary with lexical class, follow a strict order from unanalysed forms with no class differentiation to the differentiation of linguistic environments. The latter process develops in the sequence N > V > A. However, none of Kanagy's informants mastered the last step at the end of the observational period.

Huter (1996, 1998) carried out a longitudinal study of the acquisition of Japanese as a second language by Australian university students. Kawaguchi (1996) presents a cross-sectional study of JSL development. Both studies are closely related to concepts deriving from Processability Theory, and they will be presented in more detail below. However, before this can be done, we will first have to look at some aspects of Japanese syntax and how this relates to Processability Theory.

Japanese verbal morphology and word order

Japanese is an SOV language. Verbs occur in final position in main and subordinate clauses. This is evident in examples (64) - (67)[24] below. Note that the SOV pattern also applies to equational sentences (example 65). When several verbs occur in one clause, they occupy the two final positions. This is evident in (66) and (67).

(64) *Tomoko wa   ringo o   tabe-ta.*
      (name) (topic-part.) apple (obj part.) eat(-past)
      "Tomoko ate an apple."

(65) *Tomoko wa   shinsetsu da.*
      (name) (topic-part.) friendly (copula)
      "Tomoko is friendly."

(66) *Tomoko ga   Kimiko ni   denwa*
      (name) (subj-part.) (name) (indir.obj part.) telephone
      o   shi-te   mi-ta
      (obj-part.) do-(serial) try (-past)
      "Tomoko tried to give Kimiko a ring."

(67) *Tomoko ga   gohan o   tabe-te   iru.*
      (name) (subj-part.) rice   (obj part.) eat (serial) (progressive)
      "Tomoko is eating rice."

The above examples also illustrate the use of the markers of grammatical function, 'ga' (subject) and 'o' (object) as well as the topic marker 'wa'. To be precise, the canonical pattern of Japanese might be better translated as 'agent', 'action' and 'object', thus avoiding the use of grammatical functions as descriptors of constituents. We will see below that the agent is not marked as 'subject' in every clause and that there are subject-less main clauses. It should also be mentioned that although the preferred word order is "SOV", Japanese is a non-configurational language.

Japanese is a morphologically rich, agglutinative language. According to Shibatani (1990, 306f), verbal affixes usually occur in the following order:

Vstem - causative - passive - aspect - desiderative - negation - tense.

This is exemplified by several morphological forms of 'kak-u' ('write') in (68) to (71).[25]

(68) kak-areru   • passive
      stem-(passive)

(69) kak-aseru   • causative
      stem-(causative)

(70) kak-aser-areru   • causative - passive
      stem-(causative) - (passive)

(71) kak-aser-are-tai   • causative - passive - desiderative
      stem-(causative) - (passive) - (desiderative)

In other words, one morpheme usually expresses one function, which contrasts with the European languages discussed above. However, because of a large set of morphological classes and morpho-phonological variation (compare examples (70) and (71) for the form of the passive morpheme), complex form-function relationships create learning problems of a different kind.

Since the general thrust of this book is on information distribution rather than form-function relationships, I will leave aside the latter area and stay focused on predictions for learnability that can be derived from the development of processing procedures. In this context it is important to note that Japanese does not mark person or number on verbs. Nor does it mark number in noun phrases. Also, the category 'gender' does not exist for nouns. For these reasons, grammatical agreement in phrases and across phrases is not a feature of Japanese. The reader will recall, that in European languages, agreement marking is an area of morphology which is very productive and which produces many fine distinctions in processability. This does not apply to Japanese.

It may at first glance appear contradictory to think that an agglutinative language with rich morphology would not be a good testing ground for levels of processability in morphology. However, the measure of the suitability is not merely the number of morphemes, but the distribution of grammatical information involved in the morphological processes. There is no reason why most or all of the verbal morphemes listed above (expressing causative, passive, aspect, desiderative, negation and tense) could not be derived directly from conceptual structure. In other words, the only processing requirement for the insertion of these morphemes is that the formal lexical class 'verb' is so marked in the lexicon.

However, information distribution is crucial in the verbal system when more than one verb occurs. In this case, Japanese is no different from European languages in that only one of the verbs can be finite. The reader can see this in examples (66) and (67) where the penultimate verb is marked with the -te-morpheme which is a marker of non-finiteness and seriality: *"shi-te mi-ta"* [do-(serial) try (-past)] in (66) and *"tabe-te-iru"* [eat (serial) (progressive)] in (67). The verb marked '-te' appears in penultimate position and cannot be marked for any of the features causative, passive, aspect, desiderative, negation or tense. To achieve this, the two verbs have to exchange grammatical information in the encoding process.

A Japanese processability hierarchy

This means that the co-ordination of the non-finiteness marker and the set of finiteness marker on two or more verbs constitutes phrasal morphology. We have now identified three levels in the acquisition of Japanese verbal morphology:

1. no affix
2. lexical affix
3. phrasal affixes[26].

These levels which are illustrated in Table 5.4-1 are related to the general hierarchy of processability as follows: No affixes on verbs will occur when lexical material has not been classified according to lexical classes; i.e. at levels 1 and 2. lexical affixes will occur from level 2 onwards, and phrasal affixes will occur from level 3 onwards. One has to bear in mind, however,

Table 5.4-1. Processing procedures applied to Japanese

Processing procedure.	L2 process	morphology	syntax
6 • subord. clause procedure	main and sub cl		
5 • S-procedure/ WO Rules -saliency	inter-phr info		
4 • S-procedure/ WO Rules +saliency	inter-phr info		
3 • phrasal procedure	phrasal info.	V-te V	Topi
2 • category procedure	lex morph	V_{aff}	canonical order SOV
1 • word/ lemma	'words'	invariant forms	single const.

that the actual occurrence of morphemes may be delayed because of complex form-function relationships.

The above brief translation of morphological processes in the Japanese verbal system is repeated in Table 5.4-1 for the reader's convenience. Table 5.4-1 is laid out in the same way as their counterparts in the sections on German, English and Swedish, and grammatical structures of Japanese are listed at the appropriate level, depending on the required processing procedures.

The same table also lists a number of syntactic rules at levels 1 to 3. These predictions all relate to word order in a way that is parallel to the European languages discussed above. The only surprise may be that, again, canonical word order is hypothesised as the initial organising principle for syntax — as it was the case for all other languages covered in this book.

This may be surprising because the above rough structural sketch of the Japanese language may have given the impression that grammatical roles are marked very clearly by morphemes: 'ga' for 'subject', 'o' for 'object' etc. This may remind the reader of the morphological marking of grammatical functions in Turkish (cf. section 5.1) where an alternative organising principle for early interlanguage is attested, based on lexical morphological markers. However, in Japanese the markers of grammatical functions compete with the marker of topic. One can see this in contrasting example (64) with example (72) below:

(72) *Tomoko ga*   *ringo o*   *tabe-ta.*
      (name)(subj-part.)   apple (obj part.)   eat(-past)
      "Tomoko ate an apple."

The only difference between the two sentences are the markers 'ga' and 'wa'. The choice between the two depends on whether 'Tomoko' is the current topic. This creates yet another problem for the learner who has to acquire the processing procedures needed for topic tracking in order to decide whether to mark the grammatical or the pragmatic function. In other words, the lexical morphological markers for the semantic roles in the clause are subject to additional constraints which require additional processing procedures.

Therefore the canonical schema is hypothesised to be utilised initially, i.e. at level 2. This is possible because in Japanese "SOV" is the preferred word order, even though Japanese is a non-configurational language. Learners of Japanese can therefore rely on this canonical schema as the organising principle of their initial IL grammar.

The typological difference between Japanese and the European languages studied in the previous section will give us an opportunity to test a key hypothesis about L1 transfer as a principle in establishing the basic parameters of a second language. In the exposition of the psycholinguistic basis for Processability Theory in section 2.5 I made a case against 'bulk transfer'. I argued that the grammatical processing procedures of the L1 are too specific to be simply transferable to the L2 without specific adaptation.

The study of JSL gives us another opportunity to test this hypothesis empirically. If one argues that the initial hypothesis for the L2 is transferred form the L1, then one would expect that learners of Japanese as L2 whose L1 conforms to an SVO pattern to initially display such a pattern. We shall see below that this is not the case.

In Japanese. constituents not marked for subject or topic can occur in sentence-initial position. This is a means of shifting the focus to the initialised constituent. I will refer to this structure as 'topicalisation'. Sentence (73) is an example of this.

(73) *Uchi ni*   *tsui-ta*   *toki, ame ga*
      home (locative part.)   arrive (past) time rain (subj. part.)
      furi-dashi-ta.
      fall-start (past)
      "When I arrived home, it began to rain."

The principle behind Japanese 'topicalisation' is no different from their European counterparts which also constitute the learner's first deviation from the canonical schema. One would therefore expect this structure to occur at level 3 — as in all the other languages in which it is functional. At this point I will spare the reader a repetition of the alignment of this structure with level 3 processing procedures and merely refer back to earlier expositions in sections 3.3, 5.2, and 5.3.

Huter's and Kawaguchi's studies

Kawaguchi's (1996) is a cross-sectional study of seven Australian university students learning Japanese as a second language with English as the native language. Each sample was about 30 minutes in duration and consisted of a range of communicative tasks that were carried out by the informant and native speaker and non-native speaker interlocutors.

Kawaguchi's study focuses on simplification in Japanese interlanguage, and she included a range of linguistic measures from which I will adopt merely the three types of morphological phenomena discussed above, namely

no affix
lexical affix
phrasal affix.

The results of Kawaguchi's study is set out in Table 5.4-2.

Table 5.4-2 shows a clear implicational pattern with the learners 'Meg', 'Kat' and 'Sim' displaying the presence of lexical affixes and a lack of phrasal affixes, while the other four speakers display the presence of both types of affixes. This sample does not contain any learners who show evidence of a consistent lack of any affixation which is hypothesised as stage one of this sequence. I assume that this merely reveals a limitation in the database. As I noted in section 4.2, the hypothesised implicational pattern would be falsified if, for instance, learners displayed evidence of the use of phrasal

Table 5.4-2. Types of affixes in Kawaguchi's (1996) study

	Meg	Kat	Sim	Iri	Sam	Nat	Hel
no affix	/	/	/	/	/	/	/
lexical affix	+	+	+	+	+	+	+
phrasal affix	−	−	−	+	+	+	+

Table 5.4-3. Types of affixes in Huter's (1996) study

	M1	K1	K2	K3	M2	M3	M4	K4	K5	J1	J2	J3	J4	J5
no affix	/	/	/	/	/	/	/	/	/	/	/	/	/	/
lexical affix	+	+	+	+	+	+	+	+	+	+	+	+	+	+
phrasal affix	−	−	−	−	−	−	−	−	−	−	−	−	+	+

affixes in the absence of lexical affixes, however, this does not occur.

Huter's (1996) study consists of a longitudinal study of five Australian learners of Japanese who were observed over a period of approximately three years on six occasions, each time at the end of the semester, with interview 1 occurring after three months of instruction. Huter also used a range of communicative tasks and elicited about 30 minutes of speech per session.

The analysis of Huter's data in relation to the three types of affixes is set out in Table 5.4-3. Again, this is only a small subsection of the structures covered by Huter. For the purpose of this section, all of her informants are pooled in Table 5.4-3. Informants are identified by a letter. The number attached to each letter refers to the sample number. For example, K5 refers to the sample of K after semester 5.

Table 5.4-3 again displays a clear implicational pattern that supports the hypothesis to be tested here. Lexical affixes do emerge before phrasal affixes, and again, there are no data relation to the hypothesised first stage without affixation. It is highly likely that learners will stop producing such structures within the first three months of learning and therefore both studies missed this early stage in data collection.

Nevertheless, taken together, the studies by Kawaguchi and Huter provide strong evidence for the validity of the proposed processability hierarchy of Japanese. And it can be added here that both studies show very clearly that the acquisition of word order starts with an SOV pattern.[27] This observation provides additional evidence against the 'bulk transfer' of grammatical routines (cf. sections 1.2 and 2.5 and Schwartz and Sprouse, 1996).

5.5 Evidence from on-line experiments: the procedural skill hypothesis

The objective of this section

The reader will recall that the main line of argument pursued in this book is the following: the task of acquiring a second language is based on the acquisition of the *procedural skills* needed for the processing of the language. In the previous sections of this chapter, the focus was on typological evidence supported by corpus research. In this section, I will turn to evidence obtained from experiments in on-line L2 processing.

Given that the theme of the book directly addresses issues of second language processing, it is logical to base empirical evidence on data which tap into the nature of those processing procedures. Above, I made the case that L2 corpus data serve this function, since Processability Theory is a formal framework for delineating that set of grammars that is processable at a given point in development. By turning to on-line experiments, a further aspect of processability is included directly in the experimental set-up, namely that of the time-constrained nature of language processing.

The key objective of this section is to demonstrate that procedural routines, once automated, are similar in native speakers and non-native speakers. This similarity assumption derives logically from the processing-based continuity assumption (cf. Chapter 1) according to which the basic components of language processing do not change during acquisition and over age, except if they are damaged — as in aphasia, specific language disorders, dyslexia etc. If empirical evidence can be supplied to show that NSs and skilled NNSs process specific linguistic structures in a similar manner and that unskilled NNSs do not, then the key thesis of viewing SLA as the acquisition of procedural linguistic skills will be supported.

I will refer to this hypothesis as '*the procedural skill hypothesis*'. It is the objective of this section to empirically test that hypothesis.

On-line experiments in SLA research

The crucial feature of on-line experiments is that they measure language processing '*in vitro*'. In the field of SLA this type experiments is a relatively new methodological approach. In his 1987 book "Theories of Second Language Learning", McLaughlin (1987), who is a psychologist, was able to survey the literature relating to on-line experiments on automatisation within the space of four pages. The substantive research mentioned there are Dornic's (1979) study of language processing speed in bilinguals, Lehtonen and Sajavaara's (1983) study of response time by NS and NNS in grammaticality judgement tests and Hulstijn and Hulstijn's (1984) experiments on learner performance under different test conditions. The other studies are unpublished student manuscripts. McLaughlin (1987) uses these studies to provide evidence for one of his key assumptions on SLA, namely that SLA is based on the automatisation of language processing skills. The evidence he quotes demonstrates clearly that processing speed increases with proficiency.

Bley-Vroman and Masterson (1989) advocate the use of on-line experiments as an enrichment of the range of experimental data available to SLA researchers. These authors introduced the particular technique of sentence matching experiments into the field of SLA. During the past seven years this technique has proven very productive in SLA research. Below I will report on its adapted use in the present study.

In the context of SLA research, sentence matching experiments were used by Masterson (1993), Eubank (1993) and Clahsen and Hong (1995). All of these studies were modelled on the experimental design developed by Freedman and Forster (1985) with precursors in Forster (1979) and Freedman (1982). This design is based on the effect of information encoding on processing speed. For instance, it was found that informants can decide more quickly whether pairs of stimuli are identical if the stimuli are words (e.g. HOUSE/ HOUSE) than if the stimuli are non-words (e.g. HSEUO/HSEUO) even though the words and the non-words consist of the same number of characters (e.g. Chambers and Forster 1975). The reason for this effect is that words are encoded as single units while non-words are encoded as strings of characters.

Below I will return to the psychological and theoretical status of the assumptions underlying the sentence matching task. Let us first review the SLA studies which utilised this technique.

The general set-up used in these studies is basically the same: two sentences appear on a computer screen separated by a very short interval; the informant has to decide as quickly as possible if the sentences are identical or not. The test sentences may be grammatical or ungrammatical. In studies with native speakers (Freedman and Forster 1985) it was found that the identity of the sentences can be determined faster with grammatical test sentences.

Freedman and Forster interpret this as a grammaticality effect in the matching of sentences in the same way as a "real-word effect" was found in the matching of words. This 'grammaticality effect' was utilised in the SLA studies to be summarised here.

Eubank's (1993) study is designed as an empirical test of Clahsen's (1984) strategies which were advanced as an explanation of L2 acquisition sequences (cf. sections 2.2. and 6.6.). It came at a time when Clahsen's approach to SLA was being questioned, particularly by scholars who support the view that both, L1 and L2 learners, have access to UG (cf. for instance, White 1991 and several other papers in Eubank 1991). For those scholars who think that access to UG is limited for L2 learners, Clahsen's approach forms an alternative explanation which constituted an important component of the 'fundamental difference approach' (Bley-Vroman 1990; Meisel 1991; Clahsen and Muysken 1986; cf. section 6.6.).

Eubank takes the logical step to test Clahsen's strategies in the context for which they were designed, namely the real-time processing of learner language. Eubank infers the following predictions from Clahsen's strategies:

> Clahsen's Initialisation/ Finalisation Strategy (IFS) in particular predicts that uninverted, ADV-SVO sentences will exact less cost in terms of processing than inverted, ADV-VSO sentences, even though inverted sentences are grammatical in the target language and uninverted sentences are ungrammatical. Eubank (1993; 253)

Eubank empirically tests this hypothesis using German sentence matching tasks in which he measures the informants' response time which is taken as a measure of 'processing cost'. The (adult) informants are NSs of German and NSs of English.

The results of Eubank's experiments do not support the hypotheses inferred from the IFS strategy: The NNS informants (with English as NS) respond more quickly to grammatically correct stimuli (Adv-VSX) than to the IFS-supported (ungrammatical) stimuli (Adv-SVX). The NS informants (German NSs), on the other hand, do not show any differential response time for the two types of stimuli.

If the SM task at hand is sensitive to alternating verb positions, then the lack of any differential effect in NS shows that the IFS strategy cannot be taken as a general characteristic of on-line processing. On the other hand, the differential effect found in NNS is the opposite of Eubank's prediction. Eubank's study therefore casts some doubt on the validity of the IFS strategy.

The more constructive finding that emerges from Eubank's study is the observation that "... we discovered in the course of our work that the NSs and the NNSs appear to process stimulus sentences in different ways in the SM task" (Eubank 1993, 279), a conclusion that nevertheless supports the fundamental difference hypothesis.

On the other hand, Eubank's conclusion about processing differences is in opposition to the procedural skill hypothesis which is being examined in this section. Below I will display empirical evidence in support of the procedural skill hypothesis. In section 6.6 it will be demonstrated that the procedural skill hypothesis is nevertheless compatible with the view that L1 and L2 acquisition are different.

Clahsen and Hong (1995) utilise the differential effects in NNS sentence matching tasks in a different way. They argue that the limited access to UG by NNSs can be demonstrated with grammaticality effects in NSs and NNSs. In particular, they argue that one would expect grammaticality effects for *all* domains of a given UG parameter if the learner has access to UG and no such uniformity in grammaticality effects if the learner has only limited access to UG. In particular, Clahsen and Hong (1995) test Vainikka and Young-Scholten's (1994) claim that the acquisition of subject-verb agreement and non-pro drop occur simultaneously in adult SLA. Vainikka and Young-Scholten's (1994) claim is made in support of the full-access-to-UG position, and the two grammatical phenomena under discussion are linked by one parameter.

At this point the reader will notice that Clahsen and Hong (1995) use the sentence matching technique not to study language processing, but linguistic knowledge. I will return to this point below.

Clahsen and Hong (1995) test their hypotheses with Korean speakers of German and German NSs. Korean was chosen as L1 because it does not have the syntactic property of subject-verb agreement and it is a topic-prominent language which allows empty subjects and objects. In other words, Korean learners of GSL were chosen to avoid any possible influence of L1 transfer in the experiments. The two sets of informants were tested on grammaticality effects for the two grammatical phenomena, null subjects and subject-verb agreement, in SM tasks.

The results show clearly that grammaticality effects are present for all NSs on both grammatical phenomena. In contrast, NNSs showed a more heterogeneous behaviour. In order to understand Clahsen and Hong's argument one has to consider the following of their basic assumptions: Given that grammaticality effects exist with the structures in question for NSs and some NNSs, the absence of such effects in individual NNSs can be interpreted as indicating the non-acquisition of the corresponding structure. This assumption enables Clahsen and Hong to analyse which of their NNS informants have acquired the two rules simultaneously and which have acquired them separately. It turns out that the ratio is 18:13 in favour of the separate acquisition of the rules in question. In other words, unlike in L1 acquisition, the two rules are not always acquired simultaneously by NNSs. This finding is taken as strong evidence against the assumption that adult L2 learners have full access to UG.

Reflection: the focus on processing

I mentioned above that Clahsen and Hong use sentence matching experiments as a means of accessing linguistic knowledge. This assumption is stated explicitly in Clahsen and Hong (1993, 70):

> "Bley-Vroman and Masterson (1989), Eubank (1993) and Masterson (1993) were the first to apply the SM technique to study L2 acquisition. Their idea was that if the SM task provides a measure of structural representations in native speakers, then the SM task could also be used for measuring grammaticality/ ungrammaticality in L2 learners." Clahsen and Hong (1993, 70)

In fact, the use of SM experiments as a measure of structural representations is quite in line with Freedman and Forster's (1985) reasoning. Clahsen and Hong summarise Freedman and Forster's (1985) reasoning as follows:

> "The idea behind this [SM] experiment is that the presence of structure ... in the stimuli facilitates the same/different decision. In general, a subject's RT to a particular sentence pair can be taken to be a function of its grammaticality: grammatical sentences can be matched faster than ungrammatical ones. Therefore, performance in SM tasks provides a way of determining the availability of structural representations." Clahsen and Hong (1993, 69)

Freedman and Forster (1985; 117) did indeed show that "... the matching task is sensitive to degrees of grammaticality ...". This was found by comparing response times in the matching of sentence pairs which were based on word scrambles, phrase structure scrambles and grammatical sentences. In other words, 'degrees of grammaticality' refers to the rough contrast between word scrambles, phrase structure scrambles and grammatical sentences that was set up for the experiments, and it did not refer, as one might perhaps assume, to the minute nuances in acceptability which native speakers can detect in somewhat unusual sentences.

Freedman and Forster (1985) found grammaticality effects in some SM tasks but not in others, especially not in sentences with WH-extraction from NP-complements. They argue that this is so because the SM technique is sensitive only to grammaticality effects that are created early in the derivation process.

One crucial point emerges from this brief discussion, namely the fact that Freedman and Forster's reasoning about SM experiments as a measure of structural representations is closely linked to a definition of the *derivational process* in transformational grammar with its different levels of representation which have since been fundamentally revised (cf. section 1.3. above). It is therefore not at all obvious that SM experiments can validly be seen to relate to structural representations as defined in theories of grammar with an architecture that is different from that of multi-level transformational grammars. In other words, SM tasks can by no means be taken as a general-purpose measure of linguistic representation. In this context it is relevant to note that Crain and Fodor (1987) argue that SM tasks are not sensitive to the derivational process but to the correctability of the test sentences.

The fact remains that SM tasks first of all measure performance, namely the speed with which certain linguistic computations can be executed. These computations are the very procedures which are specified in a procedural performance grammar which utilises the linguistic knowledge encapsulated in a competence grammar (cf. Bresnan and Kaplan 1982, compare Chapter 2 above). In other words, the response times recorded in SM tasks are firstly a measure of the speed with which linguistic procedures are executed. It may then be possible to argue in a second step that such procedures are nevertheless linked to linguistic rules of a competence grammar and that one can therefore make inferences about such rules and the knowledge they represent. However, such a case has not yet been made.

Taking a step back from sentence matching experiments, one can see that the grammaticality effect found in sentence matching tasks is the specialised appearance of the more general phenomenon of the effect of encoding on recall tasks. As George Miller (1956) showed in his classic paper "The magic number seven; plus or minus two", the immediate memory span is determined not by the total number of items recalled, but by the number of items grouped together. Such groupings, or "chunking", can be achieved through rhythm, semantic cues or other means (cf. Kintsch 1970; Baddeley 1990).

The type of "chunking" that occurs in free recall tasks is usually determined by the skill of the subject's to form useful groups. However, if the task involves the difference between clusters of information which are grouped together in the subjects cognitive system as opposed to clusters of information for which no ready-made schemata exist, then the existing schemata serve as the 'natural' chunking principles. This is true in tasks based on hearing and seeing as well as in the recall of language. In other words, the 'grammaticality effect' found in sentence matching tasks is brought about by the structuring of the stimuli on the basis of procedural skills that form the component parts of the language processor. If the procedural skill is absent, no grammaticality effect will appear.

The objective of my own study of response times in SM tasks is to test the 'procedural skill hypothesis' according to which the ability to process specific linguistic structures is acquired gradually and the nature of the individual skill is the same in NS and NNS. In other words, I will apply the performance measure obtained from SM tasks to the notion of 'linguistic procedures'.

It is at this point that some of the assumptions inherent in the study by Eubank (1993) diverge from some of the key assumptions made in this book. One of these concerns the notion of 'processing difficulty' which surface in statements such as the following:

> "We can now make the following prediction ...: for L2 learners of German, utterances of the form Adv-SVX (i.e., uninverted) are *easier to process* [emphasis added] than utterances of the form Adv-VSX (i.e., inverted) ...".
> Eubank (1993; 257)

Eubank tests, quite logically, Clahsen's (1984) notion of 'processing difficulty' in relation to the effect of processing strategies. However, it has been known since Slobin (1966) and Goldman-Eisler (1968) that reaction times do not correlate with syntactic complexity. The reason for this lack of correlation between different measures of linguistic complexity and reaction times can be understood from within Levelt's (1989) theory according to which linguistic skills are integrated into parallel distributed routines which can all be executed at optimal times. This gain in processing time, irrespective of syntactic complexity, is one of the main features of parallel distributed linguistic routines. This also explains why ungrammatical structures and non-words usually require an increased response time in NSs (Levelt 1989; Bock 1978).

In such cases there are no ready-made routines available. This applies to syntactic patterns as much as to word access.

This brief reference to Levelt's model of language production (cf. section 2.4 for further details) highlights the reason why I assume reaction time experiments with linguistic stimuli to measure the execution of automatised linguistic routines. Processability Theory implies that the acquisition of grammatical structures entails the automatisation of the underlying routines. For instance, when SV-agreement is acquired, one can assume that the learner has acquired the routine that processes SV-agreement. It can now be predicted for this learner that the availability of this routine releases processing procedures in sentences with SV-agreement. Therefore the learner will display response times more like those of NSs.

In other words, Processability Theory predicts a gradual transition from NNS behaviour to NS behaviour. This is in stark contrast with the assumptions underlying Eubank's study. By comparing response times between NNSs and NSs he set his experiment up to test categorial differences in the processing of language between these two types of speakers. Therefore his conclusion that "... the NSs and the NNSs appear to process stimulus sentences in different ways ..." (Eubank 1993, 279) is biased by the experimental design. Given also that he presents the response times of his informants as group mean scores one will always find a difference between NSs and NNSs as long as the NNS group contains a sufficient number of informants without the requisite skills.

This opens up an interesting perspective in comparing the procedural skill hypothesis with Eubank's "processing difference hypothesis". Confirmatory results for the procedural skill hypothesis can nevertheless confirm the "processing difference hypothesis" as long as the sample includes a sufficient number of learners who have not yet acquired the necessary skill. These learners would bring the group mean score down which would then be different from that of the NNS.

A test of the procedural skill hypothesis therefore requires a different experimental design from that in Eubank's study. Since this hypothesis predicts that NNSs who have acquired a given L2 processing skill will perform in a manner similar to NSs in relation to this skill, one needs to base the experiments on three groups of informants:

(1) NNSs with the given L2 skill
(2) NNSs without the given L2 skill
(3) NSs (who will naturally have the given L2 skill)

This set-up will allow us to compare each of the three groups with the other groups, and it will be possible to establish if the following predictions are correct:

- Groups (1) and (3) perform in a similar way;
- Group (2) will perform unlike groups (1) and (3);
- Grammaticality effects will show only in groups (1) and (3).

Interestingly, Eubank (1993; 256) asks the crucial question: "... what happens to strategies like the IFS after rule acquisition."? However, he does not produce his own answer and sticks with his interpretation of Clahsen's (1984) work. While Processability Theory does not utilise strategies, the spirit of the answer to Eubank's question within the processability framework would be the following: the processing "shortcut" used by the learner before the acquisition of the necessary processing procedure will be replaced by the procedure itself. This is, in effect, the procedural skill hypothesis.

Clahsen and Hong (1995) are aware of the difference between NNSs with the targeted grammatical rule and those without it. They state:

> "We expect the same facilitating effect [as in NSs, MP] for those L2 learners who acquired agreement and the correct properties of null subjects in German. On the other hand, those L2 learners who have not yet acquired these two properties of German should not produce significant SM differences between grammatical and ungrammatical results." Clahsen and Hong 1995, 76)

This brief quotation reveals a number of significant underlying assumptions. At a conceptual level, Clahsen and Hong assume that the same grammatical properties may develop in L2 learners as the ones that are present in L1 learners. While Clahsen and Hong refer to grammatical knowledge rather than processing routines, this assumption is similar to the procedural skill hypothesis in that features of the L1 speaker are seen to develop piecemeal in the L2 learner.

At a methodological level, Clahsen and Hong assume that the absence of grammaticality effects in the L2 informants demonstrate that the corresponding grammatical properties have not developed. While I agree with this assumption I believe that its validity has to be demonstrated empirically. In fact, this assumption overlaps substantially with the procedural skill hypothesis, for which empirical support will be presented below.

Experimental design

The above discussion of the experimental design of Eubank's and Clahsen and Hong's experiments predicates the experimental design of my own study which is aimed at testing the procedural skill hypothesis. For this study, three groups of informants were included as discussed above:

(1) NNSs with the given L2 skill
(2) NNSs without the given L2 skill
(3) NSs (who will naturally have the given L2 skill).

The particular skill to be tested was German subject-verb agreement which is also one of the structures included in Clahsen and Hong (1995). All materials were taken from the Clahsen and Hong study which demonstrated grammaticality effects with these materials in NSs and NNSs.

The task of the subjects was to judge if two sentences that appeared on a computer screen with a short time interval (360 msc.) were identical or not. A computer program was used for the purpose of managing this experiment. This program was based on a 'Hypercard' stack made available by Robert Bley-Vroman and Deborah Masterson. I modified this software in several areas, most significantly to include a reliable and finely tuned method of recording response times at intervals of 5 msecs.[28], since the original program made use of the system clock which only achieves a resolution of one sixtieth of a second (= 17 msecs.) and, more importantly, is reported to be unreliable[29] for the purpose of accurate time recording within the given application.

The program recorded the subject's response time to each of the test items starting from the moment at which the second item first appeared on the screen. If no response was given within 5 seconds or an inappropriate key was pressed, a warning was given. The program also displayed the test items on the screen in a random order and in one of four random positions which were indicated by a visual clue before the second sentence appeared. This clue serves two functions:

> The first is to alert the participant that appearance of the pair sentence is imminent, encouraging a high level of attention; the second purpose is to force the participant to focus momentarily on a new image and, it is hoped,

to "erase" the visual image of the priming sentence, forcing the participant to rely more heavily on representations other than the visual. Masterson (1993, 94-95).

The experiments were carried out at the Australian National University on a Macintosh computer. Each informant was tested individually in the presence of a trained test co-ordinator who was a NS of English and a near-native speaker of German. The test co-ordinator explained the test procedure and the computer controls. Each test taker was given the opportunity to learn to use the control keys for the responses 'same' and 'different' (marked with the colours red and blue on the key board and the control key (space bar) for "next item". They were also given unlimited time to respond to 10 training items and were tested for their average reaction time using 10 stimuli.

Each of the three groups of informants consisted of seven persons. In order to determine NNS group membership GSL interlanguage samples were collected from learners of German as a second language (ANU students of German). The samples were analysed according to stage of acquisition (cf, sections 2.2, 3.3, 4.1 and 6.3), and learners whose samples were able to be classified as below Agreement and above Agreement were assigned to the corresponding group of informants. In this way it was ensured that the learners' oral production was used as an independent measure of their processing skill. One would now expect that those learners who display evidence of not having acquired Agreement will not show grammaticality effects with test items based on Agreement.

The sentence matching experiments were carried out several days after the collection and analysis of the interlanguage samples. The whole sequence of experiments was completed within two days.

The materials used in this experiment are taken from the Clahsen and Hong study. It is therefore appropriate to quote the description of the relevant material by those authors:

> The main items of the experiment were grammatical and ungrammatical German sentences containing violations of subject-verb agreement and the null-subject property. The overall ratio of grammatical an ungrammatical items was set at 1:1. The experimental items are presented in Appendix 1.
>
> *a Agreement*: Three grammatical sentences were constructed for each possible combination of three grammatical persons in singular or plural, resulting in 18 items altogether. To minimise the effect of lexical idiosyncrasy, only regular high-frequency verbs of German were used (cf. Ruoff, 1981). In addition to that, the length of the sentences was controlled with respect to

number of words and number of syllables: for each sentence, the number of words was either 6 or 7, and the number of syllables was 10 or 1. Ungrammatical sentences differed from their grammatical counterparts only in their verbal suffix, as illustrated by the following sentence pair:

8) a. Du flieg-st   nach Korea am nächsten Sonntag
        you fly-2nd sg. to Korea next Sunday
   b. *Du flieg-t   nach Korea am nächsten Sonntag
        you fly-3rd sg. to Korea on the next Sunday [sic].
Clahsen and Hong (1995, 72)

For the purpose of the present study only items related to subject-verb agreement were selected. These were complemented by filler items as in Clahsen and Hong (1995):

> c *Filler items:* Two kinds of filler items were used to make sure that the subjects were in fact performing the task accurately: 1) nonmatching pairs in which one word of the second sentence was replaced with a different one of the same length (cf. 10); and 2) pairs of meaningless word strings consisting of 6/7 constituents (cf. 11). These filler items were not included in the data analysis:

10) Du schwimmst jeden Morgen in der Schwimmhalle
     Du schwimmst jeden Abend in der Schwimmhalle
     'you swimm every morning/ evening in the swimming pool'

11) Zu Blume die kochen Auto deutsch
     'to flower the cook car German'

> The overall ratio between matching and non-matching pairs was set at 3:1; ... i.e., in the agreement condition, 11 filler items were used, ...
> Clahsen and Hong (1995, 73).

The average response times are listed for every informant in table 5.5-1 which therefore also lists all 21 informants. The age range of the informants was between 19 and 31 years with the exception of Kees who is 71 years.

Results

As in Freedman and Forster (1985) and Clahsen and Hong (1995), only those matching items were included in the analysis to which a correct response was given. The results of the experiment are presented for the three groups that participated, namely seven native speakers of German, seven post-agreement non-native speakers of German and seven pre-agreement non-native speakers of German. Table 5.5-2 lists the mean response times for all 21 informants.

The mean correct same response time for ungrammatical items was 229 msecs longer for NSs and 215 msecs for Post-agreement NNSs. The corresponding figure for Pre-agreement NNSs is 9 msecs. All NS and all Post-agreement NNSs show shorter response times for grammatical items, while

Table 5.5-1. Mean response times in milliseconds by informants

Target language: German
Structure: subject-verb agreement

Native speakers

	gram.	ungram.	reaction time	difference
Christian	1376	1470	289	+94
Gaby	1329	1624	432	+29
Walter	1356	1626	238	+270
Silke	1318	1677	257	+359
Winfried	1343	1416	191	+73
Lan	834	1055	285	+221
GŸnter	1382	1673	295	+291
Mean	1277	1506	284	229

Post agreement learners

	gram.	ungram.	reaction time	difference
Alex 08	1833	2254	276	+421
Neri 08	1290	1752	221	+462
Mel 08	1178	1349	287	+171
Julie 08	1596	1828	287	+232
Lena 08	1038	1149	286	+111
Stefanie	1833	1920	446	+87
Melanie	1330	1349	218	+19
Mean	1443	1657	289	215

Pre agreement learners

	gram.	ungram.	reaction time	difference
Dean	1999	2060	345	+61
Douglas	1921	1931	257	+10
Kees	3653	3597	493	-56
Jeremy	2054	2087	178	+33
Alex 2	2254	2260	282	+6
Guy	2331	2327	291	-4
Peter	2415	2427	283	+12
Mean	2375	2384	304	8.86

Table 5.5-2. Mean RTs for agreement

	Grammatical	Ungram.	ANOVA	Scheffe-F
Native speakers	1277	1506	F=31.734 (6,7), p ≤ .0013	31.734*
Post-agreement	1443	1657	F=11.304 (6,7), p ≤ .0152	11.304*
Pre-agreement	2375	2384	F= .428 (6,7), p ≤ .5371	.428

*significant at 95%

for Pre-agreement NNS this is not the case. The one-way ANOVA results show that the difference between response time for grammatical and ungrammatical items is significant only for the NS and the Post-agreement NNS, but not for the Pre-agreement NNS. Theses results support the hypothesis that skilled NNSs behave more like NSs than 'un-skilled' NNSs in the particular linguistic skill they have acquired.

In addition to the above comparison of reaction times within groups for the two conditions 'Grammatical' and 'Ungrammatical', an ANOVA analysis was carried out comparing the reaction time differences between the three groups of learners. The analysis supports the same trend: NSs and Post-agreement NNSs are similar, and Pre-agreement NNSs are different from the other two groups. A significant difference between groups (F= 7.697 (2,18), p≤ .0038) was found. The significance levels according to the Scheffe F-test were as follows:

Comparison	Scheffe F-test
NS vs Post-Agreement	.026
NS vs Pre-Agreement	6.146*
PostAgr vs PreAgr	5.374*

*Significant at 95%

The results of the above experiments confirm the procedural skill hypothesis. It was possible to demonstrate that for the three groups
  (1) Post Agreement NNSs
  (2) Pre Agreement NNSs and
  (3) NSs,

the following is true:
  • Groups (1) and (3) perform in a similar way;
  • Group (2) perform unlike groups (1) and (3);
  • Grammaticality effects show only in groups (1) and (3).

In other words, the grammatical skill that produces subject-verb agreement develops in NNS in the same way as in NS, and there is no fundamental difference in language processing between NNS and NS as suggested by Eubank (1993). This is strong support for the procedural skill hypothesis.

I hasten to add that the procedural skill hypothesis does not imply that there is no difference between L1 and L2 acquisition. All it implies that any such differences will be outside the domain of language processing. In section 6.6. I will show that there are, in fact, fundamental differences and that those are to be found in the initial hypotheses of the learner and the developmental dynamics that follow from those hypotheses.

Chapter 6

Hypothesis space

6.1 Introduction

Processability Theory is designed to provide a principled approach to predicting transitions in developing grammatical systems. The validity of the theory is demonstrated by the fact that the GSL data follow the predictions of the theory for syntax and morphology. Further support is provided by an application of the theory to the acquisition of ESL, to Swedish and Japanese SLA and the subsequent confirmation of predicted transitions through empirical data.

In this section I will demonstrate that Processability Theory provides a powerful point of reference in the explanation of acquisition phenomena which include variational aspects of development. I will address four major issues in SLA research, namely, (1) variation and the developmental problem, (2) the effect of formal intervention on interlanguage variation and (3) the stability and variation of interlanguages across tasks and (4) differences in primary and secondary language acquisition.

However, before I can unfold this argument, a further aspect of Processability Theory has to be introduced: Hypothesis Space. In Chapter 3, I presented a set of processing constraints and a mechanism which allows a systematic implementation of these constraints into a theory of grammar. I implied throughout that chapter that the processing procedures which are available at any one stage constrain the range of structural hypotheses, regardless of what would be logically possible hypotheses. This range of structural hypotheses will be referred to as *Hypothesis Space*.

Figure 6.1-1 illustrates this concept. The acquisition process starts at an initial state; this book refrains from speculating on the structure of that initial state. Interlanguage grammars reshape when new processing procedures emerge. This is the determining factor in the chronology of acquisition. The final state reached in SLA, as well as any intermediate stages, are not uniform

Figure 6.1-1. Hypothesis Space, development and variation

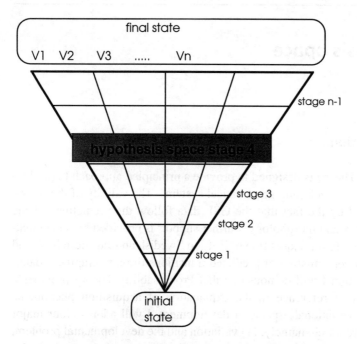

grammatical systems but they are sets of related linguistic varieties. Horizontally, these varieties are characterised by the same set of processing procedures, and vertically they are characterised by an implicational relationship of the processing procedures upon which they are based.

Conceptually, the notion of Hypothesis Space is based on Meisel, Clahsen and Pienemann's (1981) multidimensional model of SLA which also differentiates between two dimensions of SLA. The primary conceptual progress represented by Hypothesis Space is that this concept is more than a metaphor for a class of observable phenomena; it is formally defined and typologically plausible.

In other words, with the introduction of the notion of Hypothesis Space interlanguage variation can be defined in an *a priori* manner. The formal definition of variation is exactly the measure which Larsen-Freeman and Long (1991) ask for, and it overcomes one of the limitations they perceived in the multidimensional model. In their view, one of the main limitations was "...

the lack of clarity over identifying variational features *a priori*" (Larsen-Freeman and Long 1991, 285).

Admittedly, variational features were originally conceived of in the context of corpus-based analyses, where they were able to be identified through implicational scaling or simply by comparing developmental patterns between learners. However, in the context of the teachability hypothesis the stakes were raised higher and this hypothesis was falsifiable only if the features tested in a given experiment were already identified as being either developmental or variational. In other words, the falsifiability of the teachability hypothesis for any previously undefined structure depended on an *a priori* definition of variational features. As long as this definition was absent a failed attempt to teach a given structure could have been attributed to premature teaching and a successful attempt could have been attributed to the variable status of the structure in focus. This is indeed a serious limitation which I hope has now been overcome.

In this context a note of caution may be in order: while Larsen-Freeman's critique is perfectly justified in as far as it concerns the testability of the teachability hypothesis, Ellis (1994) extends this point to the multi-dimensional model itself and claims that developmental and variational features cannot be clearly distinguished from each other. That is quite incorrect. As I mentioned above, the two types of features can clearly be distinguished at the descriptive level in comparative longitudinal studies and through implicational analyses.

As I mentioned earlier, the theory proposed in this book extends the descriptive framework of the multidimensional model and links it with a typologically plausible hierarchy of processability. The explanation of variation advanced in the multidimensional model was socio-psychological in nature. In this context an *a priori* definition of linguistic features of variation was not possible. What I will develop in the following section is such an *a priori* definition, but from the same vantage point from which developmental features are defined, namely processability. In this way, the construct of Hypothesis Space defines both dimensions of SLA in an *a priori* manner.

In Chapters 4 and 5 I demonstrated how Hypothesis Space rigidly constrains interlanguage development. In this section I will look at the degree of freedom implied in Hypothesis Space and the effect the existence of such a degree of freedom has on developing systems with different initial hypotheses.

I will explore this degree of freedom in several seemingly unrelated contexts: (1) interlanguage variation, (2) the effect of instruction on interlanguage systems (3) task variation and (4) types of acquisition (first vs. second language, etc.). I will first formally describe interlanguage variation as part of Hypothesis Space. The resulting framework will then be used to analyse the effect of formal intervention on interlanguage variation and the effect of tasks on interlanguage variation. I will further demonstrate that structural (as opposed to contextual) differences between types of acquisition can be understood within the same formal constraints as interlanguage variation. In other words, I will claim that differences between child and adult L2 acquisition operate within the confines of Hypothesis Space.

6.2 Interlanguage variation and the developmental problem

In this section I will show that the degree of freedom implied in Hypothesis Space determines the possible range of interlanguage variation. In this context variation is defined as in Meisel, Clahsen and Pienemann (1981), i.e. as a dimension of SLA which is separate from development. I described this multi-dimensional conceptualisation of SLA in some detail in Section 4.2 above and pointed out its relationship to Bailey's wave model, implicational scaling (Guttman 1944; DeCamp 1973) and Labov's variable rules.

The reader will recall from section 4.2 that Meisel et al. (1981) accommodated Labov's descriptive parameters (social context, linguistic context and probability of rule application) directly in their descriptive framework: the linguistic context is part of distributional analysis and percentage values given for rule application correspond to Labov's probability of application. The social context was seen by Meisel et al. primarily in relation to the individual learner's social identity. These social variables are hypothesised by Meisel et al. to correlate primarily with interlanguage variation rather than with interlanguage development.

The focus of this section is on defining structural boundaries of variability from a processing point of view, rather than on possible non-linguistic conditions which may be seen to cause variability. Pienemann and Johnston (1987b) expressed the view that the study of the influence of "external factors" on SLA cannot, at our current level of knowledge, attain the precision where testable predictions can be made about the mechanics of the interrelationship between "external factors" and SLA processes. I believe that one can gain a deeper understanding of interlanguage variation by determining the processing procedures which give rise to the phenomenon of IL variation.

The structure of variational features

I would like to exemplify this conceptualisation of variational linguistic features with an example related to question formation. As I have shown above, the English rule "Aux-2nd" is acquired at stage 5 in the proposed system. This rule describes the observational fact that auxiliaries are placed in second position in English Wh-questions as in the following example:

(74) Where is he going?

Variability occurs in Wh-questions before this rule is acquired. At the prior stage (i.e. stage 4) some learners leave out one or more constituents, e.g.

(75) Where he going?
(76) Where is going?

Other learners produce Wh-questions using canonical word order:

(77) Where he is going?

In all these cases the auxiliary-second placement is avoided, but the effect on the interlanguage is different in each case. The omission "solution" is generally perceived by the native speaker to be more pidginised than the canonical order strategy. The crucial point behind these observations is this: while all four intermediate solutions to the learning problem are positioned at the same developmental point, namely stage 4, each of them correlates with a particular learner type.

Clahsen, Meisel and Pienemann (1983) identified 14 variational linguistic features and demonstrated that those features describe what might be called different types of interlanguage. The strongest empirical support for the concept of interlanguage type is provided by the distribution of variational features in a large group of learners. Clahsen, Meisel and Pienemann (1983) found that variational features can be ordered implicationally. This means that the presence of a highly simplifying feature guarantees the presence of less simplifying features. This justifies the concept of an individual interlanguage as being placed on one identifiable position along a continuum of norm-orientedness and simplification.

It will be obvious to the regular reader of SLA journals that the multi-dimensional model is fundamentally different from a number of other accounts of IL variation, particularly those by Tarone (1979, 1982, 1983, 1985, 1988) and Ellis (1985b).

Tarone and Ellis

Tarone claims that a learner's interlanguage represents a continuum of speech styles which differ in their degree of variability and internal consistency. In her model, the choice of an interlanguage style primarily depends on the amount of attention to language form. Her prediction is the following: the less attention is paid to form, the less variability. This is illustrated in Figure 6.2-1.

Ellis' model is very similar to Tarone's. He hypothesises a continuum of speech styles and claims that free variability, i.e. variable forms which cannot be predicted by linguistic or social context, will first occur in the carefully planned style and will spread from there to other styles. He therefore perceives free variation as the engine behind acquisition which ensures that new forms enter the interlanguage system. Ellis also allows for socially defined variation, but it is unclear in his model how this is related to attention-based variation in a principled way.

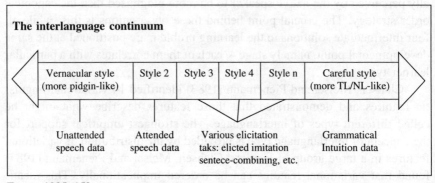

Tarone 1985, 152

Figure 6.2-1. The interlanguage continuum as seen by Tarone

Tarone's and Ellis' models conceptualise acquisition as a linear process. Different varieties are placed along a continuum, which also represents the progression of IL grammar from zero to ultimate attainment. Linguistic rules are placed along a continuum, and the learner "oscillates up and down this continuum" (Ellis 1985a, 1985b) depending on the amount of attention paid to speech production. The learner gradually moves up the continuum by adding new structures, while he or she can still move up and down the continuum from one moment to another. This model then accounts for the fact that the same learner may use two different linguistic forms for the same function in the same stretch of speech.

It has been shown by Sato (1985) and Young (1988) that in both models attention is not defined in an operationalisable way and that it is therefore difficult to empirically test the model. Those tests which have been carried out within these limitations do not support a linear relationship between IL variation and attention. Young (1988) and Tarone (1988) conclude that the relationship is probably multi-factorial.

Gregg (1989) criticises Tarone's and Ellis' models of variable IL competence on different grounds. He points out that Tarone and Ellis both assume that variable IL rules form part of IL competence. His basic point is that variable IL rules describe performance and that the assumption of variable competence "... unfortunately, explicitly erases the line between linguistic knowledge and linguistic output." (Gregg 1989, 377). He points out that describing variable linguistic output, even if one could account for all possible linguistic variants and the circumstances in which they occur, does not offer an explanation of the phenomena observed. Hence '... the variabilist [sic] is committed to the unprincipled collection of an uncontrolled mass of data" (p. 377). Gregg concludes that

> ".. to try to force variability into a theory of the acquisition of competence by claiming that competence itself is variable is self-defeating; it will neither lead to a theory of acquisition nor to a theory of performance. (Gregg 1989, 379).

This criticism has caused much debate and some confusion. Admittedly I was amongst the ones who were confused. On the one hand I can accept the criticism I summarised above, and I have my own points to add to it. Indeed, I support Gregg's attempt to bring into focus the theoretical status of interlanguage variation. On the other hand, in passages such as the following Gregg seems to be throwing out the baby with the bathwater:

"Variation is, rather, like the aurora borealis: a fascinating and puzzling phenomenon (it seems to have truly seductive appeal for a large number of SLA scholars), but one that it is not the duty of an acquisition theorist to explain." (Gregg, 1989, 379).

The generality of this strong statement makes it unclear if Gregg's critique is directed at the concept of variable competence or at variation as an object of study. In personal communication Gregg assures me that the first is the case. It is good to have this clarified.

I hasten to add that there are indeed scholars who are committed to the study of variation without the assumption of a variable competence. A prominent example is Preston (1989, 1993) who read Gregg in the same way I did (Preston 1993, 170) and who argues that "... there is no inconsistency in believing that variation arises from alternatives (not 'variation') in competence and that the probabilistically determined realisation of those alternatives is due to a variety of contributing factors, not necessarily to a built-in variability in linguistic competence itself." (Preston 1993, 170).

Preston (1993) makes the point that many of the concepts used by variationist SLA researchers are based on misunderstandings of concepts borrowed from variationist linguistics. He quotes H.D. Brown (1976, 138) who pointed out twenty years before these lines were written that the dichotomy 'systematic — variable' contradicts the basic variationist assumption that linguistic variation is systematic. It was for exactly this reason that Meisel, Clahsen and Pienemann (1981) in their multi-dimensional model did not define L2 variation in contrast to systematicity. Instead, they applied the Labovian framework to SLA in a way which maintains the systematic nature of variation and which does not necessitate the assumption of a variable competence.

Preston (1993) regrets that much of the sociolinguistic research effort in SLA is directed at studying the interface between linguistic variation on the one hand and sociological, social psychological, anthropological and pragmatic factors on the other hand and that little attention is paid to the contribution a variationist approach can make to core linguistic issues. It is exactly in this spirit that variation is framed in this chapter where I address the question as to what the formal constraints on interlanguage variability are.

In other words, this chapter constitutes an attempt to present a psycholinguistic and yet variationist approach to SLA. Let me add, however, that the objective of this chapter is not to determine the linguistic or non-linguistic factors which determine the choice of one IL variant over another. Instead, the objective is to determine the linguistic space within which IL variation can operate at any one level of development.

Let us return to Tarone's and Ellis' models. What concerns us most at this point in time is characterising the conceptual difference between Tarone's and Ellis' models on the one hand and the multi-dimensional model on the other. Tarone's model assumes a cause-effect relationship: the degree of attention causes the interlanguage to take on a certain shape. The problem with this, as Sato (1985) and Young (1988) pointed out, is testability. The multi-dimensional model, on the other hand, is not an explanatory framework in itself; instead it provides a conceptual and descriptive framework that allows the researcher to state facts in such a way that they become more accessible to explanation.

The basic distinction made in the multi-dimensional model is that between development and variation. This distinction is made in order to acknowledge the observable fact that not every change that can be observed in an IL over time will indicate a qualitative structural shift of the IL. Using this framework then makes it possible to study development, defined as qualitative structural shifts, separately from other IL processes. In other words, the framework entails a fundamental hypothesis about the nature of IL processes, namely that there are processes of qualitative of structural shifts which move the IL to different levels of "maturity" and that these processes can materialise in a variety of shapes. A commitment to this multi-dimensional hypothesis logically excludes any commitment to Tarone's uni-dimensional concept of SLA. I say this merely to state the premises on which the exposition below is based.

An *a priori* definition of variational features

I would now like to return to my claim that the concept of Hypothesis Space overcomes the "... lack of clarity over identifying variational features *a priori*." (Larsen-Freeman and Long 1991, 285). The point of departure for this is the claim that IL variation is limited by Hypothesis Space. This point can be exemplified with the variable solution of the AUX-2nd problem at stages 3 and 4, for which three types of solution have been recorded:

(A) omission: e.g.
    (78)   *Where ø he going? or
    (79)   *Where is ø going?

(B) violation: e.g.
    (80)   *Where he is going?

(C) avoidance: e.g.
    (81)   he is going *where*?

The range of possible solutions to the formation of wh-questions simply derives from the state of the learner's grammar before stage 5. The ESL processability hierarchy specifies the following for stage 5:

$$S'' \rightarrow (XP) \qquad\qquad S'$$
$$\left\{ \begin{array}{l} \text{wh} =_c + \\ \text{adv} =_c \text{'seldom, rarely ...'} \\ \text{SENT MOOD} = \text{INV} \end{array} \right\}$$

$$S' \rightarrow (V) \qquad\qquad S$$
$$\left\{ \begin{array}{l} \text{aux} =_c + \\ \text{ROOT} =_c + \\ \text{SENT MOOD} =_c \text{INV} \end{array} \right\}$$

In other words, the information "SENT MOOD = INV" has to be exchanged between XP and V to achieve the desired position of the auxiliary in second position. However, at stage 3 the IL grammar specifies merely the following:

$$S'' \rightarrow (XP) \qquad\qquad S'$$
$$\text{wh} =_c \text{'who, what ...''}$$

$$S' \rightarrow (V) \qquad\qquad S$$
$$\text{aux} =_c \text{'do'}$$

Hence at stage 3 only one lexical form of the auxiliary such as "do" can appear in second position after topicalisation. However, it will not be marked for tense and person, since these processes require an exchange of grammatical information between constituents. One confusing factor is that the learner might choose a form of the auxiliary which, in the target language, is marked for *tense* and *person* such as "does". Used in the appropriate context, the isolated sentence would first appear to be a contradiction to the above predictions as in *why does he go*. However, a full distributional analysis will reveal that the learner uses only one or a very small range of morphological forms at random: sometimes these coincide with the form used in the target language to mark tense and person.

The rules at level 3 do not permit the auxiliary to be placed in second position in main clauses after all topicalised wh-words. However, these rules do permit all of the interlanguage solutions found at this level and only those. In the case of the 'violation' of the TL rule, the learner simply applies the following existing IL rules:

$$S' \rightarrow (XP) \qquad\qquad S$$
$$wh =_c \text{ 'who, what ...''}$$

$$S \rightarrow NP_{subj} \; V \; (NP_{obj}) \; (ADJUNCT)$$

In the case of 'omission' these rules are further modified to make either the grammatical subject or the verb optional depending on semantic redundancy. In the case of 'avoidance' wh-words are simply treated as adjuncts, and the whole sentence can be generated by one level-3 c-structure rule, namely

$$S \rightarrow NP_{subj} \; V \; (NP_{obj}) \; (ADJUNCT).$$

In other words, the possible solutions to the developmental problem are defined *a priori* by Processability Theory.

Let us look at two further examples of structural problems which learners have to solve to demonstrate the limited range of solutions available. The first example refers to third person-s marking in English. The reader will recall that to produce this morphological rule the learner has to transfer grammatical information between the NP_{subj} and the verb.

[she]$_{NPsubj}$	[{eat-s} ...]$_{VP}$	(Present, imperfective)
PERSON = 3	PERSON = 3	
NUM = sg	NUM = sg	

Before feature unification across constituents is processable the learner has the following two options to resolve the logistic conflict: (1) to violate the morphological rule and thus express third person singular subjects in present imperfective sentences, albeit without morphological marking on the verb or (2) to avoid marking the present imperfective context and use progressive forms or modals, thus expressing a meaning that is different from the intended meaning.

3sg-s	(1) violation:	*"She eat her steak"*
	(2) avoidance:	*"she is eating her steak"*
		"She will/can eat ..."

Solution (1) is expressively more accurate at the cost of grammatical accuracy while solution (2) is grammatically more accurate a the cost of semantic accuracy.

The second example refers to the "ADV-INV conflict" in German interlanguage development. The reader will recall that the use of ADV (in German) creates an insoluble conflict for the learner, because ADV obligatorily requires INVERSION: ADV is a level 3 process while INVERSION can only be processed at level 5. Therefore, the interlanguage is bound to deviate from the target language every time ADV is used until stage 5 is reached. In this case, three options have been recorded (Clahsen, Meisel and Pienemann 1983, Pienemann 1981):

(A)   omission of V or $NP_{subj:}$ e.g.

 (82)   **Dann ∅ er nach Hause gegangen.*
        Then   ∅ he home   gone.   or

 (83)   **Dann ist nach Hause gegangen*
        Then   is ∅ home   gone.

(B)   violation of INVERSION: e.g.

 (84)   *Dann er ist nach Hause gegangen.*
        Then he is home gone.

(C)   avoidance: e.g.

 (85)   *?Er ist nach Hause gegangen dann.*
        He is home   gone   then.

All of these options circumnavigate the structure which is unprocessable by the learner. All of them utilise the grammar available to the learner at his/her current level of processing. This is easy to see if one brings to mind the operations involved in the processing of INVERSION: the filling of the topic position creates the information "sentence MOOD=INV", which feeds into the equation in rule (R2), and this licenses a verb in a position left of NP_{subj}. Now, if either the verb or NP_{subj} is omitted the whole process becomes superfluous, since no grammatical information needs to be exchanged, because the target of the information exchange (the verb) does not exist or because there is no such thing as "the position to the left of NP$_{subj}$", because NP$_{subj}$ does not exist. If — as in solution (3) — the topic position is not filled, no information will be created which has to be transferred into another constituent.

Looking at the effect these variable interlanguage forms have on the overall structure of the interlanguage, one can state that each solution gives a shape to the style of the interlanguage. Solution (1) increases the rate of omission, solution (2) increases the rate of non-application of INVERSION, and solution (3) decreases the rate of ADV application and results in less violations of INVERSION. Therefore these solutions all rate quite differently on an accuracy scale. One should note that they also rate quite differently on a scale of semantic expressiveness, since solution (3) implies an under-use of adverb-topicalisation, a highly productive means of attention focusing and information contrast, acquired at stage 3. Solution (3) therefore represents a regression in development.

One of the most important points in this context is that in all developmental conflicts of the type illustrated here these are *all* the options that are open to the learners at the given point in their development. There is no mysterious way to process INVERSION. After all, there is no way to "hide" adjuncts in sentence-internal position, since such rules are processable only at level 4.

This is what I meant above when I claimed that Processability Theory delimits a range of solutions to these developmentally induced logistic conflicts. It is because of this delineation effect of Hypothesis Space that interlanguage variation remains within predictable confines and is thus definable in an *a priori* manner: the rule system available to the learner at his or her current level also defines the range of solutions for developmental problems which are the basis for IL variation.

A brief postscript on variation and communication strategies

The set of phenomena which I described above as interlanguage variation are often described from the perspective of communication strategies. In the words of O'Malley and Chamot (1990, 43): "Communication strategies are an adaptation to the failure to realise a language production goal." This is exactly the phenomenon that I described as a learner encountering a developmental conflict.

O'Malley and Chamot (1990) review a wide range of research on this topic in which communication strategies are classified. What is of particular interest in the context of this book is not the classification but the possible psycholinguistic connection which was explicitly stated by Faerch and Kasper (1984) who "... assert that communication strategies entail a 'psycholinguistic' solution to the communication problem instead of one which relies upon the negotiation of meaning." (O'Malley and Chamot, 1990, 43f.)

In the Nijmegen Project, Poulisse (1990) took Faerch and Kasper's approach further by embedding communication strategies in Levelt's (1989) model of language production. On this basis predictions are made as to what choices the learner has to make when viewed from the perspective of language production.

Unfortunately, this approach is not related to the acquisition of the processing procedures which bring about the production problems which then get resolved by communication strategies. While it appears to me to be more productive to attempt to understand the nature of the mechanisms which a learner applies to overcome resource-induced production problems rather than simply list a taxonomy of strategies, it would nevertheless be necessary to link the production mechanisms to the way they are acquired in the first place before learner strategies, or IL variation, can be related to acquisition in a principled way. However, as Poulisse (1990, 196) states, this was not the intention of the Nijmegen Project.

On the other hand, this IS one of the objectives of the theory proposed in this book: By linking production mechanisms to the way they are acquired, IL variation can be related to acquisition in a principled way.

Developmental gaps or "trailers" as variational features

The reader will recall a brief discussion of developmental gaps or 'trailers' in Section 4.2 in the context of acquisition criteria. At that stage I flagged some further discussion of that point which it is now time to produce.

The notion of developmental 'trailers' was introduced by Larsen-Freeman and Long (1991, 286) in their discussion of the 'predictive framework of SLA':

> "... in an unpublished pilot study of ESL and JSL at the University of Hawaii in 1984 testing the predictive framework [a precursor to Processability Theory, MP], it was found that the general IL profile for some learners might place them, say, at stage X+4 in ESL ..., but still show them

producing stage X+3 structures in one or more domains and X+5 structures in one or more domains."

I noted above that the desired falsifiability of hierarchical stages is quite possible as long as one involves several IL samples which are sufficiently large. The example I gave is replicated in the Table 6.2-1.

It is important to note that Larsen-Freeman and Long based their analysis

Table 6.2-1. Falsifying hierarchies of rules in linguistic samples

	Sample 1	Sample 2
a	+	+
A	+	−
b	+	+
B	−	+
c	+	+
C	−	+

on the presentation of developmental schedules as set out in Table 6.2-2 (Pienemann and Johnston 1987b, 82f).

In other words, developmental schedules were presented by Pienemann and Johnston (1987b) for a range of structural domains, and it was easy to assume from this presentation that stages run uniformly across different structural domains. Admittedly, this author and his co-author are to be blamed for any misconceptions that may have arisen from this presentation.

However, in terms of the theory presented in this book there is little reason for such an assumption of uniformity. The reader will recall that Processability Theory does no predict any firm interlocking of stages with the exception of INV and SV-agreement marking which share a large number of processing procedures. However, even in this case the relationship between the two rules is somewhat variable due to the specific processes related to each of them. The relationship between phrasal morphemes and word order rules is more variable with the latter occurring between stage X and X+2 as depicted in Table 6.2-3 which was first presented in Section 3.5 above.

Let me return to the concept of developmental 'trailers'. There are two important points of reference for this concept. One is the basis for the definition of variational features in Processability Theory which is the well-defined leeway for the solution of developmental conflicts which I discussed

Table 6.2-2. Tentative developmental stages for English as a secnd language (Pienemann and Johnston (1987)

STAGE	VERB	NOUN	PN	Q	NEG	ADV	ADJ	PREP	W_ORDER
1:	Words	or	Formulae						
2:	IL-ing IRREG -ed	REG_PL IRREG_PL	1st 2nd 3rd	SVO? "	no no+X "	- -	- -	PP "	SVO "
3:		POSSESS	POSSESS	DO_FRONT WHX_FRONT	don+V	(ADV) -	- (more)	" "	TOPIC ADV_FRONT
4:	AUX_EN AUX_ING		" "	PSEUDO_INV Y/N_INV	" "	" "	(better) (best)	COMP_TO "	PART_MOV PREP_STRNDG
5:	3SG_S +"	PL_Concd	CASE(3rd) RFLX(ADV)	AUX_2ND SUPPLET	DO_2ND SUPPLET	-ly	-er -erst	" "	(DAT_TO) "
6:	(GERUND) " "	" " "	RFLX(PN) " "	Q_TAG " "	" "	" "	" "	" "	ADV VP (DAT MVMT) (CAUSATIE) 2_SUB_COMP

KEY to table 6.2-2: (Round brackets indicate tentative assignment only)

IL_ing = non standard 'ing'; PP= in prepositional phase.
DO_FRONT= fronting of wh-word and possible cliticized element. (e.g. 'what do')
TOPIC = topicalization of initial or final elements;
ADV_FRONT = fronting of final adverbs or adverbial PPs.
AUX_EN = [be/have] + V-ed, not necessarily with standard semantics.
PSEUDO_INV = simple fronting of wh-word across verb (e.g. 'where is the summer?')
COMP_TO = insertion of 'to' as a complementizer as in 'want to go'.
PART_MOV = verb-particle separation, as in 'turn the light on'.
AUX_ING = [be] + V-ing, not necessarily with standard semantics.
Y/N_INV = yes/no questions with subject-verb/aux inversion.
PREP_STRNDG = stranding of prepositions in relative clauses.

3SG_S = third person singular '-s' marking.
PL_CONCD = plural marking of NP after number or quantifier (e.g. 'many facto-ries').
CASE(3rd) = case marking of third person singular pronouns.
AUX_2ND = placement of 'do' or 'have' in second position;
DO_2ND = as above, negation.
SUPPLET = suppletion of 'some' into 'any' in the scope of negation.
DAT_TO = indirect object marking with 'to'.
RFLX(ADV) = adverbial or emphatic usages of reflexive pronouns;
RFLX(PN) = true reflexivization.
Q_TAG = question tags; ADV_VP = sentence internal adverb location.
DAT MVMT = structures with 'make' and 'let'.
CAUSATIVE = structures with 'make' and 'let'.
2_SUB_COMP = different subject complements with verbs like 'want'.

above. The other one is the structural interdependence of individual grammatical rules.

This structural interdependence became obvious in the discussion of
developmental conflicts. For instance ADV and INV, while acquired separately from each other, form a close relationship in terms of structural prerequisites. In other words, in German INV is triggered by the presence of ADV.
Similarly, the presence of auxiliaries forms the context for the application of
SEP. This relationship is depicted in Figure 6.2-2 below: in both cases (SEP
and INV) the structures that form the linguistic context for these rules can be
produced before the rule itself can be processed.

However, there is no guarantee that the learner will indeed produce a
linguistic rule as soon as s/he is able to do so. I pointed out above that one way
of coping with developmental conflicts such as ADV-INV or Aux-SEP is
avoidance; i.e. the context for the 'problem rule' is not produced and in this
way the production problem does not surface.

Figure 6.2-2 illustrates that the learner can control the onset of the
developmental conflict by holding back the context for unprocessable rules.
In Figure 6.2-2 this is illustrated with two idealised learners one of which
(type A) acquires the context for SEP (i.e. Aux) long before SEP itself, while
the other acquires the two linguistic items with a minimal, if any, gap. This
illustrates that the temporal gap between the acquisition of context and rule
may vary from learner to learner. In extreme cases the context will be

Table 6.2-3. The general picture for German

stage	exchange of information	procedures	word order	morphology
6		sub. cl. plrocedure	V-End	
5	inter-phrasal no saliency	S-procedure	INV	SV-agreement
4	inter-phrasal with saliency	simpl. S-procedure	SEP	
3	phrasal	phrasal procedure	ADV	plural agreement
2	none	lex. categories	SVO	past-te etc.
1	none		words	---

produced only when the prerequisites for the rule are acquired.

This is exactly what I found in a longitudinal study of the acquisition of German as a second language (Pienemann 1981). In this study the learner with shorter temporal gaps between the acquisition of context and rule chose avoidance solutions for most developmental conflicts and rarely deleted redundant elements, while the learners with longer temporal gaps chose omission and violation solutions to developmental conflicts and did delete redundant elements. In other words, the control the learner has over the timing of the production of context and rule forms the basis for one type of interlanguage dialect.

Looking at a given individual interlanguage from this perspective one

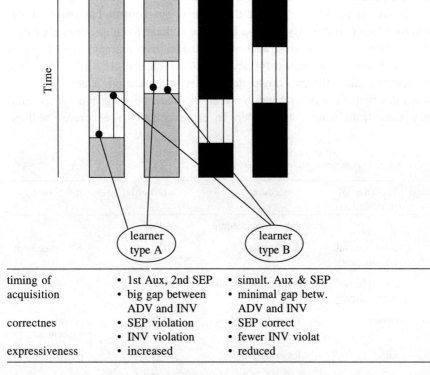

timing of acquisition	• 1st Aux, 2nd SEP • big gap between ADV and INV	• simult. Aux & SEP • minimal gap betw. ADV and INV
correctnes	• SEP violation • INV violation	• SEP correct • fewer INV violat
expressiveness	• increased	• reduced

Figure 6.2-2. Interlanguage variation and its relationship to development

can see that the avoidance of structures delays the emergence of the context for these structures. Therefore this interlanguage will lag behind in the emergence of forms that constitute the context. In other words, at least one class of "developmental trailers" is caused by the learner's preference of avoidance solutions for developmental conflicts.

It is important to note that interrelatedness of grammatical forms and functions described above exists for a wide range of linguistic forms. Here is just a brief list of linguistic items from German that are subject to this dependency relationship:

Question word	-	wh-fronting
Modal	-	SEP
Aux	-	SEP
Topicalisation	-	ADV
ADV	-	INV
subordination	-	V-END
negation	-	Neg-Final
Question	-	INV.

In other words, many L2 structures serve as the context for other L2 structures. This also applies to morphology. For instance, the presence of a grammatical subject marked for third person singular and the presence of a verb marked present and imperfective creates the context for the insertion of an s-affix on the verb.

Summing up, at least one major class of 'trailers' is caused by the learner's preference of an 'avoidance solution' to a developmental conflict. Since this type of solution was identified as one kind of variational feature, 'trailers' are variational. It is therefore not surprising that Clahsen, Meisel and Pienemann (1983) found that developmental gaps correlate with other variational features.

6.3 Teachability is constrained by processability

Theoretical significance: more about "developmental trailers"

The concept "Hypothesis Space" provides a wider theoretical context for the "teachability hypothesis" (Pienemann 1984, 1987, 1988) which predicts that

- stages of acquisition cannot be skipped through formal instruction,
- instruction will be beneficial if it focuses on structures from 'the next stage'.

This hypothesis can now be understood as a subset of Processability Theory. The latter is the formal basis for the definition of Hypothesis Space which describes orderly sequences in the acquisition of morpho-syntactic rules as well as the formal margin for variation. Within this overall concept it is logical to hypothesise that 'stages cannot be skipped' (Long 1988) through formal intervention, because each stage requires processing prerequisites which are developed at the previous stage. 'Skipping stages' in formal instruction would imply that there would be a gap in the processing procedures needed for the learner's language. Since _all_ processing procedures underlying a structure are required for the processing of the structure, the learner would simply be unable to produce the structure.

The second and more optimistic part of the teachability hypothesis ties in with Larsen-Freeman and Long's (1991) discussion of 'developmental trailers' (cf. section 6.2). This part of the hypothesis predicts that instruction will result in acquisition if it focuses on structures from 'the next stage'. One might want to extend this hypothesis in the following way: As long as developmental trailers can be related to a level of processability and it can be shown that other parts of the interlanguage are ahead of the level of the 'trailer' the teachability hypothesis can be extended to imply that the trailer can be aligned with the more advanced areas of the interlanguage because the basic processing procedures are already present in the interlanguage Formulator. This may indeed be what Larsen-Freeman and Long had in mind in their discussion of developmental trailers.

My own position on this is now somewhat more cautious. First of all, there is no reason to assume that learners will acquire a structure just because they can process it. A functional need would have to be present for the structure to emerge.

Secondly, functional constraints interact with processing constraints (cf. section 4.3). In other words, even if the basic processing of the grammatical information related to a given structure is in principle possible some of that information may not be available to the learner because of complex form-function relationships. One example is the marking of gender in German or Italian. I demonstrated in section 4.3 that gender marking does not occur in the presence of other phrasal morphemes even though gender marking itself also constitutes phrasal morphemes. The reason for this is that for gender marking to occur the corresponding diacritic feature has to be acquired for all nouns, and this is filtered through complex form-function relationships.

The third point concerning the 'catching up' of developmental trailers is related to processing. When the 'trailer' is found in a different structural area (e.g. syntax versus morphology) then the processing of the trailer structure will require a number of processing procedures which are different from the structure it is being compared with. One such example is the acquisition of INVERSION and subject verb-agreement. In this context it may be instructive to recall what was said about level 5 of the processability hierarchy, i.e. the point at which the two structures are predicted to emerge:

> "Once phrasal procedures are present, Appointment Rules and the S-procedure can be developed. This means that the functional destination of phrases can be determined and phrases can be assembled to sentences. ... "

> "What is of interest in the context of this book are the repercussions that the availability of new types of procedures have for the interlanguage grammar, and those are quite clear. Once the Appointment Rules are present and the S-procedures are complete inter-phrasal morphemes can be produced and word order can be structured syntactically according to L2 constraints; i.e. the pragmatic word order principles can be replaced by syntactic ones."

One can now see that INVERSION and subject verb-agreement utilise a number of the same processing procedures, namely lemma access, category procedures, phrasal procedures, appointment rules and the S-procedure. This is why they emerge at *about* the same developmental point. However, the procedures involved in executing INV and SV-agreement also contain components which are specific to the two rules. Therefore the presence of one does not guarantee the presence of the other.

This situation would be different if the trailer occurred in a closely related structural area because here the similarity of the procedures would be greater. One such case was discussed in the preceding section where developmental trailers were explained as a result of structural "developmental conflicts". Another similar class of trailers involves cases where the trailer coincides with one specific linguistic environment of a rule. In fact, several studies (e.g. Jansen 1991; Hyltenstam 1978) have demonstrated that certain syntactic structures occur first in some environments and later in others. One example is INVERSION which in Swedish and German occurs in questions before it occurs with adverb fronting.

In all the three classes of developmental trailers the interlanguage system gains structural diversity within the confines of Hypothesis Space from the trailing phenomenon. And this diversity can be utilised for different purposes. In the case of trailing in different linguistic environments expressive advantages can be gained from functionally more prominent environments.

Summing up, the teachability hypothesis cannot be reversed. It predicts that learners will not be able to acquire a structure even if it is functionally needed unless all processing procedures required for the structure are present. However, the presence of all processing procedures does not guarantee that the structure will emerge at that point.[30]

The teachability hypothesis - a brief overview

The teachability hypothesis was initially tested in an experiment (cf. Pienemann 1984, 1987a) which took the following form: From a population of Italian-speaking elementary school learners of GLS (the acquisition context was largely natural), ten children whose interlanguage was between stages X to X+2 were selected. The informants were "taught" a structure found at stage X+3. In order to provide a parallel for the dimension of learner's orientation, a further object of the experiment was the inculcation of standard patterns of use for the copula.

A detailed analysis of the interlanguages of the learners before and after the experiment revealed that the learners from stages X and X+1 did not acquire X+3 in their spoken language, whereas the learners from stage X+2 did. In other words, stages of acquisition could not be skipped by any of the learners and focus on from was beneficial for those who were developmentally ready for the form in focus.

These constraints on teachability are consistent with Processability Theory since learners from stages X and X+1 do not have the necessary prerequisites to process structures from stage X+3. Indeed, these finding lend additional support to Processability Theory because the conditions for constraints on teachability are more rigid than those imposed on natural development. In the case of teaching intervention an explicit attempt is made to alter the nature of the IL system at the level of its developmental maturity, whereas in the case of natural development the IL system is left entirely to its own dynamics. However, the above-mentioned experiments demonstrate that even such targeted interventions cannot alter the level of developmental maturity in an IL system.

The results of the above intervention experiments for the dimension of learner's orientation showed that this dimension of the IL is not constrained in the same way as the developmental dimension. This is completely in line with the Processability Theory, since different IL varieties that are positioned at the same developmental level are based on the same set of processing procedures.

The point I will concentrate on in this section is the delicate interplay between *constraints on processability* on the one hand and the *dynamics of structural shifts* on the other. The study presented in this section will provide further evidence for the existence of a variational dimension and describe the internal mechanics that operate on structural shifts in IL grammars under the influence of formal intervention.

The above-mentioned studies are well-documented in the literature. There fore only the research design will be briefly summarised as a background to the rest of this section. The overall design of the experiment was as follows:

1. Pre-test in natural context
2. Pre-test in formal context
3. Experiment I: focus on the copula
4. Post test (formal context)
5. Experiment II: focus on INV
6. Post-test (formal)
7. Post-test (natural)

This experimental design enables one to measure the effect of the two teaching experiments by comparing pre- and post-tests. To illustrate the overall situation with the five informants analysed in this study, Figure 6.3-1 displays their stage of acquisition and their use of the copula.

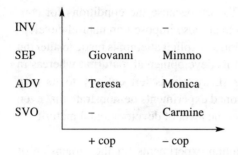

Figure 6.3-1. Stage and variation in five informants

This overview will serve as a general reference point for this and the following section.

Replication studies and further evidence

It has been noted by several scholars (e.g. Larsen-Freeman 1995) that the database of the above study is relatively small. It will therefore be useful to review further empirical evidence related to the teachability hypothesis.

My experimental study on teachability (Pienemann 1984, 1989) was replicated with 39 adult learners of L2 German in higher education in Britain by Rod Ellis (1989). This study confirms the results of my experiment.

Boss (1996) also successfully replicated my teachability study in an experiment with eight learners of German in Sydney who were observed in extended oral interaction on two occasions. Boss found that all eight learners progressed in the predicted sequence regardless of the scheduled teaching. Seven of her eight subjects produced ADV without INVERSION at time 1 of her experiment even though INVERSION had been taught before the interview. At time 2 four learners had progressed to INVERSION and one to Verb-End. The learners who acquired INVERSION had all acquired SEP before, and the learner who acquired Verb-End had previously acquired SEP and INVERSION. All of these acquisition processes occurred irrespective of the scheduled teaching.

Before I present a further semi-experimental study of my own, I would like to draw the reader's attention to the fact that the teachability hypothesis can be tested not only through replications of the original experiment but in several other ways. One of these options is to compare sequences of acquisition in naturalistic and formal L2 acquisition. It can be argued that if the teachability hypothesis is false then one would expect no sequential constraints on formal L2 acquisition. Alternatively, sequences found in formal SLA might reflect such factors as the underlying learning progression. If, on the other hand, the hypothesis is correct, one would expect the same sequence in the formal and the natural context, irrespective of the structure of the teaching interventions.

There is a number of studies which make exactly this comparison. Pavesi (1984; 1986) found identical sequences in the acquisition of English in an Italian high school context and in naturalistic acquisition by adults in Scotland. Daniel (1983), Westmoreland (1983) and Jansen (1991) found the same sequence of acquisition in German as a second language in cross-sectional studies carried out in entirely formal contexts as were previously found by the ZISA group (e.g. Meisel et al. 1981) in entirely naturalistic contexts. This is further supported by my (Pienemann 1987, 1988) longitudinal studies of German L2 in a formal context in Australia. In the latter case the sequence of acquisition was demonstrated to be substantially different from both the structures contained in the linguistic input and from the intended learning progression.

The project I would like to report on in some more detail was originally conceptualised in an applied context. It had several purposes: (1) to test the feasibility of a psycholinguistically motivated syllabus, (2) to test the teachability hypothesis for a certain range of phenomena and learners and (3) to test certain predictions of the teachability hypothesis. In the meantime, the theoretical framework within which the teachability hypothesis is situated has developed further, and some of the original assumptions of the study have changed. I will therefore treat this study as a relatively large longitudinal study of GSL rather than interpreting it in the original context.

The study is based on twelve learners whose interlanguage was observed at seven points in time. The set-up of the experiments was as follows: In a beginner's class of German (university students) the interlanguage development of the learners was monitored with the help of a linguistic profiling procedure (later described for ESL in Pienemann, Johnston and Brindley 1988). When a certain proportion of the students were found to be at a specific stage of development, a set of structures was taught which, according to the teachability hypothesis, are learnable at that particular stage.

The following structures were attempted to be taught:

Experiment 1:
- SEP
- the comparative morpheme '-er'

Experiment 2:
- INV

Experiment 3:
- Passive
- the derivational morpheme -bar (= '-able').

This study was conceived in 1984, and the motivation for this schedule was derived from an early precursor of Processability Theory according to which the sequence of the structures listed above reflects their teachability. The reader will recall that the structures PARTICLE and INVERSION are indeed acquired in this sequence. The morpheme '-er' which marks the comparative ('schnell-er': fast-er) was classified as a phrasal morpheme. This justified its combined scheduling with SEP in the experiment. In the present framework '-er' has to be classified as a 'lexical morpheme' because its diacritic feature 'comparative' can be inferred directly from conceptual structure without feature unification. The original scheduling was therefore relatively accurate. However, in the current framework lexical morphemes are predicted to be processable before SEP. One would therefore expect that a good teaching effort would produce the outcome that all those students who acquired SEP also acquired '-er', while the reverse does not have to be the case.

Table 6.3-1 displays the results of this study. It lists the informants by number, and the dates of the interviews and teaching experiments form a second dimension. The table thus contains cells for individual learners with the associated dates. Added to this one finds the experiments in chronological order. Because the information recorded for every informant is rather complex I used a graphic method of describing their interlanguage grammar. This

---

Legend Table 6.3-1   MORPHOLOGY   WORD ORDER

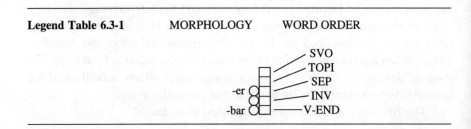

Table 6.3-1. Teaching experiments and interlanguage development - overview

method is described in the legend of Table 6.3-1 where circles represent morphological rules and squares represent syntactic rules. These circles and squares are laid out in such a way as to represent the sequence in which they are acquired in natural acquisition. Here the reader will find one difference between the 1984 precursor of Processability Theory and its current version: The distinction between lexical, phrasal and inter-phrasal morphemes was not made in 1984, and morphemes were merely attached to the last three syntactic stages. At this stage I will not alter the original analysis. Instead, I will interpret it within the current framework.

As can be seen from Table 6.3-1, our new prediction about the interplay of the acquisition of SEP and "-er" is borne out by the data: all learners acquired both structures after the teaching intervention with the exception of learner #3 who does not acquire SEP. However, this learner does acquire the earlier structure "-er".

In the period from 19 April to 17 June several learners regress, while one learner progresses. This regression coincides with the trimester break during which they received no input. The regression pattern is as follows:

learner	stable	regression by 1 stage		progression by one stage		other change
		syntax	morph	syntax	morph	
1	–	+	+	–	–	–
2	–	–	+	–	–	–
3	–	–	+	+	–	–
4	+	–	–	–	–	–
5	–	–	–	+	–	–
6	+	–	–	–	–	–
7	n.a.					
8	n.a.					
9	–	–	+	–	–	–
10	+	–	–	–	–	–
11	+	–	–	–	–	–
12	–	–	+	–	–	–

As can be seen from this analysis, half of the relevant population regresses in the area of morphology, while 40% remain stable and 10% progress in syntax only. Given the state of their interlanguage, this mean that the scarce traces of a morphological systems in regressing interlanguages disappeared completely. This is the most dramatic change documented in the entire corpus. Nevertheless, all these changes are quite orderly and fully in line with Processability Theory: no change involved more than one stage and no gap was created. In other words, these changes can be understood as orderly regression and progression.

The observation points dated 17 and 20 June form the pre and the post test for the second intervention which focused on INV. The timing for this experiment was ideal, since 11 out of the 12 informants were at stage SEP. And indeed all 11 candidates do acquire INV during the experiment. In the area of morphology one can see a further period of stagnation with the exception of two learners one of whom regains phrasal morphemes and one of whom loses them. Again, all changes are completely continuous.

The items contained in the third experiment are no longer compatible with the theoretical framework. The remaining three points in time will therefore be read simply as a continuation of this longitudinal study. The main observation is that one can further confirm the continuous nature of the acquisition process with all informants who develop further morphological and syntactic structures in the predicted sequence, even though morphology and syntax operate within their own separate schedules.

The other major observation that can be made is that all three structures (SEP, '-er' and INV) which were learnable when they were taught did enter into the interlanguage system. Unfortunately, there is only weak evidence for the amenability of the trailer effect, since the experiment with INV did not contain any inter-phrasal morphemes. On 20 June the situation would have been ideal for a 'trailer experiment' since by that time most learners had acquired INV but not subject verb-agreement. Our records show that subject verb-agreement had been part of the progression earlier in the year when the learners had not even developed phrasal morphemes. This structure was then repeated in third trimester, and our sample from 22 October shows that in this way the structure entered the interlanguage of one third of our population.

Teachability and markedness

In his review of formal instruction and second language acquisition Ellis (1994, 611-64) compares two different strands of research on formal SLA, namely universal sequences and markedness hierarchies. He observes that on the one hand studies demonstrate that the learner cannot skip stages through formal instruction. On the other hand, he quotes studies which demonstrate that structures which are positioned low on a hierarchy of markedness, improve in accuracy when the learner is taught structures which are positioned higher in that hierarchy. Ellis (1994,635) quotes Eckman's (1977) and Zobl's (1983) work as possible explanations of the latter phenomenon. Eckman's approach is based on markedness typologies while Zobl's is based on a hierarchy of markedness in parameters contained in UG. Despite the differences in their theoretical basis, these two approaches imply the same assumption, namely that the learning of an item located high in the hierarchy will facilitate the learning of items lower in the hierarchy.

In other words, the markedness hierarchy is seen as a method of packaging information about key features of the grammatical system to be learnt. Once the different rules are packaged in this way the learner needs to find clues only about the relevant packages, not about every individual rule. This principle obviously reduces the learning task and therefore offers a partial solution to the logical problem. A similar approach had been developed earlier by Bailey (1973) who applied it to the area of linguistic change.

Ellis is concerned that the two sets of observations and the explanations advanced for each of those are conflicting. He writes:

> "It is not easy to reconcile the theoretical positions of the Multidimensional Model and the Projection Hypothesis [...]. In particular, it is not clear whether instruction should seek to follow the natural order of acquisition or should try to teach the more marked features in the hope that the learners will generalise the new knowledge to implicated unmarked features." Ellis (1994, 635)

In this quotation Ellis refers to the Multidimensional Model as the basis for the explanation of universal orders of acquisition and uses the "Projection Hypothesis" as a label for the positions advanced by Eckman and Zobl.

By way of response to these observations, I would first like to point the reader to the focus of Ellis' concerns. The above quotation illustrates that he is primarily concerned that the two approaches would appear to lead to diametrically opposed recommendations for teaching practice. He does not discuss the theoretical approaches *per se* and whether they are incompatible. We are therefore left with three levels of phenomena which need to be reconciled:

(1) actual observations relating to learner languages,
(2) theoretical approaches for their explanation,
(3) practical recommendations.

Let me start with the last point. I argued in Pienemann (1985) that there is no reason to think that practical recommendations follow in an unambiguous and necessary manner from research on SLA. I argued then and I continue to believe that practical recommendations are not the immediate domain of research on second language acquisition. Language teaching is located in the domain of pedagogy which includes such factors as desired learning outcomes and their relationship to educational objectives generally. Language acquisition research can inform language teaching only if this process is mediated through pedagogy. Unfortunately, the latter domain has not been very responsive to the growing body of knowledge about language acquisition and the fact that some desired learning outcomes may not always be possible. Nevertheless, a debate of applying SLA research to practice cannot occur as a simple extension of SLA research.

What can occur in the context of SLA research, and even within this book, is to clarify the basis for the application debate, and this leads us to points (1) and (2). Let us go to the facts first; i.e. to point (1). Ellis' first observation, namely that of teachability constraints, was the subject of the previous section. The second phenomenon, namely the benefit of teaching 'high level' structures, was demonstrated clearly in Doughty's (1991) study. It will be instructive to briefly compare the research presented above with that of Doughty (1991).

Doughty (1991) carried out an experiment with three groups of informants aimed at determining the effect of teaching on the acquisition of relative clauses. She included one control group without instruction and two groups which were exposed to a different type of instruction each (meaning-oriented vs. rule-oriented). The study focused on the following types of relative clauses:

(86) The boy who was tired fell asleep.   (SUBJECT)
(87) The boy who I saw was tired.   (DIRECT OBJECT)
(88) The boy who I gave the teddy to was tired.   (INDIRECT OBJECT)
(89) I found the teddy that the girl was talking about. (PREPOSITIONAL OBJECT)
(90) They know the girl whose teddy I bought.   (POSSESSIVE)
(91) The person who is taller than is the boy went home.   (OBJECT OF A COMPARISON)

In each of the sentences (86) - (91) the NP to which the relative clause is attached has a different grammatical function in the embedded clause. Each function is listed with the corresponding example. Doughty showed that the different contexts for relativisation listed above are acquired in the order of their markedness according to the 'noun phrase accessibility hierarchy' of Keenan and Comrie (1979). What is more important in the context of the present discussion is that she also demonstrated that the teaching of marked contexts improves the learner's accuracy, not only in the marked, but also in the unmarked context, or in Doughty's (1991, 464) own words: "... instruction incorporating marked data potentially generalises not only to that marked data but to other contexts as well".

Doughty (1991, 465) is the first to raise the issue of "... an apparent contradiction to the learnability account of the importance of fixed developmental sequences in SLA, which the findings of all the relativisation studies emanating from the NPAH [noun phrase accessibility hierarchy] markedness framework seemingly constitute ...". To resolve this seeming contradiction Doughty argues as follows. She points out that the informants were selected on the basis of their readiness to acquire relativisation. In fact, 14 of the 20 informants had acquired relativisation in the context "SUBJECT" according to her 70% criterion. Doughty (1991, 465) then points out that "[w]ith respect to the psycholinguistic operations involved, it is apparent from previous studies and this one that there is a much greater difference between relativisation and non-relativisation than there is among the different types of relativisation."

The logic of this argument is quite convincing: we do not have a situation in which one set of studies show that stages of acquisition cannot be skipped while another set of studies shows the opposite. Instead, in the studies relating to the 'noun phrase accessibility hierarchy', the learners were all positioned at roughly the same stage of acquisition, with some differences in the contexts for relativisation, and all of them were 'ready' for this stage anyway.

I would like to add some of my own observations to this discussion. Doughty's intuition about the status of relativisation in a sequence of acquisition can be confirmed through Processability Theory. The reader will recall that the processing of subordinate clauses constitutes a separate 'stage' in Processability Theory because it requires a set of specific processing procedures. What distinguishes the different syntactic contexts of relativisation is the relationship between the grammatical functions of the NP in the matrix clause and that of the corresponding relative pronoun (including zero realisations) in the embedded clause. In example (1) the grammatical function is the same for both clauses, while in the other examples it varies between both clauses. In context (1) the grammatical function can therefore, in the embedded clause, be assigned in the same way as in main clause, and the canonical sequence of SVO is maintained ([who]$_{SUBJ}$ [was]$_V$ [sick]$_A$), while in the other contexts new ways of assigning a grammatical role to the relative pronoun have to be acquired. At any rate, for any of these processes to occur the learner will first have to develop the routine for subordinate clauses, and it is this requirement which places relativisation at level six of the processability hierarchy — with the exception of the SUBJECT context.

Looking at Doughty's data, we find the clearest evidence that her experiment was not set up to test the teachability hypothesis. Figure 7 of her analysis (Doughty 1991, 453) reveals that already in the pre-test all informants were using relativisation correctly in all context in at least 31% of every sample. Using the emergence criterion, one has to conclude that all structures have emerged before the experiment which is therefore the ideal testing ground for Doughty's hypothesis, namely that unmarked structures will 'improve' after exposure to marked structures. Since all structures had emerged before the experiment, none of the informants can be said to have skipped a stage of acquisition.

Ellis (1994) observes that the constellation of data in the other markedness studies is very similar to that in Doughty's study: "... none of the projection studies have examined the effects of instruction on completely new grammatical structures." Ellis (1994, 660, Footnote 3). In other words, none of these studies have produced suitable data to examine the question as to whether unmarked structures will appear in the interlanguage through exposure to marked structures.

A brief side-remark may be in order here. The above discussion highlights the significance of relating empirical methods very tightly to the concepts to be tested. The seeming observational difference between Doughty's study and mine was brought about by the use of different sets of acquisition criteria each of which are consistent and logical within their own framework. But once one compares the two frameworks these methodological differences have to form part of the comparison.

This leaves one set of contradictions to be reconciled, namely the theoretical basis of the teachability hypothesis and the projection approach (number (2) in the above list). The question is whether the two approaches do indeed make contradictory predictions and whether the assumptions that underlie these approaches are mutually exclusive.

The 'information packaging' assumption of the projection approach addresses an inferential aspect of SLA, i.e. how learners derive linguistic knowledge from the input. This approach makes the assumption that markedness hierarchies are universal (only set differently for individual languages). One can therefore conclude that the acquisition of a marked feature automatically tells the learner which unmarked features are part of the specific setting of the L2. Teachability, on the other hand, is based on the notion of constraints imposed on the interlanguage system by the development of processing procedures: what cannot be processed cannot be learnt — at that point in time.

A fundamental contradiction would arise if it was claimed that a projection of the markedness hierarchy can override constraints of processability, i.e. that stage x + 2 could be acquired by a learner currently on stage x by means of exposure to structure X+3 or greater — providing the structures x, x+2, x+3 etc. are part of a markedness hierarchy which increases from x to x+3. However, I do not think that this is the objective of the work on markedness quoted above. Instead, that work focuses on demonstrating the inferential power of the notion of markedness. This is highlighted very clearly in the above quotation from Doughty (1991, 464): "... instruction incorporating marked data potentially generalises not only to that marked data but to other contexts as well".

In order to further explore the theoretical compatibility of the processing approach with the markedness approach one would have to systematically map markedness hierarchies onto accessibility hierarchies of processing procedures in the context of typologically different languages. This exercise would reveal the full extent to which the two sets of hierarchies are compatible. However, this is beyond the scope of this book.

6.4 Effects of formal intervention on IL variation

Chapter 6 as a whole focuses on defining structural boundaries of variability from a processing point of view. In this section I will examine the effects of formal intervention on IL variation. In particular I will demonstrate that interlanguages, under the influence of formal intervention, can systematically change by altering the type of variation — however, always within the confines of Hypothesis Space.

The copula — a critical self-review

The effect of instruction on the use of the copula is presented in Table 6.4-1 which displays the relative frequencies of copula omission before and after instruction. Teresa and Giovanni obviously are the 'norm-oriented' learners: they insert the copula in the 100% of all obligatory contexts before instruction. Therefore, no effect can be measured with them.

The other learners omit the copula to a varying degree before instruction. Carmine and Monica greatly simplify this structure while Mimmo simplifies it to a lesser extent.

Table 6.4-1 describes the influence of instruction on all learners who could be tested: for all three learners the frequency of copula omission decreases considerably after the instruction has taken place. The figures from interview IV show that this influence is still present in the interlanguages after one week.

This observation seems to lend strong support to the teachability hypothesis and therefore Processability Theory: Variational features can undergo dramatic changes as an effect of formal intervention. However, generalising this individual observation to all variational features may have been somewhat premature.

When this study was conceptualised in 1980 the use of the copula in equational sentences was seen as a typical indicator of learner orientation (Meisel, Clahsen and Pienemann 1981; Pienemann 1981). The reason for this was that verbal elements (auxiliary, modal, copula, lexical verb) were shown to be acquired in a fixed order by second language acquirers (cf. Felix 1978; HPD 1976) while the *use* of verbal elements varied greatly between indi-

Table 6.4-1. Copula omission

Interview #	1	2		3	4	5	6
Carmine	/	0.7	teaching of copula structures	0.13	0.18	/	/
Monica	/	0.5		0.1	0.14	/	/
Mimmo	/	0.18		0.08	0.18	(0.33)	/
Teresa	0.	0.		0.	0.	/	/
Giovanni	0.	0.		0.	0.	0.	0.

vidual learners. At one extreme are learners who use equational sentences while hardly ever producing the copula, while others produce the same sentence type with the copula always in place.

Since the copula was perceived in this role as an indicator of learner orientation, it was natural to choose it as a learning objective to test the hypothesis that variational features can modelled through instruction.

One has to remember, however, that the original definition of variational features by Meisel, Clahsen and Pienemann was one that followed from Meisel's (1980; 1983) notion of 'restrictive simplification'. Processability Theory, in contrast, defines variational features in an *a priori* way on the basis of the current level of processing and the linguistic repertoire currently available to the learner. Distributional analysis of the type used by Meisel at al. 1981 is now seen as the analytical tool to test hypotheses made by Processability Theory.

The reader will notice immediately that the copula is not defined as a variational feature by Processability Theory, since the acquisition of verbal elements and sentence types or the development of any other aspect of c-structure is presently not captured by the theory. Looking from the theoretical perspective sketched out in Chapters 2 and 3, this reduces the value of the copula experiment, because if the structure which forms the basis of the learning objective (i.e. the copula) cannot be evaluated in terms of level of processing, one would be unable to give a reason as to why there should or should not be constraints on its processability and teachability.

Even worse, if this structure turned out to be teachable — as indeed it did in the case of the copula — one would have absolutely no grounds for claiming that other variational features would be teachable as well, since there would be no principled way that connects the various variational structures other than the way they behave in distributional analyses. Before any generalisation can be made, one has to be able to predict on the basis of a set of theoretical assumptions that feature X will vary between learners of stage Y. In this way, variational features with an *a priori* definition would act as test cases for the more general question whether structures at the learners' current level of processing can be modelled by instruction.

Fortunately, other effects of teaching were also recorded in the same experiment which will be able to be used as a basis for generalisation. These effects will be dealt with below.

The use of ADV

One set of generalisable variational phenomena relates to the use of ADV. This aspect of the experiment has been presented before (Pienemann 1987) and will now be presented in the light of the new theoretical framework because it is a very clear example of how an interlanguage can change within the constraints of Hypothesis Space.

The figures for ADV use are displayed in Table 6.4-2 below. Carmine has not reached Stage X + 1 (ADV) and therefore does not apply this rule. Giovanni and Mimmo, who are at Stage X + 2 (SEP), show fairly constant figures in the frequency of rule application.

The effect of instruction I want to focus on appears with Monica and Teresa who are at Stage X + 1 (ADV). After the introduction of INV the frequencies of ADV application fall by 75 per cent.

Table 6.4-3 gives additional evidence of this change. It shows that the initial-final ratio of adverbial positions has decreased with Monica and Teresa after instruction in INV, while the ratio has stayed stable for the other

Table 6.4-2. Relative frequency ADV

Interview #	1	2	teaching: copula	3	teaching: INV	4	5	6
Carmine	/	0.		0.		0.	/	/
Monica	/	0.56		0.53		0.11	/	/
Mimmo	0.08	0.07		0.17		0.15	0.28	/
Teresa	0.20	0.25		0.24		0.06	/	/
Giovanni	0.13	0.14		0.18		0.11	/	/

Table 6.4-3. Relative frequency ADV

Interview #	1	2	teaching: copula	3	teaching: INV	4	5	6
Carmine	/	/		/		/	/	/
Monica	/	0.56		0.47		0.20	/	/
Mimmo	0.25	0.27		0.28		0.31	0.35	/
Teresa	0.38	0.44		0.37		0.18	/	/
Giovanni	0.41	0.43		0.39		0.32	/	/

learners. Thus, out of the number of adverbials used by the two informants, fewer are preposed after the experiment.

The change which occurred in Monica and Teresa's interlanguage can be described as a transition from one learner type to another. To appreciate this transition the reader may recall from the previous section that these two learners have to resolve a developmental conflict. One the one hand they have acquired a communicatively powerful means of expression (ADV) on the other hand these means are the structural prerequisites for a rule (INV) which they can acquire only much later. The reader will also recall that this conflict has a finite number of solutions, namely the following three:

(A) **omission** of V or NP_{subj}
(B) **violation** of INVERSION
(C) **avoidance**

Tables 6.4-2 and 6.4-3 demonstrate a marked increase of the avoidance solution in these two learners which has the logical effect of increased accuracy in the suppliance of grammatical subjects and the violation of INV. In other words, the change that occurred was constrained by the solutions available in Hypothesis Space.

The omission of subject-NPs

A further change in the IL system can be observed with Monica, one of the learners with the ADV-INV conflict. This learner made extensive use of the omission solution before the teaching intervention and refined this behaviour in syntactically describable ways.

It was noted above that both Monica and Teresa do not tend towards solution (c). Instead they exploit the fronting of adverbials at least as much as Giovanni after he acquired INV (cf. interview 4 and 5), i.e. at a point in time when his ADV-INV-conflict was resolved.

Table 6.4-4 shows that Teresa almost never omits the subject-NP. Consequently this solution plays a minor role in her interlanguage. The situation is

Table 6.4-4. Omission of subject-pronouns - Teresa

Interview	I	II	III	IV	V
Omission of NPsubj	0.60	0.04	0.06	0	/

rather different for Monica. Table 6.4-5 displays an analysis of all those cases where the ADV-INV conflict is not avoided. In this situation there are two options left to the learner: (1) leave the structure that follows the adverbial in canonical order or (2) leave out the subject of the inflected verb. Part I of Table 6.4-5 documents a remarkable change in the interlanguage of this learner after the INV experiment. In interviews II and III she uses solutions

Table 6.4-5. ADV and the omission of NP$_{subj}$: Monica

1. Violation of INV

	Interview II	Interview III	INV	Interview IV
Canonical order	0.41	0.36		0.19
Omission of subj	0.55	0.57		0.71
Omission of verbal elements	0.04	0.07		0.1

2. Omission of NPsubj

	II	III	INV	IV
Average	0.35	0.34		0.13
In sentences with ADV	0.55	0.57		0.71

3. Discourse contexts for the omission of NPsubj

	II	III	INV	IV	ØNP (Same Case) all ØNP
Same Case	0.98	1.		1.	
New Case	/	/		/	
New mention	0.02	/		/	

4. Exploitation of discourse contexts for the omission of NPsubj

		II	III	INV	IV	ØNP (Same Case) all NP (Same Case)
sentences -ADV	Same Case	0.51	0.43		0.18	
	New Case	0.	0.		0.	
	New mention	0.02	0.		0.	
sentences +ADV	Same Case	0.82	0.83		1.	
	New Case Comment	0.	0.		0.	
	New mention	0.07	0.		0.	

(1) and (2) in similar proportions, while after the experiment she shifts to an almost exclusive use of solution (2). In other words: after form-focused instruction (INV) she prefers the omission of NP$_{subj}$ as a solution.

Part 2 of Table 6.4-5 reveals a further detail of this change. The average percentage of NP$_{subj}$-omission decreases after the experiment while it increases in contexts that require INV. This means that the omission of NP$_{subj}$ becomes highly predictable by the linguistic environment (ADV). Hence, the change witnessed here is one in which the learner develops a context-sensitive solution of the learning problem (INV).

This solution of the ADV-INV conflict is structurally identical with the behaviour of L2 learners just before the acquisition of INV (Pienemann 1981). It can be argued that this omission strategy goes half way towards the actual execution of INVERSION since the learner is fully sensitive to the structural context for the rule and strictly limits the omission strategy to the element to be inverted. Nevertheless, processability constraints prevent the learner from a full application of the rule.

Figure 6.4-1 illustrates very clearly how in a longitudinal study of the natural acquisition of German as a second language (Pienemann 1981) the context-sensitive omission of NPsubj precedes the application of INV.

Given that in the present study the learner develops a context-sensitive omission strategy, it needs to be clarified in what way the functionality of the interlanguage is maintained. The question is this: is the syntactic predictability of the omission of subject-NPs in conflict with the theme-rheme constraints that govern the comprehensibility of omitted phrases?

Take the following example:

(92)   * ø is a nice guy.

If the omitted NP$_{subj}$ is not coreferential with a previous mention or if a gesture does not replace a pronoun with a deictic function, it will be impossible for the listener to work out the referent of the omitted NP$_{subj}$.

In other words, the change that occurred in the interlanguage has repercussions for the organisation of coreference. I will therefore briefly look at the discourse rules that form the informational precondition for the development of the omission strategy.

Part 3 of Table 6.4-5 is intended to determine the discourse contexts for the omission of subject-NPs in Monica's speech. The contexts listed in the left column were found to be valid distinctions of discourse contexts in ESL

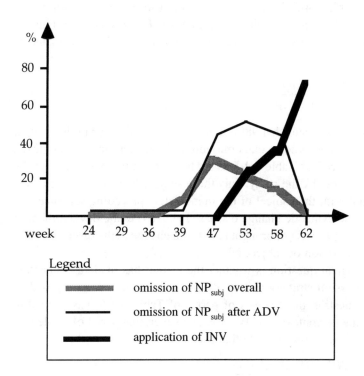

Figure 6.4-1. Omission of NP$_{subj}$ and application of INV in a longitudianl study: Concetta

development (cf. Huebner 1983). The definition of these contexts is as follows: Same Case are those referents coreferential with the subject of the immediately preceding sentence. New Case designates those referents coreferent with the object-NP in the preceding sentence. New Mention refers to those referents which were not mentioned in the preceding sentence. In a longitudinal study Huebner (1983) found that coreferent NPs are realised as pronouns instead of as zero in a fixed order which can be described within the above discourse contexts.

For reasons of structural differences in the L1s and L2s involved in the present study and in the research cited above a comparison with the actual order of acquisition in ESL would not make sense. But what is relevant for the present study is the fact that part 3 of Table 6.4-5 gives a neat description for the discourse rules governing realisation versus omission of subject-NPs.

Part 3 of Table 6.4-5 displays the proportion to which NP_{subj}-omission coincides with each of the three discourse contexts, For instance the figure in the first line of the table (Same Case) for Interview II (=98%) is calculated as follows:

$$\frac{\emptyset \ NP_{subj} \ (Same \ Case)}{\text{all} \ \emptyset \ NP_{subj}}$$

This figure therefore means that 98% of all NP's omitted occur in the context of Same Case. Slashes indicate that omissions did not occur in these contexts.

Looking at part 3 of Table 6.4-5 as a whole, it can be seen that over the whole period covered by the study, only those subject-NPs are omitted which are coreferential with the subject of the immediately preceding sentence.

Therefore the syntactic change discussed above (i.e. the development of an omission strategy) was not brought about by a change in the discourse rules underlying the omission of subject-NPs.

The next logical question is whether the learner has made a connection between the omission strategy and the discourse rules that make it possible. To study this question the analysis of part 3 of Table 6.4-5 was refined to include the syntactic context + ADV. Note, however, that part 4 of Table 6.4-5 is based on a different formula to that used part 3, namely:

$$\frac{\emptyset \ NP_{subj} \ (Same \ Case)}{\text{all NP (Same Case)}}$$

Part 4 of Table 6.4-5 therefore shows the proportion of omitted NP_{subj} in the different discourse contexts in relation to all sentences that contain the context; e.g. 51% of all sentences in interview II where NP_{subj} was a Same Case were omitted if the sentence did not contain ADV.

One can now see that the omission of NP_{subj} was already context-sensitive to some extent before the experiment while omissions of NP_{subj} still occurred at a relatively high rate in non-ADV contexts. However, after the teaching intervention the difference between -ADV and +ADV becomes categorial while the definition of the discourse context remains the same.

In summary, the case of Monica's omission of subject NPs illustrates that the mechanics of the IL can change under the influence of form-focused instruction and that this change can be more subtle than a changeover to a different solution to a developmental conflict. In this case the teaching intervention had the effect of creating a syntactically definable precursor to the form in focus. The reason for this detour was that the precursor was processable by the learner while the form in focus wasn't.

6.5 Task variation: The steadiness hypothesis

Overview

In this section I put forward the "steadiness hypothesis" for interlanguage grammars as a counterpoint to the assumption that the nature of the IL system may change from situation to situation. The steadiness hypothesis is derived from the more general concept of Hypothesis Space and it predicts that the basic nature of the grammatical system of an IL does not change in different communicative tasks as long as those are based on the same skill type in language production.

In this section the steadiness hypothesis is tested in a sample containing six ESL learners, each of whom carried out six different communicative tasks. The IL profiles of all learners were found to be *perfectly consistent* across all tasks in the area of syntax according to the emergence criterion detailed in section 4.2 above. For the area of morphology a total of three out of 324 possible cases of 'under-production' were found. This amounts to a 99.1% fit of the data in this area. In other words, the data presented here constitute strong support for the steadiness hypothesis.

Fluctuations in correctness levels across tasks do not reflect different levels of acquisition. In this section I demonstrate that such fluctuations are brought about by the specific lexical needs of individual tasks and the status of morphological marking in different entries to the learner's lexicon.

Background

There is overwhelming evidence that the shape of an interlanguage varies within one and the same learner on one and the same day depending on which linguistic task the learner performs in which context (e.g. Tarone 1983, Crookes 1989, Crookes & Gass 1993, Selinker and Douglas 1985).

For instance, Tarone (1989) observed that the frequency[31] of producing /r/ may vary between 50% and almost 100% where the latter occurs in the reading of word lists and the first in 'free speech'. The elicitation tasks which Tarone (1989, 15) has in mind range from "... word reading lists and texts, combining sentences, and elicited imitation to conversation in circumstances requiring more or less attention to language form ...". She also includes the elicitation of learner judgements of grammaticality. Tarone's interest in all these types of data is motivated by her belief "... [t]hat variability in the regular language behaviour of second language learners which is associated with the use of different elicitation tasks is caused by style shifting along the IL continuum, which in turn is caused by variable shifts in the degree of attention which the learner pays to language form ..." (Tarone 1989, 15). In other words, Tarone attempts to account for differences in accuracy levels found in the above range of 'tasks' by her concept of the 'capability continuum'(cf. section 6.2).

In the context of language testing the wide range variability reported by Tarone must be rather worrying, and indeed test developers are concerned about what a learner's performance can tell us about their linguistic ability or competence. The main concern is, of course, that the language learner might be misjudged. Douglas (1992) quotes Cohen (1992) who "... provides numerous examples of test takers 'getting an item wrong for the right reason or right for the wrong reason'." These brief quotations make it clear that the interest of language testers in 'task variation' is somewhat different from that of sociolinguists. Here the question is if test items validly and authentically test the learner's linguistic ability. This becomes even more apparent when one looks at the implicit 'mission statement' of current language testing; Douglas (1992) readily accepts J.B. Carroll's (1968) definition of a language test as

> "... a procedure designed to elicit certain behaviour from which one can make inferences about certain characteristics of an individual" (p.6). Carroll (1968) cited by Douglas (1992,1).

Looking at learner performance through the glasses of test items and right-or-wrong responses it is easy to see how task and situational variability may seem to pose insurmountable problems in achieving Carroll's objective. This must have contributed to Douglas's daunting conclusion that

> "... any factor or change in the test environment — personal, physical conditions, time, organisation, instructions, level of precision, propositional content, etc. — can lead to changes in learner perceptions and assessment of a communicative situation, and thus to change of interlanguage performance in a test." (Douglas 1992, 12).

Douglas (1986) puts it in a nutshell. He is concerned about "... the problem of characterising a learner's competence when it would appear that 'competence' varies with task." (Douglas 1986, 158)

What we see here is a world without bearings. Every linguistic measure varies and the potential number of variables is endless. A daunting perspective indeed. How did we get there? One culprit is the very legitimate premise of language testing 'maximum coverage'. It seems plausible that a language test aiming at a holistic profile of a learner's linguistic ability should cast its net as wide as possible and not be content with just a small number of linguistic phenomena. How can one ensure that the phenomena contained in the test are relevant, valid, representative? Testing communicative competence, one necessarily has to go for the big picture. With this commitment it is hard to see a way through the variability jungle, because all aspects contributing to IL performance seem relevant and leaving even just one out might invalidate the test. One can sympathise with Douglas if he concludes IL 'competence' varies with task'. Bachman (1989) has similar concerns when he writes that "... individual variations may result from different elicitation contexts, and to what extent will this affect the determination of the developmental stage?" (Bachman 1989, 204).

In other words, these are the doubts in the mind of some colleagues about the stability of the interlanguage. The crux of the instability perspective is that it lacks any fixed point of reference — presumably a consequence of its desire to encapsulate everything that is possible within human languages. I will take these doubts very seriously and will demonstrate that one fixed point of reference can achieve a very high degree of stability in the analysis of IL variation.

Before that can happen, however, I would like to reflect on a number of observations in the studies on variation quoted above. The reader will recall that Tarone relates learner performance in such diverse tasks as reading tasks and spontaneous production to the one notion of capability continuum. Form the psycholinguistic perspective chosen for this book one has to note that reading and oral production are based on rather different processes. Garman (1990) gives an extensive overview of psycholinguistic research on reading, and above I cited Levelt (1989) extensively for an overview on research on oral language production. The list of differences between the two processes is extensive, and I merely want to mention a few obvious ones: visual recognition, the visual buffer and the mediation of visual input and articulatory output. Therefore response times, word access, the availability of syntactic procedures etc. may all vary in the two sets of processes.

If one uses such tasks to make statements about the learner's linguistic knowledge, then it has to be made clear how the data one uses tap into that knowledge. Performance on each task type not only displays the learner's linguistic knowledge but it also has to pass through specific processing filters which have a bearing on learner performance. The difference between spontaneous production and reading is an example of this.

It is highly likely that task differences as described by Tarone are at least partly due to the use of different psychological mechanisms and not to different components of the learner's underlying knowledge of the IL. It is not surprising that tasks which are based on different skill components such as dictation, translation or sentence repetition would yield differences in the performance of language learners because the different skill components utilise different components of the language production or comprehension system.

Since task differences in IL performance based on different aspects of verbal skills are quite predictable I will limit the empirical study presented in this section to the domain of communicative tasks (Long 1989) and their effect on IL variation. In this context 'task' is understood as goal-oriented verbal interaction (Pica, Kanagy and Falodun 1993, Long 1989) which in the case of this study will be mediated by visual stimuli. All tasks that fall into this category produce spontaneous verbal responses which are comparable in the skills they utilise.

The study by Duff (1993) is an example of an approach where elicitation tasks were chosen to be similar in the way they relate to oral production. The study was designed to determine the influence of tasks on interlanguage performance. Duff analysed "... [e]ight hours of audio-taped oral English discourse, collected over a two-year period from a Cambodian immigrant in Canada ..." (Duff 1993, 61) using (a) interview discussion, (b) picture description, and (c) Cambodian folktale narration. The following measure were applied: (1) the amount of language produced, (2) lexicon, (3) nominal reference, and (4) negation development. Duff summarises the results of her study as follows:

> "On the whole, then, the results are somewhat ambiguous — especially in
> the light of previous research dealing with variation in IL syntax, typically
> involving just one instance of each task type. I reported that there was some

task-related variability in JDB's performance. But his performance was also different from one interview to the next, and it was consequently difficult to discern any kind of consistent association between task type and the production of specific structures." Duff (1993, 84).

In other words, no task-specific 'dialects' were found and the variation found between task types is accompanied by variation within the same task.

The question I want to address in this section is related to the sorts of performance differences that remain, as in Duff's study, when factors such as skill type, time allowed etc. are controlled and the task is more narrowly defined, i.e. when the skills required for the tasks are based on similar components of the language production system. And indeed, there is ample evidence for this more narrowly defined task variation. Several authors found that learners vary in their performance in communicative tasks when measured along syntactic, morphological or phonological parameters (Larsen-Freeman & Long 1991, 30ff, 81ff; Crookes & Gass 1993; Ellis 1994, Sato 1985).

The crucial question for a theory of SLA is what this observation of variability means for the construct of "learner grammar". As I noted above, some authors (e.g. Douglas 1986,158) have expressed the view that task variability in interlanguages indicates that a learner's L2 competence is not constant and may vary at any given point in development according to task variables. What makes it difficult to interpret this view is the fact that the term "L2 competence" is not clearly defined. I noted above in sections 4.2 and 6.2 that some authors refer to 'variable competence' (e.g. Ellis 1985b, Tarone 1983), while others quite descriptively refer to the learner's "accuracy" in the use of certain structures. And yet others (e.g. Duff 1993, 58) refer to a 'range of performance'.

The point that causes confusion here is that notions such as 'accuracy' or 'range of performance' are purely descriptive while the notions 'competence' and 'acquired linguistic rule/ system' refer to mental representation or linguistic skills. However, variations in accuracy rates across tasks do not automatically indicate differences in the rule system used by the learner or their internalised linguistic skills, much less differences in the stage of acquisition. Before any such inferences can be made a set of principles has to define the relationship between observation on the one hand and mental representation/ linguistic skill on the other.

I developed such a set of principles in section 4.2 above where the

relationship between (A) grammatical forms observed in a sample of un-
planned speech production and (B) acquired grammatical rules is defined
through a set of acquisition criteria. To pursue the objective of this section
logically and to evaluate the relationship between task variation and the
steadiness of stage of acquisition I will employ the acquisition criteria developed above. My objective will be to demonstrate that despite considerable
differences in performance the basic rule system underlying variable IL
performance does not change within one learner between tasks.

The above-mentioned principles that define the relationship between
observation and underlying linguistic skills were operationalised as follows:

> **"In an interlanguage the percentage of rule application will be greater
> than zero for rule X in all communicative tasks if it is greater than zero
> in one task providing the sample size is sufficient".**

This operationalisation of the theory-data interface is highly constrained. It
implies a commitment to a developmental perspective, to distributional analysis, to the analysis of language outside the situational context and many other
abstractions. I appreciate the pragmatic constraints that colleagues in language testing must perceive which, in their view, do not permit them to make
these abstractions. Their aim (as defined by Carroll above) is ultimately a
practical one, while the steadiness hypothesis is aimed at a cognitive concept
relating to properties of the IL grammar.

It is important to appreciate the full impact that a lack of steadiness
would have on the framework for SLA proposed in this book. If, indeed, it
were the case that one learner could be identified as being at two different
developmental levels in two communicative settings, then it would be doubt-
ful if the acquisition process could be represented as a system of steadily
developing grammars. In other words, there would be no steady development
of stages and no steadiness in the type of variation as defined within Hypothesis Space. In fact, the concept of Hypothesis Space itself would be rendered
meaningless, because its boundaries would become undefined while this is
the very objective of the notion of Hypothesis Space

To contrast the above "unsteadiness hypothesis" with the view on IL
steadiness developed in this book it will be useful for the reader to bring to
mind that the overall aim of Processability Theory is to provide a principled
approach to predicting and delineating transitions in developing grammatical
systems. The preceding two sections dealt with two different aspects of
degrees of freedom present in Hypothesis Space.

The reader will recall that a key assumption underlying the concept of Hypothesis Space is that variation and development can be captured by *one* dynamic linguistic system. At any one time and within any one learner this system, though dynamic in nature, will have a degree of stability which derives from two facts implicit in the concept of Hypothesis Space: (1) a learner will not use grammatical rules which are beyond his or her current level of processability. (2) Variational solutions are biased by the developmental history of the individual IL. In other words, Hypothesis Space treats IL variation as a highly constrained aspect of IL dynamics. And the constraints that apply are spelt out in Processability Theory.

The study

With all these preliminaries in mind I can now proceed to subject my hypothesis to an empirical test which is set out as follows: a group of ESL learners and a group of native speakers of English carried out six communicative tasks. For each speaker and each task a linguistic profile was constructed. It was then possible to determine whether individual learners were at different levels in different tasks.

This study was carried out in the context of determining the effectiveness of tasks in eliciting morphosyntactic structures for the purpose of linguistic profiling (cf. Pienemann, Mackey and Thornton 1991; cf. also Pienemann and Mackey 1993).[32] In the context of this book it provides an ideal testing ground for the relationship of IL variation and task performance.

The two experimental groups consist of six informants each with similar age range (19 - 25 years) and a similar gender composition (4 females, 2 males). The sequence in which the six tasks were carried out, the time allowed for task completion and gender and age of facilitators were controlled.

Five tasks and one informal interview were used. Two tasks and the informal interview involved one subject in interaction with one researcher. The remaining three tasks involved two subjects in interaction with each other. The researcher was present, but generally did not participate in the dyadic subject tasks.

The nature of each of these tasks and the targeted structure is described in the box below.

Task	Structure	Participants
(1) Habitual Actions	*3SG S*	*Subject + Researcher*

This task involved a set of photographs depicting "a day in the life of someone such as a librarian or a police officer". Subjects were asked questions such as "what does a librarian do every day?".

(2) Story Completion	*Wh Questions*	*Subject+Researcher*

Subjects were shown a set of pictures, which were in order, and were then given instructions to find a story behind the pictures. They were encouraged to ask for information to enable them to guess the story. One example of this task used pictures of a man who had been given poison and who needed to find an antidote.

(3) Informal Interview	*General*	*Subject+Researcher*

Subjects were interviewed informally and with sensitivity by the researcher. The situation was designed to be as close as possible to a friendly chat. The researcher asked questions of the subject and subjects were encouraged to ask questions of the researcher as well.

(4) Picture Sequencing	*Questions*	*Subject + Subject*

Subjects were each given part of a sequence of pictures. Together the parts made up one story. The pictures were lettered so that they could be identified for discussion. In order to sequence the pictures with the story, questions had to be formed and responses given which were sometimes negative. An example of this task was a story which involved a man being assaulted by three different people on his way home from work.

(5) Picture differences	*Negations/ Questions*	*Subject + Subject*

Subjects were given one picture each of the "Spot the Difference" variety. They were told that there were a number of differences. They had to ask questions and make positive and negative responses in order to find the differences.

(6) Meet Partner	*Questions*	*Subject + Subject*

Subjects in dyads asked each other questions to find out information and then were given the opportunity to introduce each other to the researcher.

The data were collected at Sydney University's Language Centre. Researchers were briefed on structures which the tasks were supposed to elicit but attempted not to produce models.

Data were collected from 6 subjects. The subjects were all short-term students at the Intensive English College in Sydney. The entire corpus of data represents 12 total hours of interaction as each subject participated in one hour of interaction with the researcher and one hour with another subject. For the purpose of the task analysis to be reported on all 12 hours of recording were transcribed and analysed in detail. The particular subjects whose interaction has been analysed are:

Subject	L1	Age	Gender
111	Indonesian	21	F
222	Indonesian	19	F
555	Indonesian	29	F
666	Korean	24	F
777	Chinese	23	F
888	Indonesian	19	M

Every session was recorded in full. It was then transcribed and analysed according to the structures found in the study of the acquisition of the ESL morpho-syntax in Section 5.2. This analysis enables us to test the variable effect of communicative tasks on IL grammar. While this is the main focus of the present chapter, the data collected in the same study also allow a test of the efficiency of the different tasks in eliciting morpho-syntactic structures.

The analysis of the NNs sample is displayed in the Tables 6.5-2 to 6.5-13 which are laid out as follows: a separate analysis was carried out for every informant for *(a) syntactic and (b) morphological structures*. For both types of analysis the structures identified in Section 5.2 in the analysis of ESL development are listed in the left-hand column. The six columns that follow to the right refer to the six types of tasks on which this study is based. Each cell of the resulting table therefore refers to the specific structure as it occurs in one individual's interlanguage in one specific task.

Two numeric values are listed in each of the cells. The value on the left hand side refers to the absolute number of occurrences. If there is a clearly definable linguistic context for the structure in question (e.g. object case for object pronouns) then a fraction is given, and the numerator refers to the number of occurrences while the denominator refers to the number of contexts. The number on the right hand side is the percentage value for rule application. This value is calculated by converting the fraction on the left-hand side to a decimal and multiplying it by 100. If the denominator is zero, i.e. when there are no contexts for the given rule in the sample in question, then the value on the right hand side is " - ". If no context is defined for the rule in question, then the value on the right is "/". In other words, a " - " denotes "rule not attempted", while a "+" means "rule is present".

As mentioned above, the sample on which this study is based corresponds to 12 hours of recorded speech which resulted in a total of 2,000 T-

Table 6.5-1. Amount of interaction elicited

	Meet Partner	Picture Sequences	Picture Differences	Habitual Action	Story Completion	Interview	TOTAL
T-Units	285	303	248	291	423	450	2,000
Turns	511	496	772	300	553	750	3382
T-Unit/ Turn	0.56	0.61	0.32	0.97	0.77	0.6	0.59

units or 3, 382 turns or two hours of recorded speech for every informant. Table 6.5-1 gives a brief overview of the size of the sample detailing the number of T-units and turns for each of the six tasks calculated for the whole group of informants. It is easy to calculate that for each task and for each informant there was an average of 55 T-units on which the analysis is based. This corresponds to the sample size of some of the extensive European SLA projects (e.g. Clahsen, Meisel & Pienemann, 1983 or Klein & Dittmar, 1979).

Testing the steadiness hypothesis

Let's return to the key question of this section: can any of the informants be said to be at two different developmental levels when performing any set of two tasks? To focus clearly on this question it will be useful to visualise what to look for in the data.

The objective of this analysis exercise is to test the consistency of IL production in different tasks in relation to the level of development. One therefore has to determine whether a learner "over-produces" or "under-produces" in any task. By "over-produce" I mean to produce structures which are at a higher level than in other samples. By "under-produce" I refer to the learner's failure to produce structures at or below the developmental level displayed in other samples.

Looking at Table 6.5-2, which displays the analysis of informant 1, one observation immediately becomes apparent: in the "Meet Partner" task the informant produces no level 4 structure, while in the other tasks she produces at least one level 4 type structure. One might wonder if this is an example of under-production which thus falsifies the "steadiness hypothesis". In my view this is not the case. All one can say is that no level 4 structure was "attempted" i.e. no linguistic context for it was produced. One is therefore not in a position to judge if in the presence of such a context the learner would have been able to produce the structure with this task. In other words, a lack of linguistic contexts for a rule means "unable to judge" (on the basis of the present observation) rather than "under-performed".

It is easy to see that a lack of linguistic context also occurs for level 5 structures in Picture Sequences, Picture Differences and Habitual Action. In a similar way structures from levels 2 and 3 are not distributed in the same way in the different tasks.

However, one thing does not occur with this informant. In none of the tasks does she fail to apply a rule which she is able to apply in other tasks. Conceivably, she might have failed to apply "Do/Aux2nd?" in the "Meet Partner" task even though she produced the linguistic context for this structure, thus producing "When she has seen this?". By producing the context for this rule she would have given away her incapacity to apply the rule in the given task.

However, this inconsistency is never produced by informant 1 in the area of syntax. One therefore has to conclude that her IL profile is perfectly consistent across all tasks. An inspection of Tables 6.5-2 to 6.5-8 reveals that the same is true for all six informants; i.e. none of them ever under-performed in IL syntax in any task over a total of 12 hours. This constitutes very strong empirical support for the steadiness hypothesis. It is important to remember, though, that "steadiness" does not refer to completely identical profiles, but to developmental consistency. I will return below to the variation evident in these samples.

The case of IL morphology is somewhat more complex. Using the above definition of inconsistent performance, one finds a total of eight cases in Tables 6.5-9 to 6.5-13. This equals 2.5% of all possible rule-task combinations for all informants. In other words, already with this rough analysis one can see that 97.5% of all data are consistent with the steadiness hypothesis.

Table 6.5-14 provides a further analysis of the eight cases of developmental inconsistency which cluster around the structure "3sg-s" and informants 1 and 8 (who make up 6 of the 8 cases).

To analyse these cases further one has to place them in the context of developmental inconsistency which was defined as that case in which a learner *never* applies a rule in the presence of its required structural context while in other samples the rule is applied to some extent. Looking at Tables 6.5-9 to 6.5-13, one notices that five of the eight cases which formally have to be counted as developmental inconsistencies are based on the one single

Table 6.5-2. Task variation and stage - Informant 1: syntax

	Meet Partner		Picture Sequences		Picture Differences		Habitual Actions		Story Completion		Interview	
6 Cancel Inv.	0	/	0	/	0	/	0	/	0	/	1/2	50
5 Neg/Do 2nd	3/3	100	0	/	1/1	100	1/1	100	3/3	100	5/5	100
Do/Anx 2nd	2/2	100	1/1	100	0	/	0	/	3/3	100	7/7	100
Do/Anx 2nd?	2/2	100	0	/	0	/	0	/	0	/	1/1	100
4 Y/N Inv	0	/	1	100	0	/	0	/	4/4	100	2/2	100
Copula Inv	0	/	0	/	1/1	100	1/1	100	2/2	100	0	/
PARTICLE	0	/	0	/	0	/	0	/	0	/	0	/
3 Topic	1	X	16	X	2	X	0	/	2	X	0	/
Do-Front	2	X	0	/	0	/	0	/	0	/	0	/
ADV	2	X	9	X	4	X	5	X	9	X	15	X
Neg + V	0	/	0	/	0	/	0	/	1	X	4	X
2 Neg + SVO	0	/	0	/	0	/	0	/	1	X	1	X
SVO	17	X	41	X	39	X	30	X	22	X	46	X
SVO?	1	X	3	X	6	X	1	/	10	X	4	X
1 Single W	0	/	3	X	0	/	0	/	0	/	0	/
Formulae	3	X	3	X	6	X	2	X	5	X	5	X

Table 6.5-3. Task variation and stages - Informant 2: syntax

	Meet Partner		Picture Sequences		Picture Differences		Habitual Actions		Story Completion		Interview
6 Cancel Inv.	0/1	0	0	/	0	/	1/2	50	0/1	/	
5 Neg/Do 2nd	1/1	100	1/1	100	0	/	2/2	100	0	/	
Do/Anx 2nd	0	/	0	/	0	/	0	/	1/1	100	
Do/Anx 2nd?	0	/	0	/	0	/	0	/	10/10	100	
4 Y/N Inv	0	/	10	/	4/4	100	0	/	2/2	100	
Copula Inv	1/1	100	13	100	3/3	100	0	/	15/15	100	
PARTICLE	0	/	0	/	0	/	0	/	0	/	
3 Topic	1/1	X	13	X	3	X	0	/	1	X	
Do-Front	2/2	X	0	/	0	/	0	/	3	X	
ADV	4/4	X	19	X	5	X	10	X	16	X	
Neg + V	0	/	0	/	0	/	0	/	0	/	
2 Neg + SVO	0	/	0	/	0	/	0	/	0	/	
SVO	15	X	55	X	51	X	27	X	25	X	
SVO?	0	/	7	X	6	X	0	/	12	X	
1 Single W	0	/	0	/	0	/	0	/	0	/	
Formulae	9	X	4	X	1	X	14	X	3	X	

Table 6.5-4. Task variation and stages - Informant 5: syntax

	Meet People	Picture Sequence	Picture Difference	Habitual Actions	Story Completion	Interview
6 Cancel Inv.				0 /	0/1 0	0 /
5 Neg/Do 2nd				1/1 100	4/4 100	1/1 100
Do/Anx 2nd				1/1 100	0 /	1/1 100
Do/Anx 2nd?				0 /	2/2 100	0 1
4 Y/N Inv				1/1 100	2/2 100	0 /
Copula Inv				0 /	15/15 100	0 /
PARTICLE				0 /	0 /	0 /
3 Topic				1/1 X	1 X	3/3 X
Do-Front				0 /	0 /	0 /
ADV				4/4 X	2 X	9/9 X
Neg + V				0 /	0 /	0 /
2 Neg + SVO				0 /	0 /	0 /
SVO				30 X	20 X	41 X
SVO?				4 X	18 X	3 X
1 Single W				0 /	0 /	0 /
Formulae				1 X	3 X	2 X

Table 6.5-5. Task variation and stages - Informant 6: syntax

	Meet Partner	Picture Sequences	Picture Differences	Habitual Actions	Story Completion	Interview
6 Cancel Inv.				0 /	0 /	0 /
5 Neg/Do 2nd				4/4 100	2/2 100	5/5 100
Do/Anx 2nd				0 /	0 /	0 /
Do/Anx 2nd?				1/1 100	1/1 100	0 /
4 Y/N Inv						
Copula Inv						
PARTICLE						
3 Topic						
Do-Front						
ADV						
Neg + V						
2 Neg + SVO						
SVO						
SVO?						
1 Single W						
Formulae						

Table 6.5-6. Task Variation and stages - Informant 8: syntax

Stage	Category	Meet Partner (n)	(%)	Picture Sequences (n)	(%)	Picture Differences (n)	(%)	Habitual Actions (n)	(%)	Story Completion (n)	(%)	Interview (n)	(%)
6	Cancel Inv.	0/0	/	0	/	0	/	2/3	67	0	/	0	/
5	Neg/Do 2nd	4/4	100	0	/	0	/	3/3	100	4/4	100	3/3	100
	Do/Anx 2nd	2/2	100	0	/	0	/	0	/	3/3	100	4/4	100
	Do/Anx 2nd?	3/3	100	0	/	0	/	0	/	0	/	0	/
4	Y/N Inv	2/2	100	3/3	100	3/3	100	1/1	100	3/3	100	0	/
	Copula Inv	0	/	0	/	0	/	0	/	2/2	100	0	/
	PARTICLE	0	/	0	/	0	/	0	/	0	/	0	/
3	Topic	1/1	X	5	X	3	X	1	X	1	X	0	/
	Do-Front	1	X	0	/	0	/	0	/	0	/	2	X
	ADV	9	X	5	X	5	X	11	X	10	X	12	X
	Neg + V	0	/	2	X	0	/	0	1	0	/	1	X
2	Neg + SVO	0	/	0	/	0	/	0	/	0	/	0	/
	SVO	21	X	27	X	14	X	29	X	24	X	58	X
	SVO?	1	X	14	X	13	X	1	X	4	X	2	X
1	Single W	0	/	0	/	0	/	0	/	0	/	0	/
	Formulae	4	X	11	X	3	X	0	X	5	X	17	X

Table 6.5-7. Task variation and stages - Informant 7: syntax

	Meet Partner		Picture Sequences		Picture Differences		Habitual Actions		Story Completion		Interview	
6 Cancel Inv.	0	/			0	/	0/1	0	0	/	0/2	/
5 Neg/Do 2nd	6/6	100			1/1	100	0	/	6/6	100	2/2	100
Do/Anx 2nd	1/1	100			1/1	100	4/4	100	2/2	100	4/4	100
Do/Anx 2nd?	0	/			9/9	100	1/1	100	2/2	100	0	X
4 Y/N Inv	2/2	100			3/3	100	0	/	2/2	100	1	100
Copula Inv	1/1	100			2/2	100	0	/	5/5	100	0	/
PARTICLE	0	/			0	/	0	/	0	/	0	/
3 Topic	2	X			3	X	2	X	0	/	5	X
Do-Front	3	X			1	X	1	X	0	/	0	/
ADV	3	X			4	X	14	X	2	X	10	X
Neg + V	0	/			0	/	0	/	0	/	0	/
2 Neg + SVO	0	/			0	/	0	/	0	/	0	/
SVO	37	X			46	X	43	X	34	X	62	X
SVO?	10	X			7	X	1	X	20	X	1	X
1 Single W	0	/			0	/	0	/	0	/	0	/
Formulae	10	X			9	X	4	X	2	X	2	X

Table 6.5-8. Task variation and stages - Informant 1: morphology

	Meet Partner		Picture Sequence		Picture Difference		Habitual Action		Story Completion		Interview	
3 sg - s	2/8	25	5/32	15	0/9	0	6/23	26	5/24	21	1/6	17
Adv-ly	0	/	0	/	0	/	0	/	1/1	100	0	/
Poss Pro	6/7	86	14/14	100	19/19	100	2/2	100	12/12	100	8/9	89
Obj Pro	3/3	100	2/2	100	0	/	1/1	100	4/4	100	0	/
- ed	0	/	0	/	0	/	1/1	100	1/2	50	1/1	100
Irr Past	0/1	0	3/3	100	2/2	100	0	/	2/2	100	3/5	60
- ing	0	/	0	/	0	/	0	/	0	/	0/1	0
plural -s	1/3	33	5/17	29	7/7	100	7/8	88	2/4	50	4/7	57
Poss-s	0	/	0	/	0	/	0	/	0	/	0	/

Table 6.5-9. Task variation and stages - Informant 2: morphology

	Meet Partner		Picture Sequence		Picture Difference		Habitual Action		Story Completion		Interview
3 sg - s	5/7	71	1/7	14	1/8	12	6/17	35	5/8	38	
Adv-ly	0	/	0	/	1/1	100	0	/	0	/	
Poss Pro	3/3	100	11	100	20	100	3/3	100	2/2	100	
Obj Pro	3/3	100	0	/	0	/	0	/	0	/	
- ed	0	/	11	100	0	/	0	/	0	/	
Irr Past	1/1	100	0/2	0	0	/	0	/	5/5	100	
- ing	0	/	16	X	14	X	8	X	5	X	
plural -s	3	100	5/6	83	5/18	83	5/11	45	0	/	
Poss-s	0	/	3/4	75	2	100	0	/	0	/	

Table 6.5-10. Task variation and stages - Informant 5: morphology

	Meet Partner	Picture Sequence	Picture Difference	Habitual Action		Story Completion		Interview	
3 sg - s				4/30	13	4/27	14	1/10	10
Adv-ly				0	/	2/2	100	0	/
Poss Pro				1/1	100	2/2	100	2/2	/
Obj Pro				3/3	100	1/1	100	0	/
- ed				0	/	0	/	1/1	100
Irr Past				0	/	0	/	1/1	100
- ing				0	/	2/2	100	0	/
plural -s				6/6	100	2/2	100	3/3	100
Poss-s				0	/	0	/	0	/

Table 6.5-11. Task variation and stages - Informant 6: morphology

	Meet Partner	Picture Sequence	Picture Difference	Habitual Action		Story Completion		Interview	
3 sg - s				7/27	25	4/4	100	2/2	100
Adv-ly				0	/	0	/	0	/
Poss Pro				7/7	100	4/4	100	1/1	100
Obj Pro				4/4	100	2/2	100	1/1	100
- ed				10/10	100	5/5	100	4/4	100
Irr Past				16/16	100	10/10	100	2/2	100
- ing				0	/	0	/	0	/
plural -s				3/3	100	1/1	100	4/4	100
Poss-s				3/3	100	0	/	0	/

Table 6.5-12. Task variation and stages - Informant 7: morphology

	Meet Partner		Picture Sequence	Picture Difference		Habitual Action		Story Completion		Interview	
3 sg - s	5/12	42		2/11	18	2/23	9	1/8	12	0/1	0
Adv-ly	0	/		0	/	0	/	0	/	2/2	100
Poss Pro	9/9	100		2/2	100	3/3	100	6/6	100	4/4	100
Obj Pro	2/2	100		0	/	7/7	100	4/4	100	1/1	100
- ed	2/3	67		0	/	0	/	0	/	0	/
Inv Past	2/3	67		0	/	1/1	100	4/4	100	3/5	80
- ing	5	X		7	X	2	X	2	X	4	X
plural -s	3/4	75		5/8	62	2/2	100	1/1	100	1/5	17
Poss-s	0	/		0/1	0	0	/	0	/	0	/

Table 6.5-13. Task variation and stages - Informant 8: morphology

	Meet Partner		Picture Sequence		Picture Difference		Habitual Action		Story Completion		Interview	
3 sg - s	0/10	0	4/9	44	3/9	33	2/29	7	4/19	21	0/6	0
Adv-ly	0	/	0	/	0	/	0	/	0	/	0	/
Poss Pro	4/4	100	11/11	100	2/2	100	6/6	100	8/8	100	6/7	86
Obj Pro	1/1	100	5/5	100	0	/	7/1	100	0	/	3/3	100
- ed	1/1	100	0/1	0	0/1	0	0	/	0	/	1/5	20
Irr Past	1/1	100	2/6	33	1/1	100	1/1	100	3/4	75	1/3	33
- ing	2/2	100	4/4	100	4/4	100	1/2	50	2/2	100	2/2	100
plural -s	0	/	1/3	33	0	/	0/1	0	1/1	100	5/10	50
Poss-s	0	/	0	/	0	/	0	/	0	/	1/1	100

Table 6.5-14

(a) Under-performances by structure and task

	Meet Partner	Picture Sequences	Picture Differences	Habitual Actions	Story completion	Interview	Total
3 sg-s	1					11	3
Adv-ly							0
Poss Pro							0
Obj Pro							0
-ed			1				1
Inv. Past	1	1					2
-ing							0
plural-s							1
Poss-s							0
TOTAL							
# cases	2	1	1	0	0	2	8

(b) Under-performances by informant

Infor. #	# of under-performances
1	2
2	1
5	0
6	0
7	1
8	4
Total	8 8/324 = 2.5 %

linguistic context for the required rule. It is difficult to see how one can categorically judge on this extremely limited observational basis that the learner *never* applies the rule — i.e. when "never' equals one single opportunity. Given that for the vast majority of the morphological rules in question the percentage of rule application is well below 100% for most informants one has to allow for the possibility that, by chance, the one context that occurred in the sample which was the one naturally associated with non-application of the rule.

This leaves a total of three out of 324 possible cases of "under-production". All of these are related to "3sg-s". The morphological rule relates to level 5 of the developmental chart. Note that all learners of this sample display evidence of the presence of an array of level 5 structures. In this context it is quite relevant to realise that by looking for "under-production" in the sample one effectively tests the validity of Tables 6.5-2 to 6.5-13 as implicational tables. Any case of "under-production" would have contradicted the implicational pattern of the scale. In other words, one would not expect rules at level 4 or below never to be applied if applications of rules at level 5 do occur.

Looking at Tables 6.5-2 to 6.5-13 one finds the strongest possible result: there is not a single contradiction to the implicational pattern. The only three cases of "under-production" occur at level 5, the maximum level of the learners with whom they occur. These cases therefore do not contradict the implicational pattern, and the scalability of the complete sample is 100%. This lends strong support to the validity of the ESL scales.

Developmental consistency across tasks, however, is a more rigid criterion than implicational scalability, and with the three (out of 324) cases mentioned one finds that developmental consistency occurs in 99.1% of the sample. This nevertheless amounts to a remarkable consistency in developmental morphology across the whole sample. This and the 100% developmental consistency in syntax strongly support the IL steadiness hypothesis.

In summary, the above analysis demonstrated that — using a rigorous set of acquisition criteria to identify grammatical rules in the corpus — the interlanguage of all informants conformed to the same grammatical rules across different communicative tasks and that the tasks did not alter the developmental status of the IL. This is what is predicted by Hypothesis Space.

Variation as an adjustment to expressive needs

There is nonetheless undeniable variation in the way in which grammatical rules were *used* across different tasks in this corpus. This observation is quite congruent with the relationship between development and variation posited in Hypothesis Space because grammatical rules can be utilised in different ways yielding different outcomes in accuracy and proficiency. Below I will demonstrate that the kind of IL variation to be found in the corpus reflects the learner's natural adjustments to the expressive needs created by the communicative tasks within the constraints of Hypothesis Space.

In this context it will be useful to remember that the present study was explicitly designed to identify tasks which would elicit the structures present in the ESL chart. In order to test that some tasks are more successful than others one has to demonstrate that the effective tasks produce a higher rate of contexts for the structures in question per linguistic units than other tasks. In other words, variable task performance is the prerequisite for obtaining any conclusive answer to the question of task effectiveness. An effective task simply increases the amount of available meaningful observations for the purpose of ESL profiling (Pienemann, Mackey and Thornton 1991). It is for these reasons that one would **expect** a high degree of task variation in this study.

There are two types of IL phenomena that vary across tasks in this corpus: one is what can be described as *data density*; the other is *fluctuation* in the percentage of rule application. Data density refers to the number of times the context for a grammatical rule is produced in relation to a fixed length of text. This can be measured by calculating the proportion of linguistic contexts per T-unit. In contrast, percentages of rule application measure the actual application of the rule. An example of fluctuations in the percentage of rule application is the rate of plural-s insertion in informant 1:

Meet Partner	Picture Sequences	Picture Differences	Habitual Actions	Story Completion	Interview
33%	29%	100%	88%	50%	57%

The above example illustrates a fluctuation of the percentage of rule application between 29% and 100%.

It was noted in section 4.2 that the number of occurrences of a grammatical rule may be related either to the number of contexts produced or to the actual rule application. The measures "data density" and "percentage of rule application" are numerical ways to express these concepts.

I will first turn to variation in "data density". To examine the differential effect of tasks on IL production, all data from Tables 6.5-2 to 6.5-13 were pooled in Table 6.5-15. On this basis one can now calculate the average frequency of specific structures in tasks in relation to the number of T-units used. To avoid making this analysis too unwieldy I selected a number of level 4 and 5 structures in order to compare their relative frequency. The results are presented in Table 6.5-16 which gives the ratio of linguistic context for structure X per T- unit.

Table 6.5-15. Pooled data of task study

1.0	Structures Elicited	Habitual Actions			Interview			Story Completion			Meet Partner			Picture differences			Picture Sequences		
1.1	**SYNTAX**	+	-		+	-		+	-		+	-		+	-		+	-	
1.11	**Negation**																		
	Neg + SVO	0	rc		1	rc		8	rc		0	rc		0	rc		1	rc	
	Neg + V	0	rc		5	rc		1	rc		1	rc		0	rc		2	rc	
	Do-2nd	11	0		26	0		24	0		17	0		2	0		4	0	
1.12	**Word Order**																		
	Topicalisation	5	rc		17	rc		6	rc		6	rc		11	rc		41	rc	
	PARTICLE	0	rc		0	rc		0	rc		0	rc		0	rc		0	rc	
	SVO	256	rc		344	rc		147	rc		154	rc		150	rc		180	rc	
	ADV	48	rc		73	rc		40	rc		34	rc		18	rc		35	rc	
	Do-Aux 2nd	5	0		19	0		12	0		17	0		1	0		3	0	
1.13	**Questions**																		
	SVO	17	rc		17	rc		76	rc		18	rc		32	rc		29	rc	
	Do-Front	0	0		6	0		3	0		12	0		1	0		0	0	
	Y/N Inversion	9	0		11	0		21	0		7	1		10	0		4	0	
	Cop Inversion	2	0		1	0		41	0		10	0		6	0		9	0	
	Do/Aux 2nd?	1	0		9	0		12	0		22	3		9	0		0	0	
	Cancel Inv	3	3		2	4		0	2		0	1		0	0		1	0	
1.2	**MORPH**	+	>	-	+	>	-	+	>	-	+	>	-	+	>	-	+	>	-
1.2.1	**Verb**																		
	- ed	10	0	0	8	3	5	6	0	1	4	1	1	0	0	1	1	0	2
	- irreg past	18	0	0	21	2	5	24	1	5	6	2	1	3	0	0	7	2	13
	- ing	12	1	rc	11	0	rc	11	0	rc	7	0	rc	25	0	rc	26	0	rc
	- 3rd sing -s	27	4	119	5	11	18	23	8	71	21	6	29	6	7	26	14	5	42
1.2.2	**Noun**																		
	Plural -s	23	2	6	28	6	13	7	3	4	14	8	7	27	2	4	13	3	2
	Possessive -s	3	0	0	2	0	1	0	0	3	0	1	0	2	0	1	3	1	0
1.2.3	**Pronoun**																		
	Possessive	25	1	1	21	1	1	32	0	0	57	0	3	43	0	0	51	0	0
	Object	19	0	0	4	0	0	13	0	0	11	0	0	0	0	0	13	0	0
1.2.4	**Adverb**																		
	- ly	0	0	0	3	1	0	3	0	0	5	0	0	0	0	0	0	0	0
1.3	**OTHER**	+			+			+			+			+			+		
1.3.1	**General**																		
	Single words	0			0			0			0			0			0		
	Formulae	26			57			23			35			19			27		
1.3.2	**Omission**																		
	Subject	37			24			15			13			35			35		
	Verb	3			5			1			4			7			4		
	Copula	1			0			2			0			0			0		
	Article	2			2			4			0			0			0		

Table 6.5-15. continued

2.0	Amount & Type of Interaction Elicited						
2.1	**Turns**						
	Total	300	754	553	511	772	496
	Group Mean	50.0	126	92.2	85.1	193	124
2.2	**T-Units**						
	Total	291	450	423	285	248	303
	Group Mean	48.5	75.0	70.5	47.5	62.0	75.75
2.3	**T-units/Turn**						
	Group Mean	1.12	0.685	0.816	1.28	1.13	1.13

+ = supplied
- = not supplied in obligatory context
> = oversupplied
nc= not coded

Table 6.5-16. Structure per T-unit by tasks

	Meet Partner	Picture Sequences	Picture Differences	Habitual Actions	Story Completion	Interview
Neg. Do-2nd	0.0597	0.0066	0.0132	0.0378	0.0567	0.0578
Do/Aux 2nd	0.0597	0.0099	0.0040	0.0172	0.0284	0.0422
Do/Aux 2nd?	0.0877	0.0000	0.0363	0.0034	0.0284	0.0200
Y/N Inv	0.0246	0.0132	0.0403	0.0309	0.0496	0.0244
Cop Inv	0.0351	0.0297	0.0242	0.0068	0.0969	0.0022
3sg-s	0.1754	0.1848	0.1331	0.5017	0.2222	0.0511
Poss-Pro	0.2105	0.1683	0.1734	0.0893	0.0757	0.0489
-ed	0.0246	0.0099	0.0040	0.0344	0.0166	0.0289
plural-s	0.0737	0.0495	0.125	0.0997	0.0026	0.0911
T-units	**285**	**303**	**248**	**291**	**423**	**450**

This ratio calculated as follows:

$$\frac{(\textit{\# of application of rule X}) + (\textit{\# of non-application of rule X})}{\text{T-units}}$$

Given that the majority of the grammatical items contained in Table 6.5-16 relate to verbs and that a T-unit does not contain more than one verb the ratio expressed by the above formula will be between 0 and 1. The only items where the ratio could theoretically exceed 1 are possessive pronouns and plural-s; but even this is highly unlikely because an excessive use of these structures would result in very unnatural language use.

Some of the differential effects of tasks which were already visible in the individualised data analysis become even more prominent in this analysis. There are marked difference in data density across tasks. A prime example is the use of "3sg-s". The density of this structure per T-unit is much higher in the Habitual Actions task (0.5017) than in any other task. For instance, in the Interview this structure is ten times less frequent (data density 0.0511). This demonstrates that the Habitual Actions task successfully creates the expressive need for the production of "3sg-s". This is congruent with the conceptual-semantic constraints of this task which requires a singular third person referent and reference to present and non-continuous action. The presence of these conceptual-semantic parameters describe the environment for English subject verb agreement marking.

These are exactly the expressive parameters that form part of the Habitual Actions task. In other words, the informants' highly frequent use of SV agreement is a logical response to the expressive needs created by the task. While the Story Completion task also provides singular third person referents it makes reference to different time relations with some of the action placed in the past. It is therefore to be expected that this task triggers a smaller number of SV-agreement environments which is exactly what can be found in the data: The figure for Story Completion is 0.2222 as opposed to 0.5017 for Habitual Action.

This conclusion is re-enforced by the fact that native-speakers of English react in a very similar way to this task as non-native speakers (NNS). Table 6.5-17 displays the comparative values for both groups of speakers. Note that the NS control group referred to in Table 6.5-17 was part of the original research on the effectiveness of tasks as elicitation devices. This group was constituted in parallel to the NNS group (i.e. same age, gender distribution, same sequence of tasks).

Table 6.5-17. *Frequency of of the production of the environment for SV-agreement*
                marking in three different tasks by native speakers and non-native speak-
                ers of English

	Habitual Action	Story Completion	Interview
NS			
3 sg-s	113	88	40
T-units	398	551	722
3-5/T-unit	0.28	0.16	0.06
NNS			
3sg-s	146	101	34
T-unit	291	423	450
3g/T-unit	0.50	0.24	0.08

Table 6.5-17 demonstrates clearly that the frequency of environments for SV agreement markers occurs in similar proportions in the NNS group as it does in the NS group. In both groups of informants the frequency declines in the following pattern of variability.

Habitual Actions > Story Completion > Interview.

The main difference between the two groups is that for NNSs the frequency of SV agreement environment is consistently higher for all tasks. This may be due to the fact that the NSs produce a greater number of T-units to accomplish the same task.

One can therefore clearly confirm the naturalness of the response produced by the NNS to the task in relation to SV agreement marking. Native speakers, like their NNS counterparts, produce the highest frequency of SV agreement environments when the task explicitly provides a singular third person referent and reference to habitual action. In other words, it is the nature of the communicative task itself which produces the variable effect on the production of SV agreement makers.

A brief side-observation: The other side of the coin is that on the basis of the structure-eliciting effect of communicative tasks one can predict that some tasks will produce poor data for specific structures. For instance, the interview is an unsuitable environment for the collection of data on SV agreement marking. When speech samples are collected in the context of tasks which produce a low data density and this is all the data the researcher has access to, then this database may lead to incorrect conclusions about the state of the learners' grammar. It is on this basis that Long and Sato (1984) caution researchers to control for task variation in empirical studies to be able to relate the learners' observed performance to their true level of acquisition.

Table 6.5-16 contains a whole range of further observations, which support the point that task variation occurs in response to the expressive needs created by the task: a further and very straight-forward example is the marking of plurals. Obviously, the Story Completion task produces the lowest, and the Picture Differences task the highest frequency of plural markers. This correlates with the number of referents depicted on the visual material on which the task is based: the Story Completion material contained no multiple referents, while the Picture Differences material had the highest frequency of all materials.

The situation is very similar for the morphological marking of past events. The Picture Sequences and the Picture Differences tasks are set out in such a way that they require no reference to past events. It is therefore logical that IL samples taken in this situation contain hardly any morphological past markers.

In the Meet Partner task, the objective is to explore open classes of information about the partner, such as age, occupation, etc. This function is fulfilled most naturally by WH-questions which necessitate do-insertion when negated and Aux-2nd placement if auxiliaries occur. In other words, the functional constraints created by this task logically bias a high rate of NegDo2nd and Do/Aux-2nd. Looking at Table 6.5-16 this is exactly what is to be found.

The Story Completion task, in contrast, involves a set of sequenced pictures. It is the informant's task to find out the story behind the picture. While this task requires some questions on open-class pieces of information, it requires a high frequency of confirmation checks on the correctness of assumed propositions (e.g. "Is he a doctor?"). This function is most naturally carried out by Yes/No questions which require Y/N inversion or copula inversion. A glance at Table 6.5-16 shows that indeed these structures have their highest frequency in Story Completion tasks.

To sum up, variation in "data density" is brought about by the functional constraints of the communicative task which bias the way the available repertoire of grammatical rules is utilised by the learner.

Let us now turn to the second type of task variation: fluctuations in percentage of rule application. For this purpose I will analyse some aspects of

Table 6.5-18. Third person singular-s and plural-s marking in six different tasks by informant 1

	Meet Partner		Picture Sequen.		Picture Differenc.		Habitual Actions		Story Complet.		Interview	
3sg-s	8	25	32	15	9	0	23	26	24	21	6	17
Plural-s	3	33	17	29	7	100	8	88	4	50	7	57

the IL of informant 1 in more detail. Comparing the percentages of rule application in Tables 6.5-8 to 6.5-13 the reader can verify that informant 1 is amongst those learners of this sample who display the greatest amount of variation in the percentage of rule application. This is evident, for instance, in the values for "3sg-s" and "plural-s" in performing the six different tasks. These percentages are reproduced in Table 6.5-18.

Table 6.5-18 is laid out in a very similar manner to Table 6.5-2 to 6.5-13. The only difference is that in Table 6.5-18 the figure on the left hand side is not a fraction, but a number which refers to the number of contexts for the rule in question.

Earlier in this section, I reflected on the application of the emergence-criterion for acquisition and I noted that the performance of learner 1 in the Picture Differences task was one out of three cases which made up the 0.9% of "under-performance" evident in this sample. In other words, the remaining 99.1% is consistent with the hypothesis that individual interlanguages will be stable to the extent that task variation remains within the confines of Hypothesis Space and will not cross developmental levels.

Looking at Table 6.5-19, it is easy to see that quantitative acquisition criteria would have produced a very different result. Applying an 80% accuracy criterion, for instance, would produce the result given in part 1 of Table 6.5-19 where "-" stands for "not acquired" and "+" for "acquired". A 50% accuracy criterion would change the picture as shown in part 2 of Table 6.5-19.

This comparison demonstrates that an 80% accuracy criterion would determine the 'plural-s' to be 'acquired in two tasks, while according to a 50% criterion it would be 'acquired' in four out of six tasks.

In Section 4.2 I argued extensively against this type of quantitative acquisition criterion because accuracy levels do not increase steadily in the acquisition process and because quantitative criteria are completely arbitrary.

Table 6.5-19. Application of quantitative acquisition criteria to the interlanguage of learner 1 in 6 different taks

Part 1: 80% accuracy criterion

	Meet Partner	Picture Sequen.	Picture Differenc.	Habitual Actions	Story Complet.	Interview
3sg-s	–	–	–	–	–	–
Plural-s	–	–	+	+	–	–

Part 2: 50% accuracy criterion

	Meet Partner	Picture Sequen.	Picture Differenc.	Habitual Actions	Story Complet.	Interview
3sg-s	–	–	–	–	–	–
Plural-s	–	–	+	+	+	+

The emergence criterion, in contrast, can be associated with the psychological level of explanation and can technically be tied into a finely-grained distributional analysis.

Leaving aside the question of the correctness or appropriateness of the acquisition criteria it is important to note that the method of hypothesis testing employed here is in itself consistent. The hypothesis about the steadiness of interlanguages is based on the particular conceptual framework of Hypothesis Space, and it was this framework that was applied when it came to empirically testing the steadiness hypothesis. That is, I applied the same set of criteria to the generation of the steadiness hypothesis as I did for testing it. It would have been quite inconsistent to apply quantitative acquisition criteria at the testing stage. The way in which the steadiness hypothesis could be falsified would therefore be by demonstrating, in a new set of data, that the initial criteria produce inconsistent results.

This leaves us with the quantitative variation evident in table 18. However, it has to be pointed out that the objective of Hypothesis Space is not to explain these phenomena. Instead, the objective of Hypothesis Space is to predict the **range of IL variation** and not which variant will occur under which condition.

The prediction that can be derived from the concept of Hypothesis Space is that the percentage of rule application will be greater than zero in all tasks if

Table 6.5-20. Plural formation in Informant I: a lexical analysis

	Meet Partner	Picture Sequences	Picture Differences	Habitual Actions	Story Completion	Interview
Suppliance in plural contexts	1 cat	2 egg 2 clothe 1 picture	4 flower 2 bird 1 button	1 thing 1 student 5 book	1 dollar 1 friend	1 parent 1 student 1 place 1 year
Suppliance in non-plural contexts	0	6 picture 2 headache 1 man 1 children 1 one	0	0	1 million	1 friend 1 dancing 1 body
non-suppliance in plural contexts	2	1	0	1	1	0
% target like use	*33*	*29*	*100*	*88*	*50*	*57*

it is greater than zero in one task providing the sample size is sufficient. This prediction was confirmed above with the qualification discussed earlier. Any predictions that would go beyond this would have to be based on a separate theoretical module or on an extended theoretical base of Hypothesis Space.

It is nevertheless interesting to note to what extent even the quantitative aspect of IL variation is determined by the expressive constraints of the tasks themselves. The one example I want to give is the insertion of plural-s in informant I.

Table 6.5-20 displays the nouns that appear to be morphologically marked for plural in the interlanguage of informant I. This table differentiates between plural contexts, non-plural contexts and non-contexts for plural.

One observation springs to mind at once: the selection of lexical items is determined by the task. Whichever pictures are used to support a task, the objects depicted there materialise, naturally, as lexical items, sometimes with high frequency (e.g. 4 x flower, 5 x book, 7 x picture).

The frequent repetition of lexical items influences the overall rate of accuracy in two ways. If an item is stored as a mono-morphemic unit, such as "pictures" and this item is repeated six times — as in the Picture Sequences task, then the overall accuracy of plural marking declines. If one discounts this one item and thereby adjusts the accuracy rate for the Picture Sequences task it will go up from 29% to 45%, i.e. very close to the rate found in two other tasks.

The second way in which accuracy rates are affected by lexical choice is the reverse of the first: a highly frequent use of **correctly** marked nouns **increases** the accuracy rate. Here we find that the highest accuracy rates (Picture Differences and Habitual Actions) occur in the only two cases where individual and morphologically regular items are repeated four times or more. In these cases the communicative task happens to require lexical items for which the morphological marking in question is active.

A further observation is relevant to the steadiness of plural marking: Low accuracy rates are not produced by the absence of plural markers but by the *oversupplicance* of such markers. The set of nouns which are over-marked (i.e. use of -s-marker in non-plural contexts) contains mostly items which are used in plural and non-plural contexts. However these items never occur in a different morphological form (i.e. without the -s-marker). This applies to items with 'irregular' plurals ("Children-s", "man-s") and to some 'regular' nouns, particularly the word "picture-s".

This distributional behaviour makes one hypothesis highly likely: morphologically 'over-marked' nouns have only one entry in the learner's lexicon, and this entry happens to coincide with the English plural form. In other words, morphological plural marking is not productive with these lexical items while it is with other lexical items. Therefore the suppliance of the plural marker is bound to vary depending on which lexical items are used and what the status of plural marking is with these items. In other words, the variable rate of accuracy in plural marking reflects two things: (1) the choice of lexical items which depends on situational variables and (2) the progress in the acquisition of morphological plural marking.

At a superficial level it is therefore correct to say that the accuracy of morphological markers depends on the communicative context. However, it is clear from the above analysis of plural marking that this is true only in a trivial sense. It is not the case that in one communicative context one can observe a set of rules for plural formation which is absent in another context. Instead, we found that communicative contexts naturally determine lexical choice which then randomly influences plural formation depending on existing lexical entries in the learner's lexicon: the more items with over-marked mono-morphemic lexical entries the lower the accuracy rate. As a result, moderating accuracy levels by discounting mono-morphemic lexical forms would produce more homogeneous levels of accuracy across all tasks.

Summary

In this section, the "steadiness hypothesis" was tested in a large sample of IL English which includes the IL production of ESL learners in six communicative tasks. The steadiness hypothesis predicts that the basic principles of the grammar will be steady across different communicative tasks while there may be fluctuations in accuracy levels in each learner.

The steadiness in the principles of IL grammars is important for the testability of the concept of levels of processability and hence of variability within grammatical principles. If the latter were to change from situation to situation, then it would be impossible to firmly test the predictions of Processability Theory, and the concept validity of the latter would be in doubt.

The IL profiles of the six informants were tested for steadiness using well-defined emergence criteria in the area of syntax and morphology. In the area of syntax, all samples were perfectly consistent (i.e. 'steady') across all informants, all structures and all tasks. In morphology, the consistency was 99.1%. This constitutes overwhelming support for the steadiness hypothesis.

It was shown that those fluctuations in levels of accuracy that remain despite the steadiness of IL principles are due to the specific lexical requirements produced by the individual communicative tasks.

6.6 Developmental dynamics and generative entrenchment

Introduction

Throughout this book I discussed one context of language acquisition, namely the acquisition of a *second* language. This was done in order to focus on one set of issues. The explanatory power of the proposed approach, Processability Theory, was demonstrated by applying it to a wide range of issues within this one context of acquisition and by applying it to a range of typologically different target languages. A full treatment of processability in other contexts of language acquisition, such as first language acquisition, will not be possible within the given space.

Nevertheless, a preliminary examination of the applicability of Processability Theory to other contexts of language acquisition will be a productive exercise because some of the most insightful work on second language acquisition has focused on differences between L1 and L2 acquisition. However, I ought to foreshadow to the reader, at this stage, the preliminary nature of these investigations which he or she might find somewhat more speculative than the rest of this book. I felt that towards the end, some speculation may be useful, if for no other reason than to prepare the ground for a research agenda that follows from the proposed theory.

The reader will recall that in sections 1.2, 2.1 and 2.2 I discussed a number of rationalist approaches to SLA which had in common that they assumed fundamental differences in first and second language acquisition (Felix 1984; Clahsen 1990; Meisel 1991; cf. also Bley-Vroman 1990). They assume that L1 learners have access to UG and L2 learners[33] do not. To account for L2 acquisition, these authors therefore have to define a UG alternative. Clahsen and Meisel are the scholars who have produced the most explicit accounts of explanations of L2 acquisition which are conceived as performance strategies. Clahsen and Muysken (1986) view the relationship of explanandum and explanans roughly as in Figure 6.6-1.

The reader will also recall the critique of Clahsen's approach in section 2.2. White (1991) claimed that processing strategies were an inadequate account of the SLA processes they were supposed to explain. The theory proposed in this book, Processability Theory, was developed in response to that critique, and I think that I have demonstrated in the previous chapters that Processability Theory has overcome the limitations of the strategies approach.

Figure 6.6-1. Explanatory devices in L1 and L2 acquisition as envisaged by proponents of the Fundamental difference hypothesis

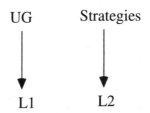

In pragmatic terms, one might now suggest a division of labour along the following lines: UG for L1 and Processability for L2. This would restore the balance of the 'fundamental difference perspective'. However, there is one problem with the logic of this approach: in this section I will demonstrate that Processability Theory can also account for L1 sequences. At first glance, this claim, if substantiated, might appear to render UG superfluous. However, such a conclusion would be premature — and incorrect.

Instead I will argue for a different relationship. In particular I will argue that the notion of universal grammar and language processing do not form a dichotomy in the context of explaining differences between L1 and L2 acquisition. I will show that the fundamental principles of language processing apply to non-native language as well as to native language use. I therefore argue that the architecture of human language processing will have a bearing on any type of language acquisition. In fact, the two explanatory devices, UG and strategies, are on quite a different scale and address different aspects of the acquisition process.

UG has been productive mostly as a property theory, addressing the issue of the origin of linguistic knowledge (i.e. the 'logical problem') and has been far less successful in accounting for the 'developmental problem' for which a transition theory is needed. I made the point above that Processability Theory is designed exclusively to address the developmental problem, and I will show that it accounts for development, not only in the L2 context but also for L1 and that it can interact with other theory modules which do address the logical problem. I therefore view the relationship of explanandum and explanans roughly as in Figure 6.6-2 where the processability components address the developmental problem while linguistic knowledge is created by a

Figure 6.6-2. An alternative view of explanatory devices in L1 and L2 acquisition

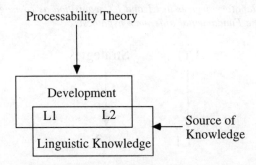

source that I leave unspecified for the time being. Some researchers would see UG in its place. This view allows the Fundamental difference hypothesis to be maintained without attributing the L1-L2 differences to a processing factor that applies equally to both types of acquisition.

Fundamental differences between L1 and L2 acquisition

There is no doubt that there are fundamental differences between L1 and L2 acquisition in ultimate attainment. Long (1988, 1990) demonstrated that age of onset "... is a robust predictor of their [the L2 learners', MP] long-term success ..." (Long 1988, 197). Long summarises relevant research as follows:

> "An AO [age of onset, MP] of 0-6 appeared to be sufficient for subjects to reach native-like proficiency (given sufficient opportunity) in all linguistic domains. Those who began SLA after age 6, on the other hand, showed decreasing levels of ultimate attainment, with increasing AO affecting long-term achievement not just phonology, but in different linguistic domains cumulatively." (Long 1988, 197)

Recent research by White and Genesee (1996) may, at first glance, appear to be in opposition to the view expressed by Long. White and Genesee (1996, 233) demonstrated that "... native-like competence in an L2 is achievable, even by older L2 learners." These authors use the existence of native-like competence in an L2 as evidence to show that even older L2 learners have access to UG. However, White and Genesee (1996) agree with Long about the overall success of L2 acquisition in a given population of learners:

> "... indeed there is a negative correlation between age of acquisition and competence in an L2 ..." (White and Genesee 1996, 234)

The crucial and open question is what the reasons are for these differences in ultimate attainment. Are they indicators of fundamental differences in the acquisition process or are there intervening variables between process and outcome that cause these differences?

Remarkable differences between L1 and L2 acquisition also exist in the developmental schedule. In his 1982 study, Clahsen found the following developmental pattern in the acquisition of German as a first language:

L1 sequence
(1) variable word order
(2) SOV
(3) V-2nd and SV-agreement marking
(4) subordinate clauses (without any mistakes in the positioning of the verb).

Quite clearly, this developmental pattern differs markedly from the one observed in the acquisition of German as a second language which follows the following sequence (cf. sections 2.2 and 4.1):

L2 sequence
(1) SVO
(2) ADV
(3) SEP
(4) INVERSION, SV-agreement marking or not
(5) V-Final in subordinate clauses (with mistakes in the positioning of the verb).

It is important to note that the differences between L1 and L2 go beyond that of the developmental path to include the following phenomena:
- The error-free learning of the position of the verb in subordinate clauses. Clahsen observed that as soon as the child uses complementisers the position of verbal elements in subordinate clauses is completely in line with the structure of the adult language.
- The interlocking of different rules in the acquisitional process. Clahsen found that in German child language development SV-agreement is acquired exactly at the same point in time as the V-2nd position. This is not the case in the acquisition of German as L2. The reader will recall that in section 6.3 the two rules were not found to closely interlock. I found the same in a longitudinal study of the acquisition of child GSL (Pienemann 1981).

Again, the issue is how to explain these differences. In Clahsen and Muysken's (1986) view all of these differences are due to the fact that children have access to universal grammar while adults do not. Instead, adults use inductive learning strategies, which enable them to reconstruct the canonical sentence schema of the target language. This implies that L1 learners are able to discover the underlying word order for German, whereas L2 learners simply infer the canonical sentence schema of German which re-flects a syntactic feature of the surface structure of the target language.

The evidence Clahsen and Muysken (1986) supply in support of their claim that children have access to UG is the following:

(1) The child's initial hypothesis about German word order coincides with the underlying word order of German.

(2) The error-free learning of the position of the verb in subordinate clauses supports the assumption that the exposure to complementis-ers is a sufficient trigger for setting this word order parameter which results in error-free production.

(3) The interlocking of different rules in the acquisitional process can be attributed to the setting of the INFL parameter, which is respon-sible for the distinction of finite and non-finite verbal elements, the crucial distinction that is the prerequisite for both rules.

Clahsen and Muysken (1986) further demonstrate that the grammatical sys-tems produced by L2 learners are not possible grammars, in particular that the rules necessary to derive the above L2 patterns from an underlying SVO order are not possible in terms of UG. This claim has inspired duPlessis, Solin, Travis and White (1987) and Schwartz (1988) to propose a re-analysis of the above L2 sequences which is indeed based on an underlying SOV order.

However, Meisel (1991, 237) points out that "... [d]u Plessis et al. (1987), in order to be able to write a grammar for L2 learners compatible with UG, have to postulate the existence of two more parameters ...". He notes that Schwartz's analysis implies a similar requirement and that in addition, both proposals rely on a poorly defined process of restructuring. Meisel quotes Chomsky (1981a) in showing that the *ad-hoc* nature of these proposals runs counter to the fundamental nature of parameters to form clusters of a number of seemingly unrelated grammatical phenomena. In view of these shortcom-ings he concludes that the above counter-proposals remain unconvincing.

Processing similarities

Let us recap: There is evidence in favour of access to UG for L1 acquisition and evidence of limited access for L2 acquisition. Throughout this book I have demonstrated that the developmental problem in SLA can be explained on the basis of processability. It is therefore quite logical to ask if Processability Theory also accounts for the developmental problem in L1 acquisition.

To test this hypothesis it has to be demonstrated that the above L1 sequence is positioned within the constraints of Hypothesis Space. Formally this is achieved by showing that the L1 sequence is predictable by the hierarchy of processing procedures on which Processability Theory is based. However, the first step in this test is to give an account of the L1 developing grammar within LFG in order to obtain a matrix for the distribution of grammatical information in the production of these structures.

Similarly to SVO structures in L2 acquisition the initial word order hypothesis in L1 acquisition (i.e. SOV) can be accounted for simply by a c-structure rule along the lines of (R-a). Since grammatical functions can be read off c-structure canonical orders, the SOV order is positioned at the lowest level in the processability hierarchy.

The Verb-2nd phenomenon can be produced by (R-b) and (R-c) in a way similar to German and English INVERSION. For the V-2nd position to be produced, the grammatical information SENT MOOD has to be exchanged by two constituents (XP and V). This places V-2nd at the same level in the processability hierarchy as INVERSION and SV-agreement.

In other words, SOV and V2nd do indeed fall within the constraints of Hypothesis Space. At this point the reader will notice that the rule SEP is absent from the L1 sequence. To explain why this is the case one has to consider the effect of the rules (R-a) to (R-c): On the basis of an SOV c-structure these three rules have the same effect as the combined application of SEP and INVERSION on the basis of an SVO c-structure. Since in (R-a) the verb is in final position, and (R-b) jointly with (R-c) permit the finite verb to appear in second position, the 'split verb' position is also permitted.

The sentence-final position of the verb in subordinate clauses is predicted to occur at level 6 of the processability hierarchy. The final stage of the L1 sequence is therefore also in line with Processability Theory.

(R-a) $S \rightarrow NP_{subj} (NP_{obj1})(NP_{obj2}) V (V)$

(R-b) $S' \rightarrow (XP) \qquad S$

$$\left\{ \begin{array}{l} wh =_c + \\ adv =_c + \\ N =_c + \\ \text{SENT MOOD} = Inv \end{array} \right\}$$

(R-c)   S' →(V)   S
$$\left\{ \begin{array}{l} \text{ROOT} =_c + \\ \text{SENT MOOD} =_c \text{Inv} \end{array} \right\}$$

Table 6.6-1 gives an overview of this comparison of grammatical development in the acquisition of German as a second and as a first language which shows at a glance that both developmental paths fall within the confines of Hypothesis Space. In other words, there are no differences in the temporal order in which processing procedures are activated. All grammars are processable at the time they develop, and each grammar builds upon the processing procedures acquired at the previous stages in a cumulative fashion. However, the L1 learner achieves this in two key 'moves', SOV and V2nd (with SV agreement) while the L2 learner takes five 'moves' most of which introduce ungrammatical structures which have to be modified in later moves.

We now find ourselves in a situation where strikingly different developmental routes in L1 and L2 acquisition have been accounted for within one and the same hierarchy of processing procedures. Therefore the formula "UG for L1 and processing factors for L2" no longer holds. And one has to ask oneself what causes the apparent differences between L1 and L2 that exist despite the common basis in language processing.

Table 6.6-1. Comparison of development in German as L1 and L2 viewed from a processability perspective

stage	exchange of information	procedures	GSL	German L1
6		subord. cl procedure	V-End	V-End (no errors)
5	inter-phrasal	WO rules S-Procedure	INV ±agr	V2nd +agr
4	inter-phrasal	WO rules S-Procedure saliency	SEP	--
3	phrasal	phrasal procedures	ADV	--
2	none	lex. categories	SVO	SOV
1	none		words	words

Generative entrenchment

My basic thesis is that different outcomes and developmental paths in language development are, at least partly, due to different developmental dynamics, caused by differences in the initial hypotheses and that the process of development can be fundamentally similar, with respect to language processing, despite fundamentally different outcomes and different developmental paths.

The basic mechanism behind developmental dynamics is the principle that developmentally early decisions bias the further development of the interlanguage system. This percolation of structural properties in developmental processes is known in biology and philosophy and has been termed *"generative entrenchment"* by Wimsatt (1986, 1991).

The concept of generative entrenchment is exemplified, for instance, by the embryonic development of animals where sections of the fertilised egg take on more and more specialised structures (e.g. Gehring 1985; Coen and Carpenter 1992; Wolpert 1992). The segmentation of the body plan occurs very early on in these processes for all animals. One example is the partitioning of the embryonic body plan of the fruit fly which I mentioned in Chapter 1. Wolpert describes this process as follows:

> A protein called bicoid marks out the space inside the egg of a fruit fly. The egg makes the protein at its anterior end, which later develops into its head. The protein then diffuses to the other end, setting up a concentration gradient which controls the pattern of segmentation. Eggs with too much or too little bicoid produce distorted segments." (Wolpert 1992, 40)

In other words, the position of head, limbs etc. is determined very early, and these structural features are maintained throughout the developmental process, and they do not have to be decided on every time a refinement of parts of the structure is made. One can say that these features are 'developmentally entrenched'.

We also know that incorrect information on the positioning of segments can have serious consequences for the ultimate shape of the organism (Gehring 1985; Coen and Carpenter 1992; Wolpert 1992). This sometimes unfortunate phenomenon illustrates the concept of the *depth* of generative entrenchment: the earlier a decision is made in structural development, the more far-reaching the consequences for the ultimate stage in structural development. This phenomenon has had extensive publicity in relation to the adverse effects of drugs on human embryo development.

Figure 6.6-3. Generative entrenchment

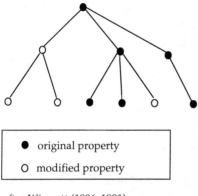

| ● | original property |
| ○ | modified property |

after Wimsatt (1986, 1991)

Figure 6.6-3 illustrates how development can be understood as a generative process where structures increase in complexity, starting with a minimal number of structural properties to which other properties are added throughout development. Figure 6.6-3 also illustrates that deeper (i.e. earlier) changes to the structure have more consequences for the overall structure resulting from the developmental process.

They key explanatory point that can be derived from the concept of generative entrenchment for language acquisition is that not all structural decisions have to be revised in the developmental process every time a structural change occurs. Initial structural features propagate in the developing system and thus determine the ultimate structure without being invoked again and again. The basic body plan stays the same.

In other words, a computational saving is made by laying structures down and keeping them. The alternative would be a developing system in which all processes of structural refinement have to be orchestrated globally for every structural refinement. In such a scenario, toes could grow anywhere on the body unless specific instructions are received as to where they have to go. In contrast, the toe-feature is entrenched in the leg feature. All that remains to be decided is where on the leg the toes are to be located (cf. Wolpert 1992).

The aspect of computational saving inherent in generative entrenchment is captured by Wimsatt (1986, 1991) in his 'developmental lock' metaphor which is based on Herbert Simon's (1962) classic paper, "The Architecture of Complexity" where he demonstrates that solutions of complex problems can be found more effectively by using the heuristic of factorising sub-problems which are solved independently, and the solutions to sub-problems are strung together to produce the solution to the overall problem.

Wimsatt's developmental lock is an idealised set of complex problems. The lock consists of ten wheels with ten positions each, very much like an extended version of a combination lock. Obviously, the total number of possible combinations on this lock is 10^{10}, which, according to Wimsatt, requires 10^9 trials to find the correct combination. In this form of unconstrained hypothesis testing, the lock is referred to as a 'complex lock'. In the developmental lock, Wimsatt constrains hypothesis testing by allowing the problem solver to factorise the combination problem. Rather than having to get all 10 digits right before the combination can be subjected to an empirical test, each wheel can be tested individually in a left-right sequence. The computational advantage of factorising the complex problem is remarkable: Only 50 trials are necessary to find the solution to the developmental lock problem, providing a strict left-right sequence is followed. In other words, in this metaphor later decisions depend on earlier decisions. If an error is made earlier on it will be very costly to recover from it, because all intervening solutions will be lost.

Summing up, the assumption that underlies the notion of generative entrenchment is that in the course of development structures are preserved and further refined. The dynamics of this process have a constraining effect on development: because of the preservation constraint, early decisions exclude whole branches on the 'developmental tree'. Once the position of legs has been decided on in the body plan, they cannot be re-located or be replaced by other parts of the body. There is ample evidence for this in biological development (cf. Gehring 1985; Coen and Carpenter 1992; Wolpert 1992).

In other words, generative entrenchment can be understood as a constraint on development that derives from the dynamics of development itself. In this way it complements the notion of processability which also acts as a constraint on language development. I will now proceed to utilise the notion of generative entrenchment as a constraint on language development in a number of empirical studies.

Generative entrenchment as a constraint on language development

The concept of generative entrenchment is a general logical-mathematical set of constraints that applies to any continuous developmental process in which structures diversify developmentally. It has been applied to many cases of biological development in ontogenesis and phylogenesis as well as population development. It is also applicable to the development of physical phenomena. Since language acquisition is another case in which structure diversifies developmentally from an initial state, the dynamics of generative entrenchment apply. The reader might object that language acquisition is different from cases of biological and physical development, because the role of input and environment is different in the case of language development. However, this objection would miss the point. Generative entrenchment models nothing but the dynamics of cumulative developmental processes, no matter where they occur. All of the non-language cases of development are also placed in an environment, be it the distribution of matter in space or the location of a body segment of the fruit fly embryo in an acidic environment. Generative entrenchment should be seen on the same scale as the logical problem where one looks at the logic of developmental dynamics.

The continuity assumption that underlies the notion of Generative entrenchment can be verified in the two developmental paths under discussion. Table 6.6-2 reveals a great deal of continuity in both developmental paths. The initial word order hypothesis of the L2 learner is maintained and refined in four developmental steps until it is finally modified to reflect the structure of the TL. It is evident from distributional analyses of large bodies of data (cf. Clahsen, Meisel, and Pienemann, 1983) that the SVO pattern continues to be produced in tandem with INVERSION and V-End. Looking at the L1 perspective, a similar picture emerges: the initial SOV pattern is maintained and refined throughout the developmental process.

In other words, pattern conservation is evident in the two developmental paths, and this gives a first indication of the initial hypothesis being a determining factor for the later course of development. However, there is also direct evidence of this. The need for the separate rule SEP arises only if the initial syntactic hypothesis is SVO. In order to modify the initial SVO order to match German main clause patterns, two developmental 'moves' are needed: one that ensures that V_i is in final position and one that constrains V_f into second position. INV on its own would not be the solution. If INV were

Table 6.6-2. Generative entrenchment of linguistic structures

	L2	L1
subordinate clause	comp SOV [comp **S V O**]	comp **SOV**
use of S-procedure for storage across constituents in S	X Vf S O Vi ±agr [(X) **S V O**]	X Vf **S O V**i +agr
use of VP-procedure for storage across constituents in VP	X **S** Vf **O V**i	---
use of saliency principle to relax canonical order constraint	X **S V O**	---
word order con- strained into canonical order	**S V O**	**S O V**

applied without SEP, ungrammatical structures like $X V_f S V_i Y$ would result.[34] In other words, both SEP and INV are necessitated by the initial SVO word order and the initial SVO hypothesis is propagated in the development of these rules.

Based on an SOV order, V2nd produces the same effect as SEP and INV combined, namely the correct target structure $X V_f S Y V_i$. This means that the development from SOV to V2nd renders the acquisition of SEP and the two developmental steps SEP and INV superfluous.

A further developmental saving is made in the acquisition of the verb final position in subordinate clauses. In L1 acquisition, where the initial fixed word order is SOV, the position of the verb does not have to change, when the distinction between main and subordinated clauses is acquired. All that has to happen is that V2 is blocked in subordinate clauses. This allows verb-final positions to be acquired with less effort than in the L2 sequence where every complementiser has to be marked for the feature ±ROOT until a lexical redundancy rule is formed for subordinate clauses. And yet again this developmental twist is brought about by the moves that followed from the initial structural hypothesis. This explains why in L1 acquisition the verb-final position is acquired virtually without errors while in L2 acquisition the development of the rule can be traced along the path of an increasing set of complementisers with the effect of an error-ridden acquisition process.

In summary, the initial hypothesis for word order in L1 acquisition renders the acquisition of SEP and V-End as separate c-structure rules super- fluous and results in a grammatically more correct output during develop- ment. Hence, the L1 initial hypothesis is far more economical, and so is the development that follows from it.

One might, of course hypothesise that L2 learners fundamentally restruc- ture the developing grammar and switch to the assumption that German is an SOV language (e.g. Tomaselli and Schwartz 1990). However, it is hard to see, in the absence of negative evidence, on the basis of which structural evidence the learner would arrive at such a conclusion, since the SVO structures they produce form a subset of the input data. But even if the learner were able to arrive at such a conclusion by some yet unknown means, a total restructuring of the interlanguage would be computationally very costly since all rules developed until the restructuring would have to be abandoned to start a new developmental path. Neither SVO, nor SEP nor INV are compatible with the SOV assumption. In this way, the developmental path known in L1 acquisi- tion becomes inaccessible once the initial syntactic hypothesis has been formed, and the development that follows is determined by the initial hypoth- esis, because the structure of the target language can be mapped only by the set of rules ADV, SEP, INV and V-END, and these rules emerge in this sequence because of their processability.

The advantage of this unified perspective on language acquisition is that it reduces the need to make recourse to UG or other epistemological sources for developmental processes. The initial structure may be derived from an epistemological source which may be identical with UG but which I will leave unspecified for the moment. Many of the other structures do not have to be specified in the epistemological source itself. They can evolve on the basis of inferencing and on the basis of the structural options allowed for by the initial hypothesis; i.e. they are generatively entrenched. For instance, the rule V-End does not have to be specified if the initial hypothesis is SOV, because the first is included in the latter.

This view also modifies somewhat the role of innate and acquired knowledge in acquisition. It was precisely Wimsatt's intention to break down the black-and-white distinction between innate and acquired knowledge with his notion of generative entrenchment. The moment one views a continuous developmental process as a chain of structural decisions which open up and close off further decisions, the question as to which of these decisions are determined by fully genetically specified information and which are determined by information that is arrived at by a combination of inferencing and genetic code becomes less relevant.

Wimsatt (1986) points out that 'innate' is not synonymous with 'fully genetically coded'. One example he gives is the partitioning of the embryonic body plan of the fruit fly which I mentioned above. In this example the logical problem is where the information comes from that determines which parts of the embryo develop into which parts of the adult body. It has been shown that the solution to this problem is a mix of genetic and environmental information (cf. Gehring 1985; Coen and Carpenter 1992; Wolpert 1992).

The reader will recall that genetic information is used to create an environment for the egg which contains a concentration gradient of the protein bicoid, and this gradient is used to mark out the space inside the egg (Wolpert 1992, 40). The information needed to produce the protein is fully genetically coded. However, the process of marking out the body plan is organised by the bio-chemical environment developed by the genetic code. In other words, there is no genetic code that orchestrates, at every step in development, the dynamics in the growth of this organism.

I propose that the dynamics of language acquisition are comparable to the developmental dynamics found in embryonic development. Some structural information has to be present to kick-start the process. However, it is presently unclear how much of this needs to be genetically fully specified, given that initial structural specifications become generatively entrenched and therefore form the basis of further structural development and given also that the development is partly determined by the environment created by the developmental process.

Let me return to the differences between L1 and L2 acquisition (and the other related contexts of acquisition). We can summarise the following points from the above discussion:

- There are two distinct developmental paths;
- Each of them falls within Hypothesis Space;
- One of the paths is superior to the other;
- Each is determined by the initial hypothesis.

One can conclude from this that one of the main reasons for L1-L2 differences is the superior initial hypothesis of the L1 learner. One can further conclude that a critical age is no *guarantee* for access to superior initial hypotheses, because weak 2L1 learners are within even the most conservatively defined critical period.

Much of the current debate on L1-L2 differences is devoted to research on the nature of the source of the type of linguistic knowledge displayed by L1 learners which permits those superior hypotheses. I have noted repeatedly above that this question has deliberately been left outside the scope of this book in which I take a modular approach to the explanation of language acquisition. I will therefore have to leave it open as to which source of linguistic knowledge permits these hypotheses.

However, I do want to highlight the interaction between genetically fully specified linguistic knowledge on the one hand and the dynamics of the developmental process on the other hand. I demonstrated above that there is a delicate interplay between these two components. For instance, the error-free acquisition of verb-final positions in the L1 context is generatively entrenched in the initial word order hypothesis. In other words, recourse to genetically specified knowledge has to be made once only for the two phenomena, and the latter results from the interplay between that knowledge and the dynamics of further structural development.

Thus the role of developmental dynamics put forward in this section constructively extends Clahsen's and Meisel's hypotheses about access to UG in L1 and L2 acquisition. The approach advocated here involves the interaction of three components, namely (1) that of genetically specified knowledge, (2) processing constraints and (3) developmental dynamics. The exact division of labour between these three components is currently unknown. Given that the validity of each of these components has been demonstrated, it appears to me that it is a more productive research strategy to determine the interaction between the above components, rather than trying to develop overall explanatory approaches from within only one of those components. Below I will show that the difference in the interaction between these components produce the L1-L2 differences discussed in this section.

Ultimate attainment and fossilisation

We have now accounted for the different developmental paths found in two different contexts in language acquisition and have seen that they can be accommodated within the overall constraints of human language processing. This nevertheless leaves a number of questions unanswered, including the following: Why is ultimate attainment better in L1 than in L2?

To address this question, let us recall the basic notion learner variation as defined within Hypothesis Space. The reader will recall a discussion of the inter-relation between different structural domains in L2 development in section 6.2 where I demonstrated that for every grammatical rule there are structural prerequisites and that there is a window of time during which the rule can develop. This interplay between rules and their prerequisites is depicted in Figure 6.2-2.

I pointed out above that many L2 structures serve as the context for other L2 structures and that this also applies to morphology. I further demonstrated that the different types of solutions to developmental problems that arise from a varying utilisation of the time window in structural development leads to different types of learner language which are characterised by different sets of variational features.

It is now time to point out that this interdependence goes further than the relationship of structural environment and rule. This is exemplified particularly well in an observation made by Malcolm Johnston (personal communication) who noticed that learners who produce English equational sentences without inserting the copula (*"me good"*) are deprived of the context for the most easily processable form of INV which occurs in direct equational questions (*"Where is he?"*). Given that affirmative equational sentences develop before questions in equational sentences, the learner's 'decision' to develop equational sentences without the copula biases the acquisition of the second rule.

This situation is depicted in Figure 6.6-4. When the learner develops equational sentences s/he has to 'decide' whether they contain a copula or not. Learners who put their bet on the copula-free structure, lose out in discovering a prototypical form of English inversion when question formation is developed. In other words, their structural choice was inferior, though easier to achieve and precludes further development.

The earlier decision then has repercussions for the acquisition of ques-

Figure 6.6-4. Equational sentences and inversion in English: a case of generative entrenchment

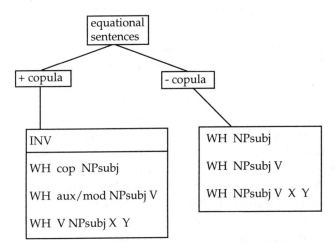

tion formation, and a developmentally early decision biases the further development of the interlanguage system. In other words, variational features can get developmentally entrenched in the interlanguage.

What we see here is a repetition of the L1-L2 differences on a smaller scale, using the same developmental dynamics. When a structural choice has to be made (within the confines of Hypothesis Space) the different options each have their own structural repercussions which vary in quality when measured against their potential for further development. The copula example demonstrates that the wrong choice can lead to a developmental dead-end.

When a learner accumulates many of such inferior choices, each of which becomes generatively entrenched, one can predict that further development is structurally precluded. This phenomenon of lack of progress despite exposure is well-attested in many of the large empirical studies of SLA (e.g. Clahsen, Meisel and Pienemann 1983). Some scholars refer to this phenomenon as 'fossilisation' (Selinker 1972).

In other words, I hypothesise that L2 development may come to a standstill when a learner has made inferior choices every time a developmental problem has occurred. This hypothesis can be tested by specifying the notions

of 'inferior choices' and 'developmental problem'. The latter term is defined
in sections 4.2 and 6.2. At this point I define 'inferior choice' as the omission
option described in sections 4.2 and 6.2.

The 'bad-choice hypothesis' can be tested empirically in a major SLA
study carried out under Jürgen Meisel's direction (Clahsen, Meisel and
Pienemann 1983). This study is based on one-hour interviews with 45 adult
learners of German as a second language. In a distributional analysis of this
corpus the six word order stages were found through implicational scaling
which are described in Chapters 2 and 3. In addition, 14 variational features
were identified which included the omission of obligatory constituents such
as the subject pronoun, lexical verbs, modals, auxiliaries, prepositions and
determiners. These variational features are also distributed implicationally.
This means that a learner with the most highly simplifying feature also
displays all other variational features. In this way, the population of the study
fell into four groups of learners, measured according to the variational features contained in their interlanguage. These four groups can roughly be
described as ranging from highly simplifying (group 3) to highly norm-
oriented (group 1a).

When one considers the group of learners below the stage SEP, one finds
that about half of these learners were recent arrivals. Their low level of
acquisition can be attributed to limited exposure. However, the other half had
between seven and fifteen years of exposure. In this group of learners,
acquisition appears to have come to a stand-still. If my hypothesis is correct
and the stand-still is caused by the developmental dynamics, then one would
have to find that these learners all produce highly simplifying and thus
inferior varieties of the IL. Table 6.6-3 gives an overview of this group of
informants.

Table 6.6-3 confirms the 'bad-choice hypothesis': all learners below level
SEP and with seven or more years of exposure belong to the highly simplifying
group 3 in learner variation. The only exception is Montse S who is the most
simplifying learner of group 2; i.e. at the transition to group 3. All other learners
are distributed across variation groups 1 to 3 with a proportion of group
membership that is similar to that of the whole population of 45 informants. In
other words, one does indeed find that all learners who do not progress far along
the developmental axis after a long period of exposure have developed a highly
simplifying variety of the L2, while beginning learners develop a wide range
of learner varieties, including non-simplifying ones.[35]

*Table 6.6-3. Informants from the ZISA study (Clahsen, Meisel and Pienemann, 1983)
below level SEP*

Name	years in G	type of variation	male/ female
• Dolores S	15	3	F
Zita P	1	3	F
Manuel P	1	3	M
• Montse S	14	2+	F
• Pascua S	7	3	F
Miguel S	1	1b	M
Estefania P	3	2	F
• Eliseo I	12	3	M
Maria P	5	3	F
• Pepita S	14	3	F
Rosemarie S	1	2	F
• Antonio S	11	3	M
Francisco S	2	3	M
• Pasquale I	7	3	F
• Rosa I	7	3	F

As in the case of L1-L2 differences, the 'bad-choice hypothesis' identifies the developmental dynamics as one cause for the lack of progress in particular L2 learners. However, it does not offer an answer to the question as to why the inferior option was chosen in the first place. Again, this epistemological question is deliberately not addressed here.

One can take the 'bad-choice hypothesis' one step further and apply it to L2 acquisition generally. This would mean that the more 'inferior choices' a learner makes, the more the progress of further development is affected by the fact that those structural choices are generatively entrenched. This hypothesis explains why there is such variation in ultimate attainment in L2 acquisition.

The 'good choices' of L1 learners

This nevertheless leaves another question unanswered: Why doesn't this type of variation occur in L1 acquisition? I attribute the more homogeneous developmental paths and ultimate attainment of (non-impaired) monolingual L1 acquisition to the superior quality of the structural hypotheses that L1 learners form and to the interaction between generative entrenchment and genetically coded linguistic knowledge. I will illustrate this point with the example of word order development.

For word order, the two developmental paths are as follows:

L2	L1
V-End	Comp: Cancel V2
INV	V2
SEP	--
ADV	--
SVO	SOV

I demonstrated above that the particular route entailed in these sequences is determined by the initial hypothesis on the one hand and the developmental dynamics (governed by generative entrenchment) on the other hand. A comparison of these developmental paths shows that there are fewer steps in the L1 sequence. One simple consequence this has is that there are fewer developmental errors in L1 acquisition. For instance, in SLA the use of ADV without INV creates such unavoidable developmental errors as is evident in the structure *adv NPs V X*. The same applies to the use of auxiliaries without SEP and the use of complementisers without V-End. None of these problems arises in L1 acquisition because the structural options do not arise within the path that follows from the initial hypothesis chosen and the fact that all the structural component parts are assembled when V2 is acquired. In other words, the high quality of the initial hypothesis in L1 acquisition prevents the learner from making 'bad choices'.

One question remains with this explanation: L1 learners not produce ADV and SEP? This cannot be answered from within Processability Theory because the latter is a constraint framework, not an epistemological framework. Processability Theory describes which linguistic structures are processable in which sequence, but it does not predict which of several possible options will be chosen. This is where the 'responsibility' of a transition theory stops. To explain why ADV and SEP do not develop in L1 acquisition a property theory is necessary. There is in fact one explanation which has been around for a few years, namely Clahsen and Muysken's (1986; 1989) analysis of the L1 developmental sequence, according to which the structures that would result from an underlying SOV order and the application of SEP would be in conflict with UG principles.

If one follows this line of argument, then one would assume that the L1 learner accesses a genetically specified source of linguistic knowledge in order to check the formal correctness of newly developed structures. Such an explanation would contain as a crucial component the interaction between developmental dynamics on the one hand and genetically specified linguistic information on the other hand. The initial hypothesis and the structural information for the creation of V2 do not come out of the dynamics of L1 development, but from a genetically specified knowledge source. However, the developmental dynamics in conjunction with the additional structural information are so designed as to create fewer choice points in L1 acquisition and fewer 'bad choices' which can get generatively entrenched.

However, there may be other explanatory components which may account for the different initial hypothesis in L1 and L2 acquisition. MacWhinney (1987a, b), for instance, would argue that in L2 acquisition the learner has to acquire the form of the second language on the basis of input and existing L1 linguistic form-function relationships. Therefore there would be a competition of cues from the input and L1 patterns which does not exist in the case of L1 learners.

As I mentioned above, this final section of the book is not aimed at completeness and engages in some speculation on potential new directions in explaining SLA. However, the fact remains that an interaction of several theoretical components would be required to generate the above explanation of L1-L2 differences and of fossilisation: (1) Processability Theory, (2) generative entrenchment and (3) an additional set of constraints for L1. I proposed that the interaction between these components is different in L1 and L2 acquisition and that these different types of interaction produce the phenomena known to exist in L1 and L2 acquisition, including open learner variation in L2 acquisition and more constrained learner variation and only exceptional cases of fossilisation in L1 acquisition.

If genetically specified knowledge plays a role in this explanatory scenario, then it does not take on the role of orchestrating the overall shape of development. I pointed out earlier that biological evidence suggests that genetic information does not take on such a role in complex developmental processes. This means that the genetically specified knowledge base would play a minor role in determining developmental schedules. The latter can be accounted for by the processability component, while variation (including fossilisation) can be inferred from the interaction between generative entrenchment and Processability Theory.

Just what exactly may be contained in a genetically specified knowledge base that is relevant to language acquisition, is the subject of a theoretical component that is separate from 'Processability Theory'. However, the construction of such a theory component would require a separate volume.

Chapter 7

Epilogue

I stated in the introduction to this book that my aim is to provide a systematic perspective on psychological mechanisms underlying spontaneous speech production by L2 learners. In the six previous chapters I developed a theory of processability of grammatical structures which formally predicts which structures can be processed by a learner at a given level of development. I demonstrated that this theory makes correct predictions for the second language acquisition of morpho-syntax in English, German, Swedish and Japanese. I further provided experimental evidence to support the view that second language acquisition is based on the development of language processing skills. I also demonstrated that Processability Theory defines the learner's Hypothesis Space on the basis of real time human information processing.

This conceptualisation of Hypothesis Space proved highly productive for an understanding of the nature of a number of key concepts in SLA research: inter-learner variation, task variation, age differences, interference and fossilisation. All of these key concepts refer to degrees of variation within universal patterns of development. I demonstrated that all this variation within universal patterns can be understood as an expression of the degree of freedom introduced into the hierarchical nature of second language acquisition by Hypothesis Space.

In essence, I described one set of constraints that is naturally imposed on human second language acquisition and which offers considerable explanatory power concerning the developmental problem in language acquisition.

Nevertheless, Processability Theory leaves a number of issues unresolved. Some of these issues were intentionally excluded at the beginning of this book. Others surfaced as the theory was described in more detail. In this brief chapter I will list some of the more prominent unresolved issues to take stock of research desiderata that follow from the exposition of Processability Theory.

Genetically specified linguistic knowledge

At the end of section 6.6 it was noted that L1 and L2 acquirers differ in their initial hypotheses and the subsequent developmental dynamics. The L1 initial hypotheses turn out to lay the foundations to a more successful developmental process. L1 acquirers also turn out to be able to link different components of the developmental process up, which again leads to a structurally more stable outcome. The question is, which source of knowledge the L1 acquirers and the less successful L2 acquirers draw from to 'fuel' these developmental processes.

Meisel (1991) and Clahsen and Muysken (1986), together with most contemporary rationalist scholars of language acquisition, assume that 'universal grammar' as specified in Chomsky (1981a,b; 1986) is a valid account of the genetically specified linguistic knowledge. I noted in section 1.2 that Chomsky's paradigm has evolved into the 'minimalist program' (Chomsky 1993; for an overview cf. Cook and Newson 1996 and Radford 1996) and that, in order to be theoretically valid, most previous UG-based work on language acquisition will have to be adjusted to the new paradigm of the 'minimalist program'.

When this adjustment process occurs it may be timely to reconsider which aspects of language acquisition are desirable to be explained solely on the basis of UG. I pointed out repeatedly throughout this book that previous UG-based research on language acquisition has demonstrated strength in explaining the logical problem while it was less successful in explaining the developmental problem (cf, also Gregg 1996). The concepts of 'generative entrenchment' and Hypothesis Space have, hopefully, demonstrated that it is a fruitful endeavour to investigate the relationship between developmental dynamics and genetically specified linguistic knowledge.

Also, an interface between genetically specified knowledge (whether UG or not) and the emerging language processor has to be constructed: how is this knowledge accessed by the developing language processor? And how specifically linguistic does it have to be to cooperate with the language processor?

Transfer

In early studies of SLA (e.g. Dulay and Burt 1973, 1974), transfer was effectively 'pronounced dead'. The reason for that pronouncement was basically an assertion of the 'creative construction process' which is now taken for granted. In the meantime, the issue of transfer has re-surfaced in different contexts.

The "Full Transfer/ Full Access (FT/FA)" hypothesis by Schwartz and Sprouse (1996) is the most radical new form of the transfer hypothesis. According to the FT/FA hypothesis "... the initial state of L2 acquisition is the final state of L1 acquisition ... " Schwartz and Sprouse (1996; 40). In other words, the notion of transfer has changed form a surface structure phenomenon of the 1950s to a UG phenomenon in the FT/FA hypothesis.

In the course of this book I pointed out a number of inconsistencies of the FT/FA position. I pointed out that one cannot take it for granted that L1 structures are processable in the L2. Given the highly specialised nature of the language processor which is sensitive to even the most subtle typological differences, a productive conceptualisation of transfer as a component of a theory of SLA has to demonstrate how L1 procedures can be adapted to feed into the automatic routines of the L2 processor. I pointed out that the procedural incompatibility between L1 and L2 processors makes a full transfer highly implausible. In the most extreme case of typological contrast, none of the L1 structures can be processed.

Conceptualising the processing interface within the process of transfer would constitute an important component of an integrated understanding of second language acquisition which will ultimately be required also for less radical positions, such as the one proposed by researchers working within the framework of markedness (e.g. Eckman 1977; Kellerman 1977; Hyltenstam 1987). According to Eckman's (1977) 'markedness differential hypothesis' (MDH) unmarked features are transferred from the L1 and marked features are not. Eckman's markedness hierarchy also allows a definition of the degree of markedness depending on typological distance.

The MDH can be more readily integrated into a psycholinguistic framework than the FT/FA position because the first implies that similar processing procedures are transferred from L1 to L2. And similar processing procedures are more likely to be adaptable to the new processing requirements. However, even in the case of similar structures it is not guaranteed that the L1 procedures can be readily integrated into the emerging L2 processor.

In other words, the role of L1 transfer in SLA, whether at the level of UG or at surface level, needs to be mediated by a processing interface which spells out exactly how L1 procedures and L1 linguistic knowledge are integrated into the developing L2 processor. Obviously, such a processing interface is another research desideratum.

Induction of form, function and procedures

Throughout this book I have taken a modular approach to the explanation of language acquisition and have concentrated on the aspect of processability which is one of the major theoretical modules needed to explain the developmental problem. One further explanatory component needed to tackle the developmental problem is the learning device that must acquire the L2 grammar (cf. Wexler and Culicover 1980, Pinker 1979).

While Processability Theory gives an account of which structures are processable, based on the development of processing procedures, one also needs to explain how the learner makes the transition from one level of interlanguage grammar and skill to the next; i.e. not only which structures to select and which not to select but also to explain what triggers or motivates the transition in the interlanguage dynamics.

Recently, this problem has received increased attention by SLA researchers who felt the need to define a UG alternative for SLA. Suzanne Carroll (1996) proposes an 'autonomous induction theory' which is aimed at explaining how and why representational systems of the learner change over time. Bley-Vroman (1996) proposes a mechanism of 'conservative pattern accumulation' to account for changes in the interlanguage system. Both approaches are designed as inferior UG substitutes that account for the inferior L2 ultimate attainment.

The need for integrating a learning device in a comprehensive theory of language acquisition is beyond any doubt. However, one has to consider exactly which aspects of the acquisition process the learning device has to explain. Given the extremely specialised nature of linguistic procedures required for the language processor to be operable, one must assume that the learning device has to be very task-specific in order to construct the component parts described in Chapter 2 of this book. The learning device will further have to have the capacity of making inferences from various types of form-function relationships described in section 4.3 as well as from a typologically diverse range of linguistic forms. And all of this will have to be integrated between the genetically coded linguistic knowledge and the real time procedures which execute plans related to that knowledge.

The above tasks imply questions such as the following: how does procedural memory develop? How do grammatical procedures develop? How do procedures used in comprehension and production relate to each other? How does the lexicon develop? How do lexical entries get entered into the mental lexicon? How do the requisite procedures for feature unification develop?

Many of these questions will no doubt require research techniques which go beyond those used in this book. While sentence matching experiments proved to be a very productive innovation, psycholinguistic experiments on SLA will need to be greatly refined to allow us to tackle some of the above questions.

While all of the above open questions illustrate our collective ignorance about the nature and mechanics of second language acquisition, it is nevertheless possible to see a glimpse of an integrated modular approach towards SLA theory in which processability acts as one component.

Notes

1. ZISA stands for 'Zweitspracherwerb Italienischer und Spanischer Arbeiter' (Second Language Acquisition of Italian and Spanish Workers). The group was founded and directed by Jürgen Meisel at the University of Wuppertal in 1974 and moved to the University of Hamburg in 1981 by which time I had moved to the University of Passau.

2. The term 'target language' is used here to cover L1 and L2.

3. One likely candidate for the source of surface difference between L1 and L2 is the different knowledge base of the two types of learners.

4. In this context 'word' is not defined as in the target language and may include chunks such as 'how are you today?'

5. Not all phrases have lexical heads. However, all phrases have unique heads, some of which may be functionally controlled (Bresnan 1982). For the purpose of this book we will simplify matters and exemplify the language generation process on the basis of phrases and clauses with lexical heads.

6. The term 'grammar development' is used here to refer to the developmental route which lexical and morphosyntactic forms take in the learner. In other words, the issue of development of form is kept separate from the issue of the acquisition of grammatical representation (i.e. the origin of those forms).

7. In the pre-minimalist as well as in the minimalist framework a distinction is made between lexical and functional heads. Lexical heads are heads of one of the four lexical phrases VP, AP, NP or PP. Functional heads are heads of functional phrases such as IP (inflectional phrase) or CP (complementiser phrase). Functional phrases may contain lexical material, such as affixes, but are not required to do so (cf. Cook and Newson 1996, 136ff.)

8. Plunkett (1995) provides a recent review of connectionist approaches to language acquisition.

9. "Child language, aphasia and general laws of phonology", MP

10. This subsection does not deal with the constraints of working memory on language processing or language learning. The volume by Harris (1992) contains a number of articles on those issues.

11. In my use of a modified and somewhat simplified LFG formalism I will focus on the the the implementation of the processability hierarchy in morphology and word order. I do not

claim that all other formal aspects of LFG are related in a similar way to the processes modelled in IPG. In particular, psychological plausibility is, at present, attributed only to the unification of lexical features, not unification generally. It may well be that other adjustments will have to be made to the formalism at a later stage.

12. Note that word order in German subordinate clauses is by no means fixed. Netter (1987) discusses several LFG-based solutions for the highly variable position of verbs and complements. Also, different types of subordinate clauses require quite different formal accounts. It was mentioned above that gaps can occur in questions (Horrocks 1987, 270). This is probably true for all complement clauses. A special problem arises with infinitive clauses in which grammatical functions may be conflated into one constituent.

13. This account is in fact a simplification, since dative can also be marked by a zero morpheme and the -e marker can also carry out other functions in German.

14. Compare section 5.3 for comments on the distinction between indefinite and definite forms of the adjective in predicatives.

15. I might add that the comment was made by a person who proved to be extremely helpful in the completion of the manuscript.

16. A brief quotation will illustrate this point:

"We have on occasion made reference to the 'closeness fallacy' in cases where an utterance produced bore a superficial resemblance to a TL form, whereas it was in fact organised along different principles ..." Perdue and Klein (1992, 333).

17. Here I refer to plural marking on nouns only. At the next level I refer to plural agreement.

18. One-constituent utterances do not form part of the implicational relationship in the same way as the other IL rules do since all other rules *accumulate* in the course of the acquisition process, while this basic pattern will be raplaced by other rules.

19. This study was carried out at the Language Acquisition Research Centre at the University of Sydney under the direction of Manfred Pienemann and was funded by a grant from the NLLIA to Manfred Pienemann.

20. This chapter is based on a paper by Pienemann and Håkansson (in press) "A unified approach towards the development of Swedish as L2: A processability account". to appear in *Studies in Second Language Acquisition*.
Gisela Håkansson's work was supported by a Fellowship Grant from the Australian National University. We would like to thank Avery Andrews, Bruno Di Biase, Elisabeth Engdahl, Björn Hammarberg, Kenneth Hyltenstam and Malcolm Johnston for their comments on this chapter.

21. As mentioned above, traditionally no distinction is made between indefinite and definite forms of the adjective in predicatives. As is shown in the chart, the indefinite and definite markings are identical in predicatives.

22. The question of whether or not Swedish also has an aspectual system and how this is acquired (cf. Noyau 1992) is not relevant here. Instead, our main concern is the morphological markings, for example, the phrasal morphology used in unification of the feature TENSE between verbs.

23.   The processability hierarchy developed in this paper for Swedish does not discriminate between the two contexts for INVERSION because we chose not to utilise the saliency principle which would indeed allow us to distinguish between these structures from a processing perspective.

24.   I would like to thank Kirsten Huter for allowing me to use these examples which are taken from her PhD dissertation on the acquisition of Japanese as a second language. (Huter 1998).

25.   I want to thank Satomi Kawaguchi for allowing me to use these examples. They are taken from her MA thesis on simplified registers in Japanese (Kawaguchi 1996).

26.   A similar hierarchy was first suggested by Malcolm Johnston (personal communication, 1992). I would like to thank him for discussing his ideas concerning processability and JSL with me.

27.   Not a single example of SVO was found even for beginning learners of Japanese in the two corpora discussed in this section (Kawaguchi, personal communication).

28.   The program itself can record time at a finer resolution. However, the computers used in the experiment introduce an error margin of 5 msecs. through variation in keyboard response.

29.   Cf. *Inside Mac*, Vol 6, p 239; D. Goodman: *The Complete Hypercard 2.0 Handbook* p. 601. I would like to thank John Tucker for his programming assistance in this project.

30.   This does not diminish the falsifiability of the teachability hypothesis which was discussed in detail in section 4.2 where I pointed out that the hypothesis can be falsified through sequences which do not scale implicationally.

31.   Tarone (1989, 15) refers to frequency as 'rule': "... the *rule* for /r/ production ..."(my emphasis) which reflects her use of Labov's framework. However, this simplifies the use of probabilistically weighted rules as conceptualised by Labov.

32.   The present study was designed by Catherine Doughty, Alison Mackey and Manfred Pienemann. The data were analysed by Doughty and Mackey.

33.   I use the term 'L2 learner' here to keep the text readable. However it should be noted that most authors base their hypotheses on the critical age of around 6 years. I will return to this point later in the text.

34.   This structure has not been reported in GSL acquisition studies.

35.   Jürgen Meisel (personal communication) pointed out that the speaker Zita from Table 6.6-4 was followed up in a longitudinal study and that this learner did develop beyond SEP. Given that Zita was assigned to learner type 'goup 3' this observation appears to contradict an inherent prediction of my generative entrenchment hypothesis. If the learner made 'bad choices' early on she ought to fossilise later on. However, a closer examination of the analysis of learner variation in Clahsen, Meisel and Pienemann (1983; 250) revealed that for Zita only 2 of the 14 variational features were marked as highly simplifying, while in the other learners the number of highly simplifying features is around 9/14 and up to 11/14. Even in the norm-oriented group 1b one finds learners with two highly simplifying variational features (e.g. Raffaela I.). In other words, Zita's interlanguage was not of a highly simplifying nature.

References

Aksu, A. 1978. "The acquisition of causal connectives in Turkish". *Papers and Reports on Child Language Development* 15: 129-39.

Altmann, G. T. M. 1990. "Cognitive models of speech processing. An introduction". In G. T. M. Altmann (ed.), *Cognitive models of speech processing. Psycholinguistic and computational perspectives*. Cambridge, Mass.: MIT Press, 1-23.

Andersen, R. 1984. "The one-to-one principle of interlanguage construction". *Language Learning* 34: 77-95.

Andersen, R. 1988. "Models, processes, principles, and strategies: Second language acquisition in and out of the classroom". *IDEAL* 3: 77-95.

Anderson, J. R. 1980. *Cognitive psychology and its implications*. Freeman: San Francisco.

Anderson, J. R. 1982. "The acquisition of cognitive skill". *Psychological Review* 89: 364-406

Anderson, J. R. 1983. *The architecture of cognition*. Cambridge, Mass: Harvard University Press.

Anderson, J. R. 1995. *Cognitive psychology and its implications*. Freeman: New York. Fourth edition.

Andersson, A.-B. 1992. *Second language learners' acquisition of grammatical gender in Swedish*. Gothenburg monographs in linguistics 10: University of Gothenburg.

Andersson, A.-B. and Nauclér K. 1988. *Språklig interaktion i en tvåspråkig förskolegrupp*. [Verbal interaction in a bilingual preschool group]. *SPRINS* 25. Gothenburg University.

Axelsson, M. 1994. *Noun phrase development in Swedish as a second language. A study of adult learners acquiring definiteness and the semantics and morphology of adjectives*. Centre for Research on Bilingualism: Stockholm University.

Bachman, L. F. 1989. *Fundamental considerations in language testing*. Oxford University Press.

Baddeley, A. 1990. *Human memory: theory and practice*. Hillsdale: Erlbaum.

Bailey, C.-J. 1973. *Variation and linguistic theory*. Washington D.C.: Georgetown University Press.

Barton, G. E., R. C. Berwick and E. S. Ristad. 1987. *Computational Complexity and natural language*. Cambridge, Mass.: MIT Press.

Bates, E. 1984. "Bioprograms and the innateness hypothesis". *Behavioural Brain Sciences* 7: 188-190

Bates, E. A. and J. L. Elman. 1992. *Connectionism and the study of change.* CRL Technical Report 9002. February 1992. University of California, San Diego: Centre for Research in Language.

Bates, E., S. McNew, B. MacWhinney A. Devescove and S. Smith. 1982. "Functional constraints on sentence processing: a cross-linguistic study". *Cognition* 11:245-299

Bates, E. and B. MacWhinney. 1982. *Functionalist approaches to grammar.* In E. Wanner and L. R. Gleitman (eds.), 1982. *Language acquisition: the state of the art.* Cambridge: Cambridge University Press, 173-218.

Bechtel, W. 1988. *Philosophy of mind.* An overview for cognitive science. Hillsdale N.J.: Lawrence Erlbaum.

Berwick, R. and A. Weinberg. 1984. *The grammatical basis of linguistic performance: language use and language acquisition.* Cambridge, Mass: MIT Press.

Bever, T. G. 1970. "The cognitive basis for linguistic structures". In Hayes (ed.), *Cognition and the development of language.* New York: Wiley.

Bever, T. G. and D. Townsend. 1979. "Perceptual mechanisms and formal properties of main and subordinate clauses". In W. Cooper and E. Walker (eds.), *Sentence processing: psycholinguistic studies presented to Merrill Garrett.* Hillsdale N.J.: Erlbaum, 159-226.

Bialystok, E. 1978. "A theoretical model of second language learning". *Language Learning* 28: 69-83.

Bialystok, E. 1981. "The role of conscious strategies in second language proficiency". *Modern Language Journal* 65: 24-35.

Bialystok, E. 1991. "Metalinguistic dimensions of bilingual language proficiency". In E. Bialystok (ed.), *Language processing in bilingual children.* Cambridge: Cambridge University Press.

Bickerton, D. 1971. "Inherent variability and variable rules". *Foundations of language* 7: 457-492.

Birdsong, D. 1989. *Metalinguistic performance and interlanguage competence.* New York: Springer.

Bley-Vroman, R. 1990. "The logical problem of second language learning". *Linguistic Analysis* 20: 3-49.

Bley-Vroman, R. 1996. "Conservative pattern accumulation in foreign language learning". Paper given at the 5th EUROSLA conference, Nijmegen, June 1996.

Bley-Vroman, R and D. Masterson. 1989. "Reaction time as supplement to grammaticality judgements in the investigation of second language learners' competence". *University of Hawai'i Working Papers in ESL* 8, 2: 207-237.

Bock, M. 1978. *Wort-, Satz- und Textverarbeitung.* Stuttgart: Kohlhammer.

Boden, M. A. 1979. *Piaget. Outline and critique of his psychology, biology and philosophy.* Brighton: Harvester Press.

Bolander, M. 1988. "Is there any order? On word order in Swedish learner language". *Journal of Multilingual and Multicultural Development* 9: 97-113.

Boss, B. 1996. "German grammar for beginners — the Teachability Hypothesis and its relevance to the classroom". In C. Arbonés Solá, J. Rolin-Ianziti and R. Sussex (eds.), 1996. *Who's afraid of teaching grammar".* *Papers in Language and Linguistics* 1: 93-103 .

Bowerman, M. 1985. "What shapes children's grammars?" In D. Slobin (ed.), *The cross-linguistic study of language acquisition,* Vol. 2. Hillsdale, NJ: Erlbaum. 1257-1320.

Boyd, S. 1985. *Language survival: A study of language contact, language shift and language choice in Sweden.* Gothenburg Monographs in Linguistics 6. Inst. för linguistik, Göteborgs universitet.

Bresnan, J. 1988. *The design of grammar.* Paper presented at the interdisciplinary Conference Women on the Frontiers of Research. Clark University, March 31 and April 1 1988.

Bresnan, J. (ed.), 1982. *The mental representation of grammatical relations.* Cambridge, Mass.: MIT Press.

Bresnan, J., 1993. *Locative inversion and the architecture of UG.* MS Stanford University.

Bresnan, J. and J. Kanerva. 1989. "Locative inversion in Chichewa: A case study of factorization in grammar". *Linguistic Inquiry* 20: 1-50.

Broadbent, D. E. 1975. "The magic number seven after fifteen years". In A. Kennedy and A. Wilkes (eds.), *Studies in long term memory.* London: Wiley, 3-18.

Brown, H. D. 1976. "Discussion of 'systematicity and stability/ instability in inter-language systems'". In H. D. Brown (ed.), *Papers in second language acquisition. Language Learning. Special Issue* No 4, 135-140.

Brown, R. 1973. *A first language. The early stages.* Cambridge, Mass.: Harvard University Press.

Butterworth, B. 1983. *Language production,* Vol. 2. London: Academic Press.

Carroll, J. B. 1968. "The psychology of language testing". In A. Davies (ed.), *Language testing symposium: A Psycholinguistic Perspective.* London: Oxford University Press, 46-69.

Carroll, S. E. 1996. "Autonomous induction theory". Paper given at the 5th EUROSLA conference, Nijmegen, June 1996.

Chambers, S. and K. Forster. 1975. "Evidence for lexical access in a simultaneous matching task". *Memory and Cognition* 3: 549-59.

Chomsky, N. 1965. *Aspects of the theory of syntax.* Cambridge, Mass.: MIT Press.

Chomsky, N. 1981a. *Lectures on government and binding.* Dordrecht: Floris.

Chomsky, N. 1981b. "Principles and parameters in syntactic theory". In N. Hornstein and D. Lightfoot (eds.), *Explanations in linguistics: the logical problem of language acquisition.* London: Longman

Chomsky, N. 1986. *Knowledge of language: its nature origin, and use.* New York: Praeger.

Chomsky, N. 1990. "On the nature, use and acquisition of language". In W. G. Lycan (ed.), *mind and cognition.* A Reader. Blackwell: Cambridge Mass, 627-646.

Chomsky, N. 1993. "A minimalist program for linguistic theory". In K. Hale and S. J. Keyser (eds.), *The view from Building* 20. Cambridge, Mass: MIT Press, 1-52.

Clahsen, H. 1979. "Syntax oder Produktionsstrategien. Zum natürlichen Zweitsprach-erwerb der 'Gastarbeiter'". In Kloepfer R. (ed.), *Bildung und Ausbildung in der Romania.* W. Fink: München, 343-354.

Clahsen, H. 1980. "Psycholinguistic aspects of L2 acquisition". In S. Felix (ed.), *Second language development.* Tübingen: Narr, 57-79.

Clahsen, H. 1982. *Spracherwerb in der Kindheit. Eine Untersuchung zur Entwickung der Syntax bei Kleinkindern.* Tübingen: Narr.

Clahsen, H. 1984. "The acquisition of German word order: A test case for cognitive approaches to second language acquisition". In R. Andersen (ed.), *Second languages.* Rowley, Mass.

Clahsen, H. 1985. "Parameterised grammatical theory and language acquisition. A study of the acquisition of verb placement and inflection by children and adults". In S. Flynn and W. O'Neil (eds.), *Proceedings of the workshop "Linguistic theory and second language acquisition".* Cambridge Mass.: MIT Press.

Clahsen, H. 1986. "Connecting theories of language processing and (second) language acquisition". In C. W. Pfaff (ed.), *First and second language acquisition processes.* Cambridge: Newbury House, 103-116.

Clahsen, H. 1990. "The comparative study of first and second language development". *Studies in Second Language Acquisition* 12: 135-153.

Clahsen, H. 1992. "Learnability theory and the problem of development in language acquisition". In J. Weissenborn, H. Goodluck and Th. Roeper (eds.), 1992. *Theoretical issues in language acquisition: Continuity and change.* Lawrence Erlbaum: Hillsdale, NJ, 53-76.

Clahsen, H. and U. Hong. 1995. "Agreement and null subjects in German L2 development: new evidence from reaction-time experiments". *Second Language Research* 11 1: 57-87.

Clahsen, H., J. Meisel and M. Pienemann. 1983. *Deutsch als Zweitsprache. Der Spracherwerb ausländischer Arbeiter.* Tübingen: Narr.

Clahsen, H. and P. Muysken. 1986. "The availability of universal grammar to adult and child learners: A study of the acquisition of German word order". *Second Language Research* 5: 93-119.

Clahsen, H. and P. Muysken. 1989. "The UG paradox in L2 acquisition". *Second Language Research* 2: 1-29.

Clancy, P. 1985. "The acquisition of Japanese". In D. I. Slobin (ed.), *The cross-linguistic study of language acquisition* Vol. 1. *The data.* Hillsdale, NJ: Erlbaum, 373-524.

Coen, E. and R. Carpenter. 1992. "The power behind the flower". In *New Scientist* 25 April 1992, 26-29.

Cohen, A. D. 1992. "Strategies and processes in test-taking and SLA". *AAAL Research Colloquium on Interfaces between Second Language Acquisition Research and Language Testing.* Seattle, February 1992

Cohen, N. 1984. "Preserved learning capacity in amnesia: evidence for multiple memory systems". In L. R. Squire and N. Butters (eds.), *The neuropsychology of human memory.* New York: Guilford Press, 83-103.

Cohen, N. 1991. "Memory, amnesia and the hippocampal system". Paper given at the *Cognitive and Neuro Science Colloquium,* McGill University, 6 November 1992.

Colliander, G. 1993. "Profiling second language development of Swedish: a method for assessing L2 proficiency". In B. Hammarberg (ed.), *Problem, process, product in language learning. Papers from the Stockholm-Åbo Conference 1992.* Dept. of Linguistics. Stockholm University.

Cook, V. J. 1988. *Chomsky's Universal Grammar. An introduction.* Blackwell: Oxford.

Cook, V. J. and M. Newson. 1996. *Chomsky's Universal Grammar. An introduction.* Second Edition. Blackwell: Oxford.

Cooper, W. E. and E. B. Zurif. 1983. "Aphasia: Information-processing in language production and reception". In B. Butterworth, *Language production*. Vol. 2.

Crain, S. and J. D. Fodor. 1987. "Sentence matching and overgeneration". *Cognition* 26: 123-169

Crookes, G. 1989. "Planning and interlanguage variation". *Studies in Second Language Acquisition* 11,4: 367-83.

Crookes, G and S. Gass (eds). 1993. *Tasks and language learning. Integrating theory and practice*. Multilingual Matters: Clevedon.

Daneš, F. 1974. "Functional sentence perspective and the organisation of text". In F. Daneš (ed.), *Papers on functional sentence perspective*. The Hague: Mouton, 106-128.

Daniel, I. 1983. "On first-year German foreign language learning: A comparison of language behaviour in response to two instructional methods". PhD Dissertation. University of Southern California.

Dato, D. 1970. *American children's acquisition of Spanish syntax in the Madrid environment: a preliminary edition*. Final Report, project No. 3036, Contract No. O.E.C. 2-7-002 637, USHEW.

de Bot, K. 1992. "A bilingual production model: Levelt's 'Speaking' model adapted". *Applied Linguistics* 13 (1): 1-24.

DeCamp, D. 1973. "Implicational scales and sociolinguistic linearity". In *Linguistics*, 73: 30-43.

Dechert, H., D. Möhle and M. Raupach (ed). 1984. *Second language productions*. Tübingen: Narr.

Dik, S. C. 1987. "Some principles of functional grammar". In R. Dirven and V. Fried (eds.), *Functionalism in linguistics*. Amsterdam: John Benjamins, 101-134.

Doi, T. and K. Yoshioka, 1990. "Speech processing constraints on the acquisition of Japanese particles: applying the Pienemann-Johnston model to Japanese as a second language". In T. Hayes and K. Yoshioka (eds.), *Proceedings of the first conference on second language acquisition and teaching*, Vol. 1. Language Programs of the International University of Japan, 23-33.

Dornic, S. 1979. "Information processing in bilinguals: some selected issues". *Psychological Research* 40: 329-48.

Doughty, C. 1991. Second language instruction does make a difference. *Studies in Second Language Acquisition* 13: 431-469.

Douglas, D. 1986. "Communicative competence and the tests of oral skills". In C. W. Stansfield (ed.), *TEFOL research reports, 21. Toward communicative competence testing:* Proceedings of the Second TEFOL Invitational Conference Princton, NJ: Educational Testing Service, 157-75.

Douglas, D. 1992. "Testing methods in context-based second language research". *AAAL research colloquium on interfaces between second language acquisition research and language testing*. Seattle, February 1992

du Plessis, J., D. Solin, J. Travis and L. White. 1987. "UG or not UG, that is the question: a reply to Clahsen and Muysken". In *Second Language Research* 3: 56-75.

Duff, P. 1993. "Tasks and interlanguage performance. An SLA perspective". In G. Crookes and S. Gass (eds.), *Tasks and language learning. Integrating theory and practice.*

Multilingual Matters: Clevedon, 57-95.

Dulay, H. and M. Burt 1973. "Should we teach children syntax?" *Language Learning* 23: 245-258.

Dulay, H. and M. Burt 1974. "Natural sequences in child second language acquisition". *Language Learning* 24: 37-53.

Dulay, H., M. Burt and S. Krashen 1982. *Language two*. Oxford University Press: Oxford.

Eckman, F. 1977. "Markedness and the contrastive analysis hypothesis". *Language Learning* 27: 315-330.

Ellis, R. 1985a. *Understanding second language acquisition*. Oxford: Oxford University Press.

Ellis, R. 1985b. "Sources of variability in interlanguage". *Applied Linguistics* 6: 118-131.

Ellis, R. 1987 "Contextual variability in second language acquisition and the relevance for language teaching". In R. Ellis (ed.), *Second language acquisition in context*. Englewood Cliffs, N.J.: Prentice Hall.

Ellis, R. 1989. "Are classroom and naturalistic acquisition the same? A study of the classroom acquisition of German word order rules". *Studies in second Language Acquisition* 11: 303-28.

Ellis, R. 1994. *The study of second language acquisition*. Oxford University Press: Oxford.

Engelkamp, J. 1974. *Psycholinguistik*. München: Ullstein.

Engelkamp, J. and H. D. Zimmer. 1983. *Dynamic aspects of language processing*. Heidelberg: Springer Verlag.

Eubank, L. 1990. "Linguistic theory and the acquisition of German negation". In B. VanPatten and J. F. Lee (eds.), *Second language acquisition — foreign language learning*. Clevedon: Multilingual Matters, 73-94.

Eubank, L. (ed.). 1991. *Point-counterpoint. Universal grammar in the second language*. Vol. 3. Amsterdam/Philadelphia: Benjamins.

Eubank, L. 1993. "On the transfer of parametric values in L2 development". *Language Acquisition* 3: 183-208.

Faerch, C. and G. Kasper. 1983a. "Procedural knowledge as a component of foreign language learners' communicative competence". In H. Boete and W. Herlitz (eds.), *Kommunikation im (Sprach-) Unterricht* Utrecht: University of Utrecht.

Faerch, C. and G. Kasper. 1983b. "Plans and strategies in foreign language communication". In C. Faerch and G. Kasper (eds.), *Strategies in interlanguage communication*. London: Longman, 20-60

Faerch, C. and G. Kasper. 1984. "Two ways of defining communication strategies". *Language Learning* 34: 45-63.

Faerch, C. and G. Kasper. 1986. "Cognitive dimensions of language transfer". In Kellerman and Sharwood-Smith (eds.), *Cross-linguistic influence in second language acquisition*. Oxford: Pergamon.

Felix, S. W. 1978. *Linguistische Untersuchungen zum Zweitsprachenerwerb*. München: Fink.

Felix, S. W. 1982. *Psycholinguistische Aspekte des Zweitsprachenerwerbs*. Tübingen: Narr.

Felix, S. W. 1984. "Maturational aspects of universal grammar". In A. Davies, C. Criper and A. Howatt (eds.), *Interlanguage*. Edinburgh: Edinburgh University Press. 133-161.

Fodor, J. 1981. "Fixation of belief and concept acquisition". In M. Piatelli-Palmarini (ed.) *Language and learning. The debate between Jean Piaget and Noam Chomsky.* 2nd edition. Cambridge, Mass: Harvard University Press, 143-149.

Ford, M. 1982. "Sentence planning units: Implications for the speaker's representation of meaningful relations underlying sentences". In J. Bresnan (ed.), 1982. *The mental representation of grammatical relations.* Cambridge, Mass.: MIT Press.

Ford, M., J. Bresnan and R. M. Kaplan 1982. Sentence planning units: Implications for the speaker's representation of meaningful relations underlying sentences. In J. Bresnan (ed.) *The mental representation of grammatical relations.* MIT Press: Cambridge. 727-796.

Ford, M. and V. M. Holmes 1978. "Planning units in sentence production". *Cognition* 6: 35-53.

Forster, K. 1979 "Levels of processing and the structure of the language processor". In W. E. Cooper and E. C. T. Walker (eds.), *Sentence processing: Psycholinguistic studies presented to Merrill Garrett.* Hillsdale, New Jersey: LEA.

Freedman, S. E. 1982. *Behavioural reflexes of constraints on transformations.* Unpublished doctoral dissertation. Monash University

Freedman, S. E. and K. Forster 1985. The psychological status of overgenerated sentences. *Cognition 24,* 171-86.

Gardner, R. C. and W. E. Lambert. 1972. *Attitudes and motivation in second language learning.* Rowley, Mass.: Newbury House.

Garman, M. 1990. *Psycholinguistics.* Cambridge University Press: Cambridge

Garnham, A., R. C. Shillcock, G. D. A. Brown, A. I. D. Mill and A. Cutler. 1982. "Slips of the tongue in the London — Lund corpus of spontaneous conversation". In A. Cutler (ed.), *Slips of the tongue and language production.* Berlin: Mouton

Garrett, M. F. 1975. "The analysis of sentence production". In G. Bower (ed.), *The psychology of learning and motivation,* Vol. 9. New York: Academic Press, 133-177

Garrett, M. F. 1976. "Syntactic processes in sentence production". In R. Wales and E. Walker (eds.), *New approaches to language mechanisms.* Amsterdam: North Holland, 231-256

Garrett, M. F. 1980. "Levels of processing in language production". In B. Butterworth (ed.), *Language production,* Vol 1. *Speech and Talk.* London: Academic Press, 170-220

Garrett, M. F. 1982. "Production of speech: Observations from normal and pathological language use". In A. W. Ellis (ed.), *Normality and pathology in cognitive functions.* London: Academic Press.

Gass, S. 1988. "Integrating research areas: a framework for second language studies". *Applied Linguistics* 9: 198-217.

Gehring, W. J. 1985. "The molecular basis of development". In *Scientific American,* Vol. 253, No 4.: 137-146.

Givón, T. 1979. *On understanding grammar.* New York: Academic Press.

Goldman-Eisler, F. 1968. "The determinants of the rate of speech and their mutual relations". *Journal of Psychosomatic Research* 2: 137-43.

Gough, P. B. 1972. "One second of reading". In J. F. Kavanagh and I. G. Mattingly (eds.), *Language by ear and by eye.* Cambridge, Mass.: MIT Press, 331-358.

348 References

Gregg, K. R. 1989. "The variable competence model and why it isn't". *Applied Linguistics* 11: 364-83.

Gregg, K. R. 1992. *UG and SLA theory: The story so far.* MS

Gregg, K. R. 1993. "Taking explanation seriously; or, Let a couple of flowers bloom". *Applied Linguistics* 15: 276-294.

Gregg, K. 1996. "The logical and the developmental problems of second language acquisition". In William C. Ritchie (ed.), *Handbook of second language acquisition.* San Diego: Academic Press, 49-81.

Grodzinsky, Y. 1986. "Language deficits and the theory of syntax". *Brain and Language* 27: 135-159.

Guttman, L. 1944. "A basis for scaling qualitative data". *American Sociological Review* 9: 139-150.

Håkansson (in press). "The verb-second rule in language attrition". A study of five bilingual expatriate Swedes. To appear in: Lund University Department of *Linguistics Working Papers* 42: 49-65.

Håkansson, G. 1996a. *"Im Winter ich laufen Ski".* *Some observations on the acquisition of German in Swedish schools.* MS University of Lund.

Håkansson, G. 1996b. *Tvåspråkighet hos barn i Sverige.* (Bilingualism in children in Sweden). Ms department of Linguistics, Lund University.

Håkansson, G. and S. Dooley Collberg. 1994. "The Preference for Modal+Neg. An L2 perspective applied to L1 children". *Second Language Research* 10 (2): 95-124.

Håkansson, G. and U. Nettelbladt. 1993. "Developmental sequences in L1 (normal and impaired) and L2 acquisition of Swedish syntax". *International Journal of Applied Linguistics,* Vol. 3: 131-157.

Håkansson, G. and U. Nettelbladt. 1996. "Similarities between SLI and L2 children. Evidence from the acquisition of Swedish word order". In J. Gilbert and C. Johnson (eds.), *Children's Language,* Vol. 9. Lawrence Erlbaum & Associates. 135 - 157

Halliday, M. A. K. 1985. *An Introduction to Functional Grammar.* London: E. Arnold.

Hammarberg, B. 1996 "Examining the Processability Theory: the case of adjective agreement in L2 Swedish". In E. Kellerman, B. Welters and Th. Bongaerts (eds.), *Toegepaste taalwetenschap in artikelen 55:* EUROSLA 6. A Selection of Papers, Nijmegen 1996, 75-88.

Harrington, M. 1987. "Processing transfer: Language-specific processing strategies as a source of interlanguage variation". *Applied Psycholinguistics 8,* 351-377.

Harris, R. J. 1992 (ed.). *Cognitive processing in bilinguals.* New York: Elsevier Science Publishers.

Harris, Z. 1954. "Distributional structure". *Word* 10 (2-3): 146-62.

Horrocks, G. 1987. *Generative grammar.* London and New York: Longman.

HPD (Heidelberg Project 'Pidgin German') 1976. *Untersuchungen zur Erlernung des Deutschen durch ausländische Arbeiter.* Arbeitsbericht III. University of Heidelberg: German Department.

Huebner, T. 1983. *A longitudinal analysis of the acquisition of English.* Ann Arbor: Karoma.

Hulstijn, J. 1987. "Onset and development of grammatical features: two approaches to acquisition orders". Paper presented at *Interlanguage Conference,* La Trobe University,

Melbourne 1987.

Hulstijn, J. 1990. "A comparison between information processing and the analysis/control approaches to language learning". *Applied Linguistics* 11: 30-45.

Hulstijn, J. and W. Hulstijn. 1984. "Grammatical errors as a function of processing constraints and explicit knowledge". *Language Learning* 34: 23-43.

Hulstijn, J. and R. de Graaff. 1994. "Under what conditions does explicit knowledge of a second language facilitate the acquisition of implicit knowledge?" A research proposal. *AILA Review* 11: 97-112.

Humboldt, W. von 1836. *Über die Verschiedenheit des menschlichen Sprachbaues und ihren Einfluß auf die geistige Entwicklung des Menschengeschlechts.* [On the diversity of human language and its influence on the mental development of the human race]. Berlin: Königliche Akademie der Wissenschaften

Huter, K. 1996. "Atarashii no kuruma and other old friends. The acquisition of Japanese syntax". *Australian Review of Applied Linguistics* 19 (1): 39-60.

Huter, K. 1998. *The acquisition of Japanese as a second language.* PhD dissertation . Australian National University.

Hyltenstam, K. 1977. "Implicational patterns in interlanguage syntax variation". *Language Learning* 27 (2): 383-411.

Hyltenstam, K. 1978. "Variation in interlanguage syntax". *Lund University Department of Linguistics Working Papers* 18: 1-79

Hyltenstam, K. 1987. "Markedness, language universals, language typology, and second language acquisition". In C. Pfaff (ed.), *First and second language acquisition processes.* Newbury House: Cambridge: Mass, 55-78.

Ingram, E. 1971. "A further note on the relationship between psychological and linguistic theories". *International Review of Applied Linguistics* 9,4: 335-346.

Issidorides, D. C. and J. Hulstijn 1992. "Comprehension of grammatically modified and non-modified sentences by second language learners". *Applied Psycholoinguistics*, 13 (2): 147-164.

Jackendoff, R. 1983. *Semantics and cognition.* Cambridge, MA: MIT Press.

Jakobson, R. 1941/69/86 *Kindersprache, Aphasie und allgemeine Lautgesetze.* Suhrkamp: Frankfurt 1969 / *Child language, aphasia, and language universals,* 1986 trans. A. Keiler. the Hague: Mouton.

Jansen, L. 1991. The development of word order in natural and formal German second language acquisition. *Australian Working Papers in Language Development 5,* 1-42.

Jansen, L. 1994. The acquisition of German subject-verb agreement — the criterion in question. Paper presented at the 9th World Congress of Applied Linguistics, Amsterdam.

Johansson, A. 1973. *Immigrant swedish phonology: A study in multiple contrastive analysis.* Travaux de l'Institut de Linguistique de Lund IX.. Gleerups.

Johnston, M. 1985. *Syntactic and morphological progressions in learner English.* Commonwealth Dept of Immigration and Ethnic Affairs: Canberra

Källström, R. 1990. *Kongruens i svenskan* [Agreement in Swedish] Diss. Dept of Scandinavian languages: Gothenburg University.

Kanagy, R. 1994. "Developmental sequences in learning Japanese. A look at negation". *Issues in Applied Linguistics* 5 (2): 255-277.

350

References

Kaplan, R. 1972. Augmented transition networks as psychological models of sentence comprehension". *Artificial Intelligence* 3: 77-100.

Kaplan, R. and J. Bresnan. 1982. "Lexical-Functional Grammar: a formal system for grammatical representation". In Bresnan (ed.) *The mental representation of grammatical relations.* Cambridge, Mass: Mit Press, 173-281.

Karlson, F. 1987. *Finnish grammar.* Helsinki : W. Söderström.

Karmiloff-Smith, A. 1986. "From meta-process to conscious access: Evidence from children's metalinguistic and repair data". *Cognition* 23: 95-147.

Kawaguchi, S. 1996. *Referential choice by native speakers and learners of Japanese.* MA thesis, Australian National University.

Keenan, E. and B. Comrie. 1979. "Data on the noun phrase accessibility hierarchy". *Language* 55: 333-351.

Kellerman, E. 1977. "Towards a characterisation of the strategies of transfer in second language learning". *Interlanguage Studies Bulletin* 4: 27-48.

Kempen, G. and E. Hoenkamp. 1987. "An incremental procedural grammar for sentence formulation". *Cognitive Science* 11: 201-258.

Kimball, J. 1973. "Seven principles of surface structure parsing in natural language". In *Cognition* 2: 15-47.

Kintsch, W. 1970. *Memory and cognition.* New York: Wiley.

Kintsch, W. 1974. *The representation of meaning in memory.* Hillsdale: Erlbaum.

Klein, W. and N. Dittmar. 1979. *Developing grammars.* Berlin: Springer.

Klein, W. and C. Perdue. 1992. *Utterance structure. Developing grammars again.* Amsterdam: John Benjamins.

Kotsinas, U-B. 1982. "Svenska svårt. Några invandrares svenska talspråk". Ordförrådet. [Swedish difficult. Immigrants' spoken Swedish. The Lexicon] *MINS 10.* Stockholm University.

Krashen, S. D. 1980. "The input hypothesis". In J. Alatis (ed.), *Current issues in bilingual education.* Washington D.C.: Georgetown University Press:, 168-180.

Labov, W. 1972a. *Sociolinguistic patterns.* Philadelphia: University of Pennsylvania Press.

Labov, W. 1972b. The internal evolution of linguistic rules. In R. P. Stockwell and R. K. S. Macauley (eds), *Linguistic change and generative theory.* London: Bloomington, 101-171.

Lahtinen, S. 1993. "Om nominalfrasens struktur och feltyperna en (gul) bilen och det gula bilen i finska gymnasisters inläraresvenska". [On noun phrase structure and the error types "en gul bilen" and "det gula bilen" in Finnish students' learner Swedish] In V. Muittari, and M. Rahkonen (eds.), *Svenskan i Finland* 2: 85-98 Meddelanden från institutionen för nordiska språk vid Jyvälskylä universitet 9.

Larsen-Freeman, D. 1995. "On the teaching and learning of grammar: Challenging the myths". In F. Eckman, D. Highland, P. W. Lee, J. Mileham and R. Rutowski Weber (eds.), *Second Language Theory and Pedagogy.* Mahwah, N.J.: Lawrence Erlbaum, 131-150.

Larsen-Freeman, D. and M. H. Long. 1991. *An introduction to second language acquisition research.* London and New York: Longman.

Lehtonen, J. and K. Sajavaara. 1983. "Acceptability and ambiguity in native and second language message processing". In H. Ringbom (ed.), *Psycholinguistics and foreign language learning*. Åbo: Åbo Akademi.

Levelt, W. J. M. 1978. "Skill theory and language teaching". *Studies in Second Language Acquisition* 1: 53-70.

Levelt, W. J. M. 1981. "The speaker's linearisation problem". *Philosophical Transactions.* Royal Society London. B295, 305-315.

Levelt, W. J. M. 1983. "Monitoring and self-repair in speech". *Cognition* 14: 41-104.

Levelt, W. J. M. 1989. *Speaking. From intention to articulation.* Cambridge, Mass.: MIT Press.

Ling, Ch. X. and M. Marinov. 1994. "A symbolic model of the nonconscious acquisition of information". Cognitive Science 18: 595-621.

Long, M. H. 1985. "A role for instruction in second language acquisition: task-based language training". In K. Hyltenstam and M. Pienemann (eds.), *Modelling and assessing second language acquisition.* Clevedon: Multilingual Matters, 77-100

Long, M. H. 1988. "Instructed interlanguage development". In L. Beebe (ed.), *Issues in second language acquisition: multiple perspectives.* Newbury House: Cambridge, Mass, 115-141.

Long, M. H. 1989. "Task, group and task-group interactions". *University of Hawai'i Working Paper in ESL,* Vol. 8, No 2: 1-26.

Long, M. H. 1990. Maturational constraints on language development. *Studies in Second Language aquisition* 12 (3): 251-285.

Long, M. H. 1993. "Assessment strategies for SLA theories". *Applied Linguistics* 14: 225-249.

Long, M. H and C. Sato 1984. Methodological issues in interlanguage studies: an interactionist perspective. In A. Davies, C. Criper and A. Howatt (eds.) *Interlanguage.* Edinburgh: Edinburgh University Press 253-279.

Maclay, H. and C. E. Osgood, 1959. "Hesitation phenomena in spontaneous English speech". *Word* 15: 19-44.

MacWhinney, B. 1987a. "The competition model". In B. MacWhinney (ed). *Mechanisms of language acquisition.* Hillsdale, NJ: Lawrence Earlbaum Associates.

MacWhinney, B. 1987b. "Applying the competition model to bilingualism". *Applied Psycholinguistics 8,* 315-327.

Maratsos, M. 1982. "The child's construction of grammatical categories". In E. Wanner and L. R. Gleitman (eds.), 1982. *Language acquisition: the state of the art.* Cambridge: Cambridge University Press, 240-266.

Marslen-Wilson, W. D. and L. K. Tyler. 1980. "The temporal structure of spoken language understanding". *Cognition* 8: 1-71.

Masterson, D. 1993. *A comparison of grammaticality evaluation measurements: testing native speakers of English and Korean.* PhD dissertation, University of Hawaii.

Mayes, A. R. 1988. *Human Organic Memory Disorders.* Cambridge: Cambridge University Press.

Maxwell, J. T. and R. M. Kaplan. 1995. "The interface between phrasal and functional constraints". In M. Dalrymple, R. M. Kaplan, J. T. Maxwell and A. Zaenen, (eds.), *Formal Issues in Lexical-Functional Grammar,* CSLI Publications, 571-590.

McLaughlin, B. 1978. "The Monitor model: some methodological consideration". *Language Learning* 28: 309-32.

McLaughlin, B. 1980. "Theory and research in second-language learning: an emerging paradigm". *Language Learning* 30: 331-50.

McLaughlin, B. 1987. *Theories of second language learning*. London: Edward Arnold.

McLaughlin, B. T. Rossman and B. McLeod. 1983. "Second language learning: An information-processing perspective". *Language Learning* 33: 135-157.

Meisel, J. M. 1980. "Linguistic simplification: A study of immigrant workers' speech and Foreigner talk". In S. W. Felix (ed.), *Second language development. Trends and Issues*. Tübingen: Narr, 13-40.

Meisel, J. M. 1983. "Strategies of second language acquisition: More than one kind of simplification". In R. W. Anderson (ed.), *Pidginisation and creolisation as language acquisition*. Rowley, Mass.: Newbury House, 120-157.

Meisel, J. M. 1991. "Principles of Universal Grammar and strategies of language use: On some similarities and differences between first and second language acquisition". In L. Eubank (ed.), *Point - counterpoint. Universal grammar in the second language*. Amsterdam and Philadelphia : John Benjamins, 231-276.

Meisel, J. M. 1995. "Parameters in Acquisition". In P. Fletcher and B. MacWhinney (eds.), *The Handbook of Child Language*. Cambridge Mass: Blackwell, 10-35.

Meisel, J. M., H. Clahsen and M. Pienemann. 1981. "On determining developmental stages in natural second language acquisition". *Studies in Second Language Acquisition* 3: 109-135.

Miller, G. A. 1956. "The magic number seven; plus or minus two: Some limits on our capacity for processing information". *Psychological Review* 63: 81-97.

Morton, J. 1969. "The interaction of information in word recognition". *Psychological Review* 76: 165-178.

Morton, J. 1979. "Word recognition". In J. Morton and J. Marshall (eds.), *Psycholinguistics: Series 2. Structures and Processes*. London: Elek.

Müller, R.-A. 1995. *Innateness, autonomy, universality? Neurobiological approaches to language*. Cambridge: Cambridge University Press.

Murdock, B. B. Jr. 1962. "The serial position effect in free recall". *Journal of Experimental Psychology* 62: 618-25

Netter, K. 1987. "Wortstellung und Verbalkomplex im Deutschen". In U. Klenk, P. Scherber and M. Thanller (eds.) *Computerlinguistik und Philologische Datenverarbeitung*. Hildesheim: Olms.

Newport, E. L., H. Gleitman and L. R. Gleitman. 1977. "Mother I'd rather do it myself: Some effects and non-effects of maternal speech style". In C. E. Snow and C. A. Ferguson (eds.), 1977. *Talking to children: Language input and acquisition*. Cambridge: Cambridge University Press.

Noyau, C. 1992. *La temporalité dans le discours narratif: construction du récit, construction de la langue*. Diss. University of Paris VIII.

O'Malley, J. M. and A. U. Chamot. 1990. *Learning strategies in second language acquisition*. Cambridge: Cambridge University Press.

Paradis, M. 1987. *The assessment of bilingual aphasia*. Hillsdale: Earlbaum.

Paradis, M. 1994. "Neurolinguistic aspects of implicit and explicit memory: Implications for bilingualism and SLA". In N. Ellis (ed.), *Implicit and Explicit Learning of Languages* London, San Diego: Academic Press 1994, 393-419.

Paradis, J. and F. Genesee. 1996. *On continuity and the emergence of functional categories in bilingual first language acquisition*. MS: McGill University.

Pavesi, M. 1984. "The acquisition of relative clauses in a formal and in an informal setting: further evidence in support of the markedness hypothesis". In D. Singleton and D. Little (eds.) *Language learning in formal and informal contexts*. IRAAL: Dublin 151-163.

Pavesi, M. 1986. Markedness, discoursal modes, and relative clause formation in a formal and informal context. *Studies in Second Language Acquisition 8* (1): 38-55.

Penfield, W., and L. Roberts. 1959. *Speech and brain-mechanisms*. Princeton, N.J.: Princeton University Press.

Piatelli-Palmarini, M. (ed.), 1981. *Language and learning. The debate between Jean Piaget and Noam Chomsky*. Cambridge, Mass.: Harvard University Press. 2nd edition

Pica, T. 1984. Methods of morpheme quantification: their effect on the interpretation of second language data. *Studies in second Language Acquisition 6 (1)*: 69-78.

Pica, T., C. Doughty and R. Young. 1986. "Making input comprehensible: do interactional modifications help?" *I.T.L. Review of Applied Linguistics* 72: 1-25.

Pica, T., R. Kanagy and J. Falodun. 1993. "Choosing and using communication tasks for second language instruction and research". In G. Crookes and S. Gass (eds.), *Tasks and language learning. Integrating theory and practice*. Clevedon: Multilingual Matters, 9-34.

Pienemann, M. 1980. "The second language acquisition of immigrant children". In S. W. Felix (ed.), *Second language development: Trends and issues*. Tübingen: Narr, 41-56.

Pienemann, M. 1981. *Der Zweitspracherwerb ausländischer Arbeiterkinder*. Bonn: Bouvier.

Pienemann, M. 1984. "Psychological constraints on the teachability of languages". In *Studies in Second Language Acquisition* 6 (2): 186-214.

Pienemann, M. 1985. "Learnability and syllabus construction". In K. Hyltenstam and M. Pienemann (eds.), *Modelling and assessing second language acquisition*. Clevedon: Multilingual Matters, 23-76.

Pienemann, M. 1988. "Determining the influence of instruction on L2 speech processing". In G. Kasper (ed.), 1988. *AILA Review 5: Classroom Research*. 40-72.

Pienemann, M. 1989. "Is language teachable? Psycholinguistic experiments and hypotheses". In *Applied Linguistics* 1: 52-79.

Pienemann, M. 1992a. *Psycholinguistic mechanisms in second language acquisition*. Paper presented at the Working Meeting on "Second language acquisition and theory construction" of the Basic Behavioural and Cognitive Research Branch of the National Institute of Mental Health, Washington, D.C., September 24-27, 1992.

Pienemann, M. 1992b. *Assessing second language acquisition through rapid profile*. LARC Occasional Papers, No 3, Feb 1992.

Pienemann, M. and G. Håkansson (in press). "A unified approach towards the development of Swedish as L2: A processability account". Accepted for publication in *Studies in Second Language Acquisition*.

Pienemann, M. and M. Johnston 1987a. "Towards an explanatory model of second language acquisition". Paper given at the *Interlanguage Conference*, La Trobe University, Melbourne 1987.

Pienemann, M. and M. Johnston 1987b. "Factors influencing the development of language proficiency". In D. Nunan (ed.), *Applying second language acquisition research*.

354

References

Adelaide: National Curriculum Research Centre, Adult Migrant Education Program, 45-141.

Pienemann, M., M. Johnston, and G. Brindley. 1988. "Constructing an acquisition-based procedure for second language assessment". *Studies in Second Language Acquisition* 10: 217-224.

Pienemann, M., M. Johnston, and J. M. Meisel, 1993. "The multi-dimensional model, linguistic profiling and related Issues: A Reply to Hudson". *Studies in Second Language Acquisition* 15: 495-503.

Pienemann, M. and A. Mackey. 1993. "An empirical study of children's ESL development and Rapid Profile". In P. McKay (ed.), *ESL development. Language and literacy in Schools*, Vol. 2. Commonwealth of Australia and National Languages and Literacy Institute of Australia, 115-259.

Pienemann, M., A. Mackey and I. Thornton. 1991, " Rapid profile: A second language screening procedure". In *Language and Language Education*, Vol. 1, No 1: 61-82.

Pinker, S. 1979. "Formal models of language learning". *Cognition* 7: 217-83.

Pinker, S. 1984. *Language learnability and language development*. Cambridge, Mass.: Harvard University Press.

Pinker, S. and A. Prince 1988. On language and connectionism. *Cognition* 28, 73-193.

Platzack, C. 1994. "The initial hypothesis of syntax: A minimalist perspective on language acquisition and attrition". *Working Papers in Scandinavian Syntax* 54: 59-88.

Plunkett, K. 1995. Connectionist approaches to language acquisition. In P. Fletcher and B. MacWhinney (eds.) *The handbook of child language*. Blackwell: Cambridge, Mass. 36-72.

Popper, K. R. 1959 (1935). *The logic of discovery*. London: Hutchinson.

Posner, M. I. and C. R. R. Snyder. 1975. "Attention and cognitive control". In R. L. Solso (ed.), *Information processing and cognition: the Loyola symposium*. Hillsdale NJ: Lawrence Erlbaum, 55-85.

Poulisse, N. 1990. *The use of compensatory strategies by Dutch learners of English*. Dordrecht: Foris.

Preston, D. R. 1989. *Sociolinguistics and second language acquisition*. Oxford: Basil Blackwell.

Preston, D. R. 1993. "Variation linguistics and SLA". *Second Language Research* 9 (2): 153-172.

Radford, A. 1996. *Syntax: A minimalist introduction*. Prepublication draft of book to be published by Cambridge University Press.

Rahkonen, M. 1993. "Huvudsatsfundamentet hos finska inlärare av svenska och svenska inlärare av finska". [The main clause foundation among Finnish learners of Swedish and Swedish learners of Finnish] In V. Muittari and M. Rahkonen (eds.), *Svenskan i Finland* 2: 199-225. Meddelanden from institutionen för nordiska språk vid Jyväskylä universitet 9.

Rochester, S. and J. Gill. 1973. "Production of complex sentences in monologues and dialogues". *Journal of Verbal learning and Verbal Behaviour* 12: 203-210.

Roeper, T. 1982. "The role of universals in the acquisition of gerunds". In E. Wanner and L. R. Gleitman (eds.), 1982. *Language acquisition: the state of the art*. Cambridge: Cambridge University Press, 267-287.

Roeper, T., S. Lapointe, J. Bing and S. Tavakolian. 1981. "A lexical approach to language acquisition". In S. Tavakolian (ed.), *Language acquisition and linguistic theory*. MIT Press: Cambridge, Mass, 35-58.

Roeper, T. and J. Weissenborn 1990. "How to make parameters work: comments on Valian". In L. Fazier and J. de Villiers (eds.). *Language processing and language acquisition*. Dordrecht: Kluwer, 147-162.

Rosansky, E. 1976. "Methods and morphemes in second language acquisition research". *Language Learning* 26, 2: 409-425.

Rotman, B. 1978. *Jean Piaget: Psychologist of the real*. 2nd edition . Ithaca, NY: Cornell University Press.

Ruoff, A. 1981. *Häufigkeitswörterbuch gesprochener Sprache*. Frankfurt: Niemeyer.

Rutherford, W. 1988. "Interlanguage and pragmatic word order". In S. M. Gass and J. Schachter (eds.), *Linguistic perspectives on second language acquisition*. Cambridge: Cambridge University Press, 163-181.

Salameh, E.-K., G. Håkansson and U. Nettelbladt. (forthcoming). "The acquisition of Swedish as L2 in Arabic-speaking preschool children. Word order patterns and double definiteness". To appear in *Scandinavian Journal of Logopaedics and Phoniatrics*.

Sato, C. 1985. "Task variation in interlanguage phonology". In S. Gass and C. Madden (eds.), *Input in second language acquisition*. Newbury House: Rowley. Mass. 181-96.

Schmidt, R. 1992. "Psychological mechanisms underlying second language fluency". *Studies in Second Language Acquisition* 14: 357-385.

Schneider, N. and R. M. Shiffrin. 1977. "Controlled and automatic processing I: Detection, search and attention". *Psychological Review* 84: 1-64.

Schumann, J. 1976. "Social distance as a factor in second language acquisition". *Language Learning* 26 (1): 135-43.

Schwartz, B. D. 1988. *Testing between UG and problem-solving models of SLA: Developmental sequence data*. MS University of Geneva.

Schwartz, B. D. and R. A. Sprouse 1994. "Word order and nominative case in non-native language acquisition. A longitudinal study of (L1 Turkish) German interlanguage". In T. Hoekstra and B. D. Schwartz (eds.) *Language acquisition studies in generative grammar: papers in honour of Kennth Wexler from the 1991 GLOW workshops*. Philadelphia, PA: J. Benjamins, 317-68.

Schwartz, B. D. and R. A. Sprouse 1996. "L2 cognitive states and the Full Transfer/ Full Access model". *Second Language Research 12* (1): 40-72.

Schwartz, B. and A. Tomaselli. 1992. "Some implications from an analysis of German word order". In W. Abraham, W. Kosmeyer and E. Reuland (eds.), *Issues in Germanic Syntax*. Berlin: Mouton de Gruyter, 251-274.

Selinker, L. 1972. "Interlanguage". *International Review of Applied Linguistics* 10: 209-31.

Selinker, L. and D. Douglas. 1985. "Wrestling with 'context' in interlanguage theory". *Applied Linguistics* 6: 190-204.

Shibatani, M. 1990. *The languages of Japan*. Cambridge University Press: Cambridge.

Shiffrin, R. M. and N. Schneider. 1977. "Controlled and automatic human information processing. II: attending, and a general theory". *Psychological Review* 84: 127-190.

Simon, H. A. 1962. "The architecture of complexity". *Proceedings of the American Philosophical Society* 106:467-482; reprinted as Chapter 7 of Simon 1981: 193-229.

Simon, H. A. 1981. *The sciences of the artificial,* 2nd edition. Cambridge: MIT Press.

Simpson, J. H. 1991. *Warlpiri morpho-syntax: a lexicalist approach.* Dordrecht, Boston: Kluwer Academics.

Slobin, D. I. 1966. "Grammatical transformations and sentence comprehension in childhood and adulthood". *Journal of Verbal learning and Verbal Behaviour* 5: 219-27.

Slobin, D. I. 1973. "Cognitive prerequisites for the development of grammar". In C. A. Ferguson and D. I. Slobin (eds.), *Studies of child language development.* New York: Holt Rinehart and Winston, 175-208.

Slobin, D. I. 1977. "Language change in childhood and in history". In J. Macnamara (ed.), *Language learning and thought.* New York: Academic Press.

Slobin, D. I. 1982. "Universal and particular in the acquisition of language". In E. Wanner and L. Gleitman (eds.), *Language acquisition. The state of the art.* Cambridge: Cambridge University Press, 128-172.

Slobin, D. I. 1985. "Cross-linguistic evidence for the language-making capacity". In D. Slobin (ed.), *The cross-linguistic study of language acquisition* Vol. 2. Hillsdale, NJ: Erlbaum. 1157-1256.

Slobin, D. I. and T. Bever. 1982. "Children use canonical sentence schemes: a cross-linguistic study of word order and inflections". *Cognition* 12, 3: 229-65.

Snow, C. E. and C. A. Ferguson (eds). 1977. *Talking to children: Language input and acquisition.* Cambridge: Cambridge University Press.

Spencer, H. 1864-7. *Principles of biology.* London: Williams and Norgate.

Sridhar, S. N. 1988. *Cognition and sentence production.* New York: Springer Verlag.

Steele, S. 1981. *An encyclopaedia of AUX.* Cambridge, Mass.: MIT Press.

Tarone, E. 1979. "Interlanguage as chameleon". *Language Learning* 29: 181-191.

Tarone, E. 1981. "Some thoughts on the notion of communication strategy". *TESOL Quarterly* 15: 285 -95.

Tarone, E. 1982. "Systematicity and attention in interlanguage". In *Language Learning* 32: 69-82.

Tarone, E. 1983. "On the variability of interlanguage systems". In *Applied Linguistics* 4: 142-163.

Tarone, E. 1985. "Variability in interlanguage use: a study of style-shifting in morphology and syntax". *Language Learning* 35: 373-404.

Tarone, E. 1988. *Variation in interlanguage.* London: Edward Arnold.

Tarone, E. 1989. "On the variability of interlanguage systems". In F. Eckman, L. H. Bell and D. Nelson (eds.), *Universals in Second Language Acquisition.* : Rowley, Mass.: Newbury House, 9-23.

Taylor, I. 1969. "Content and structure in sentence production". *Journal of Verbal learning and Verbal Behaviour* 8: 170-75.

Tomaselli, A. and B. Schwartz. 1990. "Analysing the acquisition stages of negation in L2 German: Support for UG in adult SLA". *Second Language Research* 6, 1: 1-38.

Tomasello, M. 1995. "Language is not an instinct". *Cognitive Development* 10: 131-156.

Tomlin, R. S. 1990. "Functionalism in second language acquisition". *Studies in Second Language Acquisition* 12 (2): 155-177.

References   357

Towell, R. and R. Hawkins. 1994. *Approaches to second language acquisition*. Clevedon: Multilingual Matters.

Vainikka, A. and M. Young-Scholten 1994. Direct access to X'-theory: evidence from Korean and Turkish adults learning German. In T. Hoekstra and B. D. Schwartz (eds.) *Language acquisition studies in generative grammar: papers in honour of Kennth Wexler from the 1991 GLOW workshops*. Philadelphia, PA: J. Benjamins, 7-39.

Vainikka, A. and M. Young-Scholten 1994. Gradual development of L2 phrase structure. *Second Language Research 12*, 7-39.

Viberg, Å. 1991. "En longitudinall av språkutvecklingen". *Utvärdering av skolför-beedelsegrupper i Rinkeby. Rapport 4*. Centre for Research on Bilingualism, Stockholm University.

Viberg, Å. 1993. "Crosslinguistic perspectives on lexical organisation and lexical pro-gression". In K. Hyltenstam and Å Viberg (eds.), *Progression and regression in language*. Cambridge: Cambridge University Press, 340-385.

Vigliocco, G., B. Butterworth and M. F. Garrett. 1996. "Subject-verb agreement in Spanish and English: Differences in the role of conceptual constraints". *Cognition 61*: 261-298.

Westmoreland, R. 1983. *L2 German acquisition by instructed adults*. MS University of Hawaii at Manoa.

Wexler, K. 1982. "A principle theory for language acquisition". In E. Wanner and L. R. Gleitman (eds.), 1982. *Language acquisition: the state of the art*. Cambridge: Cambridge University Press, 288-315.

Wexler, K. and P. Culicover. 1980. *Formal principles of language acquisition*. Cambridge, Mass.: MIT Press.

White, L. 1982. The responsibility of grammatical theory to acquisitional data. In N. Hornstein and D. Lightfoot (eds.) *Explanation in linguistics; the logical problem of language acquisition*. London: Longman, 241-71.

White, L. 1987. "Against comprehensible input: the Input Hypothesis and the develop-ment of L2 competence". *Applied Linguistics 8*, 95-110.

White, L. 1989. *Universal grammar and second language acquisition*. Amsterdam: John Benjamins.

White, L. 1991. "Second language competence versus second language performance: UG or processing strategies?" In L. Eubank (ed.), *Point - counterpoint. Universal Grammar in the second language*. Amsterdam and Philadelphia: John Benjamins, 67-189.

White, L. and F. Genesee. 1996. "How native is non-native? The issue of ultimate attainment in adult second language acquisition". *Second Language Research 12,3*: 233-265.

Wimsatt, W. C. 1986. "Developmental constraints, generative entrenchment and the innate-acquired distinction". In W. Bechtel (ed.), *Integrating scientific disciplines*. Dordrecht: Martinus Nijhoff, 185-208.

Wimsatt, W. C. 1991. *Generative entrenchment in development and evolution*. MS Dept of Philosophy, University of Chicago.

Wolpert, L. 1992. "The shape of things to come". *New Scientist,* Vol. 134, No 18, 27 June 1992, 38-42.

Young, R. 1988. "Variation and the interlanguage hypothesis". *Studies in Second Language Acquisition 10*, 3: 281-302.

Zobl, H. 1983. "Markedness and the projection problem". *Language Learning* 33: 293-313.
Zurif, E., D. Swinney, P. Prather and T. Love. 1994. "Functional localisation in the brain with respect to syntactic processing". *Journal of Psycholinguistic Research,* Vol. 23, No. 6, 487-497.

Author index

96, 98, 100, 102, 172, 175, 192, 220
Karlson, F. 156
Karmiloff-Smith, A. 41
Kasper, G. 29, 39, 43, 244
Kawaguchi, S. 207, 208, 213, 214, 339
Keenan, E. 262
Kellerman, E. 333
Kempen, G. 6, 9, 44, 56, 57, 58, 63, 65,
  66, 67, 70, 72, 86, 97, 115
Kimball , J.43, 44, 58, 166
Kintsch, W. 58, 78, 221
Klein, W. 50, 163, 282, 338
Kotsinas, U.-B. 195
Krashen, S.D. 29, 136

L
Labov, W. 10, 134, 140, 141, 234, 238,
  339
Lahtinen, S. 196, 197, 199, 200
Lambert, W.E. 141
Lapointe, S. 92
Larsen-Freeman, D. 137, 143, 148, 149,
  151, 153, 232, 233, 239, 244, 245,
  250, 254, 277
Lehtonen, J. 216
Levelt, W.J.M. xvi, 2, 5, 6, 8, 9, 39, 41,
  44, 51, 53, 54, 55, 56, 58, 59, 60, 62,
  63, 64, 65, 66, 67, 69, 70, 71, 72, 73,
  74, 77, 78, 89, 92, 115, 132, 221, 222,
  244, 275
Ling, Ch.X. 41
Long, M.H. xiii, xvi, 12, 13, 29, 34, 137,
  143, 148, 150, 151, 153, 232, 233,
  239, 244, 245, 250, 276, 277, 303, 311
Love, T. 62, 71

M
Mackey, A. 150, 179, 180, 279, 298, 339
Maclay, H. 56, 65
MacWhinney, B. 24, 25, 26, 28, 82, 329
Maratsos, M. 28
Marinov, M. 41
Marslen-Wilson, W.D. 58
Masterson, D. xiv, 216, 219, 224, 225
Maxwell, J.T. 91
Mayes, A.R. 61

McLaughlin, B. 5, 6, 39, 41, 216
Meisel, J.M. xiii, xiv, xv, 9, 10, 13, 16,
  18, 19, 42, 45, 49, 50, 99, 134, 137,
  141, 142, 143, 148, 149, 194, 217,
  232, 234, 235, 238, 242, 249, 255,
  265, 282, 309, 313, 319, 323, 325,
  326, 327, 332, 337, 339
Miller, G.A. 220
Morton, J. 64
Müller, R.A. 32
Murdock , B.B. Jr.78, 85
Muysken, P. 53, 217, 309, 313, 329, 332

N
Nauclér, K. 195
Nettelbladt, U. 203, 204, 206
Netter, K. 100, 338
Newport, E.L. 28
Newson, M. 16, 20, 332, 337
Noyau, C. 197, 202, 338

O
O'Malley, J.M. 43, 243, 244
Osgood, C.E. 56, 65

P
Paradis, M. 21, 40, 41, 59, 61, 62, 73, 74
Pavesi, M. 255
Penfield, W. 59
Perdue, C. 163, 338
Piatelli-Palmarini, M. 2, 30, 31, 32
Pica, T. 29, 139, 140, 276
Pienemann, M. xiii, xiv, xv, xviii, 9, 13,
  19, 45, 48, 49, 50, 82, 99, 119, 123,
  129, 134, 137, 141, 142, 144, 148,
  149, 150, 177, 179, 180, 194, 207,
  232, 234, 235, 238, 242, 245, 248,
  249, 250, 252, 254, 255, 260, 265,
  267, 270, 279, 282, 298, 312, 319,
  325, 326, 327, 338, 339
Pinker, S. 1, 2, 9, 15, 18, 24, 27, 44, 52,
  72, 89, 99, 102, 103, 104, 107, 108,
  132, 172, 175, 192, 334
Platzack, C. 21, 22, 23
Plunkett, K. 337
Popper, K.R. 132

Posner, M.I. 6, 39
Poulisse, N. 244
Prather, P. 62, 71
Preston, D.R. 238
Prince, A. 27

R
Radford, A. 16, 332
Rahkonen, M. 203, 204
Raupach, M. 40
Ristad, E.S. 92
Roberts, L. 59
Rochester, S. 59
Roeper, T. 19, 28, 92
Rosansky, E. 135
Rotman, B. 15, 30, 31
Ruoff, A. 225
Rutherford, W. 85

S
Sajavaara, K. 216
Salameh, E.-K. 196, 197, 201, 203
Sato, C. 237, 239, 277, 303
Schmidt, R. 5, 6, 39, 40
Schneider, N. 6, 39, 40
Schumann, J. 141
Schwartz, B.D. 16, 17, 18, 19, 82, 214, 313, 321, 333
Selinker, L. 273, 325
Shibatani, M. 209
Shiffrin, R.M. 6, 39, 40
Simon, H.A. 318
Simpson, J.H. 75, 92, 166
Slobin, D.I. 42, 43, 50, 78, 87, 110, 166, 167, 221
Snow, C.E. 28
Snyder, C.R.R. 6, 39
Solin, D. 313
Spencer, H. 30
Sprouse, R.A. 17, 18, 82, 214, 333
Sridhar, S.N. 58, 78
Steele, S. 103, 192

Swinney, D. 62, 71

T
Tarone, E. 11, 43, 141, 236, 237, 239, 273, 274, 275, 276, 277, 339
Tavakolian 92
Taylor, I. 59
Thornton, I. 150, 279, 298
Tomaselli, A. 16, 19, 321
Tomasello, M. 20
Tomlin, R.S. xiv, 24, 33
Towell, R. 36, 40, 42, 60
Townsend, D. 86
Travis, J. 313
Tyler, L.K. 58

V
Vainikka, A. 18, 218
Viberg, A. 195, 197, 202
Vigliocco, G. 67, 69, 71, 72, 98

W
Weinberg, A. 1, 92
Weissenborn, J. 19
Westmoreland, R. 45, 255
Wexler, K. 2, 3, 15, 37, 334
White, L. xiv, 15, 16, 18, 21, 29, 42, 52, 217, 309, 311, 313
Wimsatt, W.C. 10, 25, 316, 317, 318, 322
Wolpert, L. 25, 26, 316, 317, 318, 319, 322

Y
Yoshioka, K. 207
Young, R. 29, 237, 239
Young-Scholten, M. 18, 218

Z
Zimmer, H.D. 58
Zobl, H. 260
Zurif, E. 62, 71, 72

Subject index

In the series STUDIES IN BILINGUALISM (SiBil) ISSN 0298-1533 the following titles have been published thus far or are scheduled for publication:

1. FASE, Willem, Koen JASPAERT and Sjaak KROON (eds): *Maintenance and Loss of Minority Languages.* 1992.
2. BOT, Kees de, Ralph B. GINSBERG and Claire KRAMSCH (eds): *Foreign Language Research in Cross-Cultural Perspective.* 1991.
3. DÖPKE, Susanne: *One Parent - One Language. An interactional approach.* 1992.
4. PAULSTON, Christina Bratt: *Linguistic Minorities in Multilingual Settings. Implications for language policies.*1994.
5. KLEIN, Wolfgang and Clive PERDUE: *Utterance Structure. Developing grammars again.*
6. SCHREUDER, Robert and Bert WELTENS (eds): *The Bilingual Lexicon.* 1993.
7. DIETRICH, Rainer, Wolfgang KLEIN and Colette NOYAU: *The Acquisition of Temporality in a Second Language.* 1995.
8. DAVIS, Kathryn Anne: *Language Planning in Multilingual Contexts. Policies, communities, and schools in Luxembourg.* Amsterdam/Philadelphia, 1994.
9. FREED, Barbara F. (ed.) *Second Language Acquisition in a Study Abroad Context.* 1995.
10. BAYLEY, Robert and Dennis R. PRESTON (eds): *Second Language Acquisition and Linguistic Variation.* 1996.
11. BECKER, Angelika and Mary CARROLL: *The Acquisition of Spatial Relations in a Second Language.* 1997.
12. HALMARI, Helena: *Government and Codeswitching. Explaining American Finnish.* 1997.
13. HOLLOWAY, Charles E.: *Dialect Death. The case of Brule Spanish.* 1997.
14. YOUNG, Richard and Agnes WEIYUN HE (eds): *Talking and Testing. Discourse approaches to the assessment of oral proficiency.* 1998.
15. PIENEMANN, Manfred: *Language Processing and Second Language Development. Processability theory.* 1998.
16. HUEBNER, Thom and Kathryn A. DAVIS (eds.): *Sociopolitical Perspectives on Language Policy and Planning in the USA.* n.y.p.
17. ELLIS, Rod: *Learning a Second Language through Interaction.* n.y.p.
18. PARADIS, Michel: *Neurolinguistic Aspects of Bilingualism.* n.y.p.
19. AMARA, Muhammad Hasan: *Politics and Sociolinguistic Reflexes. Palestinian border villages.* n.y.p.